Katherine

Favored by Fortune

George W. Watts

Favored by Fortune

GEORGE W. WATTS & THE
HILLS OF DURHAM

HOWARD E. COVINGTON JR.

With kindest regards,

Howard E. Covington Jr.

THE UNIVERSITY OF NORTH CAROLINA
AT CHAPEL HILL LIBRARY
Chapel Hill

Designed and typeset in Minion with Shelly Adante display type by
Kachergis Book Design, Pittsboro, North Carolina

Manufactured in the United States of America

The paper in this book meets the guidelines for permanence and durability
of the Committee on Production Guidelines for Book Longevity of
the Council on Library Resources.

cloth 08 07 06 05 04   5 4 3 2 1

Distributed by

THE UNIVERSITY OF NORTH CAROLINA PRESS

P.O. Box 2288

Chapel Hill, North Carolina 27515-2288

Additional copies of this publication may be ordered by calling 1–800–848–6224
or from the Press's website, www.uncpress.unc.edu

LIBRARY OF CONGRESS CATALOGING-IN-PUBLICATION DATA

Covington, Howard E.
   Favored by fortune : George W. Watts & the Hills of Durham / Howard E.
   Covington, Jr.
      p. cm.
   Includes bibliographical references (p.) and index.
   ISBN 0-8078-2917-x (alk. paper)
   1. Watts, George Washington, 1851–1921.   2. Hill, John Sprunt, b. 1869—
Family.   3. Hill family.   4. Durham (N.C.)—Biography.   5. Durham
(N.C.)—Economic conditions.   6. Durham (N.C.)—Politics and
government.   7. Politicians—North Carolina—Durham—Biography.
8. Businessmen—North Carolina—Durham—Biography.
9. Philanthropists—North Carolina—Durham—Biography.
10. North Carolina—Biography.   I. Title.
   F264.D9C69 2004
   338.09756'092'2—dc22
                                                          2004046001

For George Watts Hill Jr.,
a scholar and friend

CONTENTS

ILLUSTRATIONS

Unless otherwise noted, the illustrations listed below are courtesy of the Hill family papers.

George W. Watts / ii

(Between pages 40 and 41)

George W. Watts

George W. Watts at Pinehurst

Private John Sprunt Hill during the Spanish-American War

John Sprunt Hill, circa 1900

Golfer John Sprunt Hill

Annie Louise Watts

A Watts family portrait

An infant Watts Hill with his nurse

Harwood Hall in Durham

Harwood Hall's music room
(Photo courtesy of North Carolina Collection, University of North Carolina Library at Chapel Hill.)

The main staircase and foyer at Harwood Hall
(Photo courtesy of North Carolina Collection, University of North Carolina Library at Chapel Hill.)

The smoking room at Harwood Hall
(Photo courtesy of North Carolina Collection, University of North Carolina Library at Chapel Hill.)

*Watts and Ann Hill at the National Horse Show at
Madison Square Garden in New York, 1939*

The State *magazine*
*(Photo courtesy of North Carolina Collection, University of
North Carolina Library at Chapel Hill.)*

Major Watts Hill

W. R. Kenan Jr., John Motley Morehead II, and John Sprunt Hill.
*(Photo courtesy of North Carolina Collection, University of
North Carolina Library at Chapel Hill.)*

(Between pages 264 and 265)

John Sprunt Hill in his later years

Watts Hill Jr. and his father, 1950s
(Photo by Charles H. Cooper, Herald-Sun *Papers.)*

*Three generations: Watts Hill Jr., John Sprunt Hill,
and George Watts Hill*

Early planners of the Research Triangle Park

Durham's Interim Committee
(Photo by Charles H. Cooper, Herald-Sun *Papers.)*

Watts Hill, Governor Luther Hodges, and Robert Hanes

Watts Hill, 1960s

Durham Banker John Wheeler and Watts Hill
(Photo by Charles H. Cooper, Herald-Sun *Papers.)*

The Blue Cross Blue Shield building

The first Board of Governors of the University of North Carolina

*Watts Hill christening Durham and Southern Railway's
Bull Durham engine*

*George Herbert and Watts Hill with Governors Luther Hodges,
Dan K. Moore, Robert Scott, and Terry Sanford*

Watts Hill, Kay Kyser, William Friday, and Frank Kenan

FOREWORD

ON A COLD DAY IN MARCH 1945, John Sprunt Hill dictated this message: "I am more and more interested in the North Carolina Collection, and I am determined to make it one of the outstanding Collections of State History in the whole country. For more than forty years I have kept this purpose in mind." That commitment to librarian Mary Lindsay Thornton contained more than a promise; it also revealed a trait—determination—demonstrated throughout the life of a man who chose his objectives carefully and persevered until they were reached.

That a great university library should be a party to the publication of a book about John Sprunt Hill and his family is explained by that type of determination, which is manifested throughout the pages of Howard Covington's *Favored by Fortune*. Hill's passion, and that of his heirs, was *North Carolina*, his native state. One wonders if that passion might have been heightened by the circumstances of the young man's decision to give up a lucrative career in New York City and return to a state that was still suffering from the legacies of civil war and reconstruction.

Years later, an aging John Sprunt Hill may have revealed much about himself when he sat down and wrote for his grandchildren a series of short stories about a mythical "Homer Moore." Not above a little hyperbole, the author described a young man who rose from poverty by seizing every opportunity that presented itself—homeschooling by his mother, clerking in a nearby village from age twelve to sixteen, working his way through the state university to graduate maxima cum laude, returning to his native county to teach for two years, and then coming back to the university to study law. A chance encounter on the campus with a prominent New Yorker opened a new world to Homer Moore, who, within a little more than a decade, became a highly successful big-city lawyer and a promising politician associated with Tammany Hall. Could the name of the character itself reveal something about the author, evoking as it does the *Odyssey* of the poet Homer and the search for "moore" than a Duplin County farm offered a youngster born in the lean years following the Civil War?

The autobiographical aspects of the Homer Moore odyssey are striking, and, taken with a handful of salt, they tell us much about the author of the short stories. The flesh-and-blood John Sprunt Hill, however, was more authoritatively revealed in the 1892 issue of the *Hellenian* (the annual student publication at the University of North Carolina) as a brilliant but by no means shy twenty-three-year-old member of the Sigma Alpha Epsilon fraternity, the Tennis Club, the Driving Club, the West End Whist Club, the Order of Gimghouls, the Manning Legal Club, the University German Club, the Dude Club, and, one more, the Mashing Club (i.e., the girl-watching club), in which he had achieved, according to his fellow members, "one success (?) in six and a half years." Hill was assigned the superlative, "Best prospective lawyer in the law class," and he was associated with the quotation, "A jealous man is he / Of all his 'ancient rights and privileges.'"

This image of John Sprunt Hill as a typical adolescent college student is altered significantly when his offer at commencement—to give a prize of fifteen dollars each year for the best essay on a North Carolina subject—is taken into account. Fifteen dollars in 1891 was a considerable amount of money, particularly for a country teacher who had reentered college to study law. The gesture offered early evidence of the passion for North Carolina that would culminate in the development of the largest and most comprehensive assembly of materials relating to any single state in the Union.

Back in North Carolina after his New York odyssey, John Sprunt Hill, still just thirty-four years old, delivered the alumni address at his alma mater in 1903. He began, "I have come here today on a mission of love and devotion to the State that gave me birth, and to the Institution of learning that gave me a thousand times more than I can ever repay." Was it not time, he asked fellow alumni, for them "to begin the work of making this institution a great Southern States' University, a modern directive force, commensurate with the demands of [their] people and alert to all their growing needs?" He continued: "[The work] will require the best men and we want from them the best service. Let us not beat down the market that we may purchase mediocrity cheap. But let us stand shoulder to shoulder behind our splendid standard bearer [President Venable] and give him the support that he demands. A university which has all it wants has already begun to decline, and a president of a university who is not always wanting something, should hand in his resignation." The young attorney appealed to his audience for a new library, a Young Men's Christian Association (YMCA), a hall of science, and an enhanced graduate department.

Note Hill's first priority: a new library. Inseparable from his lifelong promotion of, interest in, and knowledge and appreciation of North Carolina's history and culture was the practical businessman's recognition of the prerequisites for the physical and intellectual care of the sources of knowledge. Surprisingly perceptive for a layman of his time, he reminded his audience: "Very few people have any knowledge of the ways and means of running libraries. Such information is not picked up at country cross roads and in village factories. Library economy is a special branch of human knowledge, acquired by a few intelligent people after years of persistent study and extensive experience." He called attention to pathetic conditions on the campus:

> A feeling of sadness must needs come over the heart of every loyal son of our beloved State when his eyes fall upon our University library equipment. The building shelters 40,000 volumes and 20,000 pamphlets, but many of them are necessarily packed and jammed away in such a fashion as to largely destroy their usefulness. What is a library without research rooms, consultation rooms, seminar compartments, with but little room for the general reader, and less for the real scholar and none for the specialist, the man who digs down to the bottom of research and brings out the pure gold of human learning from the treasure houses of the world? Will not some philanthropist come to our aid and erect a memorial library building on this beautiful campus?

Hill then electrified his audience by making an audacious proposal for a huge fund-raising effort to collect $400,000 for the rejuvenation of the university. He himself set up a fund of $4,000, the income from which would finance a scholarship in history. Three years later, he and his wife gave $5,000 to assist Librarian Louis Round Wilson in setting up a separate department, the North Carolina Collection, which was given a fireproof room in the new Carnegie Library. For the first time since 1844, when the collection was started in President David L. Swain's office, North Caroliniana—books, newspapers, journals, and manuscripts—was provided its own space.

John Sprunt Hill would live to see the collection outgrow its physical parameters several times, and he was always there to help meet its needs. For example, in 1917 he provided $75.00 per month with which to pay the salary of the first full-time librarian of the North Carolina Collection, Mary Thornton, and the following year he was instrumental in the purchase of the Stephen Beauregard Weeks Collection, the largest assembly of state-related materials then in private hands. In 1923, he became chairman of the Board of Trustees' building committee and was a chief planner of the new university library (later named for Louis Round Wilson, with whom Hill had worked so closely), assuring that the North Carolina Collection and the other special collections were provided well-designed space. He was the first chairman of the Friends of the Library. When the Carnegie Library was vacated in 1929, the Hill family contributed heavily to its renovation and addition, and the building, with its state-of-the-art pipe organ, was renamed Hill Music Hall. In 1935, Hill and his wife permanently endowed the North Carolina Collection by deeding to the university the Carolina Inn with the stipulation that all income beyond what was necessary for its upkeep and maintenance was to be devoted "to the collection of books and papers known as 'North Caroliniana.'"

The pledge made to Mary Thornton in 1945 to make the North Carolina Collection "one of the outstanding Collections of State History in the whole country" became reality when between 1947 and 1953 Hill gave four valuable downtown buildings to the university. Since that time, rents from the "Hill Buildings"—138, 140, 142, and 144 East Franklin Street—have provided well over a million dollars for the purchase of North Caroliniana. The collection has never received regular state appropriations for acquisitions, so virtually all its mammoth holdings have been purchased with income from properties donated by Hill or from a few additional endowments, such as the Bruce Cotten Fund. A half century later, pull a book or pamphlet from the shelves, and its bookplate is apt to read, "The Collection of North Caroliniana endowed by John Sprunt Hill[,] Class of 1889."

Hill's beneficence, however, went beyond staffing and acquisitions, for when wings were added to Wilson Library at midcentury, the greatly expanded quarters for the North Carolina Collection were designed by librarians Charles Rush and Mary Thornton in close consultation with the Durham philanthropist. The new mahogany Chippendale-style tables, desks, and chairs were all personally selected and paid for by Hill, who, with Paul Green, also donated funds for the installation of historic interiors in the Sir Walter Raleigh Rooms and the Early Carolina Rooms. No state collection in America was more luxuriously housed. And when Wilson Library was renovated for special collections in the 1980s, the midcentury Chippendale-style furnishings were reproduced for the collection's new and larger reading room. In F. W. Wright's 1931 copy of Philip de Laszlo's painting, a dashing young John Sprunt Hill looks down on the room approvingly.

In Miss Thornton (*always* "Miss Thornton"), Hill found a soul mate, and their warm relationship flourished until his illness and death. His recognition of professional librarianship, expressed so strongly in 1903, gave Mary Thornton a degree of influence seldom exercised by a department head. Hill's conception of what a great state collection should be mirrored hers, though from time to time she tempered his enthusiasm for genealogy. She saw needs and opportunities and communicated them to Hill, and he responded generously but with a businessman's penchant for economy and leverage. Typically, the reports of the collection contained the modest statement, "The continued financial support of John Sprunt Hill is gratefully acknowledged." Mary Thornton thus was not "just another" department head, for behind her stood a benefactor whom even the head librarian dared not alienate. Oddly, however, her salary remained low, a reality that led Hill to establish a fund to supplement it. He also paid the salary of Mary Thornton's first real assistant, Elizabeth Henderson Cotten.

Still, Hill's beneficence was not at an end. In the last decade of his life, he volunteered to pay for the publication of Mary Thornton's two enormously valuable bibliographies, *Official Publications of the Colony and State of North Carolina, 1749–1939* (1954) and *A Bibliography of North Carolina, 1589–1956* (1958). When in 1957 he donated 1,000 shares of Wachovia stock for the North Carolina Collection, the *Durham Morning Herald* estimated that his gifts to the university over a period of six decades had amounted to well over $1 million—in today's dollars, several million. Upon his death in 1961, his will left 2,000 more shares of Wachovia stock to the university, the dividends from which were to supplement the retirement incomes of Miss Thornton and Mrs. Cotten "in tribute," the will specified, "to the work both of these ladies have done in promoting the growth, progress and usefulness of the North Carolina Collection." By the 1980s, his philanthropy had built not just one of the outstanding state collections in the nation but, in fact, *the* outstanding library of materials relating to a single state. Given the nature of institutional records and changing procedures of record keeping, a full accounting of John Sprunt Hill's benefactions to the various departments, programs, and campaigns of the university will never be known. What is known is that the Library of the University of North Carolina—indeed, the entire campus—bears the imprint of a man who once described himself as "[on] a mission of love and devotion to the State that gave me birth, and to the Institution of learning that gave me a thousand times more than I can ever repay." Characteristically, he accompanied his gifts with thanks to the university for allowing him to make "partial payment." In truth, John Sprunt Hill paid his debt thousands of times over.

Howard Covington's *Favored by Fortune* is, of course, about more than John Sprunt Hill's love affair with his alma mater. Here is also the unlikely story of a farm boy who carved out a promising legal career in New York City, an honest young man who associated himself with the politicians of Tammany Hall, a banker who founded credit unions to compete with his own banks, a state senator and road commissioner who defied political traditions, a citizen who argued that fluoridation of the public water supply was a communist scheme, and a religious man who generously supported black enterprise but who viewed segregation of the races as the order of the Bible. He was, without apology, a man of his time. To attempt to judge our predecessors by the standards of today is to open ourselves to the unmerciful scorn of succeeding generations with standards as yet unimaginable.

The book is also more than a biography of John Sprunt Hill. Without George Washington Watts and his daughter Annie Louise, young Hill might very well have continued his promising career as a New York lawyer and financier and thus never have resettled in his native state. Watts, a partner with the Duke tobacco brothers, had become a vigorous promoter of the once sleepy village of Durham, and John Sprunt Hill's marriage to his daughter brought together father and son-in-law, two strong individuals with mutual talents in business management. Covington hardly exaggerates when he titles a chapter "George Watts's Durham." A half century later, some might have spoken of "John Sprunt Hill's Durham." Together with the Dukes and the Carrs, the names of the Wattses and the Hills are forever imprinted on the now bustling metropolis. Their story is here told in combination for the first time.

Nor does Covington stop with two generations. Indeed, the Hill family legacy, including its influence upon North Carolina and its state university, remains very much alive. The career of John Sprunt Hill's only son, George Watts Hill, was in some ways as remarkable as his father's. His mark was heavy on business, health services, and education; a towering man with strong opinions and fierce loyalties, his name is perpetuated in the headquarters building of the Research Triangle Institute and in the Chapel Hill home of the University of North Carolina's General Alumni Association. John Sprunt Hill's oldest daughter, the late Laura Valinda Hill DuBose, presided over Meadowmont (now the centerpiece of the Paul J. Rizzo Conference Center), and a second daughter, the late Dr. Frances Faison Hill Fox, was a distinguished doctor of medicine in Durham.

This book was undertaken on the initiative of George Watts Hill Jr., whose own productive career in business, education, civil rights, and the environment ended suddenly on March 15, 2002, while the manuscript was being prepared for publication. *Favored by Fortune* thus stands as a memorial not only to the major subjects whose lives it chronicles but also to Watts Hill Jr., who ensured that the story of his parents, grandparents, and great-grandparents would be recorded for posterity.

H. G. Jones
Curator Emeritus,
The North Carolina Collection
August 2003

PREFACE

WILLIAM FRIDAY IS THE PERSON most responsible for this book. When Friday and I were talking in the late winter of 1990, he suggested that his old friend George Watts Hill was a subject waiting for a biographer. Banker, farmer, builder, philanthropist, and guiding force in the development of the Research Triangle Park, Hill was one of those people whose work touched many lives, including Friday's, but of whom little had been written.

In my earlier life as a newspaper reporter, I had covered two Hills, Watts and his son, Watts Jr., when they squared off in the contentious debate of the late 1960s and early 1970s over the reorganization of higher education. Father and son could not have been further apart. As chair of the state Board of Higher Education, Watts Jr. supported the creation of a unified system that would encompass all the state's four-year and graduate-level campuses. For his father, the *only* University of North Carolina was the campus at Chapel Hill, and he did not appreciate the politicians' meddling. The elder Hill was as steady an ally and as loyal a friend as Friday ever enjoyed during his years as president of the university, both before and after consolidation.

By the time Friday and I talked, George Watts Hill was ninety years old, so I expressed my interest in the project to his son, who warmly received Friday's suggestion. I discovered that relations between the Hills remained strained, but despite their differences Watts Jr. introduced me to his father, and the three of us spent some pleasant time together one sunny summer afternoon. Before any work could begin in earnest, however, George Watts Hill died, and for family reasons the project faded with him.

More than eight years later, I was chasing down photographs for a biography of Terry Sanford when I put in a call to Watts Jr. I knew he appreciated fine photography, especially the work of Billy Barnes. Several Barnes photos from the glory days of Sanford's North Carolina Fund (in which Watts Jr. took part) hung on the walls of Hill's Chapel Hill office, a snug, clapboard building that was once the writing workshop of playwright Paul Green. During our chat about photography, Sanford, politics, and assorted other matters, talk of this book was revived. Watts Jr. still believed an account of his father's life was overdue. During the next few months, as we explored the possibilities, it became clear that the story should begin two generations earlier with George W. Watts, Watts Jr.'s great-grandfather, who was one of the founders of Durham and the American Tobacco Company. Watts's only daughter, Annie Louise, was mother to George Watts Hill and wife to John Sprunt Hill, who had also loomed large over the university, Durham, and, for a time, the entire state.

Thus began a unique partnership between writer and sponsor. Usually, such a relationship is to be avoided. My instincts told me this was different. Indeed, for Watts Jr., this was an exploration of family and of self. I discovered that he was a serious scholar who enjoyed the search and discovery of honest research even when the facts did not agree with the stories he had heard over the years. He offered context for delicate family issues, sometimes opening old wounds in the process. Though this rummaging through the family attic was sometimes difficult, he appreciated the virtue of sound scholarship and offered thoughtful answers to my many questions. Moreover, he keenly felt his place as the last in a line of family members who over four generations had helped set the course for the university and the state. My only regret is that Watts Jr. did not see the finished book. He died unexpectedly in March 2002.

During our time together, Watts Jr. introduced me to family members who graciously shared their treasures, such as letters in the possession of a cousin, Dr. J. McNeely DuBose of Durham, that were written by George W. Watts during his early days in Durham. Another cousin, Sue Beischer of Durham, made available scrapbooks that her grandmother Annie Louise Watts had compiled in the 1890s, when she was the eligible daughter of one of the state's wealthiest families. Most helpful in understanding the dynamic and demanding personality of John Sprunt Hill were letterbooks containing three decades of his correspondence. Watts Jr. produced these from among a collection of records preserved by his father. The words on these fragile wisps of paper offered insight into the measured reasoning of a man who built banks, literally shaped the campus of the University of

North Carolina, routed North Carolina's early highways, and stood down the financial challenges of the Great Depression.

The archives of the University of North Carolina and the university's Southern Historical Collection helped fill out the Hill (John Sprunt and George Watts) years in Raleigh and Chapel Hill. Similar collections at the University of Virginia and the National Archives added shape to the shadowy story of George Watts Hill's work for the Office of Strategic Services (OSS), an aspect of his life that he kept scrupulously private. Likewise, the archives of the William Smith Morton Library at Union Theological Seminary in Richmond, Virginia, expanded the story of the unwavering evangelism of George W. Watts, whose money and leadership shaped that school and many other Presbyterian institutions.

George Watts Hill said that he liked to start things and then run like hell. Many of the details of his career in public service were lost in the dust of his escape. He was not a chatty correspondent like his father. Most of the letters and records from his years developing the state's dairy industry, Durham's hospitals and regional health care, and the Research Triangle Park disappeared when he retired and emptied his office at the top of the Central Carolina Bank (CCB) Building in Durham. Although I missed the opportunity to interview him at length, I enjoyed the generosity of Dr. P. Preston Reynolds, who spent many hours with him as she prepared her dissertation on the history of Watts Hospital in Durham. I am indebted to Dr. Reynolds, an accomplished historian and a medical doctor, for sharing with me transcripts of her interviews and the insights of a man she deeply admired.

This work was underwritten by the University of North Carolina Foundation, which received support from Watts Hill Jr., Dr. Frances Fox, and CCB. My thanks to CCB's William L. Burns Jr. for his endorsement of this project. I also am indebted to Joe Hewitt and the staff at the Library of the University of North Carolina at Chapel Hill for including this book in the library's new publishing enterprise. It is appropriate that an account of John Sprunt Hill's many contributions to the university, including the creation of the North Carolina Collection, should be issued by the library.

Thanks and appreciation are due my wife, Gloria, for her patience and understanding of this and many other projects. She shares my love for North Carolina and its people.

Favored by Fortune

CHAPTER 1

The Boy from Goshen Swamp

⌇ WITH A BIRTH DATE OF MARCH 17, John Sprunt Hill was enough of a poet to claim to be a son of Ireland. In any case, there was no mistaking him for anything other than a product of the Old South. When he was born in 1869, his arrival may easily have been considered a celebration of the end of the lingering occupation by federal troops of the lands around the Hill plantation in Duplin County, North Carolina, where his family had farmed since before the days of Andrew Jackson.

The Hills were as much a part of southeastern North Carolina as the vast fields of cotton, corn, and potatoes and the watery lowlands contained by deep pine forests. The house where Hill was born stood near Goshen Swamp at the headwaters of the Northeast Cape Fear River above Wilmington. It was part of a fifteen-hundred-acre farm worked by former slaves who were not four years out of bondage to Hill's father, William Edward Hill, when John Sprunt was born. The land had come to William E. Hill on the death of his father, William Lanier Hill, whose wife, Ann Dudley, was the sister of former North Carolina governor Edward B. Dudley of Wilmington. Local legend had it that the dogleg at nearby Faison in the otherwise arrow-straight route of the Wilmington-to-Weldon railroad was due to William Lanier Hill's political influence. He is said to have asked his son-in-law, who was one of the engineers on the project, to route the tracks away from his lands in order to discourage slaves who otherwise might have been tempted to hop the passing trains and escape to the North.

By the time John Sprunt was born, the Civil War and the years of federal occupation had sapped William E. Hill's spirit and most of his fortune. He carried the title of "Colonel" in honor of his service with the Home Guard, but the man who had once been bold enough to break with his father and the established Whig Party to join the Democrats and win election in the legislature now looked upon a world where the old rules no longer applied. He remained modestly active with his law practice, and he was interested in affairs at the University of North Carolina and in the Democratic Party, but his wife handled most of the duties on the huge farm that sustained the family.

John Sprunt's mother, Frances Faison Hill, was a strong and capable woman with a pedigree as sound as her husband's. It was Frances who stepped forward to manage her husband's affairs during this difficult and confusing period. Many newly freed slaves—who accounted for almost half of Duplin County's population—believed the lands they had once worked should now belong to them and refused to give up a portion of their harvests in payment for use of the lands. When white landowners retaliated with armed force, the federal authorities in Wilmington sent a detachment of black soldiers to investigate. A few local militia leaders were arrested, but the charges against them were later dropped.[1] By the harvest of 1870, the year after John Sprunt was born, the Hill farm was recovering. The Hills shipped sixty bales of cotton—just 15 percent less than they had shipped in the year before the war began—south to Wilmington for export at prices far above those they had previously received.

John Sprunt was the youngest of eight children. His parents named him for the Reverend John Sprunt, a noted scholar and Presbyterian clergyman from Kenansville who happened by the Hill home just after the boy's birth. As Sprunt sipped a bit of brandy to take off the chill, he had insisted the child take his name and become a preacher. The Hills agreed, having already paid homage to the immediate family in the naming of the infant's four brothers and three sisters.

Life on the farm revolved around the annual cycle of planting and harvesting. As a youngster, John Sprunt learned to drive a team and to help his mother harvest asparagus and other vegetables that were sold and shipped to markets in the North from the docks at Wilmington. He absorbed the daily atmosphere of farm life and later used the material in short stories he wrote for his grandchildren about the world on the edge of Goshen Swamp. One yarn told of a raging bull that threatened to throw John Sprunt, a young black companion, and a wagonload of ground corn into a swollen stream as the two tried to make their way home from the mill on a stormy night.

Hill's education was limited, but it was never made secondary to the demands of daily life. Since the state only paid teachers for forty days of instruction a year, Frances Hill continued the schooling of her children at home. She had been educated at the Warrenton Female Academy, and she drew lessons from the volumes in her husband's library as well as from the Bible. Each morning, John Sprunt listened to his mother read an entire chapter or the account of a particular character from the Bible. Sometime during the day he was required to write on a slate what he remembered from the morning lesson.

When John Sprunt grew older, he did not so much follow his brothers into taking on responsibilities on the farm as he replaced them. His oldest brother, Edward, left for the University of North Carolina in Chapel Hill when John Sprunt was six. Brother Christopher followed Edward to Chapel Hill three years later. Neither ever returned to tend the land. In 1882, Edward was elected to his first term in the state Senate, and he embarked on a political career that would eventually carry him to South America. After Christopher graduated from Chapel Hill, he left for medical school at the University of Virginia and, eventually, a private practice in the North.

John Sprunt was about twelve when he left his home to take a job as a clerk at a store in Faison, a farming village about four miles away. Faison had a rich history and a few fine old homes, but it was no commercial center. The handful of stores and businesses merely complemented the train depot, which was Faison's most important economic asset. The boy took the job out of necessity, in order to help support the family. He saved what he could and tried to make the best of his situation. Years later, he said the experience taught him lessons in human nature, but clerking did nothing for his love of literature or learning. After four years, when he was sixteen, his father agreed to allow him to enter the university like his brothers had. The elder Hill told his son that he would be on his own, however, because the family could not afford to pay his tuition and expenses.

In the late summer of 1885, John Sprunt left for Chapel Hill full of ambition and conviction. He arrived before the opening of classes with hopes of securing a job to help pay his way. What he found was a town with a few small stores and one decrepit hotel standing along a dusty street. It was not all that different from what he had left behind. The village was little more than an appendage to the campus's north side, whose boundary was marked by a low wall of piled fieldstones. Beyond an open park lay the heart of the campus, where the grandest of the university's nine buildings was the newly opened Memorial Hall, which had been built in honor of distinguished alumni and those who had given their lives for the Confederacy.

The new auditorium (capable of seating up to twenty-four hundred persons) was an impressive brick structure with twin turrets guarding the front entrance. It was the first new campus building to be erected since 1857, when New West and New East had opened.[2] The hall was the creation of Samuel Sloan, the same Philadelphia architect who had created the new Executive Mansion in Raleigh, and both the ornate Victorian style and the exterior of bricks made at the state's prison in Raleigh contrasted with the plain, classic lines of the other buildings that stood nearby.

For all his anticipation of entering the university like his father and three brothers had, Hill discovered his educational shortcomings when he appeared before a senior professor for his entrance examination. The professor asked him twelve questions; Hill answered most of them incorrectly. Hill later wrote of the professor's response in a short story that was largely autobiographical.

"How in the world did you hope to enter this great institution on four years of schooling and four years in a country store?" the professor asked him. "Well," he replied, "I just thought I'd make a try. I had all to gain and nothing to lose. By the way, professor, my father told me that you were the greatest teacher of Latin in the entire South. He said you could make your class in Cicero as interesting as Scott's *Ivanhoe*. I heard a great preacher say if kind-hearted old Gameliel had not allowed the poor tentmaker boy, Paul, to sit at his feet and imbibe learning, he probably would never have become Saint Paul, the greatest of the Apostles. Why not try me for the first term? Here's the money for my tuition, and I have promise of enough work on Saturday afternoons and holidays to see me through the year." According to Hill's short story, the professor then smiled and said, "Not so dumb as I thought you were. I believe I'll just try you and see what will happen. I'm warning you. If you don't pass all your work for the first term, out you go to the former life of clerking in a store."

By the end of his first term, Hill had demonstrated that he was worthy of the gamble. He earned a 75 in Latin, 98 in English, 100 in geometry, and 99 in French. The professors liked the self-assured young man, who showed an uncommon preference for his elders over those his own age. His classmates (there were fifty-three freshmen in all) called him the "boy wonder."[3] Actually, Hill found that his mother's daily lessons and instruction in the classics had served him well; he had little trouble remembering the essence of lectures on moral philosophy, literature, and ethics after the training he had received at home.

The lean years on the farm also prepared Hill for his spartan life at the university. The furnishings of his dormitory room included only a bed and mattress, a small table and chair, a homemade clothes closet, a washbowl and pitcher, and water and slop buckets, all of which he had to acquire on his own. Like most of the other students, Hill bought what he needed from his room's previous tenant. A kerosene lantern provided light. He purchased his own wood for the fireplace and paid one of the experienced black servants on campus to tend his fires and freshen his water pitcher daily. During his first two years at the university, Hill and his classmates had to use a latrine in the woods just beyond the campus's south wall.[4] An outbreak of typhoid, however, finally convinced the state authorities to install water closets and provide instruction in hygiene.

Hill's classes were small, and they were led by a faculty still struggling to rebuild the school. The university had been closed immediately after the war and had not reopened until 1868. State support barely paid for basic expenses, and alumni who were members of the state legislature had to battle for that. Leading Baptists, Presbyterians, and Methodists argued that higher education was the province of the churches, not the taxpayers. Despite the problems, the campus played on the emotions of alumni and inspired their loyalty, as it would for years to come. "Its buildings of imposing proportions, wide-spreading oaks and acres of grass, is remarkably attractive in autumn and spring," read a description in a university publication. "What with porches, yards and college campus, the town scarcely needs a park."[5]

Upperclassmen held sway within the boundaries of the stone wall. They dismissed attempts made during Hill's sophomore year to ensure that freshmen were treated with more respect. Petitioners had asked that the word "fresh" be banned and that new students be addressed as "the gentlemen who recently arrived on the Hill." The older men staunchly defended the practice of hazing, although it was formally prohibited by campus rules. They argued: "A boy entering college is like a cockerel beginning to crow. He is considered brilliant at home. What better remedy for his arrogance than to force him to trot half a mile or make a speech to jeering auditors."[6]

Membership in one of the literary societies was required of all students. The members of the Philanthropic Society, most of whom came from eastern North Carolina, had their rooms in New East, Old East, and the east end of South Building. Hill was made a member of the Dialectic Society, composed primarily of men from the western part of the state, because students from Raleigh and Wilmington were added to increase the "urban" quality of the group. "The Di's," as they were called, lived in New West, Old West, and the west end of South Building. Hill's room was in the southwest corner of South next door to John Motley Morehead III, whose grandfather had been governor. Attendance at weekly Saturday night "recitations" was required. The societies played an important role in campus life, and they had recently endowed the university's first library. In 1886, President Kemp P. Battle had persuaded the societies to consolidate their private library holdings into one collection of about twenty thousand volumes that were placed in Smith Hall and made available to all.

The university was a place designed for scholarship, and the faculty insisted on clean living. Students were required to attend daily prayers seated in the hard-backed pews of Gerrard Hall, where a member of the faculty called the roll. A most important rule banned any beer or spirits from campus, and state law prohibited the sale of alcoholic beverages within a radius of four miles. Theatrical performances and circuses were also prohibited. Women were seldom seen in the immediate vicinity of campus buildings, and if one happened to stroll across the park, men would yell "Calico on campus" from the windows. Any trips off the "Hill" had to be approved beforehand. President Battle, who had graduated with Hill's father in the class of 1849, had succeeded in raising money from alumni for the construction of a gymnasium just off the campus property, and it became a focal point for athletics and physical training. Hill thrived on the individual competition of boxing and tennis.

Most of Hill's money went to pay his annual tuition of sixty dollars and to room and board. Since there were few diversions, however, students could get along well on little. President Battle later noted in his history of the university that "a young man now standing high as a physician, by hiring a cook to bring his meals to his room, lived on $100 a year and always appeared well dressed."[7] Nevertheless, the cost of an education remained difficult to scrape together during those depressed times. Only a third of those who enrolled with Hill in the class of 1889 finished the full course of study.

Hill proved an able student. As a junior, he was chosen by the Dialectic Society to deliver a speech on poetry and progress during the 1888 graduation ceremonies. His paper on education received the essay award. By the time he was a senior, his marks were among the highest of his class, and his social life was full. He was also active in the newly organized chapter of the Sigma Alpha Epsilon fraternity.

Hill's passion was poetry, and he often spent time outside of class with his English professor, Dr. Thomas Hume, a Presbyterian minister and scholar who would read selections aloud after supper in his home. Pupil and teacher shared a "secret sympathy," as Hill later called it, which led him to write his poetry and education paper. "A teacher of poetry must have emotional responsiveness, sympathy with every kind of human experience," Hill wrote. "He must have reverence for that which is noble, right and good. He must have broadminded interest in all classes of society, and a burning desire for spiritual truth. The man who would teach poetry successfully is always a missionary to the world, for he is teaching goodness and truth through beauty, music and art."[8]

During the first week of June in 1889, the narrow dirt roads leading to Chapel Hill actually became crowded with traffic. University leaders were preparing to celebrate not only the graduation of another class but also the centennial of the chartering of the institution. Ceremonies were scheduled over three days, and in hopes of securing a large attendance, the faculty had extended word that the occasion would not be used to pressure alumni for donations.[9]

For years, local folk in southern Orange County had adopted the annual Class Day celebration as a special early summer holiday. Buggies and horses, wagons and mules, carts and oxen crowded the lanes that led to Chapel Hill. This year, the ceremonies began with graduation exercises on Tuesday the fourth. The centennial celebration opened in full on the morning of the fifth as alumni filled Gerrard Hall, where most of those on hand—including Hill's father—had received their diplomas.

Members of the state's congressional delegation, the governor, and a host of other dignitaries were on hand. Mingling with the alumni were the twenty graduates. They were a promising lot: six were prospective lawyers, another three planned careers as teachers, two were preparing for foreign mission service, and there was another minister or two among the group. Five were undecided about their futures. It was said that Tennyson was the favorite poet and tennis the preferred sport. One of the brightest among them was Hill, who, along with Daniel Johnston Currie, was graduating maxima cum laude. Currie's grades had proved to be a fraction better than Hill's; thus Currie had been named valedictorian. Hill delivered a speech for the Philosophical Society on the topic of "national moderation."

The alumni gathered for the day represented a living history of the state. The oldest was Dr. Armand J. De Rosset from the class of 1824. The Honorable Giles Mebane, a former Speaker of the state House, told the crowd about a meeting he had called in 1828 to discuss the state's first railroad. For his efforts, he declared, he had been denounced as a "visionary."[10] The empty sleeves of the Civil War veterans gave testimony to their service. The class of 1854 alone had furnished 6 or more field grade officers and surgeons, 20 captains, and as many lieutenants and privates. Half of those who had served never came home, and their names were among the 260 chiseled into the marble plaques at Memorial Hall.[11]

Among the many speakers was John Sprunt Hill's father, who had been named a university trustee in 1877 as soon as the Democrats had regained control in Raleigh. He joked with his old classmate, President Battle, about their common allegiance to the school, saying, "I have shown my faith by my works—I have sent four sons to the University."[12]

The class of 1889 was inspired by the alumni. Before the graduates left the campus for distant corners, they resolved to return in five years for a reunion, where they would present a silver cup to the first son born to a member of the class. Some said the centennial celebration gave birth to the modern alumni spirit that was captured in the Class Day song of 1884; written by Cornelia Phillips Spencer, it entreated, "Far from the Hill, but loving it still, clasp hands at parting with peace and goodwill."[13]

Hill's own future was uncertain. Two of his brothers had already embarked on exciting careers. Edward had used his political connections to secure a post as the American consul in Uruguay. Christopher was in the second year of his medical residency at a hospital in New Jersey. Isham was at home, where the family was preparing to leave the farm and move to a new house in Faison. Hill's father was not well, and John Sprunt was open to persuasion from his parents and from his mother's brother, Isham Faison, to return to Faison and become a high school principal.

If the prospect of being a schoolmaster was not exciting, the job was at least challenging. The Faison High School had been abandoned for years, and the building was in poor repair. Hill's first chore was to replace panes of glass missing from the windows. He was also responsible for recruiting a student body, and he set off about Duplin and surrounding counties to visit the parents of prospective pupils. When the school opened in 1890, he had built an enrollment of sixty-five students. The same number was on hand the following year.[14]

Hill's two years as an educator aroused his interest in teaching at the university; the place had never been far from his mind since the day he graduated, and he faithfully returned to Chapel Hill each year for Class Day. In the spring of 1891, he began making plans to enter the law school the following September. He hoped for a position on the English faculty, which would have helped cover his expenses. The appointment never materialized, but he enrolled nonetheless and began his studies for a bachelor of laws degree.

The law school was enjoying its greatest popularity in years. It had reopened in 1877 with the aging Judge William H. Battle, a former justice of the state supreme court, as dean. After Battle's death in 1879, the school had several masters until 1881, when John Manning was named professor of law. Manning enjoyed a distinguished career. He had served as a regimental adjutant in the Confederate army, had been elected to the state legislature, and had years of experience at the bar. In the fall of 1861, Hill was one of sixty students who submitted to Manning's regimen of reading all four volumes of Blackstone as preparation for a practical career.

As a graduate student, Hill was allowed to live off campus. He moved in with an old friend and fellow law student, William W. Davies Jr., who had recently graduated. Like Hill, Davies was a handsome young man and a gifted writer; he had won the Mangum Prize for oratory at the senior celebrations in 1891.

While Hill and Davies were alike in many ways, they were also a study in contrasts. Both were romantics: they created a banner for their rooms that read, "Law, Literature and Love," and they proclaimed a philosophy of "manhood, chivalry and honor," as Hill later wrote.[15] Davies had a temper and loved wine, gambling, and laughter, which he always followed on Sunday with repentance and prayers. Hill was steady, frugal, and a glutton for work. He entertained himself with boxing and long walks in the country. But the two loved poetry, good literature, good sense, and women. While Hill was quiet in his romantic endeavors and focused his attentions on one young lady, Davies seemed to have many sweethearts.

Hill's life as a law student was busy but far more social than his years as an undergraduate had been. He became vice president of the Tennis Club and a member of a riding club called the "Dude Club," the Manning Legal Club, the University German Club, the West End Whist Club, and of something called the "Mashing Club." The latter was a lighthearted gathering of young men who enjoyed watching women, although it is not clear where they would have found them in as remote a location as Chapel Hill. Hill, it was noted in the university yearbook, the *Hellenian*, had had only "one success (?) in six and a half years."[16] He was also a founding member of the Order of Gimghouls, a secret society of fraternity men who indulged themselves in rituals of chivalry and knighthood.

The Gim Ghouls—as the group was then called—suited Hill's image of himself and his time. The ideals of chivalry and knighthood conformed nicely to his romantic vision of the South and the place that the old families such as his own held in society. Members of the order exhibited impeccable manners, and throughout his life Hill would continue to charm women, as well as men, with a courtly demeanor he maintained even in the midst of heated verbal combat.

The year in law school was a time of accomplishment and happiness for Hill. At the end of his first year, at the 1891 commencement, he pledged an annual gift of fifteen dollars to the library to be given in honor of a winning historical essay. Such a promise was a bold gesture for a young man without a job whose future was clearly uncertain. After just one year with Professor Manning, Hill decided to leave Chapel Hill even though his legal education was incomplete.

He wrote of a similar decision made by his protagonist, Homer Moore, in a short story titled "Triumphs over the Shades of Night." In "Triumphs," Moore left school because of the unexpected end of a love affair with the daughter of an aging lawyer whom the young man had hoped to join in preparation for his bar examination. The lawyer died just as classes came to an end in the spring of 1892, and his daughter chose another for her husband. In a brief biography of Hill prepared for the American Historical Society in 1937, Archibald Henderson wrote that Hill was simply eager to get on with his life and that he was bound for Uruguay to join his brother, Edward, when he boarded the train and looked north toward New York City. Whatever his reasons, when John Sprunt Hill arrived in New York City in the summer of 1892, he had neither the direction nor the prospects that would have suggested much success was in store for him.

CHAPTER 2

Metropolis

———

JOHN SPRUNT HILL arrived in New York City as green and as eager as any one of the thousands of immigrants who had stepped onto the island before him. By the end of his first day, he had heard more languages, seen more tall buildings, and simply been among more people than ever before in his life. In this city of extremes, New York millionaires paid more for the rugs in the foyers of their Fifth Avenue mansions than President Battle spent to run his struggling university for an entire year. Of course, the poor were everywhere. More people lived in a single tenement than in all of Faison, North Carolina.

By the early 1890s, New York was becoming a city of skyscrapers as the new steel-cage construction enabled builders to erect structures fifteen, twenty, and even twenty-five stories tall. Yet three quarters of the city's population of 1.5 million struggled for survival in inches of space in the countless rows of three- and four-story tenements. A little more than a year before Hill arrived in the city, Jacob Riis, a writer for the *Sun*, had shocked the city, and even the nation, with the vivid descriptions of life in the tenements in his book, *How the Other Half Lives*.

Between the Bowery and the East River, Hill found the Russian, Polish, and Romanian Jews whose names were written on their shops and storefronts. He heard Hebrew and Yiddish more often than English. West of the Bowery was Little Italy. Then below, off Chatham Square, was Chinatown. Turks, Syrians, and Arabs inhabited the streets between Washington and Greenwich. North of the Bowery was Little Germany, and along Second Avenue near St. Mark's Place was Little Hungary "with its brightly lighted cafés where gypsy musicians played, where, on summer nights, the sidewalk terraces were crowded."[1] Southerners like Hill were not totally out of place. A classified advertisement in the *New York Times* for a boarding-house on Fifth Avenue offered "special rates for Southern guests."[2]

Nonetheless, Hill was a long way from Duplin County. Just how he planned to make his way in this new and very different world is not entirely clear. In one of his autobiographical short stories, Hill's hero made his way to the library of Columbia College (later Columbia University), located at Forty-ninth and Madison just north of the heart of the city, where he hoped to find work. There were no jobs available at the school, but a librarian directed him to a nearby bookstore where the management was trying to replace a clerk who had fled the city just ahead of a cholera quarantine. (Public sanitation was a new concept, and the overcrowded conditions in the tenements proved to be the perfect incubator for all manner of illnesses, including cholera and typhoid. Outbreaks of disease were common.)

In the midst of the cholera scare, Hill and the store owner capitalized on a clientele held captive by quarantine. The owner announced that Hill would teach almost any subject, from Blackstone's *Commentaries on Laws* to boxing. "Immediately, a score or more of young boys who had failed in their work in the law school, and in other departments, swarmed around the bookstore looking for somebody to help them make up their work in time for fall examinations," Hill wrote.[3]

If Hill's story is like his own experience, he worked twelve hours a day as a tutor, and with some success: all of his students passed their examinations. To boost their spirits, Hill accompanied them to their exams and took the tests himself. Based on his own results, he found that he qualified to enter the third year of the Columbia Law School. When he submitted his application, however, a professor objected. The president of the school heard of his case, overruled the professor, and offered Hill a two-year scholarship if he would withdraw his request for admission as a third-year student and enter the middle class. Hill agreed.

The law school was in the midst of major change. In 1890, the Columbia trustees had increased the course of study from two years to three and introduced the new "case study," or Langdell, approach that had recently been initiated at Harvard's law school. Columbia's most popular law professor, Theodore Dwight, the man responsible for raising the school to prominence, was so outraged at the changes that he resigned, and a number of students quit to study with him privately.

The school had yet to graduate its first class under the new three-year program when Hill entered the middle class in the fall of 1892. While the scholarship certainly made his enrollment feasible, it did not cover all his expenses. He needed work, and to find it he called on Wheeler H. Peckham, a well-known New York lawyer whom he had met a few months earlier when Peckham had visited Chapel Hill. Peckham had been out for a walk across the campus when he came upon Hill and his roommate, William Davies. Peckham was so impressed with the two that he invited them to call on him if they ever needed anything in New York. Indeed, Peckham was as good as his word, and he hired Hill as a clerk in his firm.

If Hill's short stories bear the truth, Hill's ability to impress his elders also led to his first big case. Hill's lodgings in New York were rooms in a boardinghouse owned by a man who, like Hill, enjoyed the study of history and genealogy. After the two became friends, Hill urged the man, a retired major general, to publish his memoirs, but the man was short of funds. This seemed curious to Hill, who knew that his friend had substantial real estate holdings in the city. Finally, Hill discovered that the man's financial distress was due, in part, to the fact that he had never been paid for property taken from him for the construction of the elevated railway on New York's Sixth Avenue. Working for expenses only, Hill helped find a lawyer (it may have been Peckham) who won a judgment in the landlord's favor of $94,000. The lawyer, who got a fourth of the award, was so pleased with Hill that he paid him enough to cover his living expenses in his second year at law school.

New York offered Hill one new experience after another, and it gave him insight into strange and interesting people. Hill supplemented his income at the law firm by teaching at night, but one week found himself twenty-four hours away from payday with only 15¢ in his pocket. With his funds so low, his supper was a potted ham sandwich that he purchased for 2¢ from a street vendor. As he stood at the curb eating his meal, "a man came up and with grimy hands fumbled the sandwiches to find the largest one," Hill later told a newspaper reporter. "The lack of courtesy, the uncouth manner, impressed him," Hill said. "When the man had spent three pennies and was gone, he remarked about it to the [vendor]."[4]

The vendor asked Hill if he knew the scruffy stranger. He told the man he did not. To his surprise, Hill learned that the man was Russell Sage, worth millions from his investments in real estate and railroads. The newspaper account continued: "Some months later on Long Island, Mr. Hill witnessed a man fall from a railroad car. He hurried up to assist him—picked him up and said, 'Mr. Sage, I am very sorry this happened. I hope you are not hurt.' 'How did you happen to know my name?' muttered the man half coherently. 'Why Mr. Sage—I lunched with you on Nassau street one day at the lean-to of the hunchback.'" As Hill told the story, the encounter later led to substantial legal business from Sage, certainly a boost for a young lawyer eager to build a new practice in New York City.

In the spring of 1894, Hill was nearing the end of his studies at Columbia. He had impressed the lawyers at Peckham's firm, where he had been promoted to managing clerk. That summer, as he awaited his admission to the New York bar, the senior partners asked him to take on a potentially embarrassing and even dangerous case involving fraud in a large estate held in trust for a woman and her two daughters. Hill accepted the challenge and set off to gather evidence against the trustee, another lawyer whom Hill soon discovered had stolen $758,000.

Hill was resourceful and relentless in pursuit of justice. He also wisely accepted the firm's offer to supply him with a bodyguard. Hill prepared the case for trial, but due to his lack of courtroom experience, the firm hired a respected former judge as well as a second experienced attorney to present it. The proceedings began, and the senior counsel presented the evidence just as Hill had prepared it. Then, on the day the older man was due to close before the jury, he died. The junior counsel, who had been hired to assist, agreed to present the summation but then failed to return to court after a recess. A courtroom spectator reported to the judge that the lawyer was last seen drunk and headed out of town in a carriage. "There I was with an eight-day-old law license," Hill later told a reporter. "The judge asked, 'Mr. Hill, what will you do now?' I told him I'd fight it alone." He won the case against the estate's trustee, who committed suicide before he could be sentenced. But, as Hill said, "I had won my spurs in the legal world."[5]

⚭⚭⚭

Hill's handling of the case changed his circumstances considerably. He was named trustee of the estate, and the business was sufficient for him to open his own firm—Hill, Thompson, and Sturke—in the Union Building at 52 William Street, which was one of the properties owned by the estate. Hill and his partners handled a variety of legal chores, mostly for business clients, and Hill approached his work with confidence and vigor. In one case, he upbraided opposing counsel for blocking his attempt to see stockholder records, saying, "I am somewhat surprised that a man of your ripe knowledge and wide experience should fall into the error of making a threat that is ridiculous on its face."[6]

Management of the estate, whose principal heirs were the sisters Catherine and Margaret Philipse, took much of his time. Among his responsibilities on their behalf was the disposition of hundreds of acres of land up the Hudson River near Cold Spring, New York, which required him to expand his expertise and engage in real estate development. In an effort to sell the land and realize greater value for the sisters, Hill subdivided the property and laid out roads and streets, assigning them romantic names that evoked images of the American Indians who had once lived there. "View and vista" would sell the land, he told prospective buyers.[7]

Hill was at home in New York and taking "root," as he informed President Battle in a letter. It was a good time to be in the nation's largest city. America was in a boastful mood, and New York was its financial and social center. The Fifth Avenue millionaires may have made their money in enterprises all across the land, but their grand palaces on the wide boulevard became the real measure of their success. While Hill's own circumstances were more modest, he enjoyed growing acceptance within a social circle that included other southerners as well as New Yorkers. He even joined Troop Two of the New York National Guard, a unit of cavalry volunteers whose service was as social as it was patriotic. Apparently, Hill put aside any concern that Yankee soldiers wearing his same uniform had fought his father's generation in battles across the South.

Hill also found a young woman who began to occupy much of his social calendar. She was Annie Louise Watts from Durham, North Carolina, a student at Miss Peebles and Miss Thompson's School for Girls at 32–34 East Fifty-seventh Street. Hill had handled some legal matters for Peebles and Thompson. Annie Louise was the daughter of George Washington Watts, one of North Carolina's wealthiest men. She was not quite twenty years old when she met Hill, who was seven years older. He became her regular escort to performances at the Metropolitan Opera and concerts at Carnegie Hall. These occasions were usually followed with dinner at Sherry's, one of the most fashionable and expensive restaurants in the city. From time to time, the couple was joined by Annie Louise's parents, who visited their cherished only daughter in New York with great frequency.

Watts was a full partner with Washington Duke and his two sons, James

B. and Benjamin N. Duke, in the formation of the American Tobacco Company (or the Tobacco Trust, as its detractors had begun calling the company as it gobbled up competitors in the 1890s). When Hill met Annie Louise, American Tobacco had not completed its march to dominance of the world's tobacco markets, but it was certainly on its way.

In all of Hill's musings about his years in New York, he never wrote of any woman other than Annie Louise. By the late summer of 1896, he had all but taken over her social schedule, responding on her behalf to an invitation to join the Wednesday Cotillion, a midweek evening of entertainment held at Sherry's. Hill wrote the membership chair: "Miss Watts is now almost beyond the pale of civilization climbing the rocks of the Smoky Mountains. So I will take the liberty of writing you myself assuring you of her appreciation of the compliment extended by the board of governors and also of her acceptances of this kind invitation."[8]

A generation had come of age since the Civil War. The spirit of the Confederacy was not only alive but reinvigorated in the South, where veterans and their sons and daughters were erecting monuments to the heroes of the Lost Cause. Such tributes did not dissuade young men like Hill from embracing their own patriotic stirrings in the early days of 1898 as national fever rose against the Spanish. When the U.S. battleship *Maine* exploded on February 15, 1898, sons of the South and the North united under the Stars and Stripes. Former Confederate general Joseph Wheeler, then an Alabama congressman and one of the leading proponents of war, accepted a commission to lead an invasion of Cuba. Fightin' Joe's popularity soared, and he soon became a symbol of national reconciliation.

Hill turned twenty-nine years old one month after the sinking of the *Maine*. He was beyond prime fighting age, but when President William McKinley began to raise an army to war against Spain, Hill put his name in the lottery to be chosen as a private in Troop A of Squadron A, the cavalry of the New York National Guard. He was not going to be left behind in what everyone considered to be a just war to avenge the villainy of the Spanish.

In April 1898, the American army had dwindled to a force of 30,000, but finding able men to swell that number by ten times was simple. All manner of men clamored for a chance to pull on a uniform. Officers in Hill's cavalry troop resigned their commissions so they could enter the lottery as privates, because the odds of being called were better. Those chosen were a mixed lot. According to one report, the troop included "a great variety of business interests and professions, which must necessarily suffer now that these sturdy young Americans have sacrificed all personal considerations for patriotism." There were "lawyers, physicians, artists, men of letters among them, all on the highway to success."[9] Some came from Ivy League schools and the prominent social clubs of the city. One first lieutenant was a former polo player. The sergeant who selected the mounts had been a judge at the National Horse Show, one of the premiere social events held at New York's Madison Square Garden.

Hill was eager to get to the fighting. He told Kemp Battle: "It is especially gratifying to know that we have volunteered for duty anywhere and for any length of time that may be necessary to teach the blatant and treacherous Spaniards a lesson that they will be likely to remember. Our three troops, numbering one hundred and five men each are all anxious to 'get at' the enemy, and you may feel sure that these warm-blooded, well-educated, spirited fellows will give a good account of themselves."[10]

By June, Hill's Troop A was undergoing training on the outskirts of Washington, D.C., at Camp Alger in northern Virginia. The cavalry practiced riding at full charge, stirrup-to-stirrup, across the same open fields fought over by Union and Confederate forces a little more than thirty years before. At night, when the men gathered around the campfires, they were occasionally joined by veterans of Mosby's Rangers, a notoriously mobile Confederate cavalry unit that had fought in the valleys and fields of northern Virginia.

One troop was on maneuvers late in the evening when the commanding officer asked a farmer if they could camp in his field. "He looked me over for quite a while," the officer later wrote, "and slowly withdrawing his corncob pipe from his mouth remarked, 'Well, captain, I reckon you're Federal soldiers, and the last time I seen that blue uniform I was a-shootin' at it a-back of that rock down the road. But, I suppose it's all over now and ye' can have the field.'"[11]

Equipping the units became problematic. There were few trained mounts, and Troop A spent as much time conditioning horses as it did training men for battle. Some men provided their own uniforms, and the unit purchased two machine guns with contributions sent from the city.

Annie Louise saved newspaper clippings of the daily coverage provided to Troop A. She pasted them into her scrapbook alongside the calling cards, party invitations, and concert programs she had collected during her years in New York. In late July, Troop A received orders to report to Newport News, Virginia, where they boarded the transport ship *Massachusetts* and headed for Puerto Rico. Six days later, the ship arrived at the Puerto Rican port of Ponce, where it ran upon a reef at the mouth of the harbor. Men, supplies, and horses were manhandled onto barges, and Troop A became the first unit ashore. The men prepared to face the Spanish garrison.

If there were any letters exchanged between Annie Louise and John Sprunt during his time at the front, they did not survive. But there was little time for Hill to write a word before Troop A was headed back to New York. The occupation of Puerto Rico only took two weeks. "The campaign in Puerto Rico . . . consisted of six skirmishes," Secretary of War Russell Alger later wrote. "Our total loss was four killed and forty wounded, of which [the] latter four were officers."[12] On September 10, Hill and the rest of Troop A arrived in New York City aboard the transport *Mississippi* and marched triumphantly back to the armory.

His service with Troop A would remain a proud memory for Hill, who left behind a tinted photograph of himself in his dress uniform. The army had not yet adopted standardized dress, and in full dress Hill could easily have been mistaken for a member of the Prussian Guard. The shiny leather of his belts and cartridge holders, worn over a closely tailored jacket with gold trim, was set off by a tall fur hat crowned with a feathered plume. Hill, a man of striking chiseled features, cut a handsome figure as a soldier.

∾ ∾ ∾

Hill's military service certainly added to his standing. Armed with the latest addition to his résumé, he moved into a new residence on West Seventy-third Street, which was part of a popular neighborhood west of Central Park. The new townhouses built north of Seventy-second Street had facades of brick in all shades from red to cream. They were in a style the builders called the newer "American Plan" because the entrances were at street level rather than up a raised stoop. New residents flocked to the area. "It was like a city in itself," one writer observed; "It had its own distinctive social tone."[13] Hill traveled around the city in his own carriage, which was a variation of the new two-wheeled hansom cabs whose rubber tires softened the ride.

The young lawyer's success was not lost on his friends at home. Hill maintained a regular correspondence with Kemp Battle, who supervised the annual history essay award. The university was never far from his thoughts. In September 1899, Hill told a client that he had considered applying for a junior professorship at the University of North Carolina law school but had decided to remain in New York. "Just about the time that I was considering the matter," he explained, "I became interested in a very large and important case that is likely to run along for a year or so, and the opportunity for making a great reputation and fee in this case was so sure and well defined that I could not think of giving it up."[14] His clients included not only New Yorkers but also businessmen in North Carolina who required personal attention to their affairs in the North.

Hill's growing professional stature continued to impress Annie Louise, who after finishing at Miss Peebles' continued her education at Woman's College in Baltimore. Her parents, ever protective of their only child, remained wary of this older man. At one point, Valinda Watts tested her daughter's resolve by taking Annie Louise on an extended tour of Europe and the Mediterranean with two friends and the senior minister from Durham's First Presbyterian Church. Hill was undeterred. During the months that his beloved was away, Hill wrote faithfully, and to demonstrate the intensity of his love, he punctuated one letter by burning a hole in the paper with a hot poker.

The Wattses' concerns eventually faded. George Watts became one of Hill's clients, and the family invited their daughter's suitor to accompany them to Poland Springs, Maine, the family's favorite summer spa. By the late summer of 1899, preparations were underway for a wedding that would prove to be one of the most exciting social occasions the up-and-coming town of Durham had ever seen.

The ceremony was set for Wednesday, November 29, 1899, in Durham's First Presbyterian Church, but the center of activity was Harwood Hall, Watts's grand mansion on Duke Street. From its position of prominence on Morehead Hill, Harwood Hall was a reflection of the extravagance of the age and style that first had been displayed in Durham with Julian Carr's Somerset Villa, a Victorian masterpiece built at a cost of $125,000.

Harwood Hall stood at the crest of the hill on the spot where Watts's first house had stood. (The old house was moved, intact, to another site down the hill.) The mansion was built of pink Mount Airy granite with wood trim. The upper stories featured a dazzling array of porches and gingerbread molding. A large capped turret anchored a front corner. The home's massive central staircase rose three floors beneath a ceiling of stained glass that delivered a cascade of colored light down to the center of the home. Italian carvers finished the dark wood of the interior wainscoting and mantles. Virtually every type of marble was employed in the various fronts for the fireplaces. The walls of the men's smoking room, a small octagonal space off the library, were covered with Persian tiles. An Aubusson rug was woven specially for the dining room, and the cords for the servants' bells were encased in woven bamboo.

Harwood Hall was one of the first houses in North Carolina to have electrical wiring installed in conduit. Power was provided from the W. Duke and Sons factory, located a short distance away across the railroad tracks. This caused some minor inconvenience. When the factory's generator went on standby each evening at six, the lights in the house would dim.[15]

No record survived to suggest the cost of the construction or how much Watts paid for expensive furnishings that included a gleaming white pipe organ. Nor was there ever a complete inventory of the statuary, paintings, and fine oriental rugs and items that Watts and his wife collected on their many trips abroad.

As the wedding day approached, the *Durham Sun* provided daily accounts of preparations for the marriage of a woman considered to be "the wealthiest lady in the South."[16] Even the arrival of the caterer, G. Rauscher, with his staff and food aboard a special car from Washington, D.C., rated a story. According to the newspaper, Rauscher was President William McKinley's favorite for special occasions at the White House.

The church was decorated with ropes of cedar hung from the center of the sanctuary to the four walls. These were covered with festoons of amilax, palms, ferns, and chrysanthemums. On the wedding day, promptly at 8 P.M., the bride entered to the sound of Mendelssohn's "Wedding March." She was wearing a satin dress; her head was covered by her mother's wedding veil, which was decorated with diamonds and orange blossoms. Hill's father was unable to attend because of his failing health, so Hill's brother Isham, who had moved recently to Durham to work in the Fidelity Bank, was his best man. Champe L. Andrews, one of Hill's law partners in New York, served as an usher along with other friends and one of Annie's cousins.

After the ceremony, guests were entertained at a dinner reception at Harwood Hall. The couple received some two hundred fifty guests, who passed through a line in the Louis XIV drawing room before the wedding party settled down to a supper at a heart-shaped table. The wedding presents that filled the first-floor billiard room included, according to a newspaper report, "fine cut glass and magnificent silver and goldware [that] sparkled and gleamed under the lights in the richest profusion." The report continued: "We venture to say that such a magnificent display of valuable treasures has seldom been seen at any marriage."[17] At midnight, the couple left in a special car for their "bridal tour"; once it was completed, they returned to New York City and their home on the Upper West Side.

∾∾∾

Hill had married into considerable wealth, but he was successful in his own right before he became George W. Watts's son-in-law. In addition to his growing reputation as a lawyer, he was making a name for himself in the city's Democratic Party. Hill was a leader in the Young Men's Democratic Club of the Nineteenth Assembly District and a member of the Reform Club. He proposed that the latter club should be renamed the "National Democratic Club" and that it should "draw up a platform of time-honored Democratic principles." At the same time, he was a member of the executive committee of the city's most powerful—and most infamous—political organization, Tammany Hall.

As the nineteenth century drew to a close, New York politics was in a state of change after nearly a hundred years of control by Tammany. There had been brief interludes when reformers had ousted Tammany-controlled politicians at the polls, but Tammany always returned. In the 1890s, it was under the control of Richard Croker, an Irishman born of immigrant parents who had used politics to rise from the grime of city streets to a life of wealth, comfort, and privilege. Croker made no attempt to defend the abuses that Tammany had visited on the city under the infamous William E. "Boss" Tweed. Nor did he apologize for what he called "honest graft." As one Tammany district leader said: "The politician who steals is worse than a thief. He is a fool. With the grand opportunities all around for the man with a political pull there's no excuse for stealin' a cent."[18] Croker certainly enjoyed the spoils. He lived in an $80,000 brownstone on the Upper East Side and owned a major interest in a $500,000 stock farm where he raised expensive thoroughbreds.[19]

The Tammany organization was large enough to manipulate newly enfranchised immigrants as well as wealthy business and financial leaders who, newspaper editor William Allen White said, depended on Tammany's influence over the poor to keep order in the city. John Sprunt Hill came to Croker's attention at Poland Springs, where Hill first met Croker's son on the golf course. Soon, Hill was a member of the Tammany executive committee.

As the nation and New York City prepared for the political campaigns in the fall of 1900, Tammany's control was being challenged by reformers who were fed up with the favoritism over contracts and the bureaucratic featherbedding that had been exposed by a number of investigating committees. In April, the New York newspapers had demanded action against the so-called Ice Trust. Croker's friends, who included Republicans as well as Democrats, had managed to secure a virtual monopoly on the sale of ice in the city, and they had been demanding a 50 percent price increase until public outrage forced a rollback of prices.

Croker exercised control of local politics through 90,000 precinct workers under 35 district leaders. In the first week in October 1900, the Tammany district leaders awaited their orders as they prepared to nominate candidates for the city's seats in the U.S. House of Representatives. The morning after the nominations were made, reporters were incredulous that one of the "young men" that Croker was noted for bringing into politics was a North Carolinian with "the remarkable name of 'J. Sprunt Hill.'" One article continued: "He is 32 years old. All the others are old-timers, some of them having been in Congress four and five terms, and one, Thomas J. Creamer, having been in office and in politics more than thirty years ago."[20]

Incumbent congressman William Astor Chandler had approached Croker on Hill's behalf. Croker liked what he heard about the young man, especially his name, Sprunt. Another possible contender for the Fourteenth District, Hill's law partner Champe Andrews, had also come to Croker's attention. "When the delegates got to the Narragansett Club last night for the convention few of them knew whether Champe or Sprunt was to be the nominee," one reporter wrote. "Mr. Croker, however, sent one word of admonition. 'Sprunt.' And that settled it. Mr. Croker's word made the nomination unanimous."[21]

Croker's endorsement had a practical side. Hill brought with him a broad circle of friends, including associates at the Peckham law firm who spoke up on his behalf. Croker also found it handy to back a candidate allied with the wealthy Democrats—like George Watts—who were furious that he had delivered the state's delegation to the party's presidential nominee, William Jennings Bryan, at the national convention a few months before.

The Fourteenth District covered most of the city's newly developed Upper West Side as well as a large section of Central Park and a part of the city's East Side from Fifty-ninth Street to Seventy-ninth Street. In recent elections in the district, the outcome had been a toss-up. A Republican was elected for two terms, and then a Democrat served two terms. Hill set up his headquarters just off Columbus Circle in the Virginia Hotel at Fifty-ninth Street and Eighth Avenue. Voters could find him there from 10 A.M. until two in the afternoon and most evenings after four.

Congressional campaigns were compressed into a few short weeks, and Hill made the most of his time. He compiled extensive voter lists and mailed letters asking for endorsements from men of influence in the Colonial Club, the Reform Club, and the Citizens Union. He contacted Spanish-American War veterans, Columbia Law School graduates, and his comrades from Troop A. John DeWitt Warner, a partner in the Peckham law firm, wrote to the newspapers on his behalf. He told one editor: "He was nominated without any expectation or planning on his part, on the advice of myself and others specially interested in this district, who, after looking over the ground, concluded him to be an ideal candidate, provided he would stand—as he consented to do."[22]

Hill rushed a small, four-page brochure to Ben Franklin Press, a local print shop, which turned out 60,000 campaign pieces within a few days. On the front of the brochure beneath a stiffly posed photograph of Hill were the words, "A Lawyer—A Business Man—A Soldier—No Wars for Conquest—No Grinding Trusts." Another campaign flyer promised "Equal Rights to All, Special Privileges to None, The Constitution and an Honest Dollar."[23]

Hill needed all the help he could get; it was going to be a tough year for Democrats. Incumbent president McKinley was a popular leader for the Republicans. Four years before, McKinley had defeated Bryan, whose campaign in the South and Midwest had given rise to a third party, the Populists. The Populist movement had risen in North Carolina two years before that when, in 1894, so many Democrats defected that Republicans re-gained the governor's office and won control of the legislature. To make matters worse for Hill, McKinley's running mate was the nation's newest war hero, New York governor Theodore Roosevelt.

Hill was caught between the Democratic faith of his father and the op-position of many eastern Democrats to Bryan, whose candidacy had once again caught fire with farmers. The dividing issue was whether the govern-ment should remain fixed on gold as the only standard of exchange or al-low coinage of silver, which was thought to be the answer to the financial woes of the nation's farmers.

Bryan had been Hill's candidate in 1896, but this time he put some dis-tance between himself and the "The Great Commoner," as Bryan was called, and stood with the conservatives in favor of maintaining the gold standard. "I am opposed to any interference by law with the standard fixed by commerce. I am opposed to the free coinage of any metal at an artificial rate," he declared. He lined up endorsements from Isidor Straus, Carl Schurz, and other "sound-money Democrats."[24]

Hill's Republican opponents made much of his difficult position on the silver issue, as well as of his surprise nomination by the Tammany Demo-crats. The *Sun*, a decidedly anti-Croker newspaper, reported just before Election Day on the curious lineup in the city's Fourteenth District: "There is really nothing against Mr. Hill save that he is a mere youngster and that his campaign is being conducted by battle-scarred Tammany Hall leaders who do not consult him on any subject whatever, do not ask or want his advice, and are simply carrying out a contract to squeeze him into Con-gress." "Even Tammany leaders kicked at first," the *Sun*'s reporter wrote of Hill's surprise nomination, "alleging that it was an 'awful gold brick' to load them down with."[25]

William H. Douglas, Hill's Republican opponent, drew attention to Hill's recent arrival in the city. A forty-six-year-old lawyer, Douglas re-minded voters that he was a native-born New Yorker whose pedigree enti-tled him to membership in the Society of Colonial Wars and the Sons of the American Revolution. Douglas also emphasized his experience in world trade, an advantage he held due to his law firm's dealings with the export business. He questioned Hill's position on the growing power of trusts and noted that Hill's father-in-law remained an important figure in the American Tobacco Company. The *Sun* reported that George Watts was "popularly supposed to be furnishing the money for young Hill's campaign." There is no evidence that he was or that Hill even needed Watts's help to cover the expenses of his campaign office, printed leaflets, and handouts.

Hill was not without his own resources or friends. One local booster was Jimmie Ryan, an Irishman who ran a small hotel on Broadway known as Little Coney Island. He organized a rally and pulled lumber from the side of his house to erect a grandstand "that Senator Guy, Hill and the spellbinders would not be ashamed to walk on." According to one reporter, "The meeting came off on schedule time, [and] was the success of the campaign; the Ryan homestead with one side gone stood as a mute witness to McKinley hard times and Democratic patriotism. Jimmie is busy to-day nailing back the stand to the side of his house, and he is happy."[26]

The currency issue was all consuming. On the Saturday before the election, more than eighty-five thousand people turned out for a Republican Party march through New York City. With Roosevelt at the head of the crowd, marchers withstood a drenching downpour and soggy mud. "It may be said that the parade was more than a demonstration for sound money," reported the *New York Times*. "It was an ovation to the New York governor such as few men have ever received in any country."[27]

Hill's campaign was competitive, but he was unable to overcome the overwhelming strength of the Republicans and their popular candidates at the top of the ticket. Hill won 32,167 votes to Douglas's 36,904. In the same district, McKinley ran ahead of Bryan by more than 8,300 votes.

The defeat only stimulated Hill's interest in politics. In the 1901 municipal elections, he threw himself behind the campaign of Edward M. Shephard, a lawyer and leader within the reform movement in the city who had campaigned against the Tammany candidate in an earlier campaign. Hill turned his law offices into the headquarters for the Committee of Independent Democrats for Shephard. Weakened by the scandals of the previous administration, Croker and his district leaders had no strong alternative to Shephard, and they finally gave him their support.

Shephard's opponent was Seth Low, the president of Columbia University, who had the full support of a fusion ticket that included Republican grafters from the previous administration, disenchanted Tammany leaders, reformers, and others bound by the cry of "Down with Croker."[28] The race drew attention outside of the city, particularly in the South, where newspaper editors were outraged over Low's opposition to the inclusion of a bust of Robert E. Lee in a proposed Hall of Fame to recognize noteworthy Americans. "The man who does that puts an affront upon every man, woman and child in the South," wrote the *Louisville Courier-Journal*.[29] Southerners in the city—and there were an estimated forty thousand voters of southern birth in New York—were plied with circulars that included quotes like this to remind them of their allegiances.

Shephard lost the election, and it was the end of Croker, who sailed for England, where he vowed his thoroughbreds would win the Derby. He never returned, and he died twenty years later at his home at Glencairn, a huge castle in Ireland. His widow, a young woman he had married late in life, inherited an estate valued at $5 million that was largely consumed in defending her husband's will against challenges by his children.

Hill was disappointed in Croker's departure. Writing Lewis Nixon, Croker's immediate successor at Tammany, in 1902, he said, "I have always been a believer in Richard Croker, and generally speaking I will stand with him through thick and thin." He questioned the loyalty of some of those around Croker and reported that voters in his neighborhood were defecting to the Republican and fusion campaigns in growing numbers. "I believe in straightforward, aggressive politics," he wrote. "No figure heads, no 'monkey' business, and in assuming any duties that may be placed upon me by you. . . . It is with this understanding that I have consented to cast my fortunes with the organization."[30]

Nixon responded by saying that with more men like Hill, the Democratic Party "would never know defeat." He wrote: "I hope you will come in to see me and I assure you that your welcome will never wear out."[31] Unfortunately, Nixon himself was deposed a few months later.

The upheaval in city politics came just as Hill was struggling with a difficult personal decision. Almost from the day of his marriage to Annie Louise, her parents had encouraged the couple to leave New York and settle in Durham. The family pressure increased with the birth of their son, George Watts, in the city on October 27, 1901. Annie Louise's parents had pampered her through her pregnancy, and her younger cousin, Nellie Watts, had stayed at her side constantly while the family vacationed in Atlantic City the summer before the boy was born.

Hill did not want to leave New York, the city that had become his home. Even before he married Annie Louise, when his prospects were less secure, he had passed on opportunities to return to North Carolina. In 1902, he was so involved in city politics that he had missed attending the commencement exercises at Chapel Hill, an annual pilgrimage that he had made without fail since his own graduation. He wrote Battle that his law practice and the season's political campaigns would keep him from making the trip south. Perhaps as important as all other considerations was Hill's own pride. He believed that he had laid the foundation, through determination and his own resources, for a successful future in politics and the law. He was not without influential friends and a solid bank account. By some reports, he had more than one hundred thousand dollars in the bank.

Moving to Durham would be like starting over, and with a formidable challenge at the outset. Many believed the talk that John Sprunt Hill was nothing more than the son-in-law of George Watts, Durham's most respected citizen.

CHAPTER 3

George Watts's Durham

THERE WAS NO MORE IMPORTANT or highly regarded man in Durham in the first decade of the new century than George Washington Watts. He had begun to put his imprint on the emerging city almost from the day he had arrived in March 1878. The Dukes accumulated greater wealth, but Watts, the Marylander, was the one who made Durham his home and the place where his money built businesses, churches, colleges, and hospitals, as well as one of the finest mansions in the state.

Watts helped transform Durham into a thriving community of some respectability. When he arrived to become a partner in W. Duke, Sons, and Company, Durham was a dirty, rough-and-tumble town; the Dukes ran just one of the dozen or so tobacco manufacturing houses that operated out of factories built along the shoulders of the North Carolina Railroad's tracks. Aside from the money that Watts and others believed could be made in the sale of small, cotton bags filled with shredded smoking tobacco, there was little to recommend Durham as a place to live. There were no city services, not even a public school. Most of Durham's houses were plain one-story structures made of whitewashed yellow pine that stood in stark contrast in a landscape stripped of trees. Here and there an occasional picket fence had been erected to keep the wandering cows and goats away from the front door. The dusty streets turned to mud in the rain.

This was a working man's town with no pretense of greatness. One of the town's main thoroughfares had been called Hen Peck Lane until it was renamed just a few years before Watts arrived in Durham. Four trains—two each from the east and west—arrived daily, but Durham had no direct connections to the major cities in the South. And while the population had grown tenfold to two thousand in a decade, a casual visitor would hardly

31

have taken notice. The town remained little more than a railroad stop in a state still laboring to overcome the waste of a civil war.

Watts moved to Durham from Baltimore, one of the most sophisticated cities on the eastern seaboard, where his father, Gerard S. Watts,[1] managed a successful wholesale tobacco business. The elder Watts was a man of money and property whose country home, Beverly, was a pleasant retreat from the city's bustling harbor and streets of commerce, where he did business among the fiercely competitive tobacco manufacturers. Only a year before George W. Watts's arrival in Durham, the owner of Durham's leading tobacco house, W. T. Blackwell Company, whose Bull Durham brand had put the town on the map, was in the elder Watts's office burdened with concern over the way the Dukes' Pro Bono Publico brand was winning away Blackwell customers throughout the West.[2]

George Watts had gone to work with his father, calling on merchants from New York City to St. Louis, in 1871, soon after he finished his studies at the University of Virginia. As a student, he had concentrated on chemistry and mathematics and graduated with a degree in engineering. The only product of his engineering skills, however, was his father's country house, in the design of which Watts had demonstrated a fine touch for architecture. The home was built of native stone and sat atop a hill with a commanding view of the lush, rolling Maryland countryside.

The contrast between Baltimore and Durham was extreme, but even amidst the town's dirt and rough appearance Watts found the prospect of a place where he could make a name for himself. As he made his way from the depot at the foot of Corcoran Street, he passed boardinghouses, dry goods and grocery stores, drugstores, confectioneries, a hotel, restaurants, barrooms, and a newspaper office where job printing paid most of the bills. His destination was the office of Washington Duke.

ᴏᴠᴏᴠᴏᴠ

At the time, Duke was in his late fifties. He had served the Confederacy only to return home from a Yankee prison to find a ruined farm. In the years since the war, he had parlayed a wagonload of tobacco into a going concern. His Pro Bono brand competed with Blackwell's better-known Bull Durham and a dozen others for the attention of smokers across the land who had developed a taste for Carolina bright leaf tobacco mixtures. Duke, Blackwell, and the others all smiled when the farmers' canvas-covered wagons lined up outside their factories to deliver tobacco, creating a "cloud of white." Blackwell's factory was said to be the largest of its kind in the world.[3]

George Watts's presence in Durham was evidence of the competitive nature of the tobacco business. For years, his father had been the sole distributor in Baltimore for Bull Durham; then, Blackwell gave the distribution to a Philadelphia wholesaler. Gerard Watts sought out the Dukes, who were eager for new capital, and they sold him a one-fifth interest in their growing business for $14,000. As part of the exchange, George Watts became a full partner with Duke and his three sons, James, Benjamin, and Brodie.

The growing popularity of the Duke brands was largely due to the hard work of James B. Duke, whom everyone called "Buck." In addition to supervising the manufacturing end of the business, he traveled the country in search of new outlets for Duke brands. Watts arrived with more formal schooling than any of his partners, and he eventually became the company's chief financial officer. In the early days, however, he joined Buck on the road and spent a portion of his first year working from an office in Chicago. He was not particularly happy about the distance that his work placed between him and his wife, Valinda, and their three-year-old daughter, Annie Louise, who was born September 15, 1876. His family remained in Baltimore until the summer of 1880, when Watts finished building a handsome new house on Morehead Hill just south of Durham's central district.

Laura Valinda Beall Watts, also known as Linnie, was three years younger than her husband, and she joined him in Durham reluctantly. She was a delicate woman who wore her curly brown hair pulled back from her face in a fashion that emphasized her expressive eyes and her soft pleasing appearance. Her family was from Cumberland in western Maryland, where the Bealls were prominent in the early history of the state. The couple married in 1875 and enjoyed the luxury of a long honeymoon before they settled in Baltimore, where she was at home with the comforts of the city.

George Watts had come south as more than the Dukes' new business partner. He was seeking a secure future for himself. Wholesalers like his father were seeing their markets crumble as tobacco manufacturers began selling directly to retailers in an effort to make their prices competitive. In a short time, the business world that Gerard Watts had known would change dramatically. Thus, George was the point man on the family's southern frontier. An alert venture capitalist, Gerard Watts would soon have his money invested in a Durham bank, an Alabama steel mill, and North Carolina textile mills, as well as in the Dukes' tobacco company.

❦❦❦

One of George Watts's early acquaintances in Durham was Eugene Morehead, the son of former North Carolina governor John Motley Morehead. Like Watts, Morehead was a recent arrival, having moved from Greensboro to open the Eugene Morehead and Company Banking House. He was lured away from Blandwood, his family's Tuscan-style villa, by Julian S. Carr, who had been a classmate at the university in Chapel Hill before the Civil War. Carr and other Durham boosters were ecstatic when Morehead opened his bank, Durham's first, in January 1879 and became the manager of the federal government's new revenue office. With Morehead on hand, tobacco manufacturers no longer had to travel to Raleigh to obtain the tax stamps they were required to put on their products.

The irrepressible Carr was the Blackwell tobacco faction's principal tub-thumper and promotional genius. He owned a sizeable portion of the Blackwell firm, and he put the Durham bull, the symbol of Blackwell's smoking tobacco, on anything and everything imaginable. Signs, posters, sample cards, and buildings carried illustrations of the hulking black bull. On one occasion, he attached its image to the heads of horses pulling carriages from Durham to Chapel Hill for university commencement. He was equally adept at promoting himself. Carr left the Confederate army a private, but by the time of his death in 1924 he was known as "General Carr" by virtue of his success in organizing veterans who had worn Southern gray.

Carr also knew the Wattses through their earlier association with Blackwell's tobacco, and he may have been the one who introduced Watts to Morehead. Morehead was six years older than Watts, but the two newcomers had sufficiently common backgrounds and interests to form a bond. Both were deeply religious men and were among the early members of Durham's small community of Presbyterians. Both constantly looked for new investments and business opportunities, and they would soon venture into a variety of projects together.

They also shared an appreciation for the finer things in life. Watts was a careful and meticulous dresser who kept his dark mustache neatly trimmed. Morehead was a self-confessed dandy. "I like to wear the longest coats, the biggest legged pants, the slenderest canes," he once wrote.[4] Both had left fine, comfortable homes to come to Durham with an eye to capitalizing on new opportunities, and they were often among the guests at

Carr's own expansive manor house, which he called Waverly Honor. There, Morehead and his wife, Lucy, the daughter of the founder and president of the Cotton Exchange of Savannah, Georgia, found the surroundings more to the tastes they had grown accustomed to in years past, when their needs had been taken care of by slaves. By the summer of 1879, Watts and Morehead had selected adjacent lots on a prominent rise south of town that would become known as Morehead Hill. It was said that the two tossed a coin to see whose house would sit closest to town. Morehead won.[5]

"Anything you do toward improvement of the lots we bought will be approved by me," Watts wrote Morehead from Chicago in July 1879, "but don't clear any of the woods on my portion. I would be well satisfied to find upon my return that everything there was in apple-pie order and two nice houses on our building sites. When do you propose to raise your house?"[6]

The Wattses and Moreheads moved into their homes in 1880, just as Durham was about to become the official seat of a new county. When Watts and Morehead had arrived, Durham was part of Orange County, and the county seat was in Hillsborough, fourteen miles to the west. In the spring of 1881, armed with data showing that Durham's population had increased, the General Assembly created Durham County, carving it out of portions of Orange and Wake counties. Washington Duke, a prominent Republican, was named to the county's first board of commissioners. At about the same time, Watts became a member of the city of Durham's board of aldermen.

During the 1880s, Durham would shake loose from its primitive beginnings and assume the trappings of a modern municipality. After businessmen found they could not secure fire insurance at reasonable rates because of a rash of fires on Main Street, the city's first fire company was formed. An electric light company brought arc lights to town, and a gas company was organized along with a central water system. The first public schools were opened. Local officials also began to heed the warnings of Dr. Albert G. Carr, Julian Carr's brother, about the health hazards created by polluted surface water and the absence of a general sewerage system. At one point, typhoid fever was so prevalent that residents in neighboring communities called it "Durham Fever."[7]

George Watts seemed to be in the middle of virtually everything. In 1880, he and Morehead helped organize the Durham Literary Society and Lyceum, which began making plans for a city library and the promotion of musical performances. He was appointed to the fire department, and he developed a concern about the health of Durham residents after discovering the extent of the sanitation problems while searching various corners of the town to find a site for the public cemetery.[8]

Watts joined others to help save the newly organized public schools after opponents—among them Washington Duke—filed lawsuits to close them. Duke and others argued that it was unfair to tax everyone for the benefit of a small group, principally the poor and black, who could not afford to send their children to the private schools then operating in town. Watts also joined with Morehead to form the Durham Electric Lighting Company in 1885. Three years later, with Julian Carr as one of his partners, he helped organize the gas company. In 1884, Watts's father became one of the principal investors in Morehead's bank. This new relationship gave Watts and the Dukes a slight edge over their competitors. Since the Morehead bank handled federal revenue stamps for all manufacturers, Watts could easily learn the sales volume of other manufacturers; it was slipping farther and farther behind the Dukes.

The Morehead and Watts families often shared their holiday celebrations with Gerard Watts, who, with his wife, joined them from Baltimore. "Yesterday morning I went hunting with Mr. Watts," Morehead wrote his wife a day or so after Christmas in 1882. "We had the finest sport yet. The day was magnificent, clear, cool, delicious. We got 7 rabbits. I took John with me. We got back to Mr. Watts's 'big turkey' dinner and did full justice to it. Annie Watts had her biggest Christmas! Lots of things: from home and abroad. Mr. and Mrs. Watts leave this p.m. I have enjoyed the old gentleman. She is quiet you know."[9]

❧❧❧

Durham was surely as good a place as any for men of wealth like Gerard Watts to invest their money. Certainly W. Duke, Sons, and Company proved a smart bet. At Buck Duke's insistence, the company had thrown itself into the production of machine-made cigarettes. With the advent of the new Bonsack machine, a contraption that eventually virtually eliminated hand-rolled cigarettes altogether, Duke began outproducing every competitor. By 1884, Buck Duke had moved to New York City to open a factory there, leaving management of the Durham office in the hands of his brother, Ben, and George Watts.

The bond between Watts and his partners grew stronger with each passing year. It was a comfortable relationship founded upon the shared virtues of hard work and right living. Watts's personal devotion to the Presbyterian Church was matched by the Dukes' deep faith in God and the Methodists. Whenever the company opened a factory, the partners built a church for workers nearby. Watts became a regular visitor at these factory churches, where he faithfully conducted Sunday school classes and Friday evening prayer meetings.

Competition among the tobacco companies was fierce, and the Dukes earned the eternal enmity of Blackwell and Carr. But Watts moved easily among the feuding factions. Unlike his father, who was high-tempered and impulsive, George Watts softened his own manner; according to someone who knew him later, he did so "without abating a scintilla of his natural firmness, and he gained strength by practicing self-possession, while he learned to abhor duplicity and to admire frankness, openness and honesty in purpose and action."[10]

Certainly Watts saw the advantages of Durham businessmen pulling together to improve conditions. In 1884, he was one of the organizers of the Commonwealth Club and was elected its first president. As such, he turned his attention to one of Durham's most pressing needs: improved rail service to handle the ever growing shipments of tobacco products. When Durham businessmen announced a public subscription in 1886 to build the local portion of a rail line between Sanford, North Carolina, and Lynchburg, Virginia, the Duke factories alone were producing more than 177 million cigarettes a year. Promoters said the new railroad would give the city far superior connections to new markets not readily available through the main lines running north and south.

Watts, Morehead, and Carr led the promotion of the new railroad and urged Durham County voters to approve the sale of $100,000 in bonds to pay for the construction of rails to be laid in the county. Samuel T. Morgan, another of Morehead's business partners, caught the enthusiasm of Durham in a letter he wrote a year later. "Well, the Town is on a regular 'Birmingham Boom' and they say will be the R R center for N.C. It looks like it now."[11]

Durham's exuberance turned to bust in 1888, however, when Blackwell's Bank of Durham went under. The financial panic also took down a number of businesses and created uneasiness in many quarters. The Morehead bank remained firm, however, as did the newly organized Fidelity Trust

Company and Savings Bank that Ben Duke, George Watts, and other investors had established the year before. For the most part, the bank accounts of Watts and the Dukes grew with each passing day, as cigarette sales expanded almost exponentially. While others scrambled to make do, the Duke company's revenue more than tripled. Even with heavy investment in advertising gimmicks and promotion, the partners enjoyed an annual profit of more than $300,000 at a time when other businesses were failing.

Watts's problem was not a shortage of money, but how to satisfy bankers looking for his business. Late in 1888, he responded to a scolding letter from Morehead, who had pointedly asked why he did not maintain a larger balance in the Morehead bank. "Boss, I have tried to be liberal to you," Watts responded, "but sometimes I can't, especially as I have to also carry a reasonable balance with Fidelity and a good one in N.Y. I am sorry you intimate I haven't done the 'whole thing' as there is nothing I would not do for you and Pa."[12] A few days earlier, in another letter to Morehead, he had accounted for his cash on hand of nearly $20,000, a third of which was in Morehead's bank.[13]

Morehead's health was failing, and he had begun spending more time in Savannah in the comfort of his wife's family home. He tried in vain to find relief from a malady that doctors from New Orleans to Baltimore could never diagnose. Certainly the unhealthy conditions in Durham did little to relieve him of his chronic ailments.

Durham's frontier appearance and unhealthy atmosphere may also have contributed to the frequent absences of Watts's wife Linnie. During the family's early years in Durham, she made extended visits to Maryland, especially during the hot days of summer. Durham was not her "home," she wrote a friend one day in July. "As I told George I feel as if I never wanted to see Durham again. I felt like taking a hearty cry when I got to Clara's. Everything looked so familiar, and brought so vividly to mind the happy days of yore. Annie is like a caged bird set free."[14]

In January 1889, Linnie Watts left for Baltimore to undergo medical treatments for painful cramping in her legs and feet that had been a problem for some time. (Her condition was later identified as chronic nephritis.) Her husband wrote her almost daily and brooded that he could not be there with her. "Ben [Duke] is giving no attention to business," he complained, "is not in the office 30 minutes a day and expects very soon to return to N.Y."[15] By the middle of February, Linnie had moved to the

Woman's Hospital in Baltimore, where her doctor, H. P. C. Wilson, finally responded to George's insistent demands for a medical report. In late February, he wrote that the cramping had eased; "I am now able to keep her womb comfortably in place and am making good progress in reducing the chronic inflation," he explained.[16] It was a puzzling diagnosis.

Watts's concern for his wife's health remained in his thoughts daily, even as he set aside the details of business to make arrangements for the funeral of Eugene Morehead, who died on February 27, 1889. At the request of Morehead's widow, Watts chose the pallbearers and selected a cemetery plot for his close friend and business partner. In the tribute he delivered at services in the First Presbyterian Church, Watts recalled an evening some eight years earlier when he and Morehead had sat by a fire talking of "this life and the next." Watts told the mourners: "[Morehead] said, 'I am not afraid to die. I am ready whenever the summons comes.' His last words to those about him were 'Lay me down.' They laid him down but Jesus picked him up."

A prominent figure at the funeral was Gerard Watts, who remained on for several days to make arrangements for a reorganization of the Morehead bank, which was now Durham's largest. Like others, Gerard Watts had anticipated Morehead's death. Just days after the funeral, he was among those named in the *Daily Tobacco Plant*'s announcement of the reorganized Morehead Banking Company.[17]

After attending to the details of the funeral and his father's business arrangements, George Watts was more than ready for his wife to return to Durham, but it was another two months before the stream of letters that flowed between Durham and Baltimore came to an end and she finally headed south. One of the last letters, written in late April after Linnie had been away for nearly four months, contained Watts's complaint about the mounting medical bills, including those from the doctors who would not provide a clear diagnosis of her condition. "I think it is an outrage or a mistake, if not a mistake he will have to wait for a good while for his money," Watts fumed in one letter.[18] When Linnie Watts did finally return home, she found a new telephone installed on Morehead Hill. But even more profound changes were in store.

❧❧❧

Late in 1889, James B. Duke was negotiating with four of his competitors to form an even larger concern, and on January 31, 1890, the American

Tobacco Company was born. With a total capitalization of $25 million, the Dukes and Wattses held $7.5 million worth of the common and preferred shares in the new company. The others taking shares in the new enterprise were the Allen and Ginter Company from Richmond, Virginia; Kinney Tobacco Company and Goodwin and Company of New York City; and Kimball and Company of Rochester, New York. Together, the firms produced most of the 2.1 billion cigarettes made in 1889, with the Duke firm accounting for 940 million of that total.[19] For George Watts and his father, the cigarette combine meant that the family's initial $14,000 investment made a dozen years earlier had grown to about $1.5 million. In March 1890, W. Duke, Sons, and Company became a "branch" of the American Tobacco Company, with Ben Duke and George Watts named as the managing partners. American Tobacco began consolidating its production at factories in Durham, Richmond, and New York.

The creation of American Tobacco took place only a few months before the passage of the nation's first law designed to restrain the power of the economic interests that had begun to monopolize all manner of American businesses. The Sherman Antitrust Act, passed in April 1890, was named for U.S. senator John Sherman of Ohio, who emerged as one of the most ardent foes of John D. Rockefeller's Standard Oil Company. At the time, Standard Oil controlled the nation's growing petroleum industry, but it was only one of a number of trusts that fixed prices and eliminated competition from the sale of everyday products from whiskey and sugar to screen doors and steel. Neither the new law nor the growing howl from American voters over the political corruption spawned by the trusts deterred the barons of Wall Street. Standard Oil continued to operate virtually unchanged, and other trusts and huge business combinations, such as the new American Tobacco Company, joined it. Sherman's law was derided as the "Swiss Cheese Act" because it was so full of loopholes.[20]

James B. Duke was clearly the driving force behind the creation of American Tobacco Company and the one who continuously pushed his brothers, his father, and their partner to raise W. Duke, Sons, and Company to a position of dominance. He had maneuvered the business into the mass production of cigarettes and won a concession from the Bonsack manufacturers so that the Duke firm would always be in a position to make cigarettes at a lower cost than its competitors. He embraced the full gospel of Wall Street and the rush to bigness in the same way that his father, Wash-

George W. Watts.

George W. Watts (second from right) with his golfing partner and their two caddies, probably at Pinehurst at the beginning of the twentieth century.

*John Sprunt Hill was a private in Troop A of Squadron A, the cavalry of the
New York National Guard, during the Spanish-American War.*

John Sprunt Hill, probably during his years in New York.

*John Sprunt Hill began playing golf during his courtship
of Annie Watts.*

*Annie Louise Watts, the only daughter of George and Laura Valinda Watts, met
John Sprunt Hill while she was attending school in New York City.*

A family portrait. From the left, standing, are George Watts's mother Mrs. Gerard Watts, John Sprunt Hill, Annie Watts Hill, and George W. Watts. Seated are Gerard Watts and his daughter-in-law Laura Valinda Watts, who is holding her first grandson, George Watts Hill.

The infant Watts Hill with his nurse.

George W. Watts's mansion, Harwood Hall, on Duke Street in Durham.

Harwood Hall's music room.

The main staircase and foyer at Harwood Hall.

The smoking room at Harwood Hall.

The second Watts Hospital in Durham opened in 1909. It later became the home of the North Carolina School of Science and Mathematics.

John Sprunt Hill's home on Duke Street reflected the Spanish mission style design that architects used in building Watts Hospital.

John Sprunt Hill, seated fifth from left, in Budapest with a national commission that traveled throughout Europe in 1913. On this trip, Hill learned of the potential of credit unions for American farmers.

Annie Watts Hill.

The three children of John Sprunt and Annie Hill: George Watts and his younger sisters Frances (left) and Valinda.

ington, had accepted the faith of his fathers and the Methodist Church. For James B. Duke, the merger made good business sense. In addition to eliminating competitors, the combination of the firms gave him a level of support for further ventures that would otherwise have been out of reach.

In testimony given nearly twenty years later in the federal government's antitrust proceedings against the American Tobacco Company, Duke explained his strategy this way:

> Well, my father was a very old man and he had practically retired from business. Mr. Watts and my brother, B. N. Duke, they were in very bad health and my brother, B. L. Duke, had nothing at all to do with the business, so that practically left the management of the business in my hands, and I had not had time really to build up an organization to help me conduct the business except to do the clerical work, or to do what I directed to be done.
>
> I thought in selling our business to the American Tobacco Company in connection with other manufacturers would get a good organization of people who would be of assistance in conducting the business, and then besides that I expected to make a profit by it because you can handle to better advantage a large business than a small business.[21]

The potential of the American Tobacco Company was not lost on the Dukes' competitors, nor on Richard H. Wright, one of their former partners and a prominent figure in Durham business affairs. In 1880, Wright had purchased Washington Duke's share of the company and become a full partner with the sons and George Watts. Five years later, however, when Buck pushed his partners to put more money into the business, Wright was unable to come to terms with his partners, and he threatened to sell his interest to a competitor until the Dukes and Watts settled with him for nearly $40,000 in cash. In 1891, Wright sued the Dukes and Watts, claiming they had defrauded him by failing to disclose the existence of the Bonsack agreement, which gave them an edge over their competitors. Wright said he only learned about the special discounts offered by Bonsack when he discovered a letter written by Watts in which he asked the machine's patent holders to keep their arrangement with the Duke firm a secret. Wright claimed that one-fifth of the American Tobacco Company's assets were rightfully his.

The case was decided against Wright in 1893, when a New York trial judge ruled in favor of the defendants. Wright subsequently appealed, and as the case lingered it became particularly vexing for Watts, who was held up to ridicule by Al Fairbrother, the feisty editor of the *Durham Globe*. It was not the first time that Fairbrother had taken aim at Watts. Two years earlier, he had accused Watts and his business partners in the Durham Fertilizer Company, including Watts's brother-in-law Louis A. Carr (no relation to Julian Carr), of defrauding farmers and attempting to avoid payment of taxes on fertilizer shipments.[22]

Fairbrother applauded the judge's decision in the Wright case but accused Watts of duplicity in the affair. "So far as we are concerned, with the evidence at hand, we expect that no honest man would believe as sorry a creature as George Watts," he wrote. Watts canceled his subscription in the wake of the insults; Fairbrother, however, would not let the matter drop. He published letters of praise that Watts had written about the paper before the fertilizer incident, and, continuing his attack, he wrote, "It may be that he would be believed—but since he wrote us that he could not sleep without the *Globe*, and that he still sleeps, we think he remains the polite Presbyterian liar that he seemed to have been in the old days."[23]

Within two weeks of publishing this damning claim, Fairbrother was visited by a delegation of leading Durham men that included J. S. Manning, city council members C. H. Norton and E. G. Lineberry, and a "Mr. Erwin"; they demanded that Fairbrother cease his attacks on Watts. Fairbrother challenged the delegation in a subsequent edition, which turned out to be one of his last as editor of the *Globe*. He soon gave up his job and left town.

⌒⌐⌒⌐⌒⌐

At the time of the incident with Fairbrother, Watts was one of Durham's wealthiest residents; he was also one of the town's busiest men, as the wheels of commerce greased by the tobacco millions turned even faster. Often found in tandem with Ben Duke, Watts expanded his investments into an increasing variety of business ventures, not the least of which was one that involved the "Mr. Erwin" referred to by Fairbrother. Ben Duke and Watts brought W. A. Erwin to Durham in 1892 to run their newly organized Erwin Cotton Mills Company. Searching for a name for the business, Duke had suggested they use Erwin's, since the eventual success or failure of the business depended on him.

The new mill they built on Durham's western edge began manufacturing the cotton fabric that was used to make bags for tobacco; it entered into direct competition with Julian Carr's Durham Cotton Manufacturing Company, which had begun business eight years earlier. Two years later, Duke and Watts took over the Pearl Mill, which had been founded by Brodie Duke but had stalled after Brodie lost most of his fortune in the 1893 financial crisis. By 1895, Watts and Duke and their partners had a combined textile operation that employed nearly six hundred workers. They also invested heavily in a Danville, Virginia, textile mill, and they would eventually take over mills in Morganton, Oxford, and Cooleemee, North Carolina.

Watts followed the Dukes and invested in other ventures, such as the Keeley Institute in Greensboro, whose founder, Dr. Leslie Keeley, claimed to have had amazing success in curing drug addicts and alcoholics. Ben's brother, Brodie, underwent Dr. Keeley's treatment at his hospital in Illinois, but it did not take. Brodie continued to be plagued by alcoholism.

At the same time, Watts kept his lines open to Julian Carr, who, like Watts, was one of the town's most energetic developers. One of Carr's latest projects was the Hotel Carrolina, a huge, rambling seventy-room hotel with broad verandas and an imposing tower. Lavishly decorated rooms featuring frescoes by local artists pushed the building cost to $85,000 by the time the hotel opened in 1893. In 1894, George Watts, Julian Carr, and Louis Carr formed the Interstate Telephone and Telegraph Company after an earlier effort by Southern Bell Telephone and Telegraph Company failed to satisfy customers. The new company offered home service for $20 a month, compared to Southern Bell's $36, and subsequently it bought the Bell facilities.[24]

None of these business ventures produced a more amicable business partnership than the one Watts enjoyed with the Dukes. The men had much in common: good business sense, wide-ranging contacts, a strong Protestant work ethic, and deep religious faith. After 1890, however, the men saw one another as often in New York as in North Carolina. Buck visited mostly during the holidays. Ben talked for ten years about building a large home in Durham, but at the turn of the century he purchased property on Fifth Avenue for his New York residence before he began work on Four Acres, the estate he eventually built on the western edge of Durham's business district.

According to some writers, Ben Duke's move to New York City was hastened by the growing intensity of the attacks on the American Tobacco

Company and the ferocity of the political campaigns in the mid- to late 1890s. Opponents lumped the Dukes, Republicans, trusts, and the evils of cigarette smoking all into one easy target.[25] A particularly vocal antagonist was Raleigh newspaper editor Josephus Daniels, who accused the Dukes of supporting a competing newspaper in Raleigh in 1897 in an effort to undermine his investment in the recently purchased *News and Observer*. Daniels produced a newspaper that openly supported the Democratic Party, and he fired regular broadsides at the enormous power of the American Tobacco Company.[26] The Duke-sponsored paper supported Republican governor Daniel L. Russell.

Washington Duke remained the venerable patriarch and absorbed the criticism that sprang from his son Buck's aggressive marketing and empire building. The elder Duke was well regarded in Durham, where he had built his home adjacent to the factory. Over the years, he had heard all manner of objections to his family's business practices. Methodist clergymen complained about the promotional cards featuring curvaceous models that accompanied early packs of cigarettes. The anger of tobacco farmers and competitors over the growing "Tobacco Trust" left him uncomfortable. Daniels would later write that the old man confided to him on one occasion that he was having second thoughts about his son's ambition. Daniels wrote that Duke told him, "I wish Buck had never put us into the [American Tobacco] company and that we could carry on our business like we used to do it. We were making lots of money and did not have any criticism."[27]

∾∾∾

Although he had his differences with Fairbrother and the *Globe*, Watts escaped much of the public criticism that Daniels heaped on the Dukes and the American Tobacco Company. His name was not Duke, for one thing, and unlike his partners he was a practicing Democrat. He also seemed more skillful in dealing with touchy public issues. After all, he had campaigned successfully for public schools over Washington Duke's opposition, he had fought for community improvements such as a fire department and paved streets, and he had even become involved in the agrarian movement in the late 1880s when failing farm prices had impoverished North Carolina and Virginia tobacco farmers. When more than two hundred tobacco farmers met in Durham in December 1888, Watts represented his partners at the gathering and urged farmers to establish their own collective sales warehouses rather than pay a portion of the income from their sales to brokers and dealers. Watts's credentials with the farmers were sufficient to help the Durham Fertilizer Company, in which he held a considerable stake, secure the endorsement of Leonidas L. Polk, founder of the *Progressive Farmer* and one of the best-known leaders of the emerging Farmers' Alliance.

Watts joined the Dukes in their support of Trinity College. The school was struggling financially in 1893 when Watts and Ben Duke arranged for the Travelers' Insurance Company of Hartford, Connecticut, to buy the school's entire subscription of $40,000 in bonds.[28] He helped pay for Durham's first YMCA, and his work as a Sunday school teacher was much admired in a town that put a premium on piety. Watts and his father also helped underwrite the operation of Elizabeth College in Charlotte, a small Lutheran girls' school where Gerard Watts's son-in-law, C. B. King, was president.

Perhaps George Watts's most generous contribution was the hospital he built on more than four acres on West Main Street and dedicated to the city on February 21, 1895. The hospital project was the culmination of a series of incidents that had aroused Watts to an awareness of the desperate need for adequate local health care. On the evening of the inauguration of the facility, Watts cited his own recent hospitalization—he suffered from debilitating headaches that he blamed on his diet and a busy schedule—as well as the continuing medical care required by his wife as important factors in his decision to build the hospital. At the same time, he said that building the hospital was a way for him to return something to a community that had proved to be so beneficial to his financial health.

"I had never seen the faces of but three residents of Durham previous to our coming here," Watts said at the inauguration of the new facility. "Yet, we were warmly welcomed, received into your homes, invited to your churches, and encouraged in every way to make ourselves part of the commonwealth. From that day to the present we have cheerfully reciprocated the feelings as then expressed, and we have endeavored to become fellow citizens with you; we have to the best of our feeble abilities striven to aid in the growth and progress of the town, have been jealous at all times of her good name and rejoined in her continued advancement and progression in numbers, education, morality and wealth."[29]

Another important factor in Watts's decision to build the hospital was a decade of association with Dr. Albert G. Carr, the Watts family physician. Carr had been pushing for a hospital since the mid-1880s, when he and Watts had seen the unhealthy condition of Durham's back streets. (In truth, the entire state ranked near the bottom for availability of health care.) Watts also may have been influenced by his own brother, who was trained as a doctor but died at the age of twenty-nine in 1889. Whatever the reasons for it, Watts's generosity spoke to the needs of the community and his own conscience.[30]

In addition to providing medical care, Watts designed the hospital to provide training for nurses. He told his audience at the dedication that when he was convalescing in Baltimore, the nurse who cared for him was "an angel of mercy at the bedside of the sick." When such a woman cares for a patient, he explained, "she knows his needs, she realizes his condition, her hand is always ready to make him comfortable, her earnest sympathy encourages him, her firmness stimulates him, and her training enables her to faithfully carry out the physician's instructions." He commented, "More than once I have been told that her services are more valuable than physic."[31]

Watts Hospital was built at a cost of $30,000, and it included five buildings, four of them connected by covered walkways. Described as a "cottage hospital," the buildings provided separate pavilions for men and women, a surgical center, and an administration building on a four-and-a-half-acre tract on West Main Street. The facility was equipped with the latest in heating, ventilating, and sanitation, as well as a system of electric bells that allowed patients to summon a nurse from their beds. It was, Watts emphasized, the finest facility money could buy, and its twenty-two beds would be open to all white citizens regardless of their ability to pay. Watts also provided $20,000 in stocks and bonds as an endowment to underwrite the operation of the hospital. He put the facility under a board of trustees composed of representatives from his family, Durham's mainstream religious denominations, the Hospital Aid Association, the Academy of Medicine, the town commissioners, and Trinity College, whose president, John F. Crowell, harbored dreams of opening a medical school.

Three years earlier, when the Methodists had relocated small Trinity College from rural Randolph County to Durham, Crowell had encouraged a plan to incorporate the training of medical students and the operation of a hospital. Those ambitions evaporated with the financial crisis of 1893. It must have become apparent to Watts that if Durham was going to have a hospital, it would have to come from somewhere other than Trinity; this realization may have influenced his decision to move on his own.

The construction of the hospital was a major undertaking, and Josephus Daniels said that Watts's benevolence was an example to other men of wealth. "There are twenty cities in the State that need such a hospital," he wrote.[32]

∾∾∾

Watts's dedication to improving the physical health of Durham citizens was matched only by his devotion to their moral well-being. Watts had been raised in the Lutheran Church, but when he brought his family to Durham they joined the Presbyterian Church at a time when the total Durham congregation numbered only forty-three souls. He became quite comfortable among these Durham disciples of John Calvin. They were serious followers of the Lord, even too much so for some. One minister called to fill the pulpit for a period in the summer of 1885 found the Durham congregation suffering from a "a collective Calvinistic frigidity." The Reverend Joseph Ruggles Wilson wrote his son Woodrow, the future president of the United States who was then teaching at Bryn Mawr College: "In addressing them from the pulpit, I find only unresponsive hearers, while at the prayer meeting I conducted the other night, the air was chilled by their freezing manner."[33]

If members were missed at communion or worship services, the church elders, who included George Watts, called upon them to account for their absences. The elders considered it their duty to monitor the spiritual health of the membership, and on occasion they suspended membership on charges of "conduct unbecoming a Christian."[34] Public intoxication was more than sufficient to qualify for censure.

Watts enjoyed good preaching and the authoritarian, stiff-necked gospel delivered by the church's early ministers. If for some reason the church's regular minister was away from the pulpit, Watts would seek out a good sermon wherever he could find it. In 1889, when his wife was convalescing in Baltimore, he wrote her that he was "thinking of going over to Hayti and hear the Negro preacher who is said to be a fine one."

Watts energetically shouldered more than his share of the work of the Lord. He assumed personal financial responsibility for Presbyterian foreign missions in Korea and Cuba as well as a Lutheran college in India, and he helped the Durham church support other missionaries—thirteen in all—who were working in Africa and Brazil. In 1885, he took on the super-intendency of the Sunday school, a job he would hold for more than thir-ty-five years. In 1894, when the Presbyterians sponsored a church at Brodie Duke's Pearl Mill, where a Methodist mission had been built as well, Watts paid for the construction of a small, frame chapel. He ministered there reg-ularly, praising the work of his Sunday school pupils who attended Friday prayer meetings and Sunday classes. After each meeting, as folks left ser-vices he led with fellow church member Leo Heartt, the cashier at Julian Carr's bank, he "democratically shook hands with all and sundry," as one congregant recalled.[35]

Watts's generosity spread to many Presbyterian institutions. He built and furnished a cottage for girls at the Barium Springs Orphanage and named it for his daughter. When Annie Louise was married in 1899, a light was hung in every window, and at the same hour as the wedding in Durham the girls performed a mock ceremony of their own. When his grandson, George Watts Hill, was born, Watts made another donation that he repeated each year on his grandson's birthday. For years, the children in the cottage held a birthday party for a child they never knew. Among the annual rituals was opening small gilded nutshells that contained a picture of the baby.

Watts and his father also contributed to Elizabeth College in Charlotte and to three other Presbyterian schools: Flora MacDonald and Davidson colleges and the Lees-McRae Institute, a mountain school tucked away on the north side of the Blue Ridge Mountains in Avery County. The school that received Watts's closest attention, and much of his money, however, was Union Theological Seminary in Virginia, where he was elected a trustee in 1894.

The primary training ground for Presbyterian clergy in Virginia and the Carolinas, Union Seminary was located on the campus of Hampden-Syd-ney College in Farmville, Virginia, when Watts became one of the first lay-men elected to the Board of Trustees. Church leaders worried that the school's location in a rural backwater was responsible for its declining en-rollment, so with the election of a new young president, the Reverend Wal-ter W. Moore, they began a campaign that led to its relocation to Rich-mond. Major Lewis Ginter, a business associate of Watts and one of the tobacco manufacturers who had been part of the original American To-bacco Company, offered the school thirty-three acres in a new residential section that Ginter was beginning to develop northeast of downtown. Title to the land hung like a carrot before Moore, who was challenged to raise $50,000 to make the deal. Finally, Watts provided the needed cash, and the trustees named their first building on the Richmond campus in his honor.

Opened in 1897, Watts Hall was built in the popular French Renaissance style and set at the head of a quadrangle of campus buildings. The building's central tower stood more than four stories tall—inside was the school's water supply—and was flanked by gabled sections clad in brick of a deep, rich red color. In 1900, Watts sent the school another $20,000 to add a chapel capable of seating 500 persons. Paneled in dark wood, with an overhead choir loft and wraparound gallery under a high, vaulted ceiling, the chapel became the focus of campus events. At the faculty's request, Watts commissioned a portrait of himself that a century later still hung on a landing on the building's broad stairs.

In later years, Walter Moore often told of Watts postponing important New York business meetings so that he could attend sessions of the Union trustees. In 1905, Watts became the first layman elected president of the Board of Trustees, and he was reelected each year until 1911, when he was made its permanent president.

⊶⊶⊶

Watts spread his money around liberally during this very expansive period. He certainly had plenty in the bank, as the American Tobacco Company continued to increase its share of the tobacco market. By 1899, the company had even absorbed the famous Bull Durham brand and had brought the Reynolds tobacco operations from Winston-Salem into the fold. Buck Duke enlisted the financial aid of Wall Street barons like Oliver Payne of Standard Oil to continue his consolidation, and the company shed many of its original directors. A decade after the company was organized, the only directors who remained from the first board were the Dukes and Watts, whose fortunes grew with each passing year.

Yet with his grand house, his servants, and his frequent travel across the country and abroad, Watts was not ostentatious. "He is not given to any of the amusements that engage many men of wealth," a Durham writer once observed.[36] Watts invested himself in civic affairs and church work; he closely followed the example of America's most famous millionaire, the pious John D. Rockefeller, who believed that his great riches were a gift from God to be used for good works.[37]

The one thing that Watts's wealth and influence had not been able to move was his son-in-law, John Sprunt Hill. Watts and his wife were unhappy that their only daughter lived hundreds of miles away in New York City. The parents visited New York often, and the two families spent time together during the holidays and on vacation in the summer at Atlantic City, New Jersey, and Poland Springs, Maine. That was not enough for the Wattses, however, especially after the birth of their grandson, George Watts's namesake, on October 27, 1901. The family pressure on Hill only increased, and at one point the Wattses even considered leaving Durham themselves and relocating to New York. It was said that prayer meetings were held in Durham against that eventuality.[38]

For his part, Hill was not impressed with his father-in-law's offer to ensure that his income would remain the same if he moved to Durham. If Hill made the change, he would make it on his own terms. For the sake of family harmony, Hill did look at opening a law practice in Durham, but he set that idea aside when he discovered that even the best lawyer in town made one-fourth his annual income. Finally, Hill arrived at a plan that he presented to George Watts during the Christmas holidays in 1902. Hill proposed a business enterprise that would ultimately change the way Durham bankers treated their customers. Watts gave his endorsement, and in 1903, John Sprunt Hill began to make the transition from lawyer to businessman.

$\mathscr{A}$ $\mathscr{N}$ew $\mathscr{C}$entury, a $\mathscr{N}$ew $\mathscr{S}$tart

---

JOHN SPRUNT AND ANNIE WATTS HILL SPENT most of August 1903 at the comfortable resort hotel at Poland Springs, Maine, in anticipation of their move to Durham, a change that would profoundly shape their lives. Hill joined his father-in-law in golf, his favorite pastime, while back in Durham workmen readied his new home. It was the tall frame house with striking Victorian lines that George W. Watts had built when he first moved to Durham and had later moved down the hill to make way for Harwood Hall.

The move was a real homecoming for Annie, who had longed to be closer to her parents. The decision to leave New York was more problematic for her ambitious husband. He loved his law practice and had achieved some notice as a leader in Democratic Party politics. He left all that behind, along with a fashionable home and other pleasures of city life such as his tailor, whom Hill had kept busy creating a splendid wardrobe. Like his clothes, the carriage he shipped south was out of place in a town where pavement was considered an extravagance and politics was settled in one of the town's twenty-three saloons. "It was a raw place," Hill later said of the Durham he found in 1903, "[with] more bastards and illegitimates than any place you ever saw."[1]

Yet Hill approached the move to Durham with anticipation. For all his affinity for New York, he remained close to the state of his birth and especially to the university, which had raised him up high enough to see the broader horizons. He also felt obliged to help his mother, widowed since 1900, and his unmarried sisters who lived with her in Faison. While Hill had good reasons to move to Durham, it was of paramount importance to him that he remain in control of his own destiny. If he was going to take advantage of his father-in-law's wealth, it would be as a backstop for new business enterprises, not as a sinecure. One morning not long after he arrived, he found a $1,000 check from Watts, who later explained it was compensation for Hill's help in managing his investments. Hill returned the check; he said there was not that much work to do. George Watts never spoke of such a thing again.

❧ ❧ ❧

Hill and Watts had worked out the details of an ambitious real estate and banking business during the Hills' visit to Durham over the Christmas holidays of 1902. Hill returned with his family to New York after the holidays, but then he headed back to Durham alone, quietly checked into a hotel, and began preparations for his new business, which included acquiring property on which to erect an office building. He proceeded with as much secrecy as possible. Certainly, once word leaked about his plans, he and George Watts would pay the price. Hill did not intend to suffer anyone with plans to dig a few more nickels out of Watts's pockets.

"I slept most of the day and worked all night," he later told his grandson, Watts Hill Jr. "You had to never be seen." He roamed the city and the surrounding area looking at property. Finally he settled on a lot at the corner of Market and Main streets as the site for his building. He bought the lot as well an adjacent building, which had formerly housed a saloon. A large tract that included an abandoned warehouse just west of downtown in an area later known as Five Points also caught his eye. He bought that and was looking for more when he received a telegram from Watts, who was in New York with Annie and the family. Word of Hill's buying spree had reached Ben Duke, who wrote Watts to tell him his son-in-law had gone crazy. "Mr. Watts was awful worried about it," Hill said later. "He telegraphed back here to two or three friends to talk to me about it and see what I was doing. I was cagey as I could be."[2]

In a few weeks, however, Hill's plan became public when he carried draft legislation to Raleigh that asked the General Assembly for charters for two new state banks. One bill authorized the creation of the Home Savings Bank (Hill originally planned to call it the Watts Savings Bank), which would conduct regular banking business. The second created a company Hill called the Durham Loan and Trust Company. It would have no tellers, nor would it take deposits; instead, Hill planned to use the company to manage investments, sell insurance, and secure bonds, as well as buy and sell real estate.

What Hill had in mind was a radical departure from banking as local businessmen knew it. In Durham, as in most of the state, the rule that only those who had money could borrow more was honored at Durham's principal banks: Fidelity, the city's largest, which had been started by Ben Duke, and the smaller First National Bank, which was owned by Julian Carr. Neither bank did much to solicit new business, and both paid interest on savings accounts only when depositors insisted. Moreover, to secure a loan, borrowers were required to pay commissions to agents—mostly lawyers cozy with the bank officers—that could add as much as 20 percent to the legal limit of 6 percent interest.

Hill reasoned there was a place in Durham for a well-funded and well-managed savings bank that would succeed without these payoffs and at the same time serve the working man and the farmer. Such a venture had done well in Wilmington, North Carolina, Hill told Watts in a detailed memorandum, and Wilmington was a market with less potential than Durham. He explained: "A good savings bank with large deposits, paying 4% to depositors who will rely upon the good name of George W. Watts, as well as the 4% will be the means of furnishing large amounts of money to be used in loans on good real estate, to cotton mills, tobacco factories, Durham Loan and Trust Company, Fidelity National Bank at 5% and 6% interest."[3]

Hill also appealed to his father-in-law's Presbyterian ethic and thrifty nature. He argued that the bank would build up Durham and "would teach [working people] to save their earnings and improve their condition." He wrote: "The improvement in the general character of these people which always follows in the wake of widely distributed savings bank accounts would, in the long run become a great monument to the example and memory of George W. Watts."[4]

Meanwhile, Durham Loan and Trust Company would concentrate on managing trusts, floating bonds for commercial ventures, developing real estate, and selling a wide range of insurance. Implied, but never stated, was the fact that the business would also make the perfect platform from which to manage a portion of Watts's millions. Hill also anticipated picking up a respectable portion of the insurance business of American Tobacco Company, which paid about $9,000 a year in commissions on fire insurance to Durham agencies. Hill predicted that in return for a share of Durham Loan and Trust's business, the Fidelity Bank would serve as the depository for all the trust company's accounts. He also advised Watts that the state-chartered Fidelity—where Watts was a director—would be better served if Ben Duke would convert its charter to a national one to avoid what Hill called the "populistic" tendencies of legislators in Raleigh to tax banks. (Duke did not follow his advice.)

Hill showed a keen appreciation of sales promotion. He told Watts that the trust company representatives "should be the first persons to meet the person who moves to town." He continued: "Rent him a house—sell him a house—take his money away from him and put it in the savings bank or in the Fidelity National Bank, to be turned over four or five times during the year in business deals around Durham. This business has proven very successful at Greensboro, Charlotte and Burlingham [sic], and [Greensboro banker E. P.] Wharton agrees with me that Durham is a better field now than any of the places mentioned ever was."[5]

Hill's confidence in the eventual success of his venture could only have been augmented by the lazy habits of Durham's bankers. Hill told Watts that Fidelity had broken one of the cardinal rules of banking by putting too much of its money into large loans to its directors and their good friends. It made money in spite of itself, largely because of the reputation of its directors, Ben Duke and George Watts, and of the American Tobacco Company. Carr's First National Bank suffered from the same weakness, Hill said. When the financial markets failed—and they had demonstrated erratic behavior with alarming frequency—large lenders would default, and the banks would be in jeopardy. Hill discounted competition from the Morehead Banking Company, Durham's first bank, where Gerard S. Watts remained a director, and from the Citizen's Savings Bank, which was struggling to remain afloat. According to Hill, "It was barely organized before its directors frightened depositors by turning all the deposits into law offices, schemes and speculations."[6] The close comparison that could be made between their actions and his own plan seemed not to matter.

While Hill's office building was under construction, he took an office above a clothing store at 213 South Main Street, located across from the construction site. By February 1904, masons were laying the last of the exterior brick of the five-story building, which would be, when finished, the tallest in the state and fashionably distinctive. The structure's curved southeastern corner, set at an acute angle to Main Street, was reminiscent of the prow of a ship when viewed from the east. As work on this building proceeded, Hill announced plans for the construction of a second building immediately across Market Street from the Trust Building. His announcement was premature, however. It would be another five years before work on that building would begin.

The Trust Building opened in late June 1904 to high praise with an impressive list of tenants, the largest of them companies in which George Watts had an interest. The building cost $89,000 to build, considerably more than the $60,000 Hill had asked Watts to put up for construction. It would not be the last of Hill's building projects to go over budget. The front entrance opened onto a wide central terrazzo-tile concourse that ran from Main to Parrish Street at the back and separated the offices of the Fidelity Bank on the right from those of the new Home Savings Bank on the left. The building had an elevator—the first in town—that carried passengers to the upper floors, where the offices of the Virginia-Carolina Chemical Company and the city's chamber of commerce were located. The Life Insurance Company of Virginia took space on the third floor near the offices of Fuller and Fuller, a law firm closely associated with the American Tobacco Company, and Watts, who moved from W. Duke, Sons, and Company. Smaller offices were available for rent on the fourth and fifth floors. Just below street level on the right was a barbershop that was directly across from the offices of the Postal Telegraph and Western Union. The telegraph's staccato could be heard from the curb on Market Street, where the Western Union boys parked their bicycles. "Our little city is ever forging to the front," the *Durham Sun* boasted, "putting on more metropolitan airs as the days go by. We are bound to be a big city some day."[7]

The Home Savings Bank commenced business with the opening of the Trust Building. Just one day earlier, Watts and Hill had completed the merger of Home Savings with the Citizen's Savings Bank. Watts was named president of the new company, and Hill vice president. A month later, near the end of August, the Board of Directors for the Durham Loan and Trust Company held its organizational meeting. Hill was elected president and his brother Isham, who had left his position at Fidelity, was elected secretary and treasurer.

The merger with the wobbly Citizen's Savings Bank had not been part of Hill's original plan, but shifting financial markets and anxious investors may have forced the change in strategy. Some potential stockholders had been scared away by Hill's plan to voluntarily pay interest on savings accounts.[8] He was called a "wildcat in the banking business,"[9] Hill later recalled. "If I had shot somebody, it wouldn't have made more of a sensation," he said. Ben and Buck Duke remained cautious. Old-timers in Durham had scoffed at his plans for the new office building. Sixty days before the bank opened, Watts confided to Ben Duke that he had quietly acquired a controlling interest in Citizen's and he hoped that Ben would join in the new venture. Ben subsequently invested in both the Home Savings Bank and Durham Loan and Trust, and, perhaps more important, he rented a large portion of Hill's building for the offices of Fidelity Bank.

An unexpected turn in the nation's financial market created problems for Hill just as his plans began to unfold. Around the time that Hill and Watts went looking for investors early in 1903, the usually profitable Virginia-Carolina Chemical Company failed to pay dividends and its stock price plummeted. At the same time, cotton mills throughout the South introduced short hours as business slowed. After the glorious economic run in 1902, Wall Street had grown nervous when President Theodore Roosevelt's attorney general filed antitrust actions following the fight among Wall Street titans for control of the Northern Pacific Railroad. Gilt-edged stocks such as American Tobacco took a beating. The price of Standard Oil fell from $800 to $650 in one day.

Watts was so badly shaken in the summer of 1903 that he appealed for help to Buck Duke, who was occupied with final negotiations to reorganize the American Tobacco Company into a worldwide enterprise. "You have no idea how humiliated and ashamed I feel of my experiences on Wall Street," Watts wrote Duke in August before heading to Poland Springs with the family, "not so much that I have lost a fortune and cut my income in half, as because some of my bonds were sold contrary to our agreement, while you was worried & harassed to protect the bonds & other tobacco securities on the market." He continued:

> I have always, that is for over 20 years, regarded you & Ben as my closest
> friends outside of my family, but the last few years your responsibilities
> have become so large & your interests so many that I had no idea that you
> gave me and my affairs more than a passing thought, so when Ben told
> me what he did down deep in my heart I felt God bless Buck, not that you
> were willing to help me but that the old friendship was there, even busi-
> ness & cares couldn't keep it down. This is a very bright spot to me

among the clouds. I have admired you as a great genius, but I have esteemed you more as an intimate friend & I am glad my foolishness & blunders have not estranged you. I would sooner lose my arm than to lose your personal regard & friendship.[10]

Even with his losses, Watts remained one of the wealthiest men in the state. Out of about four thousand millionaires in the entire country, Watts was one of five in Durham (the others were Washington Duke, his sons Ben and Buck, and Julian Carr), certainly a signal honor for a town that had barely existed a quarter century before.[11] There is no way to calculate the value of Watts's holdings in 1904, but at the time of his death in 1921, after a quarter century of philanthropy, his estate was worth more than $15 million, an amount equal to about $255 million in 2002 dollars. His investments included the American Tobacco Company, Durham utilities (including the telephone company), banks, Alabama steel mills, cotton oil, a chemical company, railroads, and textile mills. His connections with the Duke brothers had provided an entrée to many moneymaking, and money risking, opportunities, including the expansion of Erwin Mills at an entirely new town, Duke (later renamed Erwin), in Harnett County.

Watts stood by his son-in-law, and that commitment proved essential, especially after Hill discovered the details of the shocking portfolio of bad debts and past due notes in the Citizen's Savings Bank that he and Watts had just purchased. Hill was going through the bank's books when the cashier told him, "Mr. Hill you better go outside and loose [sic] your lunch because this bank is busted, broke. The big people in Durham have borrowed all the money."[12] With that tip, Hill set about to collect every dollar that was owed.

Hill ignored competitors who said he was headed to bankruptcy when he declared that the only thing borrowers needed for a loan was collateral and a signature. He stuck to his plan, in part because the prevailing system offended Hill's deep-seated sense that the little man and the underdog deserved fair play. Hill later joked that his first customer at the Home Savings Bank was a farmer, a man known as something of a roughneck, who asked about a $500 loan. The man offered as collateral a "blaze-faced cow with a stocking foot, a good bull calf with one horn, a good blind mule and a yoke of oxen." The two talked at the teller's counter, and together they made quite a pair: Hill in patent leather shoes, striped trousers, and a fashionable cutaway, and the farmer in brogans, work clothes, and a slouch hat. As they talked, Hill's cashier whispered from behind him, "He'll shoot you if you don't lend him that money." Hill made the loan.[13]

Borrowers off the farm seldom got such attention in a bank. If they made application for loans at all, they were led into a complicated and expensive maze of double-talk and outright bribery. According to Hill, who later explained the customary banking practices at a congressional hearing, a bank customer was likely to be told by the cashier that "money is tight" and a loan was impossible, but the cashier would refer the customer to a lawyer who, he was told, might be able to help. When the customer reached the lawyer, who usually did legal work for the bank, again he was told a loan was impossible. "The purpose," Hill said,

> was, in my opinion, to shake down the applicant, to reduce him to a state of mind where he would pay his charges. When that was reached, [the lawyer] said, 'I think I can arrange it for you as a special favor to you, but it will cost you $50 for that $1000.' That $50 was divided as follows: $10 each went to the attorney and three of the directors of the bank for commission on the bank's money. The remaining $10 was divided between the attorney and the cashier of the bank. The victimized A then got his money, but he did not get all of it. He only got $850. Fifty dollars had already been paid out. That left $950. The bank then required him to deposit $100 in the bank so as to take care of any possible contingencies, out of which was deducted the interest in advance for the first three months. That is the rake-off of the bank.[14]

Such commissions were prohibited at Home Savings Bank. Hill hung a banner in the window declaring he would fire any employee who accepted a kickback on a loan. In a story he loved to tell over the years, Hill said that after the banner went up he got a visit from O. T. Carver, who was Brodie L. Duke's secretary. Carver had just told his boss that a leading bank in town charged a 20 percent commission for a $20,000 loan, and the news sent Duke into a fit of rage against all banks in Durham; he accused them of being "loan sharks and criminals." When Carver told Duke about Home Savings' offer, "Duke handed him a handful of tobacco stocks [to use as collateral] and told him to close out the deal, which was promptly consummated."[15]

Shortly thereafter, an intoxicated Brodie Duke appeared at the bank and handed Hill a check for $2,000, which represented a 10 percent commission. Hill refused it and insisted that Duke tear up the check then and there. As Hill told the story, "Mr. Duke walked up and down the hall, outside the bank, with his hands over his ears, singing 'Angel Wings, Angel Wings.' He stopped at the [Home Savings] cashier's desk and said, 'You won't live long in this damn town.' He went back to his office and gave the Home Savings Bank his bank account and turned over to Mr. Hill the management of all his financial affairs."[16]

❧ ❧ ❧

The century's early years—some called them the best years—inspired men like Watts and Hill to believe they could shape their communities into whatever they desired. America was safe behind the protection of two oceans. Such relative peace reigned in the world that Watts and his wife casually embarked on trips abroad, especially to Europe and the Middle East. Anything seemed possible when Durham, a mere crossroads village a quarter century before, could boast of the largest tobacco factories in the world, five cotton mills, electric lights, churches, secret societies of all description, beautiful homes, a public library, and residents with personal property worth more than $9.5 million.[17] The city's schools, presided over by a board that included Julian Carr, George Watts, and fellow prohibitionist James H. Southgate, were considered some of the best in the state, and they offered classes for 140 days a year. As Durham became more attractive to new businesses and new residents, Hill profited handsomely from the sale of the property he had acquired on his first quiet trip to Durham.

Durham would be righteous, clean, and wholesome, the city fathers declared as they launched a campaign to rid Durham of saloons. Durham's prohibitionists opened the city to the notorious saloon-smashing Carry Nation. Hill shouldered his local duty and campaigned for the public good, becoming a dues-paying participant in the temperance movement, a favorite of his father-in-law. Sundays were honored as the Sabbath; the city council prohibited any business transactions or entertainments on that day, as they were thought to distract the citizens from piety. Each Sunday, the Hills joined George and Linnie Watts at the First Presbyterian Church, where Watts personally welcomed the three hundred fifty or more persons who turned out for Sunday school. Promptly at 9:30 A.M., he began the morning program with gospel hymns and Bible study, challenging parishioners to find selected verses. He knew each "pupil" by name and was alert to newcomers. A Presbyterian clergyman later recalled the summer he came upon a Davidson College classmate who was working his way across the state selling stereopticon slides. He was astonished to learn that his friend had eaten Sunday dinner with Watts, who had picked him out as a visitor at First Presbyterian. Before the young man left Durham, Watts had placed a $30.00 order, which proved to be the visitor's largest sale of the season.[18]

∾∾∾

With the Hills close at hand, Watts must have felt his life was complete. Annie Louise was a comfort to her mother, whose health remained frail. While her husband busied himself with his new affairs, Annie Louise reconnected with her hometown. Only a few months after she arrived, she was hosting regular meetings of the Tourists, a gathering of ladies of similar station who enjoyed six-course luncheons and entertained one another with presentations about their travels abroad.

The Hills' home on the southern slope of Morehead Hill was only a short distance from the center of Durham. John Sprunt often left his New York carriage at home and walked to his office in the Trust Building, as did his father-in-law. Hill moved along briskly with purpose and dignity. Always well-groomed in a dark suit and vest with a jeweled stickpin positioned just below his stiff, high collar, he would have been recognized as a man of means by strangers alighting from the morning train from Raleigh at Union Station. Durham's streets were unpaved but clean. In the summer, the city water trucks sprayed the streets to settle the dust, and sweepers regularly removed manure dropped by passing horses and mules. Automobiles remained a novelty.

Hill's offices were in the center of Durham's business district, a five-block stretch of Main Street. As shopkeepers and merchants prepared for the day, the trolley passed by on the way to the interchange at Five Points and beyond to Durham's only park, Lakewood, which the trolley company had opened to inspire ridership. At the Trust Building, Hill took the elevator to the third floor, where he was greeted by his secretary, Miss Childs, one of the first females to hold such a job in the city. He often took his midday meal at home and then returned to work.

Hill's relocation to Durham was a success by any measure. In less than two years, he had launched two major financial concerns, built the tallest office building in town, and mounted a noticeable challenge to the status quo. In March 1905, the *News and Observer's* Josephus Daniels called Hill a hero after a federal judge threatened to throw Hill in jail for defending Durham officials in their dispute with the Southern Railway Company. The matter arose in the early hours of March 20, 1905, when a Southern train pulled into downtown Durham just before two; the train unloaded about two hundred workers, and they started building tracks up Peabody and Pettigrew streets. Before the mayor and council could react with a state court order to halt construction, new tracks had been laid within four feet of the sidewalks, effectively closing the streets to carriages or wagons. The *News and Observer,* no friend of the railroad company, called it "A Night Invasion By The Southern."[19] When the city's suit against Southern was heard in state court, Hill was there, sitting with city officials, waiting to post bond for the city against any damages the railroad company might bring for the delay in construction.

The dispute between Durham and the railroad was a long-simmering affair. It arose from the question of who controlled the right-of-way for the railroad tracks that lay like a steel spine through the center of Durham. Southern claimed to control a hundred-foot swath on either side of the rails. In 1903, Durham had conceded Southern's control of Pettigrew Street but disputed any claims the railroad had on Peabody Street. The issue became more contentious with the increase in rail traffic and the growing danger for pedestrians who had to cross the busy tracks. Hill himself went to Raleigh to support legislation that would have allowed the city to control where Southern put its tracks in order to provide for safer crossings; it was met with resistance from the powerful railroad lobby, which objected to such local control.

After Durham officials secured a restraining order from a state court to halt the railroad's "midnight" construction, Southern's lawyers immediately headed to Asheville to appeal to a federal judge. He ordered the mayor and the council, as well as Hill, to appear in his court and answer contempt charges. The railroad argued that the city's action violated the federal court order that had been issued two years earlier, when the city had, in effect, acquiesced to Southern's claim on the property.

It was a perfect contest for a scrapper like Hill. He had a personal stake in the outcome; he and his family crossed the tracks regularly to get from their home on Morehead Hill to downtown. His family's fortune was invested in the Seaboard line, not the Southern; when Seaboard officials came to town, they often dined with company director George Watts at

Harwood Hall. And Hill had a most unpopular villain; one of the more infamous acts of the last Republican administration in Raleigh had been to grant Southern control of the state-owned North Carolina Railroad tracks for ninety-nine years.

Two days before Hill's contempt hearing in Asheville, the city settled with the company. Nonetheless, Southern's lawyers pressed legal action against Hill and asked for sanctions. After a two-day hearing, U.S. District Judge J. C. Prichard found Hill not guilty and charged the cost of the action against the railroad.

Daniels was ecstatic. "Good for Mr. Hill, who has set an example of fighting corporate tyranny that is needed by rich men and others in North Carolina," he wrote. He said that Hill's crime had been in challenging Southern in the General Assembly with legislation to require safer crossings. Daniels explained: "That was his unpardonable sin and the Big Boss marked Mr. Hill for slaughter. It was decreed that he should be made an example of and held out as a warning to others[;] it is safer to put one's head into the Southern halter than to dare to criticize the Southern. Mr. Hill stood his ground. He could not be cajoled, scared, bull-dozed, or bought. The Southern crowd do not understand a man who cannot be controlled by one of these methods, and so they thought it best to teach him a lesson for disobedience to the Railroad Boss."[20]

～～～

Hill's tangle with the railroad was consistent with his politics, which was an undiluted brand of Jeffersonian democracy that valued individual rights and praised the virtues and strength of the yeoman farmer and the small businessman. It was a political faith that he had held since his days in New York and his work with the young reformers eager to revive the national Democratic Party. One of the national journals that he read faithfully was the *World's Work*, a New York newsmagazine edited by Walter Hines Page, a North Carolinian who prodded the state relentlessly to shake off the past and support a new generation of leaders. One time, in a state of high pique, Page wrote that what North Carolina needed was "a few first-class funerals."

Before moving to New York, Page had been a newspaper publisher in Raleigh, where he helped organize the Watauga Club, a group of like-minded young reformers who barred from membership anyone old enough to have fought in the Civil War. Among its members were Charles Aycock, who was elected governor in 1900; Clarence Poe, editor of the *Progressive Farmer*; Josephus Daniels; Josiah W. Bailey, the editor of the *Biblical Recorder*; and up-and-coming educational reformers Charles McIver, founder of the state teachers' college in Greensboro; state superintendent of public instruction J. Y. Joyner; and University of North Carolina president Edward Alderman. McIver, Joyner, and Alderman had graduated from the university less than a decade before Hill, and they were among a group of young men who turned first to education, rather than to the law, as a way to effect change in the state.

Hill cast his lot with this generation of leaders upon his return to North Carolina. In a speech to the alumni in Chapel Hill in the summer of 1903, he challenged the university trustees to take more interest in their work, to support an overhaul of the trustee selection process, and to allow the General Alumni Association, which Hill proposed be revived, to have greater influence. Hill chastised the crowd of aging trustees—many of whom still addressed one another by the rank they had held in the Confederate army—for letting their participation sink to the point where only a fourth of the seventy-eight members of the board even bothered to attend meetings. Such contempt for their jobs did not provide the support university president Francis P. Venable (who had succeeded Alderman in 1900) needed to accomplish his mission, Hill declared. At the same time, he argued, Venable should not expect much from alumni if the Alumni Association had no voice in running the university. Hill argued that an invigorated alumni alliance, which would be allowed to name candidates for the Board of Trustees, could move the institution out of its depths and raise the money the university needed. "Is it not time for us to begin the work of making this institution a great Southern States' University, a modern directive force, commensurate with the demands of our people and alert to all their growing needs?" Hill asked in a finely crafted speech.

Hill laid out his plan: secure legislation to permit the alumni to elect one-third (twenty-six members) of the university's Board of Trustees; build a proper library; and erect a new building for the YMCA, the focus of religious life on the campus. The alumni also needed to support Venable's plan for graduate studies and organize a committee to "make a thorough study of the problems of education in North Carolina with a view to uniting [its] loyal sons and daughters in the common hope and upon the common purpose of upbuilding this institution for the higher education of the whole people."

Before he left the podium, Hill pledged the income from a gift of $4,000—roughly $200 a year—to the university. In the first year, Hill said, he wanted the money to go toward the erection of a new building for the YMCA. In subsequent years, he offered it in support of a fellowship in North Carolina history. Though his gift would appear modest a century later, $200 was sufficient to cover all but $65.25 of a student's tuition and board in 1903. Four thousand dollars was almost 10 percent of the total amount appropriated by the General Assembly for the maintenance and upkeep of the university.

Before giving his speech, Hill had told Venable that he would pay for the reorganization of the Alumni Association. "I have had this matter in mind for the past four or five years, but have been so burdened with work and engagements of all kinds in New York that I preferred to await my opportunity to do the wise and profitable thing, rather than give to the university a hundred dollars here and there in an unorganized manner," he explained. "I expect therefore, to bear the expense personally of the plan for reorganization of the alumni association and if I succeed in my undertaking I feel sure that I will have done a great work for the University."[21]

The Board of Trustees appointed the committee Hill proposed and named him a member. Working with him were Venable, McIver, Joyner, Samuel M. Gattis, and Thomas S. Kenan. Hill prepared an agenda and hosted the first meeting of the group at his home in Durham in the fall of 1904. Among the issues Hill raised with the committee was the possibility of expanding the university's curriculum beyond Chapel Hill through extension programs and graduate study. Such an expansion of the university's role had begun under Venable's predecessor, and it would later flourish and become the hallmark of the administration of Edward Kidder Graham, then a faculty member, who became Venable's successor in 1914.

The North Carolina General Assembly was about to open its 1905 session when Hill wrote Venable to inquire whether his name was among the nominees to the Board of Trustees that had been recommended to the legislature. "Two years ago," Hill told the president, "Governor Aycock asked me to go on the board, but I was not a resident of the state at that time and had to decline. I am now eligible and would like to go on the board." Venable replied two days later that he had submitted Hill's name for appointment.[22] On March 2, just a little more than a month before Hill was hauled into court by the Southern Railway Company, he was among twenty-nine members elected to serve as a trustee.

Hill's election to the board gave him a formal outlet for his devotion to the university, and it continued a tradition in the Hill family. His father had served on the board from 1877 until 1899, the year before his death. It also raised his stature in state politics. Hill's appointment gave him a seat among the men of influence within the state Democratic Party. Elected at the same time for a similar eight-year term were former governor Aycock, former lieutenant governor Rufus A. Doughton, Greensboro insurance executive A. M. Scales, and Goldsboro lawyer Frank Daniels, whose brother edited the *News and Observer*.

Hill became a determined supporter of Venable's ambitions for the school. Between 1905 and 1910, the university received increased appropriations for campus facilities, including $50,000 for new chemistry laboratories and classrooms, the first state-financed buildings since Old East was built a half century before. (Other campus buildings had been erected, but they had been paid for by private donations.) Hill put himself and his money behind Venable's campaign for a new library and better preservation of the university's collection of books and pamphlets, which was the largest in the state. Hill told the trustees when he addressed them in 1903 that the conditions at the library were a disgrace. Much of the collections were "packed and jammed away in such a fashion as to largely destroy their usefulness." A new building was required, he said. "Will not some great-hearted son or daughter of the 'Old North State' give our people a great library, the head of the library system of the State, to illumine the homes of all the people of every creed and of every station, and show them the hidden paths to the kindly fruits of earth and to the eternal blessings of heaven?" he asked.[23]

The university got its library, but it was from a Scot, not a son of the Old North State. In April 1905, Venable announced that Andrew Carnegie had pledged $50,000 for a new library if alumni and others would raise a like amount for maintenance and improvement. Hill converted his earlier endowment of $4,000 into a direct gift of $5,000 in American Tobacco Company stock on the condition that it be used to create a collection of what he called "North Caroliniana." Hill's gift represented one-tenth of the amount needed to match the Carnegie's grant, and when the library opened in 1907, a portrait of John Sprunt Hill was hung in the reading room.

The library campaign was just the first of nearly fifty years of building projects for Hill at the university. One of his first assignments as a trustee was to serve as a member of the committee overseeing campus construction, and he commented liberally on the building plans submitted by architects. While he had no training in design or construction, he knew from experience what he liked and what he did not. He also pestered Orange and Durham County officials until they paid for the improvement of the narrow, rutted dirt road that connected Chapel Hill and Durham. Travel to Chapel Hill from the train depot in Durham was uncomfortable by day and downright dangerous at night. On occasion, Venable asked Hill to allow university guests who arrived in the late afternoon to overnight at Hill's home before they continued on to Chapel Hill the next morning.

∽∽∽

The university's building projects began just as Hill became involved in more construction in Durham, including a new home for his growing family. A daughter, Laura Valinda, was born January 12, 1905. A second daughter, Frances Faison, was born October 14, 1908. In the months prior to Frances's birth, Hill asked Boston architect Bertrand Taylor to prepare designs for a home. Taylor's early renderings did not excite Hill or his wife, and they postponed a decision until after they completed a summer tour of New England coupled with a stopover in Tuxedo Park, New York, where they hoped to be inspired by homes.

Hill may also have put off the construction of his new home because he was too busy with other projects. Construction on a second Watts Hospital began in May 1908 at about the same time as the construction of the office building on Main Street that Hill had announced he would build five years earlier. The so-called Temple Building took its name from its principal tenants—the Elks, Masons, and Order of Odd Fellows—and featured a Mediterranean style with a pebbled stucco finish and a mansard roof covered in tile. It was built with some of the same materials used to build the hospital. It opened in 1909.

The hospital was an entirely different matter. The hospital George Watts had given the city in 1895 had been a source of both pride and disappointment. It had raised the level of health care in Durham well above that available elsewhere in the state. It may also have saved the life of Watts's wife, Linnie, who had undergone an emergency appendectomy there in March 1909. "I rejoice in having the institution," Watts wrote Walter W. Moore at Union Theological Seminary, "as I am much pleased with the treatment that she has received."[24]

At the same time, it had taken years for the poor—who needed the hospital services the most—to overcome their fear that a hospital, or "pest house" as they were called at the time, was a place where the sick went only to die, or worse. (Some suspected that doctors were performing experiments on the sick.) Community use had grown in the early years of the century, however, and demand now required the hospital to expand. Watts was discouraged that his dream of community support for the institution had never materialized. Durham still looked to him to cover the hospital's annual operating costs. Nonetheless, he was intent on improving the hospital.

Watts planned to expand the existing facilities on Buchanon Street near the Trinity campus, but Betrand Taylor returned with drawings for an entirely new hospital complex at a new location away from the smoke and noise of trains and factories. To find the most desirable site, Taylor had exposed bacteriological plates to the air to measure contamination, and he finally settled on a sixty-acre tract west of the city.[25] The new campus, set amidst a grove of hickories and oaks, would be designed for patients and their visitors to enjoy the clean country air.

Since designing the first Watts Hospital, Taylor had become the nation's leading hospital architect, with more than two hundred designs to his credit. The second Watts Hospital would be his last; he died soon after the dedication on December 2, 1909. What Taylor created cost far more than the $75,000 Watts had planned to spend. The complex of five buildings, designed in the Spanish mission style with large overhanging roofs shading stucco walls, cost more than $217,000. Altogether, the land, buildings, and equipment represented the largest single gift Durham had ever received.

More than a thousand people turned out for the hospital dedication. Before guests were allowed inside to see everything from the richly paneled walls and tile floors of the lobby to the steam disinfection equipment in the laundry, they sat through an afternoon of speeches that began with Watts's presentation of the deed to the city and his announcement that he would give the hospital a $200,000 endowment. In addition, Watts pledged to build a home for nurses in the coming year at a cost of $45,000.

As before, Watts offered his gift on the condition that the hospital be open to charity cases from throughout Durham County. "May it ever be conducted in the true Christian or Christ-like spirit, where all distinction of class or creed fade away in the one universal desire to bind up the wounds, to relieve the pains and strengthen the courage of our common humanity," Watts said in his remarks. The hospital continued to receive white patients only. Watts had planned to build a wing for African Americans, but he had been persuaded by Durham's leading black doctor, Aaron Moore, to instead encourage the Dukes to build Lincoln Hospital, where black doctors, who were prohibited from practicing at white hospitals, could treat their patients.

Watts's fellow civic warrior, James H. Southgate, praised his friend's philanthropy and put him in a class with Andrew Carnegie, Leland Stanford in California, and John D. Rockefeller. He told the crowd, "The world has never seen such philanthropy as we have seen in our times and no country has ever seen it as we Americans see it, and let me say, in all this broad land I challenge any city, on a comparative basis, to point to more philanthropists than are to be found in our own town of Durham, North Carolina."

The new hospital incorporated the latest in modern medical care, including isolation rooms, accommodations for ambulances, more space for surgery, and improved housing for nurses. The two-story patient pavilion with beds for twenty-eight patients offered a "homelike atmosphere."[26] It was connected by an enclosed walkway to the three-story main building, which had forty-five beds. Telephones connected every corner of the complex. The complex even had its own power and steam station. Watts hoped the impressive array of modern facilities would encourage more paying patients, which would improve the hospital's bottom line.[27]

⤳⤳⤳

The Hills revived their interest in building a new home in the spring of 1910. They chose a site just over the crest of Morehead Hill south of Harwood Hall on land that belonged to George Watts's cousins. The sketches that Hill drew of the home he wanted reflected the Spanish influence that Taylor had adopted for the hospital and the Temple Building. He sent these drawings to architects in Atlanta and Charlotte, as well as to the Taylor firm in Boston, which continued in business after his death. The Taylor firm got the job.

Hill was not one to leave such work solely to the builders, and he occupied himself with every detail of the construction, which began in April 1911. He altered plans for the southeast side to accommodate a screen porch that could be enclosed with glass in winter and used as a conservatory with potted palms. Over the objections of his architect, he added a bay window on the west side of the second floor to enhance a bedroom on the corner of the house. The professionals said it took away from the lines of the house, but Hill replied that since he owned all the land to the south, no one would care. "I am not quite so keen on sacrificing comfort to appearances on this corner," he told the architects.[28]

Hill stipulated that concrete, not fill dirt, be used under the outside terraces to prevent settling of the earth that could lead to cracks in the tile floor such as he had seen in houses he had visited in New York. And he stipulated that the house be as near to fireproof as possible. "I have in mind the construction of the new Watts Hospital as about the construction to be used in the building of my residence," he wrote just before construction began.[29] Hill and the rest of the city had been reminded of the danger of fire just months before, when a blaze destroyed the Washington Duke Building on the Trinity campus. Nearly one hundred years after it was built, Hill's home was as solid as it had been on the day it was completed; this was largely due to the three hundred tons of rock and the thousands of yards of sand and concrete that builders poured in the walls and foundation.

Hill created a distinctive mansion with broad piazzas across the front that was the focus of an urban estate with gardens, stables, and carriage house. More than a hundred gallons of paint were required to cover the house's stucco exterior. The interior rooms were large and custom-tailored in carved woodwork from Irving and Casson of Boston, then considered one of the finest firms of its kind in the country. Some walls were covered with silk damask and others in Spanish leather stamped with gold. The music and dining rooms featured elegant colonial revival woodwork. The elevator installed just off the large kitchen was near a walk-in vault for the family's silver.[30]

Outside, Hill adapted landscaping ideas he received from Thomas Meehan and Sons, a Philadelphia landscaping firm. In the spring of 1912, he placed orders for fruit trees, willow trees, privet hedge, hydrangea, and a host of garden plants, including 400 asparagus roots like those his mother had cultivated on the farm and sold in produce markets. He did not adopt the landscapers' entire plan, however. "Some other day I may lose my mind and commence building the tennis court, rose garden, pergola, etc., on the southwest corner of the property and then erect gates there as laid out, but this is such a remote possibility that I will not trouble you to bother about it now."[31] In the years to come, he kept nurseries and seed companies busy filling orders for plants and all manner of vegetation. The Hills moved into their new home in September 1912 while workmen were still busy with the finishing touches.

∞∞∞

The entire period of construction had been a troubling one for the family. On May 29, 1911, just after work had commenced, the U.S. Supreme Court upheld the federal government's antitrust suit against the American Tobacco Company. The lawsuit had begun four years earlier when American's influence and control spread across 250 related companies and accounted for four-fifths of U.S. tobacco output, including more than 80 percent of cigarette production. American's annual advertising budget alone amounted to more than $10 million. George Watts remained a director of the company, and once the Court's decision was announced, this righteous Presbyterian and humanitarian benefactor found himself personally liable for crimes that even high officials in Washington said deserved a stay in prison.

The chief justice read the decision himself in chambers so crowded that senators could not find a seat. The Court returned the case to a lower court to decide just how to dismember the company that a year before had been valued at more than $101 million. On hearing of the Court's decision, Buck Duke reportedly said, pointing to a log cabin: "In England if a fellow had built up a whale of a business outa that he'd be knighted. Here they want to put him in jail."[32]

Farmers and others who had long complained about American's predatory methods hailed the decision as a victory. When the suit was filed, Josephus Daniels had said: "The trust's desires are modest. All it wants is the earth with a barbed wire fence around it. The tobacco trust is a hog and wants all the swill. The tobacco crop is short this year. It ought to have brought twelve cents a pound, but the trust fixed it at seven or eight cents, and that is all that is being paid."[33] Some farmers had taken matters into their own hands and burned American warehouses in Kentucky. Rallies against the company in North Carolina drew farmers by the thousands. Buck Duke had dismissed the opposition as "socialist agitators."[34]

Many in the country were not satisfied with the Court's apparent remedy of simply requiring a breakup of the company. Within days of the decision, men in Washington were talking about jail terms for Watts and twenty-eight others, including the Dukes and important Wall Street figures. A Tennessee congressman declared that "a prison sentence would have a healthy effect on violators of trust laws, who have been as deservedly denounced in this case by the highest court in the nation."[35] President William Howard Taft's attorney general was quoted as having said that "he believed prison sentences would be the most effective means of enforcing respect for the anti-trust law" when he spoke before a congressional committee.[36]

Watts was especially distressed, and the entire family worried with him. At home, in Durham, he found some consolation. When the Court's decision was announced, the city was caught up in graduation exercises at Trinity College and in the expansion of the campus. Engineers had been rolling a cart holding a huge statue of Washington Duke about the lawn for several days trying to determine the best location for it. The greatest local concern appeared to be how the Court's decision would affect the fate of a new $135,000 hotel that had been announced for downtown the month before. Ben Duke, George Watts, and their corresponding banks were among the underwriters.

Durham was inclined to accept the Dukes' explanation that they had not created a predatory trust like Rockefeller's Standard Oil that was said to grind down competitors unmercifully. Rather, Ben Duke said, the American Tobacco Company simply created a more efficient company by acquiring other businesses. If they were doing anything illegal, they did not know it, and they would do whatever was necessary to correct the error of their ways. Watts remained out of the news, but he was shaken by the experience.

Lawyers for the company and for the government met through the summer and into the fall until a dissolution plan was adopted in November 1911. Under it, the Durham factories would be divided between two companies. The old Blackwell firm, whose Bull Durham brand had started it all, would remain under the American Tobacco Company, while the old W. Duke, Sons, and Company factories would go to Liggett and Myers Tobacco Company. The R.J. Reynolds Tobacco Company in Winston-Salem would keep its brands, while a fourth firm, P. Lorillard, would share in the remainder. All four companies would be required to operate independently. American would control 33 percent of the total smoking, plug, and cigarette tobacco business in the United States, while P. Lorillard, Reynolds, and Liggett and Myers would control about 23 percent each.

Unlike those who believed that the men who had run American Tobacco should serve time in jail, the *Durham Sun* was sympathetic to the Court's decision to simply break up the company. "The American Tobacco Company has never shown any disposition other than to obey the law when once the law was interpreted and defined," intoned an editorial. "All who have taken anything like a sane view of the situation have believed that the plans submitted to the court were an honest attempt to comply with the mandates of the Supreme Court."[37]

The paper seemed to express Durham's relief that now that the case was resolved, local business could return to normal in a town where tobacco remained a mainstay of the economy. It had brought "health" and "wealth" to Durham and made it a city "Renowned the World Around," according to a lighted sign, thirty feet tall and forty feet long, that the Durham Traction Company put atop a downtown building.

Even after the terms of the breakup of the company were decided, the threat of criminal sanctions remained. The aggressive leader of the North Carolina Farmers' Union (formerly the Farmers' Alliance), Dr. H. Q. Alexander of Charlotte, sent delegations of farmers to Washington to urge the attorney general to prosecute. "The farmers' Union has a large clientele among the tobacco growers of the state and is anxious to do what it can for their welfare," Alexander was quoted as saying; "There is no question that the tobacco trust has been guilty of the greatest violations of the Sherman anti-trust law and that the tobacco growers of the state have suffered untold injuries as a result of the manipulation of the great corporation."[38]

President Taft reviewed the Court's decision and sent a message to Congress just before the end of the year. He said he was satisfied that the order restricting the defendants from buying any further tobacco company stocks for three years was sufficient punishment. No one went to jail.

Relief settled on Watts and his family. While the threat of criminal charges was real, prosecution would not have been realistic. Most of Wall Street would have been vulnerable if the government had used the American Tobacco directors and executives to prove the point. There were no penalties against any individuals. Watts's fortune, which he would continue to use for good works, remained safe. An ironic outcome of the affair became apparent less than two years later as John Sprunt Hill launched a vigorous campaign for rural credit unions that he hoped would free farmers from the crippling burden of crop liens. The same leaders of the Farmers' Union who had been eager to imprison his father-in-law became his most devoted allies.

CHAPTER 5

Rural Credits

———————

IN THE YEARS PRIOR TO THE OUTBREAK of World War I, North Carolina had more farmers ruining more land than any other state in the South. The annual plantings of cotton and tobacco sapped life from soil that was left to erode and degrade even further when farmers moved to more fertile fields nearby. Corn was another staple, but little of the harvest actually made it to market. Rather, the grain was needed to feed the horses and mules required to cultivate and harvest the so-called money crops that only drove farmers deeper and deeper into debt. It was a destructive cycle with no end.

As if that was not enough, entire counties had long ago given up their forests to loggers. In little Ashe County, on the west side of the Blue Ridge Mountains in the state's northwest corner, any tree of sufficient size to support rail or roof was cut and hauled away to feed the new century's appetite for construction. In 1913, a farmer in the Sandhills region reported he had to drive sixty miles from his home in Moore County to find a stand of native longleaf pine that resembled anything like the trees that had inspired a line in the state's official song. By some estimates, more than fourteen million acres were wasted by farmers who had neither the techniques, the tools, the labor, nor the money necessary to break out of a cycle of one-crop farming, or, as Raleigh's Clarence Poe, the editor of the South's leading farm journal, the *Progressive Farmer*, called it, "one-armed farming."

"There are two great arms for producing agricultural wealth—plant production and animal production," Poe argued at farm meetings across the region. Southern farmers not only lagged behind the rest of the nation in the numbers of horses, mules, and cattle they owned, but they also further complicated their lives by planting the same crops—cotton and tobacco—on the same land year after year. Poe spoke from experience. His own family had been forced to leave a Chatham County farm after it failed.

Not only did North Carolina have a surplus of Poe's one-armed farmers, the number was growing as families from the Deep South, dispossessed from cotton fields ravaged by the boll weevil, migrated into the Carolinas. They signed on as tenants or sharecroppers and settled on small plots to make do for themselves and their families. With the cultivation of tobacco and cotton dependent on the number of hands available to harvest it, the average tract of land actually under cultivation in North Carolina was only about five acres per farm; millions of acres were left to degenerate into gullies and weeds.[1]

Throughout his life, John Sprunt Hill considered himself to be a farmer in addition to his other professions. Living in New York had kept him away from the land, but his mother and sisters remained dependent on the family's farm in Duplin County. Not long after he moved to Durham, he purchased several hundred acres of land west of town and put it into cultivation. Hill called the farm "that old Jones Land," and he had to roust bootleggers from their moonshine stills before he could plant a crop. Like others, he grew corn and tobacco, but he also turned to his father-in-law's family for some of the finest Guernsey cattle in the country and began building a dairy herd.

When Gerard S. Watts died on February 26, 1905, he left a large portfolio of investments as well as a herd of prize Guernseys, a breed known for milk rich in butterfat. When Hill brought some of the Watts Guernseys to Durham County, there were fewer cows per farm resident in North Carolina than there had been when he was a boy. The state's rural economy was so unbalanced that even farm families were dependent on others for a steady supply of milk. These prize cattle were a rare contribution, indeed.

It took Hill six years to adequately prepare the land and the herd for full commercial production, so he accepted Poe's call for diversification. With the help of two tenants and a foreman, he launched a truck farming operation that soon produced a variety of fruits and produce, which Hill shipped to market each week from spring through summer.

Of course, Hill had few of the worries of most farmers. His wealth allowed him to operate without regard to financial success, much like his wealthy neighbors Julian Carr and Ben Duke, who ran trophy farms of their own. Carr's Occoneechee was a showplace of 663 acres near Hillsborough; there, he had been demonstrating innovative farming methods and raising cattle, sheep, and swine since the mid-1890s. At about the same time, Duke acquired large tracts of land near University Station west of Durham where he experimented with new techniques in landscaping and cultivation. Neither of these farms compared with Buck Duke's estate in New Jersey, or with the 120,000 acres surrounding George W. Vanderbilt's estate south of Asheville, where the Biltmore dairy herd was the pride of the region. Hill's beginning was modest in size, but not in ambition. He would eventually acquire more than 7,000 acres in Durham and surrounding counties and become as expert in the pedigrees of his cattle as he was in the genealogy of his forebears.

∾∾∾

Not all of Hill's farm was given over to cows, grass, orchards, asparagus, and potatoes. By the winter of 1908, he had staked off a section just north of the Hillsborough road where he planned to build a nine-hole golf course.[2] Hill was as addicted to golf as George Watts was. Both were among the first regular guests at Pinehurst, North Carolina, where Leonard Tufts, the son of a Boston millionaire, was transforming thousands of acres of cut-over timberland into a mid-South resort with golf courses, stables, and hunting. Watts was consistently the better golfer, according to the club's early records.[3] Watts's favorite midwinter course was in Palm Beach, Florida, however, and in February he would head south with his wife and the Hills for a month of golf and relaxation at the Royal Poinciana Hotel. In the summer, when all were vacationing at Poland Springs, Watts hired a professional to teach his grandchildren the game. Now, with a course close by at his son-in-law's Hill 'in Dale farm (a name later changed to "Hillandale"), both Watts and Hill could indulge their passion whenever they wished. Hill's brother Isham and the senior minister at First Presbyterian Church, the Reverend E. R. Leyburn, made up the rest of the foursome for the weekly game.

The course was laid out along a broad, rolling creek valley and followed a design drawn by Donald Ross, who also created the Pinehurst course for Leonard Tufts. Hill probably introduced some elements that he picked up from other courses he had played with his father-in-law, however. Like most Ross courses, the Hillandale course used the existing contours of the land and its natural hazards, such as a stream that bisected the property, to challenge golfers.

Hill also hired an architect to design a clubhouse, and construction began on it in 1911. The designer adopted a Dutch Colonial style, including wide porches on the first and second stories of the building, which cost a surprising $15,000. "It is cool and restful in appearance and standing on the crest of a hill it overlooks hundreds of acres of beautiful landscape," the *Durham Morning Herald* reported.[4] In the fall of that year, Hill negotiated with a New York golf club manager, Alex Pirie, to come to Durham to manage the golf course, provide lessons for Durham golfers, and run a small pro shop.

The following spring, in March 1912, the Durham Country Club was organized, and the first round at Hillandale was played on April 8. Hill won the trophy with a low score of 114 for eighteen holes.[5] The Reverend Leyburn was second with a score of 115, and Watts was third with a score of 116. Leyburn's son later recalled that from that day on, his father and Watts seldom missed a Monday afternoon on the course, and their scores never changed.[6] For Hill, golf was a gentleman's game, but he accommodated ladies as well at half the annual $12 membership fee. Among the women who played the course were Ben Duke's wife, Sarah, and their daughter, Mary. In 1915, Hill added another nine holes.

❧ ❧ ❧

Aside from his love of the land, Hill had little in common with most of the sixteen hundred farmers in Durham County, more than half of whom worked and lived on property owned by someone else. Yet his devotion to the romantic ideal of yeoman farmer–citizens prompted him to feel a gnawing concern that the nation's very soul was in jeopardy as farmers left the fields and flocked to factory jobs in the textile mills that had sprouted like mushrooms across the landscape since the turn of the century.

North Carolina had more textile mills than any other state by 1910. Work in the mills was a strain on a man's body and offered little more than subsistence pay, but even a modest paycheck allowed families to escape the uncertainties and hardship of rural life. One writer compared the change reshaping the South to the "exodus from Egypt." The flight from the farm was viewed with alarm by some. One commentator described the changes as follows: "[Farmers] move out of a world of measurable sovereignty into a world of measureless subjection, in which they have no share in conducting the business from which they draw their support, and no voice in its management." He continued: "Their share of the wealth they help to produce depends upon the righteous will of their employers. They have entered a world of feudalism. We like to think that is increasingly a benevolent feudalism; but it is feudalism nevertheless."[7]

Poe's editorials in the *Progressive Farmer* raised the specter of another threat to the established order of life in the South. Mill jobs were for whites only, and as white farmers left for the factories, African Americans migrating into the Carolinas ahead of the failing cotton crops in the Deep South replaced them on the land. Poe commented:

> The greatest danger to [the] social order in the South is the menacingly rapid encroachment of the Negro farmer upon white territory—the fact that the Negro farmers are increasing relatively too fast, and actually driving out the white settlers in many sections. We do not say this with any ill-will toward the Negro, whose rights we have always defended. We say it regretfully, because, and only because, we feel and know that some remedy must be evolved to save our white communities from this danger, if the high purpose of all our workers for rural betterment is not to be cruelly defeated. We must save the rural south for the white race.[8]

A week after Poe ran this editorial, he published the response of a black farmer who objected to Poe's premise that African Americans lowered the level of civility in a community. This was not the case where he lived, the man wrote. He said he was "constantly pestered" to teach neighboring white children how to read and write.[9] Poe answered the following week: "It has long been a disgrace to our race, for example, that thousands of white boys and girls at tender age are shut up in factories, gaining neither education nor physical development, while Negro children are out on the farms building up strong bodies and going to school as regularly as the school house door opens."

Poe declared the need for a compulsory school attendance law and public condemnation of "loafing white men and boys." He added: "Finally, let us teach that in the fierce struggle for industrial supremacy, that white man is untrue to his race who weakens himself by whiskey drinking or other forms of vice and dissipation."[10] Poe also began to promote an amendment to state constitutions that would have allowed the majority race in any community to use local referenda to impose land segregation. Since relatively few blacks were registered to vote, whites would be empowered to keep blacks from owning land in rural communities or townships.

The intensity of Poe's campaign was just beginning to build in 1913. Although his newspaper gave a measure of dignity to African Americans by capitalizing the word "Negro" in print (a courtesy ignored by virtually every other publisher), neither he nor other proponents of segregation made any apology for their racist plans. African Americans had been disenfranchised by the controlling Democratic establishment in 1900, and whites had not looked back. It was a time when the cost of pensions for Confederate soldiers absorbed almost as much of the state budget as support for the university at Chapel Hill did. It was a time when Governor Locke Craig, a popular orator, used the word "nigger" in his inaugural address and never heard even a hint of reproach.

∾∾∾

The concern about migration off the farm was not limited to the South alone. But the changes taking place in North Carolina were perhaps more pronounced than elsewhere in the South, since the state had the largest number of manufacturing workers in the region. As part of its response, the 1913 General Assembly approved a plan to establish farm-life high schools in counties around the state. Local school boards were given an extra $2,500 a year to help pay for schools that offered promising white, teenage boys and girls the standard curriculum plus courses in agriculture and homemaking. Earlier, three prototypes of such schools had opened in Guilford County near Greensboro. In the fall of 1913, additional schools opened at Lowe's Grove, a crossroads community between Durham and Chapel Hill, and at Harmony in Iredell County.

While Hill's sympathies certainly lay with the prevailing enthusiasm for protecting the order of life in rural North Carolina, he never publicly joined Poe's campaign for land segregation. But he took great interest in a companion plan of Poe's to organize farmers into cooperative associations for marketing and credit. The daily flow of loan applications into Hill's Home Savings Bank and the accompanying stories from sharecroppers and renters were clear testimony that Durham farmers suffered outrageous treatment at the hands of their creditors. Individual cases varied from farm to farm, but Poe's newspaper estimated that farmers forced to make time payments to merchants for seed, fertilizer, and machinery paid as much as 25 to 60 percent more per year than those who could pay in cash. Long-term mortgages were virtually unheard of. The ninety-day notes available at banks were useless to farmers who took longer than that to plant, harvest, and sell their crops.

"Understand us," Poe wrote, "we are not blaming the merchants. They have to stand so many losses from wandering, penniless Negroes and from dishonest persons of both races that they must make time prices exorbitant; so exorbitant that an honest white man in the South can't afford to pay them—certainly not until he has tried his local banks and exhausted all other efforts to get money at a reasonable rate of interest."[11]

∽∽∽

In early March 1913, Hill was among a group of Durham businessmen who had gathered to hear an organizer from a national commission established by Congress to study all aspects of rural life, including farm credits, or a system of lending for farmers. The speaker arrived in Durham with the hope of recruiting southerners to join an upcoming tour of Europe, where the commission planned to investigate farming practices. A few days later, Hill accepted Governor Craig's invitation to join the commission even though it left him but a few weeks to arrange his affairs before leaving on a three-month trip abroad. It would be his first, and only, trip out of the country.

The American Commission on Agricultural Finance, Production, Distribution, and Rural Life included representatives from twenty-nine states, four Canadian provinces, and several independent organizations. Members gathered for the first time in late April for a reception and dinner at the White House. Hill missed the evening with President Woodrow Wilson, but he was in New York on April 26 when the SS *Saxonia* sailed for Italy. Since he had enrolled late, he ended up sharing a berth across the Atlantic with North Carolina lieutenant governor E. L. Daughtridge of Rocky Mount, who postponed the meeting of a commission studying changes in the state constitution to make the trip. By the time the commissioners reached their first stop in Genoa, Hill had been named chairman of the committee on rural credits.

Europe was on the verge of war in the late spring of 1913. The major European powers had imposed a temporary peace upon the Balkan states, where a conflict of the most brutal sort had changed the balance of power and aroused a fierce nationalistic spirit in Serbia. In March, the king of Greece was assassinated. An armistice was signed in April, less than a week before Hill and the American Commission left for Italy, and an uneasy calm settled on the region. Before the Americans would leave the continent and return to New York, however, fighting would resume, and in a year's time the freak assassination of Archduke Franz Ferdinand, the heir to the throne of Austria-Hungary, would ignite a world war.

The commission steered clear of the Balkans but planned stops in eighteen nations. Traveling by special trains, the members visited private farms, stock markets, government-run farms, and mines. It was an itinerary that was quite different from the European excursions taken by Hill's in-laws and his wife, Annie, whose schedules included the relaxing quiet of fashionable spas, the salons of large cities, and stops in bazaars and markets where Watts picked up tapestries, rugs, and even tiles to furnish Harwood Hall.

As the commission traveled throughout Germany, it would have been hard for Hill and the others not to notice that the nation was preparing for war. The kaiser was busy increasing the size of his army while building a fleet of warships to equal the British navy. Such turmoil and uncertainty was far removed from Main Street in Durham, where bankers, businessmen, and merchants had enjoyed one prosperous year after another for more than a decade. Like most Americans, Hill believed in his nation's detachment from world affairs and the safety of a homeland defended by two broad oceans. He also shared the growing national confidence that if trouble came, Americans could certainly take care of themselves just as they had in 1898, when the Spanish had been dispatched in a matter of weeks. Even with all their problems, American farmers still received the best prices in years for their crops. Cotton prices inched their way up to all-time highs.

Hill and those interested in farm credits spent the first two weeks in Italy, where the king welcomed them, before they moved on to look at the operation of a farm credit society in the northern town of Vigonova near Padua. There, they heard about the so-called Wollemburg bank, which had been formed in 1885 with 40 members who together had pooled a total of only $100 and opened for business. Over the years, the bank had steadily increased its membership and assets. By 1912, the Vigonova credit society's assets included 318 members, deposits of $12,500, and an operating surplus of $4,000.

Hill was fascinated. He learned that borrowers were not required to put up their land as security for small loans ($200 was the limit), but accounted for themselves based on their moral character and earning capacity. He later reported that Dominico, a farmer, had borrowed $200 to buy cattle and farm implements on nothing more than his pledge of repayment. Another member, Fiola, had taken a loan for steel for his blacksmith shop. Of the 180 loans that commission members were permitted to review, 6 had been made to acquire land, 29 were for commercial purposes, 15 were for family needs such as sickness, and 120 were for farm supplies such as seed and fertilizer. In thirty-eight years of operation, the society's losses amounted to only $300.

Hill found the Italian experience repeated elsewhere in Europe. He attended day-long sessions in Frankfurt where he absorbed all he could about a system of small cooperative banks called *landschaften* that were designed to aid farmers with long-term mortgages as well as short-term financing for seasonal needs. Everything he heard ran counter to the customs of most American bankers. Hill knew that his own decision to lend money on land at the Home Savings Bank was the exception; most bankers considered real estate to be a bad risk. He quickly became convinced that the concept of cooperative credit blended well with the brand of banking he practiced.

Hill's train was pulling into the Hungarian capital of Budapest when one of the hosts approached him and asked, "How is Carolina today?" Before Hill could respond, the man was struck with a thought. "I have it—Carolina—Karolyi," he said, comparing the sound of the name of Hill's home state to the name of Count Karolyi Sandor, the man credited with building a vast organization of cooperative credit unions in Hungary. "I will order the gentleman from North Carolina to make the speech on cooperation at the monument erected in the park to Count Karolyi."

Hill had only a few hours to prepare, but he seldom failed to rise to the occasion; his effort in Budapest proved to be no exception. He began by comparing the desperate situation in the American South following the Civil War to similar postwar devastation in Hungary in the mid-1800s. "Your wonderful lands, your blue skies, your noble women, and a few of your men were about all that was left to you. But like your true friends across the seas, you did not waste much time brooding over defeat. You bravely undertook to place your country once more in the front rank of the great nations of the earth," he said.

Hill then recounted how Karolyi's work had eventually led to the creation of more than twenty-four hundred small cooperative societies that made loans to farmers and villagers at 5 and 6 percent interest and helped members pool their purchasing power to gain lower prices for seed, fertilizer, and machinery. European financial institutions were staggering under a current crisis, Hill said, but not one of the cooperatives had gone bankrupt.

While American industry had grown at the expense of American farms, European farming was far stronger than its industry. "Let us co-operate," Hill said; "You give us copies of your wonderful plan for bringing cheap and sound and elastic financial credit to the doors of your humblest citizens, and we will give you our plan for building Macadam hard-surface roads for these citizens at the expenses of the great industrial enterprises located in our cities and our towns."[12]

After a month in Germany and stops in Russia and other Central European countries, the commission headed to Paris by way of Belgium and Holland. The group remained in Paris for ten days. Hill attended an international forestry meeting before embarking for London and Ireland. This last stop was perhaps the favorite of a man who claimed that his March 17 birth date made him an honorary Irishman. On a visit to the Lakes of Killarney, Hill's friends hung him by his heels over a wall so he could kiss the Blarney stone. Hill also visited with Sir Horace Plunkett, a leading proponent of cooperative farm efforts in Ireland, whose name he would mention often in the months to come.

Hill returned to the United States with a mission. Building cooperative credit organizations for farmers would occupy his attention for a decade or more. He had no sooner arrived in Durham than he was off to attend the annual convention of the North Carolina Farmers' Union. More than seven hundred farmers were gathered in Raleigh in late August for the three-day meeting, the highlights of which were speeches on a range of topics, from politics to farming methods, and sumptuous meals prepared with fresh vegetables, beef, and pork from the campus of the State College of Agricultural and Mechanic Arts, the forerunner of North Carolina State University.

The day before Hill spoke to the farmers in Raleigh, the leaders of the American Commission made a formal report to a gathering of the nation's governors in Colorado. In this report, U.S. senator Duncan U. Fletcher of Florida "made it clear that emphatic recommendations would be made for a system of rural banking through which farmers could secure better loans, and through which they could finance their own co-operative production, buying and selling organizations."[13]

Hill brought the same message to Raleigh, and he preached the need for small, community-based credit associations similar to those he had seen in Europe. "Give North Carolina co-operative societies and the usurer will be put in jail where he belongs," Hill said during a forty-minute speech that was often interrupted by applause. He said that bankers should not fear losing business to the new credit associations (the term credit union had not come into wide use), because most farmers were not bank customers to begin with. "This is a very unusual body of farmers," he told the crowd, "yet I doubt if many of you have bank accounts."

He said he had already demonstrated that banks could make money by paying 4.5 percent for money and loaning it at 6 percent. In a cooperative, the rates could be even lower. "There is a bank in Germany that lends money at 3 percent," he told his audience. "Remember there are no dividends paid by these co-operative banks." Hill also encouraged the development of cooperative marketing. "If somebody were to show you that by getting together you could get 25 percent more for what you sell, you would get together, wouldn't you?" he asked. "Well, that's what is being done in Europe."

In December, Hill and the other members of the commission from North Carolina made their report to Governor Craig. "We have a great many banks in North Carolina, but we have scarcely any banks willing to do the banking business of the poor man," the report said. It predicted that more banks extending business to small farmers in the state "would work wonders in upbuilding agriculture and bring much new business to . . . commercial banks."[14]

The report bore Hill's unmistakable touch; the language was direct and to the point. North Carolina farmers were "subjected to many kinds of extortion, usury and exploitation," the report said. And the farther the farmer lived from town, the higher the usury, the larger the commissions and fees, "and the more exacting the oppression and the extortion."[15] The report insisted: "Our farmers need to develop a complete system of co-operation in (1) getting credit; (2) buying supplies; (3) buying and using machinery; (4) converting raw products into more finished forms as in ginning cotton, grinding grain, converting cotton seed into meal and oil, milk into cream, butter and cheese, etc., and (5) marketing the finished product to the consumer."[16]

A few months later, in March 1914, Hill traveled to Washington to testify before a joint congressional committee on banking and currency. Hill argued that his experience in turning a small savings bank into a profitable institution, all on 6 percent interest without fees and commissions, was sufficient evidence that fair dealing with small borrowers was sound business and good for the country. "I tell you, gentlemen, frankly, I do not know anything that a man can do in this country higher and better than helping the man to build his home and helping a man to improve his home," he said, "and that is why I am here today, to make this fight if I can."

After more than an hour in the witness chair, Hill's passion was aroused when he heard a New York congressman question whether banks should be in the business of making risky farm loans or taking chances on wage earners who wished to build small homes. Replying to the congressman's question, Hill argued: "That shows that there should be an organization of the farmers and the poor people of this country to demand their rights. It is the poor people's money that is there [in the bank] and the poor people some day, in my judgment, will rise up and demand their rights. It is a matter of education of the men who are sitting there and directing the great banks and never see the poor man that is on the ground." Congress should set the example, Hill said. "That is one of the most important things in this business, is to educate the people of America to get away from the skinflint's business, oppressing the poor man, taking from him his savings and spending it somewhere else. I tell you that the mortgage on land at home is just as good as the mortgage on a railroad in Colorado or any Southern state."[17]

The legislation that came out of Congress was not to Hill's liking. The congressional sentiment was in favor of joint-stock banks; a cooperative feature had been introduced to make the bill more palatable. Hill favored more direct government support for cooperative credit and mortgage lending associations that would be underwritten by the sale of bonds. Hill said, "The joint-stock idea is absolutely and fundamentally opposed to the cooperative altruistic idea, and I can not imagine how any man's mind can associate the two."

Hill's appearance as a witness must have shocked some on the panel. The challenge he put before the committee sounded like a verse from the leftist radicals of Europe rather than the carefully crafted legal argument of a Southern banker wearing a high collar and jeweled tiepin. He left Washington impatient with the cool reception his ideas had received and took to the road.

A month after his appearance in Washington, he was in Lexington, Kentucky, where he addressed a meeting of the Southern Educational Association. The speech drew newspaper coverage around the South and the Midwest. Hill received an enthusiastic response from a Kentucky farm demonstration agent, who wrote: "I have heard your address severely criticized by some of our business men; but in each case they are the type we all know as usurers and extortioners. On the other hand, every man who is recognized as fair and square in the state of Kentucky, who heard your address, is outspoken in its praise."[18] The following month, Hill corresponded with a banker in Illinois who wanted to use a portion of the speech in an address of his own. And Hill heard from Ernestine Noa, a member of the American Commission from Nashville, Tennessee, who asked for copies of his speeches for distribution in her state.

"The great masses of people appear to be very much interested in co-operation," Hill told Noa. "Strange to say, however, our political leaders are opposed to co-operation, and are only going to permit advancement along this line when forced by the masses." He said he planned to "make it hot for some of our politicians in North Carolina." "I have been somewhat engaged in politics myself for the last twenty-five years," Hill explained, "and am not much averse to engaging in red-hot political campaigns."[19]

Hill was about to take his proposals to political leaders in North Carolina when he received a letter from E. C. Branson, the president of the State Normal School of Georgia in Athens. Branson was preparing to leave Georgia for North Carolina to organize a department of sociology at the University of North Carolina at the request of President Edward Kidder Graham. He learned about Hill from Noa, who was one of his former students. Branson warned Hill that organizing the state's farmers would not be easy: "Getting under the skull-caps of the democratic multitudes is a great, big, difficult undertaking." But he suggested that a biweekly publication might be one good way to reach them. "Your thinking and counsel about our getting every fortnightly, say, into the homes of 50,000 North Carolina farmers who own, live on and till their own farms would help us get into direct touch with the most valuable elements of country life regeneration." That fall, after Branson arrived in Chapel Hill, the first issue of the *University News Letter* was published, and Branson had established a lifelong bond with Hill and his "gospel of co-operative democracy."[20]

∾∾∾

Branson was a native of Morehead City, North Carolina, and eight years Hill's senior. He was a graduate of Trinity College with an advanced degree from Peabody Normal College in Nashville, Tennessee. Like Hill, he had begun his career as a teacher and high school principal, and by the time he reached the state teachers' college in Athens he had published several texts on the teaching of reading, arithmetic, and spelling.

Branson had a consuming interest in the ebb and flow of rural life. While in Athens, he organized the Georgia Club to familiarize teachers with the state and its people. The University of North Carolina's President Graham was eager to extend the reach of the university, and he hoped that Branson would replicate his program in North Carolina. He adopted Branson's plan of "taking stock of a state" by "fingering the resources, conditions, causes, tendencies, drifts and movements that have made history in the past, that have determined the present and that are operating to determine the future." Graham's plan was "to do this thing county by county," using the university's resources to undertake "an enormous economic study" over the course of "ten or fifteen years devoted to laborious toil."[21]

The plan was more sophisticated than what Hill had proposed a decade before in his 1903 speech to the university trustees, but the message was the same. Over the coming years, Branson's tenure at Chapel Hill would prove to be a significant turning point in the involvement of the university in the life of the state. Branson's pioneering work in the social sciences would touch many lives, including that of a young law professor named Albert Coates, whose own life's work produced the Institute of Government, which provided specialized training to state and local officials.

Hill's best opportunity to advance his plan for a system of rural credit associations was to appeal to the North Carolina General Assembly, which convened in Raleigh in January 1915. By that time, Europe had become engulfed in war, and the impact of the conflict was being felt all across the South. The cotton market was a shambles after Germany's submarine warfare in the Atlantic led to the suspension of shipments of American cotton abroad.

Hill's appeal to the legislature was successful. On March 6, 1915, just as the General Assembly was about to adjourn, legislators approved the

McRae Credit Union Act, which was considered at the time to be one of the most progressive laws on the subject in the nation. In addition to authorizing the creation of credit unions, the legislation also directed the state Department of Agriculture to promote cooperative marketing and credit organizations.

The day before the bill passed, the state Senate rejected Clarence Poe's proposed constitutional amendment on land segregation. A deciding vote came from Charles A. Jonas of Lincolnton, a Republican mindful of his own party's historical relationship with African Americans. Said Jonas: "I almost fear to say what I am going to. Because of my party affiliation I am afraid there will be charges of ulterior motives. But I can't sit here silent when such legislation is proposed. The great state of North Carolina and the people of North Carolina cannot afford to deprive a lower race of its rights."

Poe vowed to return in 1917 for another attempt at land segregation, but the movement later dissipated into oblivion as war fever swept the nation. At the same time, Poe applauded the legislature's approval of the credit union bill. Credit unions had failed to grow in other states, Poe wrote, but the provision in the North Carolina law requiring the state to promote cooperation was "an advanced step that other states [would] undoubtedly adopt."[22]

Hill accepted the term "credit unions" in place of "credit societies" to describe the new cooperatives. "We want to lay the emphasis upon the word 'union' in all of our movements," he wrote Branson. What he had in mind was really no different from the small credit unions that had established toeholds elsewhere in the United States by 1915. The first were formed in New England in 1909, where they served wage earners in the factories of New Hampshire and Massachusetts. The first rural credit unions were organized by Jewish farmers, who by 1915 had eighteen associations operating in four northeastern states. "The borrowers paid only 6 percent upon their loans and the 18 unions earned 13¾ percent upon the capital invested," Branson wrote in an article for the *Progressive Farmer*. "When Jews try out a business proposition and find it sane, safe, sound and practicable little room is left for argument or doubt."[23]

The cooperative movement was a direct threat to a system that produced enormous profits for lenders and merchants, particularly those in small rural communities where farmers had few choices. One study showed that in North Carolina alone, farmers paid $3.3 million more for credit in 1913 than they would have if interest rates had been enforced and farmers had not been bound to crop liens. At the same time that Hill's credit union bill passed, the legislature turned down a bill that would have eliminated crop liens within three years.

The success in Raleigh invigorated Hill. He drew on Branson's research when he spoke to a statewide meeting of merchants in Asheville that summer before heading to Atlantic City, New Jersey, for a brief vacation with his family. In the fall, he organized a meeting of farmers in Durham and invited Branson to stay with him during the three-day session. "Mrs. Hill will be away with her father at Pinehurst, but all of my servants and children will be there so that you will be at liberty to come and go as you please," he wrote. "I promise not to talk you to death about rural credits."[24]

This was a subject that aroused his passion. Credit unions made eminently good sense not just for the farmers but also for the state. "Any movement that can persuade the average small farmer of North Carolina that his real prosperity is tied up closely with that of his neighbor, that they should cooperate with each other in the use of credit," Hill argued, "would bring the greatest possible benefit, not alone to the farmer, but to every one who lives in North Carolina." "Banks were aggregations of money," he told the meeting of farmers in Durham, "while credit unions were aggregations of men."

Hill continued: "Practically every farmer here knows a few things about the workings of so-called country banks, the so-called friends of the farmers. Some of the foul financial concoctions turned out by some of our country banks for the farmers to feed upon and grow strong and great are so disgraceful that I am ashamed to mention them in detail in a public address." He declared: "Let the aim of the Tar heel farmers be to abolish the heart-breaking, single handed struggle for existence on North Carolina farms, and put into its place co-operative union for prosperity."[25]

In December 1915, Hill met with a group of farmers at Lowe's Grove (where the new school was being developed between Durham and Chapel Hill) to talk about including a credit union in the school's expanding curriculum, which was fast becoming one of the models for the state's farm-life program. By the time Hill arrived, the school included an eleven-room dormitory for boys and girls and a barn for prize stock that housed a pair of Percheron mares, a Guernsey bull, two Jersey cows, and a Berkshire sow.

Teachers and students had turned what was once a worn-out, mismanaged farm into a thriving place that produced crops of corn, soybeans, and enough tomatoes to support a cannery. The *Progressive Farmer* declared it the result of the "co-operative spirit." For Hill, it was the natural location for the state's first credit union.[26]

Before a receptive audience, Hill outlined what he had seen in Italy and urged the group to be the first to act. A week later, he attended a similar meeting near Charlotte in Mecklenburg County. The Lowe's Grove Credit Union began business January 20, 1916, five days before the Carmel Credit Union opened for business outside of Charlotte. While Lowe's Grove had the first credit union in North Carolina, farmers in Catawba County had voted two years earlier to form one but had decided subsequently to establish a traditional building and loan association.

Over the next two years, Hill conducted his private campaign to extend the credit union movement to all corners of the state. By the end of 1916, six credit unions had opened. Six more were chartered in 1917. They sprang up in farming communities such as Bahama in Durham County, Eureka in Moore County, and Oakdale and Providence in Mecklenburg County. More often than not, Hill was one of the first to buy shares in the new institutions.

Opposition dogged Hill every bit of the way. Securing the legislation and organizing the first credit unions had been a struggle, Hill told a friend in Raleigh. The state Department of Agriculture had been no help at all. Agriculture officials hired a person to assist the credit unions, as directed by the General Assembly, but his attention had been turned to other matters. Hill became frustrated with the impenetrable bureaucracy. "The truth is that some powerful, but unseen hand appears to reach out and block the way to the formation of credit unions in North Carolina," he complained. "I have letters in my office from prominent and patriotic North Carolinians to this effect."[27]

Another obstacle was the farmers themselves. As Branson had warned, the same individualism among farmers that Hill held in such high regard also contributed to what Branson would later call "rural mindedness." Among the farmers' outstanding characteristics were "social aloofness" and "non-co-operativeness." One of Branson's students later wrote: "The rural mind is private and local—almost inescapably so. And the culture of the countryman has long been the main-spring and the measure of our civilization. As the countryman thinketh in his heart, so are we in North Carolina—or so it long has been. Both the best and the worse of us lies in this fundamental fact."[28]

Hill remained undeterred; he simply increased his personal evangelism. "What is a credit union?" he asked a gathering of Tennessee farmers in the summer of 1916. "It is a savings society. It is not a bank. A few men of means form a bank to make money out of their friends and neighbors. A credit union is a union of farmers without much means, but strong in moral character and earning capacity. It is a new kind of corporation founded on sound business principles plus democratic manhood."

Hill's personal crusade for credit unions continued into 1917. The progress had been steady, but only a fraction of those who could benefit were being served. Then, in the spring, forces well beyond Hill's control interrupted his work. On April 6, 1917, Congress declared war on Germany in response to President Woodrow Wilson's call to "make the world safe for democracy." The nation's attention shifted to the war in Europe. Personal savings that might have gone to the credit unions went into war bonds. Young men left both the fields and the factories to enlist.

Hill's patriotic spirit was equally aroused. In early October 1917, he wrote army captain A. C. Michie of Durham, who was organizing a company of home guards. "[If] you can use a real stout young man of about forty-nine years, with considerable military experience," he told the captain, "I shall be glad to volunteer for service."[29] There was another in the Hill household also anxious to contribute to the war effort. That fall, Hill's son, George Watts Hill, organized a drill team among his fellow students at Durham High School and hoped that the war would not be over before he could get into a real uniform.

CHAPTER 6

Passing Generations

—————————

BECAUSE HE WAS ONLY SEVENTEEN YEARS OF AGE in the fall of 1918, George Watts Hill was too young to enlist in the army. Instead, he enrolled at the University of North Carolina, where he reluctantly settled for a spot on the sidelines while the university focused on older students in the Students' Army Training Corps (SATC).

Watts Hill would have made a fine-looking soldier. He was an energetic and athletic young man with the same lean physique and classic facial features of his father. He had his grandfather's height. At more than six feet, he stood nearly a head taller than his father. Watts Hill had been eligible to enter the university in 1917 following his graduation from Durham High School, but his parents thought he was too young for college and sent him off to prep school. Their decision proved a boon for his good friend, William D. "Billy" Carmichael Jr. The university scholarship Hill won at Durham High School was passed on to Carmichael.

Life at the university gave Watts Hill a measure of freedom that he had never known before. While the family's governess, Bessie Fritz, tended mostly to his sisters, Watts had been raised under the watchful eye of his grandfather, who imposed his own rigid Presbyterian discipline on the boy. In addition, his father impressed upon him at an early age the importance of responsibilities. John Sprunt Hill provided every luxury for his family (servants were always on hand to perform work throughout the house), but Watts and his sisters were still given daily work. Watts milked a cow or two and made his own bed before he left for school each morning. Meanwhile, Annie Watts Hill imposed full upper-class decorum upon the household. Adults and children dressed for dinner, which was served in the large dining room with everyone seated straight and tall. Children did not speak unless spoken to by an adult; one false move and the child was sent from the table.

❧❧❧

As the oldest of the children and the only boy, Watts Hill spent considerable time with George Watts, whom he called "Far." Watts often escorted his grandson to classes at Morehead Elementary School, prodding the youngster to walk erect as he scrambled to keep up with an adult's pace. The two shared morning and evening prayers, and from time to time George Watts asked his grandson to lead. George Watts also taught the value of order and precision. The boy's school notes were thorough, and his clothes were arranged just so, a habit that he kept into adulthood. He was a precocious youngster who enjoyed baseball, golf, tennis, and swimming. When not outdoors, he was reading. *Ivanhoe* and *The Last of the Mohicans* were among the favorites he named in a brief childhood account that he wrote in 1913 with a clear hand. (He once sent a letter to President Theodore Roosevelt when he discovered they shared a common birth date. The president's reply became a lifelong keepsake.) On Sunday afternoons, when outside play was forbidden, Watts Hill joined his grandfather in the library at Harwood Hall. While his grandfather studied the Bible and prepared his Sunday school lessons, the boy read Walter Hines Page's newsmagazine, *World's Work*. Around four, Watts Hill would gather up the reins of the carriage and drive his grandfather to Bible classes at the Pearl Mill's mission church. The boy enjoyed the time with his grandfather and would later count him among those he was closest to in life.

Watts Hill inherited his father's fiercely competitive spirit, love of the outdoors, and at least some of his religious devotion. Watts was bored by the sermons at First Presbyterian, but he faithfully attended Sunday school, learned his catechism, and endured the services from his place on the family pew in the fourth row. The boy much preferred outings to the American Tobacco Company factory, where he scooped up the uncut cigarettes that were spilling out of the machines. "You couldn't smoke one longer than six inches because you couldn't get a draw," Hill later recalled. "I'd have fun passing them around to kids." He also accompanied his grandfather to Quail Roost, the hunting preserve north of Durham where George Watts and other tobacco millionaires had leased thousands of acres for their shooting enjoyment. If Watts Hill was not driving the buggy, he snuggled close to his grandfather beneath heavy buffalo robes to escape the cold winter air.[1]

⊙⊙⊙

The boy's companionship was a comfort to George Watts, who had watched his wife's health decline with each passing year. She was bedridden for nearly a year before she died on April 26, 1915. Linnie Watts had been as devoted a member of Durham's First Presbyterian Church as her husband. She had dedicated her talents to the church's music program, singing in the choir. A new sanctuary was under construction at the time of her death, and when it opened the following year, it included a new $10,000 pipe organ that George Watts had provided in her memory. George Watts also presented the church with paired sets of brilliant stained glass windows for the church sanctuary. Designed by the Von Gerichten glassworks in Munich, they were bound for a church in Philadelphia. When the church refused delivery and the war prevented a reshipment to Europe, Watts bought them at a discount and had them installed in Durham.

Two years after his wife's death, as Watts Hill prepared to leave Durham for prep school, George Watts sat his grandson down and told him he was going to marry "Aunt Sarah," as Sarah Ecker, the family's longtime nurse, was called by younger members of the family. A part of the family for quite some time, Ecker had cared for Watts Hill when he was an infant and more recently had nursed Linnie Watts through her prolonged illness. The marriage bothered some, including Watts's daughter Annie, and the ceremony was performed quietly in Syracuse, New York, Ecker's hometown. After a honeymoon, the couple returned to Durham and Harwood Hall.

⊙⊙⊙

Watts Hill had received a first-rate education in Durham schools, where he advanced rapidly, bypassing the third grade. Community leaders such as George Watts, Julian Carr, and others shared leadership of the city's school board. The city's schools for whites were kept in good repair and operated in good order. Classes were strictly segregated in the upper grades, with the girls on one floor and the boys on another. "Dating by high schoolers was so rare that the word was not even in our vocabulary," one of Hill's classmates later recalled. Dancing was known to only a few.[2]

By the time Watts Hill got to high school in an imposing neoclassical building on the edge of downtown, any student who remained in the upper grades was presumed to be preparing for college. Most of the students from the mill villages had already left for factory jobs. Watts Hill was drilled in English grammar and literature, Latin, algebra, civics, and hygiene. For hygiene, he memorized the bones of the body and the proper names of the muscles, and he drew diagrams of the circulatory system. Girls chose from electives such as domestic science; boys took shop. Drawing, another option for both sexes, was one of Watts's favorite subjects. The concepts of shape, form, and depth of field kindled a lifelong interest in architecture.

In the regular classroom, he was partial to history and math. He did well and skipped a grade, just as he had in elementary school. Even though he was younger than his classmates, Watts helped organize a drill team and was elected captain after the United States entered the war against Germany in the spring of 1917. His soldiers-to-be practiced close order drill and the order of arms with wooden rifles.[3] The February 1917 issue of the *Messenger*, the school's literary journal, included a short story he wrote about a daring encounter a lone French plane had with a zeppelin over the lines of the European western front.

Before Watts Hill finished his last year at City High, his parents had already made plans for him to enroll at the Hotchkiss School, a prep school in Lakeville, Connecticut. The school headmaster, H. G. Buehler, was an acquaintance of George Watts, but he made no exceptions when Watts Hill failed the admissions test for the senior class. John Sprunt Hill explained to Buehler that his son had not done well on the test because he was distracted by Red Cross work and the drill team. He promised that his son would be ready by fall.

That summer, Watts spent some of his time at Camp Winape in Charleston, Vermont, studying French, English, and algebra as well as hiking and paddling his canoe. His father was philosophical. "I regret very much your failure to pass has brought on you such a lot of trouble and expense," he wrote his son in July 1917, "but reverses come in a man's life once in a while, and the best way to overcome them is to take your medicine like a man and buckle down to serious work."[4] In September, Hill packed his son off to Hotchkiss and told Buehler to send him home if he did not pass his entrance examinations. "I am an old school teacher," he wrote Buehler, "and my own experience prompts me to say that it would be almost ruinous to a big, manly fellow like my son to put him back into a class of small boys. His ambition needs to be stimulated and with boys somewhat his own age, he will apply himself and desire to become a leader."

The elder Hill sounded like every other parent frustrated with the whims of teenagers. He told Buehler that he had high hopes his son would become a "strong leader of his fellow men in his native state," where he could be a "power of good." At the same time, he said that his son could, "like many other boys in his circumstances, become a lightweight sport, a disappointment to his family, and the means of promoting a tremendous amount of evil."[5]

Watts Hill's summer study was sufficient for him to qualify for Hotchkiss. He had barely settled into the prep school routine, however, when he injured his left leg playing football. It was his first opportunity for organized sports, and he had begun his assignment as a tackle when he was hurt. The injury was serious enough for his parents to admit him to a New York hospital, where doctors prescribed a daily treatment of alternating hot compresses and cold showers. The treatment was worse than the cure. New York was experiencing an uncommonly severe winter, and for several days the hospital was without coal. By Christmastime, when Watts Hill arrived home in a wheelchair, he was suffering from a severe case of bronchitis. His father canceled the rest of his term at Hotchkiss.

Watts Hill spent the next two months in treatment and rehabilitation at Watts Hospital. As he recovered, he hobbled around on crutches and became such a fixture about the place that surgeons invited him in to watch them operate. This constant exposure inspired an interest in medicine that was probably encouraged by the attention of his uncle, Dr. Christopher Hill, who had left his practice in New Jersey to become superintendent of Watts Hospital in 1913. By the time Watts was admitted, the hospital had achieved a reputation as one of the finest in the South. The teenager finally recovered the use of his leg, although the months of limited use atrophied his muscles and made his left leg one-half inch shorter than his right.

⌒⌒⌒

When Watts Hill got to Chapel Hill in the fall of 1918, the campus had been converted into an army post. The university was part of the war effort. Patriotic fever was high, and submission to the military was a near necessity. The year before, 68,000 college men around the country had volunteered for military service and emptied the nation's campuses of tuition-paying students. Altogether, 800 Carolina men were in the field, 2 of them as brigadier generals. Another 125 were privates or noncoms, including a young Marine corporal named Frank Porter Graham.

In order to meet the military's need for a larger army and to keep educational institutions solvent, the federal government created the Students' Army Training Corps. Men of draft age who had a high school diploma could enlist in the army and undertake college work at the same time they participated in military training. Based on the University of North Carolina's record of voluntary training the year before, university president Edward Kidder Graham was put in charge of the SATC program in the Carolinas, Virginia, Georgia, and Florida. He had been relieved of his administrative duties in Chapel Hill by an army colonel who assumed control of all campus activities down to assigning work details to rake the leaves. A report that appeared in the *Alumni Review* described the SATC: "The SATC unit at Chapel Hill is a war department camp just as much so as Camp Jackson, the only difference being that the 18- to 20-year old registrant could enter this unit on October 1st, while he could not enter Camp Jackson until he was sent." The report responded to critics who had charged that the SATC was little more than a way for young men to dodge their responsibility to enlist.[6]

Chapel Hill was khaki and olive drab. The dormitories were called barracks, Memorial Hall was renamed Armory Hall, and SATC men took meals in the Mess (Swain) Hall. The old University Inn, a broken-down hotel on the edge of campus, was converted into the Post Exchange. War films played at the Y, where evening lectures and readings by faculty members offered some diversions.

The University of North Carolina men—all but 32 of the 1,200 students on campus were men—began the day with reveille at six followed by physical training; breakfast and military classes began promptly at eight. Two hours every other day were devoted to military subjects, and training continued on Saturday. "Men rose with the sun, went to bed—imagine it—at ten o'clock, after a day spent washing windows, peeling potatoes, drilling in close order formation—with occasional class attendance and possibly a bit of study now and then," according to the *Alumni Review*.[7] All athletic schedules were canceled to open playing fields for close order drill, attack maneuvers, and practice of the manual of arms. The army dug trenches and set up wire obstacles on land at Piney Prospect owned by the Order of Gimghouls.

In September 1918, Watts Hill was still weeks away from his eighteenth birthday, and he was sorely disappointed that when he enrolled at the university he was classified as a non-SATC student. He carried the normal freshman load of classes, but with the dormitories filled with SATC men, he had to live off campus. He found a room in a boardinghouse on Columbia Street near where the Ackland Art Museum would later stand. He joined a non-SATC drill unit along with about 140 others who could not qualify for active duty. They were given uniforms with special insignia, and their training was led by Lieutenant J. Stuart Allen, a Canadian who had served in France in 1915 with the Royal Fusiliers. Allen was home recovering from wounds he had received the previous year when he accepted the offer to conduct the voluntary training. He promoted Watts to sergeant.

∾∾∾

Young Hill came naturally by his patriotic fervor. The entire family had committed to the war effort. John Sprunt Hill even set aside his work on his beloved credit unions, turning down an appointment from the governor to represent the state at a national farm credit meeting in the fall of 1917. "Just at this time," Hill wrote his friend E. C. Branson, "I am more interested in pushing the war than any other matter, and I feel it my duty to the country to 'do my bit' along this line."[8]

John Sprunt Hill offered Hillandale Farm as an army training camp and organized a speakers' bureau to arouse patriotism in the rural areas. As chairman of the Durham County Board of Agriculture, he chaired the Food Conservation Commission when food supplies were curtailed and shortages arose. He became state treasurer of the Salvation Army War Service Fund and volunteered to lead the Durham County drive for war savings bonds. Annie Watts Hill helped organize the Red Cross Gray Lady volunteers in Durham, while her father chaired the state's YMCA war fund. In one magnanimous gesture, the Hills paid for an ambulance and had it shipped to France, where it went into service with the Red Cross.[9]

As America's involvement reached its peak in the spring of 1918, John Sprunt Hill presented British and French flags to the voluntary training companies at Chapel Hill as a reminder of the debt that Americans owed their European allies. "I have made a great many speeches on subjects pertaining to the war," Hill wrote a friend, "and I have mingled with a great many people in different parts of North Carolina, and I am astonished to find the tremendous amount of prejudice against the English. There is a great misunderstanding of our relations with England, and I believe this misunderstanding is doing a great deal of harm at this particular time."[10]

Some of the resentment toward the British stemmed from Great Britain's decision to sever American access to the cotton markets in Europe before the United States entered the war. There was also a general feeling that old Europe should be left alone to settle its own problems. Others in the outlying areas just resented the military draft and the intrusion of the federal government into their lives. In the summer of 1918, Governor Thomas Bickett went after what he called "the poolroom aristocracy and the Coca-Cola gentry" to see that they answered the call to arms. He ordered the state militia into the backwoods of Ashe County in search of eighteen deserters after they failed to return to their training camps. Bickett later excused the mountain boys' absence, saying they were all sons of deserters from the Confederate army and that they had believed that if they stayed out until the war was over, they would not be prosecuted for desertion.[11]

John Sprunt Hill's blood came to a proper boil on several occasions when he detected what he believed were weak hearts or worse among his countrymen. In the summer of 1918, Hill reported that Durham County had not met even half of its goal in the sale of bonds, and he asked the state director of the bond drive, Colonel F. H. Fries of Winston-Salem, what the government could do about "wealthy slackers." Hill wrote: "The responsibility should be fastened directly upon these slackers and near-slackers and the officials at Washington should in my opinion, advise us promptly how to put pressure on these people. Many of these people have been more or less engaged in the whiskey business, and are naturally against the government on everything." Hill said that if the government did not do something, "hot-headed neighbors will take the law in their own hands and commit acts of violence that will bring discredit upon us all."[12]

Hill was equally upset over reports emanating from Chapel Hill—reports that he said were encouraged by the "denominational" schools—that certain University of North Carolina professors were guilty of "pro-German sentiment." Much of this discussion arose from an article in the *Charlotte Observer* that quoted philosophy professor Horace Williams as having questioned whether America should be involved in what he said was essentially a European war. In a lengthy letter to President Graham, Hill complained, "There is a small coterie at the University quite indifferent to the great issue [of the causes of the war] and at times indiscreet and foolish in speech and conduct." One professor, he reported with alarm, had allowed Rose Pastor Stokes, a socialist opposed to the war, into his classroom. "The thought is rising in the minds of many of us about the advisability of continuing to permit any professor to hold a position in our state university who is not known to be absolutely and actively loyal to our cause in mind, body and spirit," Hill told Graham.[13]

Hill received a conciliatory letter in reply from Charles L. Raper, a respected economics professor and faculty leader who had been one of Hill's steady allies on campus projects. Raper did not deny that Stokes had spoken to his classes, but he reassured Hill that he himself was no socialist. Hill wrote off the affair as a misunderstanding.[14]

❧❧❧

Watts Hill's first term at the university was unlike any other he would experience. The SATC regimen eliminated the usual freshman, sophomore, junior, and senior designations for all except the non-SATC students like Hill. He had barely settled in at his boardinghouse when the Chapel Hill community was stricken with an outbreak of influenza. Two weeks after the SATC enlistees were sworn in, the university infirmary was overwhelmed with more than five hundred cases. The campus was quarantined.

The flu epidemic first swept through Europe, where it flourished in Spain (hence the name Spanish Influenza), before reaching the Atlantic seaboard. Twenty-one people died in Boston in one day alone. The virus ravaged army camps as it spread easily among men living in the close quarters of barracks and tents; half as many soldiers died of influenza as had died overseas.[15] People were panic-stricken. Public gatherings were banned. In the cities, people took to wearing face masks.

It was the worst epidemic North Carolina had ever seen. Governor Thomas Bickett reported fifteen thousand victims statewide in the fall of 1918. More than 10 percent of the twenty-one thousand people living in Durham County took sick. John Sprunt Hill packed his wife and two daughters off to Poland Springs aboard the Dukes' private railroad car so they could avoid exposure at public rail stations.[16] In Chapel Hill, medical classes were suspended, and the faculty and second-year students cared for patients.

Three SATC students and two female nurses succumbed to pneumonia and other complications in Chapel Hill. The most devastating loss was President Graham, who had worked himself to a point of exhaustion in his efforts to organize the SATC program. He fell ill on October 21 and died five days later. The entire university community was left feeling shock and disbelief. Albert Coates later wrote that he had felt "there had passed away a glory from the earth."[17]

ᴓ ᴓ ᴓ

The epidemic produced John Sprunt Hill's first serious financial crisis since he had discovered the state of the books at the old Citizen's Savings Bank. Two years before the flu outbreak, in 1916, Hill and George Watts had formed the Home Security Life Insurance Company with two Durham men, A. M. and E. N. Moize. The brothers were experienced insurance men who in the previous decade had been with the Durham Life Insurance Company. After they had a disagreement with the Durham Life management, they approached Hill about creating a new company. The brothers had put up half the necessary capital and George Watts had put up the other half. John Sprunt Hill handled the legal work and took a small amount of stock for his efforts. The company did well in its first two years, selling policies to factory workers who paid modest weekly premiums. The value of the policies was small, between $250 and $1,000. The smaller ones generated just enough money to pay for a decent burial, while the larger policies were designed to provide a man's family with a bit of a financial cushion.

The flu epidemic drained the reserves of insurance providers across the country, but it hit new companies like Home Security especially hard. At the height of the epidemic, Watts could see nothing but trouble ahead. He stepped into Hill's office and dropped all his Home Security stock certificates on his son-in-law's desk. "Here," he said, "take this stock. You can have it, all of it, as a gift." Hill took the stock and set about refinancing the company. He put in a substantial amount of his own money to forestall bankruptcy and thereby saved Home Security from collapse, but it would be another two years before the company reported a surplus. At the end of 1919, the company had only $29.05 on hand.[18]

ᴓ ᴓ ᴓ

The epidemic had virtually disappeared from Chapel Hill by early November 1918, just as Watts Hill prepared to enlist and upgrade his SATC status. Then, the war in Europe ended with the armistice of November 11.

Watts never forgot the sight of a future fraternity brother, later a doctor in Winston-Salem, running naked across campus yelling, "Weeeee, the war is over, the war is over!"[19] Almost immediately, the War Department issued orders to shut down SATC. All those in uniform, SATC and non-SATC alike, stood for their last formation on Saturday, December 7. Demobilization began the following Monday. When the term closed a few days later, the campus was relieved of its military command and returned to normalcy.

During the holiday break, the faculty readjusted course outlines, campus organizations that had been on hold for the duration were revived, fees were established for the new order, and a drive was started to attract upperclassmen who would be returning from military duty. But it would be months before the men in Europe returned home. As a result, enrollment for the spring term dropped to less than nine hundred as SATC men deserted the campus.

Enrollment swelled to more than fourteen hundred in the fall of 1919. No longer distracted by visions of battlefield glory, Watts Hill settled in to the routine of college life. His inclination was to prepare for the serious study of medicine and to pursue his dream of becoming a doctor. His father, however, had other ideas, and he pushed his son to concentrate his course work in the university's new School of Commerce. After Watts Hill graduated, his father planned for him to attend law school. Watts responded to his father's wishes and performed reasonably well in the classroom throughout his remaining three years. He never could master accounting, however, and this failure kept him from being admitted to Phi Beta Kappa.

As a sophomore, he joined the Dialectic Society (membership was now elective), and he later became a photo editor of the campus yearbook, the *Yackety Yack.* He took some interest in the new Carolina Playmakers under Professor Frederick H. Koch, whose star pupil was a writer named Thomas Wolfe. In the spring of 1920, when Wolfe's play *The Third Night* was staged, Watts played the streetcar operator in *Who Pays?*, a tragedy about a labor organizer whose daughter is killed in a riot. On many a Sunday evening, friends piled into his Marmon automobile (a car that his father's bank had repossessed), and they drove to Durham for a meal at the imposing Hill home on South Duke Street.

From time to time, as John Sprunt Hill's business obligations increased, Watts became his father's surrogate. Watts was in his senior year when his father asked him to become involved with the Chapel Hill Presbyterian Church. The church's minister, Dr. H. Howe, had written to Hill asking for financial support. The elder Hill in turn asked his son to meet with the minister and see what was needed. "I will stand behind you on the financial side of the matter," Hill wrote his son, "but that Church needs more than financial support and I am unable to give any time and attention to it."[20] He went on to tell his son that he had spoken in 1903 of the need for all the major denominations to open churches on the campus perimeter, and George Watts had helped underwrite the establishment of the Chapel Hill congregation. Hill urged his son to become one of the "pillars of the church."

Watts Hill's lasting memories of his undergraduate years were not of the classroom, but of extracurricular activities that often had an entrepreneurial bent. In his first quarter, in the fall of 1918, he earned extra money selling candy and fruit to the SATC students, who were given only limited privileges to leave the campus. In his junior year, he managed a small dining club called The Cabin, where he supervised a cook and kitchen helper who prepared three meals a day for nearly three dozen paying members.

While his knee injury kept him off the playing field, Watts maintained his interest in football. In his junior year he was assistant manager of the team as the Carolina boys suffered through a disastrous season. Most of the losses were complete shutouts; the only successful outing was against South Carolina. Student athletics were controlled largely by the alumni, who had taken over five years earlier after Carolina's humiliating 66–0 defeat by the University of Virginia. With another embarrassing season on the books, the alumni brought in two brothers, William McKeithan and Robert Fetzer, to take charge in 1921.

The Fetzers were rumored to be drawing $7,000 a year each in pay, which set off a howl from those who compared the coaches' salaries to those of professors, who received half as much. The investment paid off, however. Carolina lost to Yale, 34–0, and to State College in Raleigh, but the team beat Maryland 16–7 in a game in which Johnny Johnson ran for a total of 353 yards. The alumni focused their attention most on the annual Thanksgiving game against Virginia, which at one point was canceled after the Carolina faculty questioned the eligibility of a Virginia player. Under pressure from alumni who cherished the annual reunion, however, the game was rescheduled, and it was played before a tremendous crowd. As team manager, Hill collected the gate receipts and watched the game from a hillside with a cashbox stuffed with money at his side. Carolina won, 7–3, saving the Fetzers for another season.

Hill led a modest social life. He dated a girl from Asheville for a time and once escorted Buck Duke's daughter Doris to a campus dance. For the most part, he was uncomfortable around girls thanks to his segregated schooling in Durham and to the little exposure to girls he had received on the virtually all-male university campus. Once, he arrived to pick up his date and had the girl's sister halfway down the steps before he realized his mistake.[21] As for drinking, gambling, and other assorted transgressions reputed to be part of college life, Hill carefully followed the example of his grandfather and remained a teetotaler. He did "nothing more derogatory to his dignity than to take an occasional smoke," his class notes said, and he earned a reputation as a tough enforcer of prohibition among his Sigma Alpha Epsilon fraternity brothers.

Hill was invited into the Order of Gimghouls, the exclusive club of leading fraternity men that had grown in prestige since his father's day. The son seemed as suited as the father for the secret order. "How like a noble knight he looks!" Watts Hill's yearbook description said. "Yea, and verily it is impressed on those who know him. If he knows, he will tell you; if he does not know he will tell you anyway. Nothing from the fine points of football to the achievements of the recent disarmament conference will find him at a loss conversationally."

❧ ❧ ❧

Hill was midway through his junior year in early 1921 when his grandfather, George Watts, fell gravely ill. The previous year Watts had suffered through an attack of flu and then undergone surgery to correct recurring stomach ulcers. After his recuperation, he appeared much improved and left with his wife for an extended trip that included attendance at the World's Sunday School Convention in Tokyo, where he was due to be elected a vice president.

The Presbyterian Church remained the focus of Watts's life. Until his health failed, he continued to meet the Sunday school classes and lead his Friday prayer meetings at the mission church. The trip to the Far East gave him an opportunity to visit Soon Chun, Korea, a village south of Seoul where a Presbyterian mission school had been built with his $250,000 gift to the Presbyterian Church. The salaries of eight of the thirteen missionaries assigned to Soon Chun were paid for by Durham's First Presbyterian

Church, largely with money provided by Watts. While at Soon Chun, he was asked to intervene on the Christians' behalf before the Japanese barons governing Korea, who had forbidden the use of the Bible.

Watts returned home in early fall, and his health began to fail. His condition did not appear life threatening, so John Sprunt Hill organized a bird-hunting party at Quail Roost Farm over the Thanksgiving holiday for a number of friends, including his old university classmate William R. Kenan Jr., tobacco executive W. D. Carmichael, and a friend from New York. Hill was anticipating an enjoyable reunion with old friends who were not like some New Yorkers who came south and "went in heavy for Scotch highballs and hunting clothes." He counseled each on how to ship dogs down for the hunt and made preparations for a great feast at the lodge on the farm. At the last minute, however, he canceled the hunt when Watts's condition worsened.

Doctors tried to relieve Watts with transfusions, and his grandson Watts Hill came over from Chapel Hill to provide blood. The transfusions helped, and Watts recovered sufficiently to enjoy a large Christmas dinner with his entire family. Doctors could never fully control the bleeding from what they considered to be ulcers in his stomach, however. By the first of the year, Watts's condition had declined.

In February, a team of doctors was called in from The Johns Hopkins University in Baltimore. Watts was too sick to be moved to Watts Hospital, so the doctors performed surgery in Watts's bedroom on the second floor of Harwood Hall. He received further blood transfusions, including blood donated by his chauffeur, Billy Bryant, but the doctors were unable to do anything about the cancer they found in his midsection.[22] George Watts died on March 7, 1921, six months shy of his seventieth birthday.

All of Durham came to a standstill on March 9, the day of the funeral. Workers in factories and offices throughout the city were released in time to attend services at Harwood Hall, where Linnie Watts's services had also been held. Thousands turned out, although most were forced to stand on the lawn in a steady rain that continued until just before 3 P.M., when the services began. The Reverend David Scanlon from First Presbyterian; Union Seminary's president, the Reverend Walter W. Moore; and the Reverend E. R. Leyburn, who had been Watts's golfing partner and longtime pastor, officiated in a service that was as simple as the surroundings were grand.

Among those attending were Presbyterian clergymen and college presidents from across the South. Governor Cameron Morrison came, as did Lieutenant Governor W. B. Cooper. They were joined by Watts's partners, Ben and Buck Duke, and other associates from the old American Tobacco Company days. Even Al Fairbrother, the newspaper editor who had been forced off the *Durham Globe* for his attacks on Watts more than twenty-five years earlier, paid his respects. Many of those attending followed the cortege to Maplewood Cemetery for a short interment service.

The flag over Watts Hall at Union Theological Seminary in Richmond was lowered to half-staff in honor of the loss of the school's most generous benefactor. Presbyterians around the world had been touched by Watts's generosity, especially in the missions in Korea, Cuba, Africa, and India. Had he lived another thirty days, he would have learned that Japanese officials had lifted a six-year ban on the use of the Bible, but only for the Presbyterian mission schools.

∽∽∽

George Watts left his son-in-law, John Sprunt Hill, in charge of his estate, which amounted to almost $15 million. In his will, Watts remembered his favorite institutions and his church. He provided for a $500,000 endowment for the Korean mission and gifts of $200,000 to Watts Hospital, $150,000 to the First Presbyterian Church, and $50,000 to Union Theological Seminary. The Durham YMCA received $10,000 and the Presbyterian Church $50,000 for missions at home and abroad. He gave $25,000 to the Barium Springs Orphanage at Troutman, North Carolina, where the celebration of the birthday of Watts Hill remained as a tradition. Equal shares of about $5 million each went to his daughter and to his widow, who planned to remain on at Harwood Hall. In a touch of irony, Watts left $200,000 in cash to John Sprunt Hill. It was an amount roughly equal to what Hill would have received had he accepted Watts's $1,000-a-month offer in 1903.

In noting Watts's death and the recent deaths of two others from the early days of the state's tobacco business, the *Southern Tobacco Journal* wrote, "The old guard is passing." Yet at the time of his death, George Watts's legacy was more than a record in business. Watts had helped to create a modern city, build one of the best school systems in the state, erect a grand church where hundreds gathered for his Sunday school classes, and establish the only hospital in North Carolina that merited a Class A rating by the American College of Surgeons.

He had left unfinished business at the hospital, which Watts hoped would become part of a medical school. In 1909, he had offered Trinity College the original Watts Hospital buildings as well as the use of the new hospital as a training clinic if Trinity could raise an endowment of $300,000 and open a medical school. Nothing had come of his offer.

After the war, Trinity president William P. Few revived discussions with George Watts, Ben Duke, and Dr. Abraham Flexner of the General Education Board, an arm of the Rockefeller Foundation. Flexner had recently completed a study of medical training in the United States that resulted in the closing of many small institutions, including two in North Carolina. The only viable medical training that remained in the state was the two-year program at Chapel Hill, which was limited because it had no hospital where students could complete their clinical training.[23] Few had an unwritten understanding with Flexner that if Rockefeller would endow the school, Trinity would provide the buildings and use Watts Hospital for clinical training.[24]

The year before Watts died, John Sprunt Hill reported to the University of North Carolina trustees that he knew of plans by those outside of the university for a "high-grade medical college" that would provide the final two years required for a medical degree. The school would be "amply supported" and require no financial responsibility from the university.[25] The university trustees appointed a committee to investigate Hill's report, but nothing had materialized by the time of Watts's death.

Watts's passing all but stopped Few in his tracks. For the time being, at least, a medical school at Trinity remained an open question. There also appeared to be little motivation from the trustees at Chapel Hill to expand the scope of the medical training the university offered.

❧❧❧

The full burden of managing George Watts's estate—and especially the future of Watts Hospital—fell on John Sprunt Hill at a most awkward time. In the months leading up to his father-in-law's death, Hill had become an important figure in the statewide movement for better roads. Watts was in his last hours when the General Assembly passed the most ambitious highway-building program in North Carolina history. In the week of Watts's funeral, Governor Morrison asked Hill to become a member of the State Highway Commission. Hill accepted immediately.

The appointment came as Hill was entering one of the most productive periods of his lifetime in business and public affairs. He could not ignore the affairs of Watts Hospital, which became his responsibility after his father-in-law's death, but he did little more than dispense money from the Watts estate to meet the needs of the institution. His primary interest was in a host of public projects, not the least of which was building a network of hard-surfaced roads to connect North Carolina communities from border to border. The new state public works program—the largest in its history—would become the hallmark of Governor Cameron Morrison's four years in office. It would also make John Sprunt Hill one of the most powerful figures in central North Carolina.

CHAPTER 7

Building North Carolina

ON A STEAMY SATURDAY IN JUNE 1920, the lead vehicle in a convoy of sixty-five automobiles, heavy trucks, and motorcycles turned the corner on Capitol Square in Raleigh and paraded down Fayetteville Street. Amazed onlookers watched as the vehicles rolled on to the State Fairgrounds, where the convoy was to bivouac for two days. When the last vehicle rolled to a stop, the convoy commander announced proudly that his men had traveled the final leg of the journey from Oxford to Raleigh—a distance of about fifty miles—in less than nine hours.

The convoy had left Washington, D.C., four days earlier under the eyes of President Woodrow Wilson and with the blessing of members of his cabinet and other dignitaries. Its mission was to motor across the United States, and the military had equipped itself for the journey as thoroughly as it had for any effort since the Great War. Forty officers and more than a hundred enlisted men traveled with a field kitchen, a telegraph outfit, tank cars carrying gasoline and oil, two hospital cars, and a special unit with materials to repair bridges found too weak to support the heavy trucks. A pair of motorcycle riders scouted the road ahead and carried messages between vehicles.

The convoy had stopped for lunch in Wake Forest before covering the seventeen miles to Raleigh on a hard-surfaced road. Travel was relatively easy on this leg, and the vehicles made the expected average speed of nine miles per hour. From north of Wake Forest to the Virginia state line, the sand-clay roads slowed the advance to a crawl thanks to recent rains that had turned them to mud.

Governor Thomas Bickett, North Carolina's first governor to have an automobile at his disposal, welcomed the convoy with elaborate fanfare and praise. He did not mention that he had resisted efforts to launch a state-financed road-building effort during his three years in office. Bickett opposed building roads on credit, and he would leave that knotty issue to his successor, Cameron Morrison of Charlotte. As the convoy arrived, Morrison was waiting for the state Board of Elections to determine whether he or Lieutenant Governor O. Max Gardner had won the Democratic gubernatorial primary election held just the week before. The margin of difference had been less than a hundred votes. Morrison would win the nomination in the ensuing runoff election a few weeks later, and eventually the election.

The leaders of the convoy said the purpose of the Washington-to-Los Angeles expedition was to determine the viability of ground transport by truck. Along the way, army engineers and others were to test the durability and reliability of pneumatic tires for trucks with loads of up to ten tons. They were also to determine whether roads could withstand the strain of heavy transport. But the most important—and unstated—purpose of the convoy was to demonstrate America's desperate need for a dependable highway system. It did not require a four-month expedition to discover that most of America's roads were in sorry condition and direct routes from one place to another were limited.

North Carolina had a few hundred miles of solid, all-weather roads like the hard-surfaced route from Wake Forest to Raleigh. Concrete and asphalt roads were in use around Greensboro, Durham, Asheville, and Charlotte, where county commissioners had paid for construction. Travelers were on their own when they ventured much beyond city limits, however. The few roads worth the name in the rural areas were impassable in bad weather and rutted and dangerously narrow when dry. Travelers had difficulty even reaching adjoining counties. Some farm-to-market roads simply stopped at the county line, because local merchants refused to pave the way to neighboring counties for fear their customers would go there to shop.

North Carolinians had only lately become aroused about the pitiful condition of state roads. Some of the leading proponents of building a statewide system were looking to a special session of the General Assembly scheduled for the fall of 1920 to do something about it. One group favored a $50 million bond issue. Governor Bickett and legislators who disapproved of bonds believed that local governments and property owners along the roads ought to pay for them.

The day the convoy rolled into Raleigh, John Sprunt Hill was on a train returning home from Asheville, where he had been attending a three-day meeting of the North Carolina Good Roads Association, one of two such organizations in the state. The one Hill belonged to was the oldest and probably claimed the broadest support; in the last year, the association's membership had grown from several hundred to more than four thousand. A competing good roads organization had been put together more recently with the goal of building a hard-surfaced "military" highway linking Wilmington and Asheville on a route that passed through Charlotte. At the Asheville conference, the disagreement between those who wanted to concentrate the state's highway money into one cross-state artery and those who wanted to spend state and federal road money more broadly had produced a contentious meeting. Members quickly became divided over the election of a president for the association and finally elected a Wilmington man with a foot in both camps. At one point, Hill had been nominated, but he withdrew in the compromise that finally brought peace.

In advance of the Asheville meeting, Hill had worked on the speech he planned to deliver there. It would prove to be one of the most important of his life. During his first decade back in North Carolina, Hill had labored largely in local affairs in the shadow of his father-in-law, George Watts. While he had focused mainly on his business, he had also served two terms on the Durham City Council and helped rid Durham of saloons. Later, his efforts on behalf of the credit union movement and his membership on the University of North Carolina Board of Trustees had expanded his reputation beyond Durham, but the campaign for good roads and his appointment to Governor Morrison's highway commission would give him a statewide reputation. In the coming decade, he would emerge as Durham's best-known as well as its wealthiest and most influential public servant.

Hill enjoyed the public pulpit, and he was never at a loss for words. His speeches were often long, but they were seldom boring. He took a position and defended it with cold logic and hot rhetoric. His combination of combative language and colorful description usually aroused the interest of his audience. His fever was up on the issue of roads, and he threw himself into the Asheville speech. Hill believed the proposed bond issue was bad business, and he called it "a political and economic blunder." He declared that he also did not support the "pay-as-you-go philosophy" of the legislature, which he said was filled with "high priests of mud-turtle philosophy." Furthermore, he argued, the 1919 state road law was "mere makeshift," because it relied too much on the cooperation of individual counties and failed to create a true statewide highway system. As long as local officials picked the routes for thoroughfares, Hill maintained, drivers would have to settle for a disjoined patchwork shaped by local politics rather than good sense.

Hill proposed that the state create a strong state highway commission with the authority to choose routes and supervise construction after all interests had been aired in public hearings. Roadways should be widened to provide a "wearing surface" of at least eighteen feet, and rather than borrow money for roads, Hill proposed that the state pay for a proposed $200 million, 5,000-mile network with license fees and property taxes. Furthermore, he called on the association to prepare a plan for the 1921 General Assembly that would "lift the vision of . . . lawmakers away from county lines, penny-wise economy and mud-turtle philosophy." He declared: "Let us take time by the forelock and decide right here today to go forward with a clear-cut program that will appeal to the good horse sense of all the people of North Carolina."[1]

Hill had been a student of road engineering ever since he had laid out a network of streets and supervised their construction when he was in New York and managing the affairs of clients. During his two terms on the Durham City Council, he had served on the streets committee. Before the war, Bickett's predecessor, Governor Locke Craig, had appointed him to the North Carolina Geological and Economic Survey, which as early as 1916 had begun sponsoring seminars on road- and bridge-building techniques at the university in Chapel Hill.

The seminars were a modest effort to prepare the state for the growing demands of the automobile, which by the time of the Asheville meeting was reshaping life across the state. Yet solid action by state officials usually trailed the rhetoric. There were far more constituents in the country willing to let well enough alone than there were in the cities, where automobiles were more likely to be found. It had been seven years since the legislature had provided for a so-called Central Highway to be built from Morehead City to Asheville, and still there was no reliable all-weather highway across the state. In the meantime, there were more than one hundred forty thousand automobiles on the roads, compared to only sixteen thousand five years before.

❧❧❧

Hill's traveling companion on the train home to Durham was Harriet Morehead Berry, a woman of uncommon organizational skill and political savvy who was the paid secretary of the Good Roads Association and one of the state's leading good roads evangelists. After graduating in 1903 from the State Normal College in Greensboro (later the University of North Carolina at Greensboro), she went to work for the Geological and Economic Survey as a stenographer and statistician for State Geologist Joseph Hyde Pratt, an early believer in the necessity of creating a statewide road system. When Pratt left his state post to serve in the war, Berry carried on doing his work and ran the agency for nearly two years. She was responsible for the remarkable growth of the association's membership.

Hill had come to know Berry through his service with the survey, where it was Berry's job to cultivate powerful and influential people who favored good roads. With allies like Hill, she had become one of the most nimble political organizers in the state as well as a fearless competitor, a quality that Hill admired. When the crosscurrents of the recent fight within the association threatened Berry's job, Hill staunchly defended her in a manner just short of calling her opponents out.[2] He trusted her judgment. She was one of just a few people he had asked to review his Asheville speech.

Berry was not a one-issue woman. At the same time she was preaching on behalf of good roads, she was also working as a leader in the women's suffrage movement and lobbying politicians to vote for a pending constitutional amendment that would give women the vote. The question was due to be considered at the 1920 special session, and Berry hoped to see North Carolina become the thirty-seventh ratifying state, the threshold for adoption. That honor would go to Tennessee, however, which approved the resolution two days before North Carolina legislators finally brought the matter to the floor, where it was defeated.

For all her other interests, Berry's passion was good roads. She had written the draft of the bill that the 1919 General Assembly had used to reorganize the State Highway Commission. She was determined to see a better law come out of the 1921 session that would create a bona fide statewide highway system. By the late fall of 1920, the plan Hill proposed in Asheville was being widely circulated. Before the legislature convened in January, Hill, Berry, Heriot Clarkson of Charlotte (Cameron Morrison's campaign manager), and two others had completed a final draft of the speech that was printed and circulated to legislators and others around the state. Hill had modified his position. He now supported a small bond issue, with additional money to come from auto license fees and a modest property tax. He remained skeptical that New York bankers would buy the state's bonds unless they were backed by property taxes, since the state had only recently recovered from an embarrassing lawsuit rising out of its refusal to honor worthless bonds sold during Reconstruction. In his inaugural address in January 1921, however, Governor Morrison heartily endorsed the road program and called for a $75 million road bond issue.

Berry became an important contact in Raleigh for Hill in the early months of 1921 as the legislators chewed on the roads bill. In addition to the roads bill, Hill was interested in legislation put forward by the North Carolina Forestry Association, of which he was president. The forestry bill would allow county officials to work with the state Geological Board (which oversaw the survey) to protect forestland within county boundaries.

The state's future road-building program was being determined in the state House just as Hill's attention was diverted by family matters and the failing health of his father-in-law. Hill did leave Durham for Raleigh long enough to make an appearance at a public hearing at which he endorsed the bill and Morrison's bond issue, which the governor had said would be repaid with revenue from a new gasoline tax.

The passage of the bill was not assured, however, until its backers promised to pave the main thoroughfares of more than four hundred towns in the state that had populations of less than three thousand and to link every county seat to its neighbor. Such a promise left opponents of the bill defenseless. If they voted against it, their constituents would ask why they had opposed paving Main Street. The bill sailed through the legislature, and in the week of George Watts's death, Governor Morrison asked Hill to become a member of the new commission.

⤿⤿⤿

Hill joined eight others on a commission led by Frank A. Page of Aberdeen, the highway chairman whom Bickett had appointed under the 1919 law. Page was a member of a prominent Sandhills family. His brother, Walter Hines Page, had been a New York newspaper editor and President Woodrow Wilson's ambassador to Great Britain. Another brother, Robert Page, was a prominent banker. Frank was an experienced businessman who had learned about road building at home and in France during the war. He was well respected in state circles and had demonstrated his administrative ability during his time on the commission.

Membership on the commission was balanced both politically and geographically, with each member assigned to a specific district. More important, Morrison chose members who had either considerable wealth or political influence. With Hill, he got both. The group included businessmen like Word Wood, a Charlotte banker, and W. A. Hart of Tarboro, a textile executive. Three of the nine were Republicans, including J. Elwood Cox of High Point, a banker who would later become a trustee of the Duke Endowment. Rufus A. Doughton of rural Alleghany County, a former Speaker of the House and lieutenant governor, brought more than thirty years of political experience to the job. J. G. Stikeleather, an Asheville real estate developer, was, like Page, a carryover from the previous commission. Hill was the nominal representative of the Good Roads Association, while W. A. McGirt of Wilmington could speak for the Wilmington-to-Asheville road crowd. The quality of Morrison's choices was confirmed over and over again during the next ten years. Through the tenures of three governors, only fourteen men filled the nine slots, and two of them were appointed to fill vacancies caused by death.

Hill's Fourth District reached from the Virginia line across the center of the state to just north of Fort Bragg in the Sandhills. It included one of the major highway entries into the state at Clarksville, Virginia, as well as the cities of Raleigh and Durham and the large farming area to the south. All across the state, small towns and rural counties competed with the road-building demands of growing cities, where automobile traffic was increasing daily. Hill would balance it well, but the job he and the others accepted required considerable time, attention to detail, a thick hide, and integrity. Under the decentralized arrangement, a commissioner's word was virtually law within his district.

The job paid no salary, but Hill threw himself into it as he did every endeavor. He arranged for the district engineer's office to take space in his bank building in downtown Durham, which put the engineering staff at his fingertips and provided some rental income for his real estate division as well. He became active in national good roads organizations including the Bankhead National Highway Association, of which he was vice president, and the U.S. Good Roads Association, which held its sixth annual meeting in Greensboro in the spring of 1921.

Hill was particularly suited for the daunting task of absorbing the pressure that could be brought to bear from the interests of competing communities. A generation earlier, the location of railroads had demonstrated how access to transportation could reward one town while causing another to wither and die. As a man too rich to be bribed and too well founded in the basics of road building to be fooled, Hill weathered the inevitable charges of favoritism to Durham (which were not altogether unfounded) and the brickbats of local politicians. Early on, he was hit by a storm of protest from Wake County after he approved a road (later North Carolina 98) connecting Wake Forest in northern Wake County to Durham. Raleigh people objected, but Hill argued that the colleges and universities of Wake and Durham counties should have easier access to one another, and the road brought Wake Forest College into the loop. Much of the criticism died away when a new road (North Carolina 54) was later built west from Raleigh to Chapel Hill without passing through Durham.

When Hill was challenged on his decisions, he usually responded with a mountain of statistics and a detailed accounting of how each county had fared in the distribution of roads built and dollars spent. He also made it hard to argue against a system that incorporated countless public hearings and public posting of proposed routes, something he took pride in encouraging as the process moved along. By the end of his terms on the commission, he had conducted more than six hundred public hearings around the district. Nevertheless, angry landowners often slowed progress. In 1924, Hill paid the lawyer's bill for a highway department employee who was arrested and thrown in jail by the Franklin County sheriff after a landowner complained.

Hill could be equally persuasive in competing with other districts for cash. He compared the number of automobiles in the remote First District in the northeastern corner of the state against the number of automobiles in his own and discovered that his district was being seriously shortchanged. The tipping point for paving a highway was a daily count of 400 cars. By 1925, there was that much traffic on half of the roads in his district, and he asked for an adjustment to make up the difference. More money soon flowed into the Fourth District.

The engineers were not always right, he found. When the people of Pittsboro objected to the way intersecting roads were routed away from the Chatham County Courthouse, Hill overruled the professionals and told them to respect the local wishes. "Our elders didn't know anything about automobiles and trunk lines," he explained, when they located the courthouse in the middle of what had become a major intersection.[3] The traffic circle around the courthouse would remain into the next century.

The job gave Hill a powerful seat from which to wage an ongoing fight with the railroads over grade crossings, particularly where the tracks intersected with the so-called intrastate trunk routes. "So far as I know I am one of the largest holders of railroad stock in North Carolina," Hill told O. B. Hester, the state's chief locating engineer, "and I have no prejudices against railroads, but I do think that the long suffering public has stood punishment from railroad crossings on trunk lines of state highways long enough."

It just did not make sense to Hill that the rail companies objected to paying the costs of building bridges and underpasses when their legal costs from court claims won by motorists who collided with passing trains were mounting daily. "Some of our railroads insist upon having little narrow-gauge folks represent them about these matters, who are unable to take the larger view and spend $1.00 and save $3.00," he told Hester. Hill threatened to take the matter to the railroad company directors, if necessary.[4]

Hill knew his district, and he was on the road constantly, usually with a highway engineer in tow and always with a driver. He had been one of Durham's first automobile owners, but neither he nor his wife learned to drive. His son Watts said years later that his father had forsaken driving after he ran the car into a tree during one of his first efforts behind the wheel. Meanwhile, Watts was only fourteen when he first drove the family's Buick to the railroad station to pick up his father when he returned from a trip out of town. By 1922, John Sprunt Hill owned a Buick as well as a Pierce Arrow, a seven-passenger 1917 Hudson limousine, and a Studebaker. Watts drove a Marmon during his years at Chapel Hill, and his sister Frances started driving a red Jackson when she was just a teenager.[5] Hill felt that it was important that a man of his generation and position have a chauffeur. It was the logical move for someone who had arrived in Durham with a distinctive New York carriage that always had someone else at the reins.

Hill's position afforded him the personal freedom to explore construction sites as he investigated complaints and reviewed construction progress. On occasion, he got closer than he should have. One morning, while walking out the route of a proposed extension of Cameron Avenue in Chapel Hill, he was shaken by a dynamite blast that sent an eruption of tree roots, dirt, and rock into the air. One large stone penetrated the roof of a nearby house. Hill and members of the building committee from the university ran for cover into a nearby barn to escape the falling debris.[6]

True to Hill's prediction, the New York bankers were tentative about buying the first issue of North Carolina's road bonds. As work progressed, however, another bond sale was authorized, and this time Hill and the bankers had changed their minds. It sold within the limits of the interest requirements set by the legislature. Hill purchased a sizeable share for himself and became an outspoken advocate of the state's ambitious program. He wrote a friend in England who had a road-building firm in Canada and encouraged him to send his machinery to North Carolina, Tennessee, or Virginia, where there was work aplenty.

⚬⚬⚬

By the mid-1920s, North Carolina had become a stopover for a growing stream of travelers, many of whom were on their way to and from Florida, which was enjoying a boom in resort home sales. Hard-surface roads were still the exception rather than the rule, and traveling long distances by car was not easy. Just keeping track of the route numbers required close attention. Hill calculated that a motorist on his way across the center of the state had to recognize seven changes in route numbering between the South Carolina and Virginia state lines. Early on, Hill joined the campaign for a transcontinental highway that would carry the same route number from Canada to Florida. He focused his attention on the federal government's Route 15 (later U.S. 15), which would enter the state from South Carolina near Laurinburg, connect Sanford and Pittsboro, and then pass through Durham before reaching Virginia at Clarksville and continuing north to Niagara Falls, New York.

Community boosters all along the eastern seaboard hoped to cash in on the growing interest in interstate route designations, and all wanted their share of the money that could be made off the motoring public. The take was considerable. In North Carolina, the state's Motor Club estimated that in 1925 893,000 cars carrying an average of three passengers each passed through the state and left behind about $37 million in payment for meals, hotel rooms, and purchases.[7] Hill prodded the manager of the city's new Washington Duke Hotel to see that the hotel was mentioned on the new road maps and travel booklets circulated by auto clubs and gasoline companies. He told the hotel's manager, "Some time ago a gentleman that I happened to meet in New York remarked to me that it was worth at least $25,000 to his hotel to be located on a great trunk line highway."[8]

Hill lobbied highway associations and highway commissioners in the adjoining states. Just as he did for other causes in which he became interested, he reached into his pocket to expand his efforts by hiring additional help. During the campaign to win the U.S. 15 designation, Hill paid the expenses and salary of a Washington, D.C., law student to set up shop as the Atlantic Transcontinental Highway Association in Pennsylvania, where he was to drum up interest for a "local" effort to connect with the roadway in that state. "The quickest and safest way to get the road clear through to Niagara Falls and Rochester is to form a Route 15 association somewhere in Pennsylvania," he wrote.[9]

He even encouraged the involvement of local schoolteachers. Hill told fellow commissioner Charles P. Upham that when he was a boy students were required to draw, from memory, a map of the United States. "I think now it would do a great deal of good to require each high school pupil to prepare a road map of North Carolina showing the main routes on the map," Hill argued.[10]

∞ ∞ ∞

Just as the governor's highway program moved into full swing, Hill assumed another demanding job at the request of the university trustees who named the building committee. In January 1923, he became chairman of the committee after the death of Secretary of State J. Bryan Grimes. Hill took over just as the university was about to receive a second infusion of state funds to continue the expansion of the campus south of Cameron Avenue in the grove below South Building. Among the construction projects approved by the legislature that year were a men's dormitory, the first women's dormitory, a new chemistry building, additions to the library, completion of the new law school building, and the remodeling of older structures.

The building program became President Harry Woodburn Chase's top priority after he succeeded Edward Kidder Graham in April 1919. That fall, more than fourteen hundred students competed for lodging and classroom space designed for half that number. A year later, Chase reported that Gerrard Hall could not seat every student at chapel and Swain Hall, the main dining hall, was feeding two hundred more than capacity. Memorial Hall, which was built before the days of electricity and central heating, was usable only for daylight events in good weather, and the acoustics were bad. Classrooms had become so overcrowded that the geology department had limited registrations. Space for the law school, then meeting in ivy-covered Smith Hall, was inadequate, and the new School of Commerce did not have enough classrooms. Moreover, Chase told the trustees, "There is not in the town today so much as a comfortable room—to say nothing of a house—in which any new member of the faculty could be installed."[11] To illustrate the state's neglect of the university, Chase reported that since 1917, when the state appropriated $500,000 for a power plant and two dormitories, the Baptists had raised more than $6 million for their institutions and the Presbyterians had raised $1 million for theirs.[12]

The campus also lacked a coherent style or design. The buildings were a hodgepodge, from the gothic Memorial Hall to the medieval-flavored Carr dormitory and the YMCA. The Alumni Building was modeled after the Boston Public Library, while the Battle, Vance, and Pettigrew buildings had the flavor of old English colleges. The original campus buildings were ivy-covered classics and indeed picturesque, but they now showed signs of serious neglect.

In the fall of 1920, more than forty alumni had responded to Chase's call for help and gathered at a boardinghouse known as the "Coop" to organize a public campaign to raise the money necessary for delayed and unfunded construction projects. The prospect of raising the $20 million Chase said was needed was formidable—some said impossible—in the face of the economic hard times that had settled over the South. Once again, cotton prices had fallen, and so had the rest of the region's economy.

The Coop meeting was followed by a larger meeting two weeks later in Greensboro, where a public campaign was launched to enlist supporters of public and private higher education who favored meeting the university's immediate needs. John Sprunt Hill attended the Greensboro meeting and with eight others put up $500 to underwrite the new Citizens' Committee for the Promotion of Education. The campaign culminated in February, when Greensboro real estate developer A. M. Scales led a delegation of 500 people to the legislature to demand action. Speakers from across the state "called for an end to the faintness of heart and expediency when the education of youth, the one bright hope of North Carolina's future, was at stake."[13] With the endorsement of Governor Morrison, the legislature approved an appropriation of $1.5 million in new building funds for the coming two years along with a regular appropriation and a promise of $6.7 million more for the university from a proposed bond referendum.

When Hill succeeded Grimes as the chair of the building committee, it included other strong figures in state affairs, including George Stephens, a Charlotte banker and real estate developer; Asheville lawyer Haywood Parker; James A. Gray, a top executive of the R.J. Reynolds Tobacco Company in Winston-Salem; President Chase; and university business manager C. T. Woolen. Hill knew them all well and had done business with Stephens. George Watts, along with the Dukes, had invested in Stephens's company, which was developing Charlotte's new suburbs. Hill's proximity to the campus, his standing among this committee, and his irrepressible urge to build would give him extraordinary influence within the university community during a period of construction that literally reshaped the Chapel Hill campus by expanding it into a virgin grove south of South Building. Landscape designer John Nolen, who had worked with the Tuftses at Pinehurst, said the new buildings should be built in the grove.[14]

∾∾∾

By the time Hill assumed the chairmanship, he had already completed several major building projects. One was the rebuilding of fraternity houses that had been destroyed by fire. Hill had arranged for an exchange of property owned by the fraternities on the east side of Columbia Street for a tract of similar size on the west side. Construction began in March 1920 on new houses for Hill's own Sigma Alpha Epsilon chapter along with new quarters for the local chapters of Sigma Nu and Pi Kappa Phi. A Durham contractor, I. G. Lawrence, won the construction bid.[15]

Hill had also done the early work to expedite the delivery of construction materials and workers to the campus for the early stages of the building program. In the summer of 1920, Hill and two other trustees, John L. Patterson and George M. Rose, had opened discussions with the Southern Railway Company about extending the Carrboro tracks east to the campus. A route roughly parallel to Cameron Avenue was chosen, and by the time the legislature approved the first appropriation of building funds for the university in the spring of 1921, the Southern had agreed to build the track. The trustees approved $50,000 for construction of the rail extension after Hill said that that much money would be saved in delivery costs alone. Hill personally negotiated the purchase of land for the track and on at least one occasion browbeat Chapel Hill property owners into giving up the right-of-way. He reminded one reluctant landowner that "the old folks, a hundred forty years ago, gladly gave their lands, which they purchased with their blood, for the university," and he argued that present-day citizens could certainly part with a bit of their gardens on behalf of the future of the school. By summertime, construction of the railroad line and a camp to house fifty convict laborers was under way. Hill was also helpful from his seat on the State Highway Commission in providing for the construction of a new twelve-mile stretch of concrete highway between Durham and Chapel Hill. It opened in late November 1921.

◌〜◌〜◌〜

President Chase energized the campus with more than new buildings. He helped launch the University of North Carolina Press, upgraded the law school, established a School of Journalism, and endorsed E. C. Branson's proposal for a School of Public Welfare.

Branson had first talked to John Sprunt Hill about the new school before the war. The two men shared a common interest in using the university to develop the rural areas of the state as well as provide a foundation for the training of local officials. Branson was particularly taken with what he called Hill's philosophy of "cooperative Democracy," and at one point he asked Hill to lecture on the subject at the university.[16] While planning a study trip to Europe at the end of 1918, Branson had told Hill, "I want to see how co-operative enterprise is developing in Ireland and also to talk out with them your great idea of 'cooperative democracy, the opposite and antidote of socialism.'"[17]

Hill enthusiastically endorsed Branson's plan for what he first called a school of social science, where Branson hoped to train judges for the state's new juvenile court system, county welfare workers, and probation and truant officers. Branson flattered Hill by suggesting it be named the John Sprunt Hill School of Social Science, although both men were becoming concerned about the common misunderstanding of the terms "social," "sociology," and "social science." They were "fatally linked in the North Carolina mind with 'socialism,'" Branson told Hill.[18] Branson and Hill settled on calling the new venture the School of Public Welfare, and Hill offered to put up $500 of the $2,000 needed to get it started. He told his fellow trustees that he would do more if necessary.

The school was established in 1921 under Howard W. Odum, who came to Chapel Hill from Emory University to fill the new chair of sociology. Odum was not Hill's first choice. He had told Branson that the university should recruit former governor Bickett or some other high-profile public figure such as historian R. D. W. Connor. Most certainly the dean should be a native son, Hill said, and not someone "infused with socialistic ideas."[19] Odum would prove to be an important choice and a leading figure in the university for the next thirty years.

∾∾∾

Construction on the new campus buildings was getting under way when a medical school proposal, dormant for two years, was revived. In the summer of 1922, the Board of Trustees adopted a recommendation supporting a four-year medical program at the university and declared that the school should have a teaching hospital. A week later, the trustees voted to ask the legislature for money to build a hospital in memory of the state's Civil War dead. Six months later, in December, President Chase and this group were preparing a report for the 1923 session of the legislature when Trinity College president William P. Few asked to meet with the committee at the Executive Mansion in Raleigh.

George Watts's death had only delayed Few's timetable for a medical school on his campus. Once interest had been revived, Few was ready to push forward. At the meeting at the Executive Mansion, Few outlined a plan only slightly different from what he had discussed with Watts. He proposed an $8 million medical school independent of both Trinity College and the University of North Carolina that would be built with a combination of state and private money. Control would be vested in a joint board. The first two years of study would be based in Chapel Hill on the university campus, while the final two would be in Durham. Nothing was said about the site of a teaching hospital, but Few had always planned for Watts Hospital to serve that function. Few left the meeting with the endorsement of the governor and a few key members of the Board of Trustees. Others remained cautious.

News of the proposed school reached the newspapers just prior to the Christmas holiday. Chase's committee's report argued against such joint ventures based on what the members had found elsewhere in the country, but the downfall of Few's plan was religion. The joint venture began to lose favor after the *Charlotte Observer* and Raleigh's *News and Observer* questioned the use of state funds for a church-supported institution. There were other problems, including municipal jealousy. Boosters in cities larger than Durham believed they had the makings for a medical school campus, too.

Chase stayed out of the public debate. "It is in all the line of education endeavor unique," he told the *Durham Herald*.[20] Privately, he had serious misgivings about a joint venture. One of the troubling issues, Chase confided in a letter, was that the Rockefeller Foundation originated the plan, and undoubtedly the foundation would want some say in how the school would develop and be run. "I think frankly that the situation as offered is in a way dangerous in that it puts the General Education Board, because of its authority and financial resources, in the position of dictating about medical education in North Carolina."[21] In another letter, he called the Few plan a "slippery proposition." He outlined his objections in a letter to the governor and began looking for a way to postpone a decision. Chase was also anxious about the timing of the medical school request. Legislators were already gathering in Raleigh for the 1923 session, and the university was looking to secure the money to continue the building program begun two years before, not to expand into something new and controversial.

When the university trustees met in the governor's office late in January, the study committee had filed its report. Few's joint venture was not part of it, although in some respects the committee's recommendations were similar to Few's. The majority favored the creation of a four-year school for the university. Students would spend the first two years studying at Chapel Hill and the last two in Durham, where Watts Hospital was available for use. The committee said that Chapel Hill was simply too small and remote to supply adequate patients for a hospital or a teaching faculty. Chase almost had the matter postponed for two years when a delegation from Charlotte was ushered into the executive offices to offer their city's Presbyterian Hospital as the teaching hospital. Morrison, whose political base was Charlotte, backpedaled and asked for the postponement of a final vote for ten days to allow any interested city time to prepare a bid.

Delegations from Raleigh, Greensboro, Durham, and Charlotte arrived in Raleigh on February 9, 1923. Greensboro offered a hundred acres of land and $3 million from the estate of Moses H. Cone. Raleigh tendered the site of the former state Institute for the Blind and offered the inmates at the state mental institution and Central Prison as "clinical material." Charlotte supporters promised a $1 million endowment and $500,000 in property.

John Sprunt Hill organized the Durham plan, whose centerpiece was Watts Hospital. While the hospital only had about hundred beds, Hill said there was $200,000 immediately available from George Watts's estate to build an additional wing. Another $100,000 had been promised by the chamber of commerce. He lauded Durham's central location in the state and its ready access by rail. If the city's proposal were to be accepted, he said that his wife would donate the twenty-eight acres adjacent to the hospital to the university. She said it was land her father had purchased with the hope that a medical college would be located there.

After hearing all the proposals, the trustees endorsed a legislative request for start-up money for a four-year school but did not pick a site. A few weeks later, however, the state budget office vetoed the request. The proposal never reached the legislators, and it would be nearly thirty years before a four-year medical school opened in Chapel Hill.

∾∾∾

John Sprunt Hill did not wait for his son Watts to graduate before turning to him for help with his many projects, particularly the construction work in Chapel Hill. Watts had shown an early talent for architecture, and his father appreciated his son's keen sense of design. Ever since he took drawing classes in high school, Watts had often turned his father's rough sketches into finished presentations. Watts later recalled, "[My father] couldn't draw a straight line so asking me to do the scaled drafts was a perfectly normal and natural thing for him to do."[22] By the time Watts was a rising senior in the business school, his father asked him to help supervise the construction of the Sigma Alpha Epsilon fraternity house going up on Columbia Street.

John Sprunt Hill was so confident of his son's ability that as the university's architects finished the plans for the new campus dormitories he gave the drawings to Watts and asked his opinion. Watts studied them and returned with suggestions, including the observation that the closets were too small. Before the final drawings were completed, the closet space was enlarged. Watts later claimed that his suggestions helped cut the construction cost of the dormitories.[23] Not long afterward, father and son began work on the Carolina Inn, which would become a Chapel Hill landmark.

John Sprunt Hill, who never missed the opportunity to tell a good story, said that plans for the hotel began to take shape one hot night when he was awakened in a room in the old University Inn by the noise of rats racing across the floor. He arose, dressed, headed out for a walk in the night air, and ended up sitting on a rock in front of the Graves boardinghouse at the corner of Columbia Street and Cameron Avenue.[24] It was time, he decided, for Chapel Hill to have something like Princeton's Nassau Inn, which offered comfortable accommodations and served as a familiar reunion spot for alumni and friends of the university.

In May 1920, Hill had proposed a joint venture to classmate W. S. Roberson and John W. Umstead Jr., both of Chapel Hill, and to Clem G. Wright. Together, they applied for a charter and made plans to erect a hotel. The site most often talked about was on Franklin Street at the corner of Henderson Street near the location of the old University Inn, which had burned in 1919. Hill's attention later shifted to the corner of Columbia and Cameron, his resting spot on that hot summer evening. That location fit well with Hill's vision for the new south campus. A hotel just outside the west entrance would be more centrally located than one on Franklin Street.[25]

In September 1920, Hill purchased the Graves property for $20,000. The property extended 200 feet along Cameron Avenue to the west of the campus entrance and was 520 feet deep south along Columbia. Even with the rush of events in Raleigh and George Watts's death, Hill had plans drawn for a hotel with fifty rooms. He referred to it as the College Inn in correspondence with his friends. He told his old friend Joseph Hyde Pratt, "We are hoping to have a resting place for overworked friends of the University where they can forget all about the cares of business and politics and enjoy the fresh cool air of Chapel Hill and its delicious intellectual atmosphere and democratic surroundings."[26] He also told Pratt he was willing to donate the property along with $10,000 in cash if the university would take on the project and the building of the hotel, which he estimated would cost $100,000.

In the meantime, Hill began developing plans to build brick cottages on the southern portion of the property, which he planned to rent to students. He signed a contract for the construction of two cottages and had plans for ten more. With eight students in each, he planned to house about a hundred students a year.

More than a year passed with no progress on the hotel until finally, in the fall of 1921, a Greensboro newspaper urged that the project move ahead. In December, Louis Round Wilson, the university librarian and editor of the *Alumni Review*, wrote a lead editorial entitled "Let's Build One" in an effort to revive interest. A month later, Hill offered the university the property at Columbia and Cameron, which had cost him $30,000, as well as $10,000 to build the hotel.[27]

No one leaped at Hill's offer. Instead, a committee was organized to study the proposal. A year later, Hill reported to the trustees' executive committee that a committee of alumni proposed to organize a company to build the hotel, which would be home to the Alumni Association. Hill's offer of land and money was conditional upon the contribution from 500 alumni of $200 each. For their money, the contributors would become charter members of the alumni club that Hill proposed for the hotel.

Hill's vision for the building was clear. He favored a traditional Southern Colonial style, and he asked Arthur Nash, the Durham architect who was already at work on other campus buildings, to come up with a design. Nash was Harvard-trained and a graduate of the école des Beaux-Arts in Paris. He practiced in New York until 1922, when he became a partner in the Durham firm of Atwood and Weeks.[28] While the plan for the new south campus bore the stamp of the well-known New York firm of McKim, Mead, and White, it was Nash who translated the ideas of W. M. Kendall of the McKim firm into the actual designs.

The north side of Nash's new inn was reminiscent of George Washington's Mount Vernon, with a long pillared veranda facing Cameron Avenue. There was a smaller veranda on the south side. Guests could enter through French doors on the front that opened into the broad comfortable lobby or, if they were arriving by automobile, on the east side off Columbia Street by way of a porte cochere. The three-story building included fifty-two guestrooms, all with private baths, and a ballroom, a dining room, and parlors on the main floor. Nash's original design called for an exterior of brick painted white with white wood trim. Hill liked everything except the painted brick.[29] The final plans left them in their natural red. The building, with its gabled roof and dormers, would make an impressive anchor to the west side of the campus.

Plans also called for the old Graves home, which was in the way of the new building, to be moved back from the front of the lot to the rear, where it would be remodeled into a cafeteria. (It would be the first of three to operate in the inn in the next seventy years.) The upper floors of the old house were to be remodeled to provide rooms for student employees of the inn. A nine-car garage was added on the far south side, just beyond the temporary railroad line used to deliver construction materials to the campus.

Watts Hill was in his first year of law school and living with three friends in one of the cottages that his father had built on the south side of the property when work began on the Carolina Inn on March 24, 1923. While taking a full load of classes, Watts also assumed the role of on-site manager for his father. John Sprunt Hill, who had been impatient with the project all along, soon wearied of the lagging support of other alumni and assumed complete control of the project along with all the expenses.[30] The Carolina Inn became a Hill project from top to bottom.

Construction moved slowly, and completion of the building was several months behind schedule by the end of 1923. John Sprunt Hill held out some hope that the building would be adopted by alumni and managed for the benefit of the university by something he called "the Carolina Club." A year before the inn opened, Hill told one supplier that he did not see it operating as a "regular hotel."[31]

Rainy weather and disagreements among the contractors made an opening by the summer of 1924 impossible. To be fair, some of the delay was due to John Sprunt Hill himself, who fussed over every detail. He picked H. B. Emery, the interior designer for Tufts's Pinehurst properties, to design the inn's interior, and he told Emery to seek out reproductions suitable for the "colonial revival mode" from specific local furniture makers in the state. "It is my purpose to make [the inn] as nearly a North Carolina product as possible," he told a friend.[32] In the summer of 1924, Emery waited while John Sprunt and Annie Watts Hill picked a pattern for the inn's dining room china.

John Sprunt Hill insisted that the inn, like all his buildings, be as fireproof as possible, a fact promoted widely to assure any who were anxious that the new hotel would be reduced to ashes like the old University Inn. And he bought the best equipment available. The kitchen was equipped with an icemaker that could produce 1,600 pounds of ice in ten hours, a mechanical potato peeler, and huge mixers and ranges.[33] He also changed Nash's plans and had telephones installed in every room. "Our friends occupying rooms will be seriously inconvenienced by having to come down to the first floor to call up their friends in various parts of the state over a pay station telephone 'quarter-in-the-slot' plan," he explained. "A great many small hotels are run on this plan and they find it very satisfactory."[34]

With a summer opening out of the question, Hill had hoped to have the inn ready by October, perhaps in time for University Day, when Chase had asked him to present an address. Hill declined the invitation, saying, "I am so embarrassed and chagrined at the delay in the opening of the Carolina Inn that in all probability the least said about the Inn on this occasion will be the best." He advised the president's wife Lucetta that she had better find another location for a reception that she had planned.[35]

Despite his early hopes of uniting the inn and the Alumni Association, Hill finally resigned himself to the fact that he was in the hotel business and set about to find a manager. He settled on I. M. Gattman, whom he had come to know from his visits to the Mid-Pines Country Club in Pinehurst and to Poland Springs.

The inn's first guests arrived in late November. Workers were still applying finishing touches and the dining room was not ready, but Gattman agreed to accept reservations from guests who knew of the inn's limitations. With the doors of the inn finally open, the *Chapel Hill Weekly* devoted an entire section to the new hotel and mailed copies of the special edition to 6,000 alumni. The final cost of the building's construction was reputed to be $200,000, but the figure was probably higher.[36]

The first formal event at the Carolina Inn took place on the evening of Tuesday, December 30, 1924, when the Hills gave a dance in honor of their daughters, Frances and Valinda. An orchestra played from the raised platform in the ballroom for more than a hundred guests, who shortly after midnight were entertained with dinner "served with all the precision and finish to be found in one of the famous hotels of New York or Washington or Pinehurst." Among the group were older guests, many of them Carolina alums, who were dazzled by their old college town's newest accommodations.[37]

A month later, John Sprunt Hill hosted a luncheon for alumni, legislators, and members of the state supreme court who were on campus for the dedication of the Manning Law Building, one of three new buildings on the campus's south lawn. After the crowd of 200 guests found their places for the meal, Jonathan Daniels noticed that the one person left standing was Hill, who "was so busy seeing that everyone else had everything they could possibly want that he took no time for eating himself."[38]

Hill fairly gushed over the place. He personally supervised the waiters and told one guest after the other about the inn's furnishings and architecture, which Daniels said fit well with the "spirit of Chapel Hill." Daniels wrote, "The Inn is new but already it is a place of personality."[39] He said Hill hoped to be able to recover his investment in two to three years. That would prove to be wishful thinking.

∾∾∾

Watts Hill missed all the celebrations. He had finished law school in June, and after a vacation break in Asheville, where the Hills had begun to spend their summers, he returned to Chapel Hill to prepare for the bar examination in mid-August. His father wanted him to continue his legal education at Columbia University in New York, but Watts made plans to be married in September.

His bride was Ann Austin McCulloch, the daughter of the Reverend and Mrs. Duncan McCulloch of Afton Waters, Glencoe, Maryland, where her father was headmaster of Oldfields School, a girl's college preparatory boarding school. The family was modestly situated, but with a distinguished lineage. On her mother's side, forebears included Charles Carroll, a signer of the Declaration of Independence. Watts had met Ann in the spring of 1922 when his sister Valinda invited him to a spring dance at Shipley School in Bryn Mawr, Pennsylvania, where Valinda and Ann were classmates. Watts had two dances with Ann and was quite taken with her. He saw her the following summer in Europe, where she was studying art in Grenoble and he was traveling with a college friend. After returning to the states, Ann was attending the School of Applied Design in New York when Watts invited her to Durham for the Christmas holidays.

The holidays provided the occasion for a "bal masque," as the *Durham Herald* called it, in honor of Ann and another friend from Shipley, Marcia LeMoyne, who was from Pittsburgh. Everyone dressed in costume including John Sprunt Hill, who appeared as "the Rajah." Annie Watts Hill came as Anne of Austria. Watts Hill wore an Oberammergau costume, and Ann McCulloch masqueraded as a "Chinese lady." Guests danced to an eight-piece orchestra that played until two in the morning. A buffet supper was served at 11:30 P.M.[40] Before Ann headed back to Baltimore, Watts proposed marriage.

"I remember vividly what I said," he recalled. "I asked her to marry me and she was 'so and so' and I said, 'I'll give you 'til tomorrow. I'm going to put you on a train tomorrow night for Baltimore and I want to know by tomorrow. Period.' So I found out later that she sat up all that night and talked with my sisters' governess and told me the next morning that she would marry me."[41]

For her part, Ann was swept away by Watts, whom she later said was the handsomest man she had ever met. She was nineteen, nearly three years younger than Watts, and the product of a world quite different from her fiancée's. Her family had founded Oldfields and made a life educating the children of privilege, but they were far from wealthy. There were further contrasts. Ann thrived on intellectual challenge and the excitement of the offbeat artists' world of New York City, where her prospective sisters-in-law would never be found. Marriage to Watts Hill, she later confided to a friend, offered permanence and the promise of his absolute devotion.

The engagement lasted more than eighteen months while Watts finished his second year of law school. Ann continued her studies at art school and for a time worked as a designer and newspaper illustrator. In the summer of 1924, she joined the family for a time in Asheville, but everything was on hold until Watts learned if he had been admitted to the North Carolina bar.

He stood his examination before a panel of North Carolina Supreme Court justices in Raleigh in mid-August—it was the last year that candidates for the bar were personally examined by the justices—and hopped on an overnight train for Asheville, where Ann was vacationing with his family at the Grove Park Inn. When Watts arrived, he telephoned his classmate Jonathan Daniels, who checked the late edition of the *News and Observer* and told him he had passed. Watts and Ann were married September 30, 1924, in Baltimore.

❦ ❦ ❦

By the time the Carolina Inn opened in December, the two were halfway around the world. Their ten-month honeymoon carried them first to New York, where they boarded a ship to Cuba, and then on through the Panama Canal to the west coast of the United States. They stayed two weeks in Los Angeles while Watts recovered from the flu before continuing on to Hawaii, where Watts tried his hand at surfing on the heavy, long boards of the islanders. A primary destination was Japan, and from there Korea. John Sprunt Hill had agreed to underwrite a portion of the trip if Watts would make an inspection tour of the Presbyterian mission in Soon Chun, which continued to receive thousands of dollars in annual support from Annie Watts Hill.

When the young couple arrived in Japan, the nation had not fully re-covered from a devastating earthquake and tidal wave that had killed more than 125,000 people the year before. One of the few Tokyo hotels to with-stand the quake was the Imperial, which had been designed by Frank Lloyd Wright to survive a trembling earth. A well-connected friend loaned the couple a car and driver, and they toured Japan before they boarded a ferry for Korea. There they were met by a missionary and his wife, who took them on a harrowing drive over the mountains to the mission hospital and school built with George Watts's money.

The excursion to Korea took them into rugged countryside and rudi-mentary lodgings. On their first morning at the mission, a maid awakened them early so they could visit the four-seat outdoor privy ahead of the schoolchildren who were soon forming lines to wait their turn. Such priva-tions were rare during the rest of their honeymoon. Most often, the couple enjoyed the pampering of accommodations in the finest hotels, where porters handled their twenty-eight pieces of luggage, including two golf bags that proved to be all but useless weight. Both were accomplished golfers and enjoyed the game, but in their ten months away from home they played only once at a British rest camp in Colombo.[42]

Leaving Japan, they traveled on to Shanghai, Hong Kong, French In-dochina (Vietnam), Bangkok, and the ancient temples at Ankor Wat in Cambodia. The trip was not without adventure. The scenes of destruction in Japan were followed a few months later by the frightening uncertainty of an attempted mutiny. On their way to Suez aboard a freighter with about two dozen other passengers, Watts remained locked in a cabin with an American officer, both of them armed and waiting for the turmoil to subside on deck. When they arrived in Rome, Mussolini's Fascist govern-ment had just consolidated its power.

Along the way, the couple picked up souvenirs, some of which they had shipped back to the United States. One trinket, a Chinese headdress they found in Hong Kong, prompted a letter to John Sprunt Hill from the cus-toms office in Savannah, where customs inspectors had delayed shipment because the headdress included feathers from a kingfisher, a protected bird. The elder Hill tried to explain his son's mistake, saying, "[Watts] is a young fellow just out of College, who probably never heard of a Kingfisher or ever saw one in his life, and would not know Kingfisher feathers from rooster feathers."[43]

The young couple's funds were running low in Rome. Watts wired his father to forward him $3,000. When that money arrived, Watts and Ann planned to spend the summer in France, but they received a wire from Annie Watts Hill, who asked them to meet her, Valinda, and Frances in London. They complied since she was paying their fare, but not before they experienced one further bit of excitement. They crossed the English Channel riding in the open cockpit of a biplane.

The family left for the States in June aboard the SS *Aquitania*, a huge four-screw liner that crossed the Atlantic at an average speed of 24.63 knots. When Watts and Ann arrived home, he discovered that the money his father had sent him in Europe had actually come from his own savings account. "I had $3.61 when I got home," he joked some years later.[44]

Watts Hill's resources were certainly far greater than this pocket change. His grandfather had left him with a trust fund worth more than a million dollars. Nonetheless, his future was uncertain. His father had several assignments in mind for him, including assigning Watts to oversee Watts Hospital, which had become a steady drain on the family's finances as deficits continued year after year. Yet just like his father a quarter century before, Watts Hill was not going to be content to remain in the shadow of an elder, more influential patron. He would have to find his own place and time to make his mark. It would not be easy with a father like John Sprunt Hill.

CHAPTER 8

Good Times and Bad

NORTH CAROLINA WAS ENJOYING the full blush of prosperity in 1927 when Durham celebrated its Manufacturers and Educators Dinner. Durham had begun to call itself the "City of Industry and Education" thanks to James B. Duke's remarkable $6 million gift, which transformed Trinity College into Duke University. The elaborate dinner, which took place at the new Washington Duke Hotel, included addresses by Governor Angus W. McLean, Associate Justice W. J. Brogden from the state supreme court, and the city's leading capitalist, John Sprunt Hill, who spoke on the virtues of Durham's educational institutions.

Durham had much to offer those willing to take a second look. The city once known for its diseases and saloons now showed signs of grace and style. Annexation in the mid-1920s had expanded the city's boundaries to make it the fourth largest in the state. Municipal bonds had paid for handsome public buildings. The city had a new water system, and construction had begun on a civic auditorium that would seat more than two thousand persons. South of town, just beyond John Sprunt Hill's mansion on Morehead Hill, was the classy Forest Hills subdivision. Developer J. O. Cobb billed it as the "place to build your dream home." Among the amenities were a golf course, riding stables, a swimming pool, and dancing at the clubhouse. Another development at Hope Valley promoted its access to both Duke University and Chapel Hill.

Civic boosters were still preening over changes planned for Trinity College. All the land for the new campus had been acquired by the time James B. Duke announced his name-changing gift. In the summer of 1925, Duke himself helped select the stone for the new Tudor-style campus. A year later, as the city was preparing for the opening of a sixteen-story downtown hotel named for the patriarch of the Duke clan, James B. Duke died unexpectedly on October 10, 1926. He was sixty-eight. The hotel manager had to accelerate final preparations to accommodate mourners who arrived aboard the seven private railroad cars that brought Duke's body and the funeral party to Durham for services and burial.

The hotel occupied a full city block immediately behind John Sprunt Hill's Trust Building. The city's Academy of Music had been razed to make way for it. The Washington Duke offered 300 rooms—all with baths—and a ballroom with a seating capacity of 600. It was formally dedicated on the evening of October 20 with speeches from local dignitaries and others from across the state. John Sprunt and Annie Watts Hill were "chaperones" at the dance for the public that followed.

The Hills were among the more than eleven hundred local investors who put up money for the $1.8 million venture. The outpouring of local support was hailed as an example of Durham's maturity; the city no longer needed to wait for millionaires to decide the future. It was the first of Durham's proud buildings that had not been handed to the city by someone named Carr, Duke, Watts, or Hill. Nonetheless, it drew on the resources of some of the city's richest citizens like the Hills, W. D. Carmichael, and others. The project was speculative. More than half of the money needed for construction was raised through an Atlanta broker who sold bonds and took half of the hotel corporation stock as security. The lion's share of the bonds was due to mature in twelve years, but the future looked bright from downtown Durham. No one imagined they would not be paid in full.

John Sprunt Hill had little to do with the hotel promotion. Some even considered him a spoiler despite the fact that he and his wife had purchased 10 percent of the $400,000 in bonds sold locally. The night before the grand opening, he faced down a crowd of angry townspeople, merchants, and hotel investors who accused him and the city council of reneging on their promise to construct an extension of Parrish Street to Market Street to provide an entrance on the hotel's north side across from the Trust Building. Hill refused to provide land for a right-of-way as large as the hotel owners wanted, so the city settled for a street twenty-four feet wide rather than one thirty feet wide. The *Durham Morning Herald*—whose owners were among the hotel incorporators—ridiculed Hill's stubborn resistance as the only dark spot on the otherwise joyous occasion.

❧❧❧

The late 1920s were a high point in the lives of John Sprunt and Annie Watts Hill. Their daughters were close to home. Valinda had married Watts's fraternity brother, David St. Pierre DuBose of Baltimore, who had been the best man at his wedding. Frances—her father called her Frank—had finished at Shipley School and was living at home while she studied at Duke University. When she told her father she wanted to become a doctor, he said, "Well, if you want to do it, do it." Her mother was appalled.[1]

Watts, his wife Ann, and their infant son George Watts Hill Jr. had recently moved into Harwood Hall rather than build a home as they had planned. George Watts had left his home for the use of his wife, but it was to pass on to his grandson after her death. He also left the young Hill a trust valued at nearly $1.5 million. The mansion, complete with furnishings and collectibles that included a full-size stuffed bear, came available in 1925 after the marriage of Sarah Ecker Watts to former governor Cameron Morrison. The Morrisons moved to Charlotte into their own large home on an estate they named Morrocroft.

Watts and Ann Hill made a strikingly attractive couple. He was tall, with a strong, muscled physique and the same chiseled good looks of his father. His hair would fade to gray early in life, but in his mid-twenties it was dark brown. He wore it combed straight back with a deep part in the center. He had deep-seated blue eyes and a strong, square-cut, dimpled chin. Ann had an air of sophistication polished by private schooling, studies in Europe, and a year in New York's art community. She was petite, with burnt-orange hair. Her small size and narrow hips had created serious problems during her pregnancy. In the latter weeks of pregnancy, she went to her home and doctors in Baltimore, where she gave birth to Watts Jr. on August 3, 1926.

She was called Ann although she had been christened Anna Austin McCulloch at her birth on July 30, 1903. She was fluent in French, spoke a little Italian, and was a voracious reader and an accomplished horsewoman. Though sociable, Ann was shy, and her reticence among strangers was taken the wrong way by some people in Durham. Even Watts's sisters were not among her close friends. She preferred her old acquaintances in New York, especially her classmate Marcia Zimbalist (the daughter of the great lyric soprano Alma Gluck) and the coterie of artists and writers she had befriended while living in the city before her marriage.

❧❧❧

Watts Hill spent one summer during his college years on Heaton's dude ranch in the western United States.

Watts Hill as a student at the University of North Carolina.

While a student at the University of North Carolina, Watts Hill ran a student dining room called The Cabin. He is seated on the right of the center post.

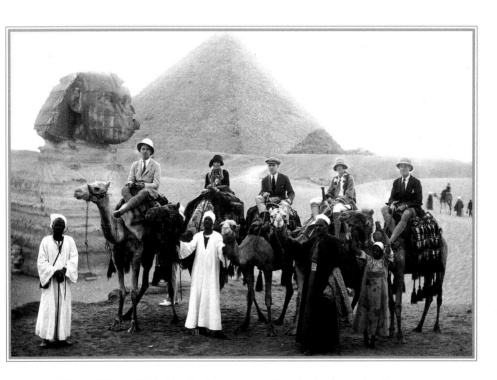

Watts Hill and his bride, the former Ann McCulloch of Maryland, spent their honeymoon touring the world. Watts is on the first camel on the left. Ann is second from the right.

A family portrait. From the left, standing, are John Sprunt Hill, Watts Hill, Ann Hill, and the Reverend Duncan McCulloch. Annie Watts Hill is holding George Watts Hill Jr. Ann's mother is seated beside Mrs. Hill.

The University of North Carolina's new library was dedicated on October 17, 1929, completing the extension of the new campus below South Building. Standing with John Sprunt Hill (front left) on the steps of South Building are Andrew Keogh, Governor O. Max Gardner, and university president Harry W. Chase. In the back row, from the left, are newspaper editor Josephus Daniels, W. D. Moss, university librarian Louis Round Wilson, and architect Arthur C. Nash.

Watts Hill used this photograph in his campaigns for the
Durham City Council in the 1930s.

VOTE FOR

JOHN SPRUNT HILL

CANDIDATE FOR SENATOR, 16TH SENATORIAL DISTRICT

SUBJECT TO DEMOCRATIC PRIMARY, SATURDAY, JUNE 2, 1934

A

FRIEND

OF

MANKIND

NOT

AFRAID

TO DO

RIGHT

A LIFE-LONG DEMOCRAT

With Much Experience in

Farming, Banking, Road Building, Educational Work Public Welfare, and Military and Legislative Affairs

MY RECORD AS STATE SENATOR SHOWS THAT I STOOD OPENLY AND FOUGHT FOR:
GOOD SCHOOLS, GOOD ROADS, BETTER FARMING CONDITIONS, A SQUARE DEAL
FOR THE MAN OF SMALL MEANS, AND BUSINESS-LIKE ADMINISTRATION OF
ALL STATE DEPARTMENTS.

John Sprunt Hill poster for the state Senate campaign in 1934.

John Sprunt Hill donated the Carolina Inn in Chapel Hill to the university.
This photograph shows the inn as it appeared in the late 1930s.

The Hill Building in downtown Durham during various phases of construction in 1936 and 1937.

*The Hill family at Quail Roost. From the left: Watts Hill, Ann Hill, Watts Jr.,
Dudley, and John Sprunt II.*

*Watts Hill revived Quail Roost as a model dairy farm with purebred
Guernsey cattle.*

The entrance to Quail Roost at Rougemont north of Durham.

Watts Hill staged an annual birthday party for High Point Prince Maxim, his prize Guernsey bull and father of much of the Quail Roost herd.

Watts Hill was host at cow sales and farm shows at Quail Roost.

Watts and Ann Hill at the National Horse Show at Madison Square Garden in New York, 1939.

THE STATE

A Weekly Survey of North Carolina

FEBRUARY 3, 1940   TEN CENTS

"JINGLE BELLS!" George Watts Hill, of Durham, out for a drive on the streets of that city during the recent heavy snow.

Travels of De Soto   Bracebridge Hall
By J. B. Hicklin   By John M. Gregory

VOLUME VII   —SUBSCRIPTION PRICE—$3.00 PER YEAR—   NUMBER 36

Watts Hill was a favorite of Carl Goerch, publisher of the State *magazine. This photo appeared on the cover of an edition in December 1940. With Hill are his daughter Dudley, his son John Sprunt II, and their governess, Doris Castle.*

Watts Hill was commissioned an army major and served in the OSS during World War II.

Three of the University of North Carolina's most generous benefactors in 1947. From the left, William R. Kenan Jr., John Motley Morehead III, and John Sprunt Hill.

The Hills were easily Durham's first family, socially and financially. When John Sprunt Hill paid his federal income taxes in 1924, the bill was more than $27,000, a sum many in Durham would not earn in a lifetime. Hill owned two banks and a controlling interest in a growing insurance company, and his influence reached into a host of other enterprises whose owners came to him with investment opportunities. The real estate he had bought that caused Ben Duke to question his sanity had paid off handsomely; he sold some of it at ten times what he paid for it. In 1915, he had created Durham Realty and Insurance Company to handle the real estate, bonding, securities, and insurance business of the Durham Loan and Trust after the bank commenced regular commercial banking operations. He had built one of Durham's earliest subdivisions, Oval Park, near his Hillandale Golf Course and used the proximity of the course to enhance the sale of lots in the West Durham "street-car" suburb.[2] Easily the largest property owner around, Hill had holdings that included two office buildings on Main Street, a dairy farm, and the controlling interest in the 800-acre Quail Roost Hunt Club, once the exclusive shooting preserve of George Watts and other tobacco millionaires.

John Sprunt Hill nurtured a deep patrician pride in his family, and he assumed that it was the responsibility of people of wealth to devote themselves to public affairs for the good of the community. He was never shy about telling anyone how to run a business, a city, a university, or even the state. While his manner was often considered pompous, it was more a reflection of his own self-confidence than of egotism. He was not ostentatious, he was considered warm and genuine by his friends, and he followed George Watts's example of simple living. His pleasures were literature, self-improvement, and golf. He was a lifelong student, and books filled the shoulder-high cases on the walls of the large library on the first floor of his Duke Street mansion. Hill's favorite overstuffed chair sat to the left of the room's huge fireplace near the end of a long table. In the evenings, Annie would sit at the opposite end of the table working on her needlepoint.

He and Annie often had guests for dinner and then adjourned to a quiet evening of bridge. They enjoyed simple foods of the country, and the family's Scottish gardener tended a large bountiful plot, part of the eight acres surrounding the house that also included an orchard and grazing for two saddle horses and two cows. Hill used the fresh vegetables and fruit from his garden to entice William R. Kenan Jr., his former classmate who had also become a millionaire and university benefactor, to overnight in Durham prior to the 1924 commencement exercises. "We have plenty of room and plenty of fried chicken and strawberries to eat and plenty of automobiles to run you over to Chapel Hill whenever you feel like it," he wrote Kenan.[3]

Hill occasionally ventured outside of the state on trips to New York City, but seldom for pleasure. His wife was the traveler. She took frequent extended trips abroad in the grand style she had enjoyed with her parents. The entourage usually included her children and, after the girls grew older, her cousins. Viola Fritz, the sister of the girls' governess, was a constant companion who served as secretary and travel agent, changing currency and handling other details that Annie did not consider fit chores for herself.

Through John Sprunt Hill's seat on various corporate boards and state commissions, he was well known to persons of influence and power. As a highway commissioner, he made decisions that determined the economic fortune of cities and towns across an important cross section of the state. His seat on the executive committee of the university's Board of Trustees gave him easy access to the state's political leadership. (There was no question he was a Democrat, but he had passed on attending the party's 1924 national convention due to his lack of enthusiasm for the national platform.)

Hill loved grand occasions like the 1926 Manufacturers and Educators Dinner that gave him a platform to advance his personal credo of self-reliance and to share his nostalgia for a simpler time. In preparing his long, detailed speeches, he drew upon his study of North Caroliniana, as he called it, for patriotic color. He was particularly proud of a speech he delivered in January 1924 to the Atlanta Retail Merchants Association. Hill had 8,000 copies of his address, which he titled "North Carolina—A Story of Triumphant Democracy," printed for distribution to anyone who asked. He even had it translated into Spanish for the benefit of a South American delegation that visited the state to see the results of Governor Morrison's road program.

In his speech to the merchants, Hill argued that North Carolina's growth and success were due to the same widely touted "Atlanta Spirit" that had lifted that city from the ashes following the Civil War.[4] Hill believed North Carolina had succeeded after the Democratic Party had been able to overthrow a corrupt Republican regime that was founded on the votes of "120,000 ignorant negroes." Hill praised the white Democratic Party candidates elected in 1900 for their leadership in introducing universal education, encouraging health care, building good roads, and taking advantage of the dedication of wealthy men like himself who were willing to shoulder state affairs. In a statement that clearly defined his own philosophy, Hill told the merchants, "There are no idle rich in North Carolina. Everybody works including father, hence there is little or no prejudice against drafting for service to the state rich men who have already won success in business."[5]

Department store retailers around the South had been courting Hill as a partner for a Durham store, but he had resisted invitations from those who would impose "foreign domination." Hill wanted a locally owned operation, and he finally enticed A. P. Tilley, a Birmingham, Alabama, department store manager, to relocate to Durham and open Tilley's Department Store in 1927 in an elegant new building Hill erected on Main Street. The cost of the store building had been estimated at $100,000, but overruns pushed the figure to $120,000. Across the front were three wide arched windows that reached from the second to the fourth floors and were flanked at the top by cartouches bearing the Hill family crest.

∽∽∽

If there was any excess in John Sprunt Hill's life, it was his passion for golf. He had built the Hillandale course in Durham, and even after the Durham Country Club declared bankruptcy he continued to maintain the course, pay a professional, and keep golf a local option. In 1922, Hill had been one of the charter members of the Mid-Pines Country Club in Pinehurst, which opened with a select membership of men who had been long-standing guests at the Carolina Hotel. Leonard Tufts's Pinehurst Company was one of the backers of the new development, as was Donald Ross, who had created the Pinehurst courses and was just launching his career as a course designer. Ross devoted special attention to the Mid-Pines course. Until Hill's son Watts joined the club in 1927, John Sprunt Hill was one of only a few North Carolinians (with the exception of the year-round Pinehurst residents) with regular memberships. William N. Reynolds of Winston-Salem, the brother of R. J. Reynolds, was another. Hill had recommended Reynolds for membership along with W. S. Lee of Charlotte, Smith Richardson of Greensboro, and Kemp Plummer Lewis of Durham.

Membership was by invitation; the $2,500 joining fee entitled members to special rates on accommodations at the Mid-Pines clubhouse.

Mid-Pines satisfied Hill's midwinter golfing needs. The club was close enough for a weekend visit and comfortable enough for an extended stay. The entire family was frequently at Pinehurst during the season, which opened in December and continued through March. As for his summers, Hill preferred the courses around Asheville, which by the mid-1920s had become his substitute for Poland Springs, long the family's summer retreat. In 1926, he began making plans for a new home in Biltmore Forest, an exclusive colony of summer residents at the edge of the estate of the city's most famous resident, George W. Vanderbilt.

∾ ∾ ∾

The Hill family had been regular visitors in Asheville before the war. "I am looking for a good site for a summer residence near Asheville," Hill wrote a friend in 1911. "I would like from twenty-five to one hundred acres of land, ten or fifteen acres cleared and the balance woodland with plenty of large trees. I prefer a site close to the [French Broad] river, and close enough to town to have city water and light and sewerage facilities."[6] No real estate agent could satisfy Hill's requirements. For a time, the family rented homes on Sunset Mountain, but they soon became regular guests at the nearby Grove Park Inn, a favorite of rich and famous travelers. The accommodations were superb, and the North Carolina location allowed Hill to return to Durham easily if that was required. More often than not, many of the people that Hill wanted to see ended up in Asheville, often at the Grove Park Inn. The Hills' favorite suite was on the northwest corner of the second floor just off the Palm Court. He had a view of the golf course and of stunning sunsets.

In August 1926, Hill finally found a suitable building site for a home. He paid $36,500, a sum inflated by Asheville's building boom, for four lots—eight acres—on a hillside overlooking the Donald Ross golf course at Biltmore Forest Country Club.[7] The Durham architectural firm of Atwood and Nash completed plans for his new home in the spring of 1927, and work began immediately on a massive structure built on a solid frame of concrete and steel. The home was faced with the same type of granite used in construction of both the State Capitol and Christ Church on Raleigh's Capitol Square. Hill chose an Ohio sandstone for the trim that matched stone used in his home in Durham.

The two-story house with an attic level large enough for servants' quarters was completely different from anything Hill had built before. It was designed in the style of an English manor house and was set on a hillside with a commanding view of the course's fourth fairway and the mountains far beyond. Two wings extended at obtuse angles from a large central foyer that opened to a lawn, which sloped down to the golf course. On one side of the ground floor was a large sitting room; on the other was an equally large dining room where the Hill family crest was molded in plaster over a large fireplace. The interior plaster walls were set off by dark millwork. Bedrooms and baths occupied the second floor. Over a heavy wooden front door, mounted vertically on the wall, was a sundial.

Hill filled the house with specially designed furniture and personally selected the silver service and linens. His wife later joked that she went to Europe and when she returned her husband presented her with a house. It cost more than $117,000 to build.[8]

Life with the Hills was something totally different for the family's newest member, Watts Hill's wife Ann. She had never known the wealth, mansions, and servants that her husband accepted as requisites for daily life. Instead, her family's wealth was measured in the stimulation of lively dinner conversation and in intellectual pursuits. When Watts told her they were moving to Harwood Hall from the modest rental house they had taken when they first arrived, she had asked how they could afford it on his $250-a-month salary as a vice president at the Durham Loan and Trust Company. Only then did her husband explain that he would soon have access to the trust fund established by his grandfather. Even secure financially, Ann was never comfortable in what she later called a "fifty-room monstrosity, the satisfied desire of dead ancestors."[9]

Watts Hill also harbored some anxiety about life in Durham. He returned resigned to do what he had to do to satisfy his father, who had eagerly anticipated that his son would relieve him of some of his business and civic responsibilities. As the eldest son in a family whose affairs affected the lives of many in the city of Durham, Watts Hill felt that his first duty was to the family. "I didn't have a brother," he said some years later. "I had to go to work."[10] Work, of course, was a relative term. He was a lawyer, but he took only one client, collected a modest fee, and never accepted another. He rented an office near his father at the bank, but he showed little interest in the intricacies of finance. He once listed banking as a hobby on a biographical summary.

Despite their differences, father and son were close, and the elder Hill catered to his son's abiding interests. Watts Hill had not been home long when his father turned the responsibility of Watts Hospital over to him. John Sprunt Hill had never given his full attention to the hospital, which continued to operate in the red. He had told one friend just before young Watts returned to Durham that he was "somewhat fed up on hospital work." "The work of acting as president of the board of trustees," he confessed, "worries me very much."[11] When Watts Hill joined the hospital Board of Trustees in 1926, the administration had accumulated losses of $32,000 in the previous two years.

The hospital's red ink came primarily from the charity cases that it accepted according to the wishes of George Watts.[12] The community had never responded with support, as George Watts had hoped it would. For all Durham's civic success, the community did not shoulder its public burdens. Year after year, the newly organized Community Chest failed to reach its fund-raising goal. The city seemed perfectly willing to let the Hills provide medical care for the poor.

Given Watts Hill's love of medicine and his frustrated ambition to become a doctor, the hospital work provided an outlet for his interest that he would enjoy for the rest of his life. It also engaged him in medical care in ways he could not even have imagined at the outset. The doctors and medical professionals at the hospital, and later at Duke and at the university in Chapel Hill, would become his closest friends, and he would thrive in the atmosphere that had so frustrated his father. After taking his seat on the board, Watts Hill moved into an office in the administrative wing, and he could be found there almost daily with his attention focused on two pressing needs: improving the hospital's financial condition and supervising the construction of a new wing.

∾∾∾

Demand for medical care had increased drastically as Durham's population grew larger. Business also improved after both the extension of the city trolley lines to the hospital's front door and the growing number of automobiles made the facility more convenient to all. In 1924, more than seven thousand patients were admitted than had been in the year before, and occupancy was pushed to capacity. The number of major and minor surgeries performed in the operating rooms doubled.[13]

When Watts Hill arrived, plans called for a new hospital wing—the last expansion paid for with George Watts's money—that would be dedicated to the care of private patients. A three-story addition to the 1909 building would provide space for a maternity department, pediatrics, and general surgical and medical services. Hill questioned the amount of space devoted to pediatrics, and he set off on a personal tour of hospitals around the country to collect ideas for the best use of the new space. Based on what he learned, the final blueprints were changed to enlarge the new facilities to accommodate medical and surgical specialties, an emergency room, a delivery room, and fifty private rooms that Hill hoped would attract more patients with the ability to pay.[14] The Valinda Beall Watts Private Patient Pavilion opened in 1927 at a cost of $273,000. Included in the cost was the renovation of the administration building, nurses' home, kitchen, and dining room.[15] The additions prompted Dr. Watson S. Rankin, director of the Duke Endowment's hospital section, to call Watts Hospital "a model institution."[16]

Watts Hill immersed himself in the details of hospital administration with the very practical goal of reducing the burden of support that his family had to carry. He began to whittle away at the hospital's operating deficit. It took three years of work for the hospital to even approach becoming a break-even operation, but in 1928 the losses amounted to only $1,200.

Part of the problem was the hospital's own good fortune. Since George Watts had left money to pay for the new wing, local citizens and public officials believed that the hospital had accumulated wealth to pay for the mounting costs of charity care. Even after Watts Hill convinced the city council to increase its annual support of the hospital from $5,000 to $8,000, some council members remained convinced that public money was going into bricks and mortar rather than into patient care.[17]

The hospital's financial health improved in 1927 after it began receiving annual payments from the Duke Endowment, which provided up to $1.00 a day for each indigent patient, about a fourth of the daily cost. James B. Duke had been impressed with the need for medical care in his home state, and he had stipulated in his will that one-third of the endowment's income be set aside for support of nonprofit hospitals in the Carolinas. This provision was one that John Sprunt Hill had helped to prepare during one of Duke's visits to Durham in the months before his death.[18]

Watts Hill knew that public money alone was not going to solve the hospital's problems. What was required was a change in attitude among hospital users. He discovered that because the institution had a reputation as a "charity" hospital, even some patients who were able to pay did not do so. But even when faced with serious deficits, the hospital board refused to take deadbeats to court lest the lawsuits create even more controversy within the community.[19]

∽∽∽

In the spring of 1929, Hill discovered what he hoped would be a steady and reliable source of payment for patient care. Hill and Dr. Wilburt C. Davison, the dean of Duke University's new medical school, began putting together a plan that they hoped would serve Watts Hospital as well as the new hospital under construction on the Duke campus.

After Duke president William P. Few's dream for a joint Trinity–University of North Carolina medical school evaporated, he had shifted his attention to James B. Duke, who included an additional $4 million in his bequest for the construction of a medical school. Few lost no time in making use of Duke's money. Less than a year after the tobacco millionaire's death, Few had hired Davison as the school's first dean.

Davison came to Durham from Baltimore and The Johns Hopkins Medical School, where he served as pediatrician and associate dean. He was a Princeton graduate and Rhodes Scholar who had begun his medical training while studying in England. He had graduated early from Johns Hopkins so he could serve with Army Field Hospital Number One in France. After the war, he returned to Johns Hopkins and took a position in the medical school's children's clinic. He was teaching there when Few asked him to come to Durham and prepare the Duke University School of Medicine for its first class. For his faculty, Davison drew heavily upon his colleagues in Baltimore, which immediately added credibility for the new school.

Included in the new medical complex was a 416-bed hospital. Watts Hill and the other trustees at Watts Hospital greeted the news with concern, but as the new school began to develop it became clear that the Duke medical program and Watts Hospital could coexist. Davison told the Watts Hospital trustees that experience had shown that an additional medical facility generally drew more patients into a market. In addition, he said that as a teaching hospital where patients would be needed for the training of medical students, Duke would attract a different type of patient from those who would use Watts Hospital.[20]

Not long after Davison arrived at Duke, he and Dr. Watson Rankin began talking about establishing a low-cost hospital care plan for workers in large manufacturing plants. Such a plan had been organized in 1914 by Dr. T. W. Long of Roanoke Rapids, North Carolina, for that town's six industrial employers. Members made small contributions—by 1929 they amounted to twenty-five cents a week—for complete family coverage including home visits by nurses and physicians. These payments generated enough money for patient care and the operation of a small hospital.

Davison circulated a similar plan in Durham and found Watts Hill very interested. On March 14, 1929, the *Durham Morning Herald* announced the creation of the Durham Hospital Association, which was to serve all four of the city's hospitals: Duke University Hospital, Watts Hospital, the privately owned McPherson Hospital, and Lincoln Hospital, which operated solely for the care of African Americans. According to the newspaper, the new program would be supervised by a board of trustees that included Davison, Hill, Dr. D. S. McPherson, Dr. Foy Robertson from Watts Hospital, Superintendent of Public Welfare W. E. Stanley, D. T. Carey of the Durham Chamber of Commerce, and the Reverend J. W. Smith from the ministerial association.[21] The organizers took care to call the plan an "association" so as to avoid having to come under the management of the state insurance laws, which would have required the investment of a considerable amount of capital.

Coverage under the plan would be open to any resident of Durham County, but the organizers had their eye on large employee groups such as the workers at Erwin Mills, the tobacco factories, and Duke University. Davison and Hill believed this hospital care plan could provide medical care for those least able to afford it and enable all to contribute something for hospitalization "without jeopardizing their future welfare by sacrificing other needs equally important to them."[22]

In an effort to reduce collection costs, Davison and Hill restored old savings stamp machines that had been used a decade earlier to sell war bonds. These machines were to be placed in mills and other work sites for the convenience of workers. Plan members would buy stamps and post them on membership cards to show that their payments were current. In that payments were made weekly and the plan was administered without paid agents, it was similar to a British program that Davison had seen in which neighborhood volunteers collected the payments.

Despite all the preparation, the plan was not well received in Durham. Millowners said that workers would never part with a quarter out of week- ly wages of six dollars. Some doctors complained that the plan was the first step toward socialized medicine. Dr. Isaac Manning, the dean of the Uni- versity of North Carolina Medical School, warned Davison that if patients were able to select their own physicians then the hospitals would be forced to admit any doctors, even African American physicians.[23] Unable to se- cure broad support, the proposal that Hill threw himself into with such enthusiasm died before the first client could be enrolled.[24]

ᦙᦙᦙ

All the while that Watts Hill immersed himself in work at the hospital, he also was creating a model farm on the old Quail Roost Hunt Club prop- erty north of Durham near Rougemont. Like his consuming interest in health care, the farm would become as much a part of Hill's life as his fu- ture in business. And just as he had taken on the hospital, he took on the rehabilitation of Quail Roost only after his father gave up his hope of mak- ing something of the place.

Watts Hill was still on his honeymoon in 1925 when C. W. Toms, the head of Liggett and Myers Tobacco Company, came to see John Sprunt Hill about the future of the Quail Roost property. The land belonged to the Quail Roost Hunt Club, and only Toms and Hill, who had acquired the stock of some of the original owners in 1919, remained as investors. In re- cent years, the management of the land, buildings, and tenants had fallen to Hill, and the occasional bird outings had become a very expensive luxury.

Toms offered his shares to Hill, who said that he was not interested in buying them but that his son might be. Actually, Watts Hill had probably spent more time on the farm as a youngster than his father had as adult. One day soon after Watts Hill had settled in Durham, his father ap- proached him waving a sheaf of papers and asked, "Do you want this?" "Sure, I'll take it," Watts had replied. "What is it?" His father handed over his shares in the club.[25]

What Watts Hill found on his first visit to the property was not encouraging. Club members had never wanted the property to produce anything but birds, so the tenants had been chosen for their skill in cooking and raising good hunting dogs rather than their ability to care for the land. As a result, a quarter century of neglect had left the sloping hillsides rutted with gullies and the fields tangled with briars and weeds. Aside from a few tenant houses, the only structure on the property was the old log clubhouse where the members had once gathered after a day's hunting for a big meal and card games around a large, round mahogany table. The linens and silver from the clubhouse had been secured, but the lodge at the edge of the woods was in shambles. At the end of Watts Hill's first season as owner of the property, he calculated the operating cost at about $1,000 for each bird shot that year. He took his figures to Toms and offered to either sell his interest or buy Toms's stake. Toms sold, and Watts Hill became a farmer.

Over the next two years, Watts Hill's efforts at producing a paying crop on the land proved no more successful than his attempt to operate a hunt club had been. In his first year of raising tobacco, he failed to cover the cost of planting and harvesting. The next season, he added a few fields of corn, but that ended up costing him $1.25 for each bushel sold at 60¢.[26]

Hill had the resources to absorb losses, but only for so long. He was looking for a way to make the farm pay when he met H. T. Hodnett, a Durham man who had graduated from State College in Raleigh and had five years experience in dairying. Hodnett told Hill that he believed he could turn Quail Roost into a dairy farm. In 1927, the farm stirred with new activity as workers began erecting barns and silos. Fields were plowed and planted in barley and clover. Hill put in another crop of corn, but this time the cob, stalk, and leaf all went into cattle feed. When Hill did the math, he figured that corn worth $1.00 could sell for $1.40 as milk. The tall silos flanking the main barn were filled to the top. Hill himself enrolled in classes at State College, and he mined the resources of the U.S. Department of Agriculture on Guernsey cattle, the favored breed of his great-grandfather Gerard S. Watts.

Hill joined the American Guernsey Cattle Club and began tracking bloodlines as closely as his father, whose own herd at Hillandale included the registered Guernseys brought south from the Watts farm in Maryland. For his own stock, Hill bought prize Guernseys by the names of Hines Buttercup, Jennie's Pet, and Belle of Lakewood from a South Carolina farmer who was forced to sell due to financial problems.

Hill's investment proved to be an example of what money and determination could do when applied to worn-out farmland. In 1929, a Quail Roost cow took home blue ribbons from the North Carolina State Fair. A year later, Quail Roost Guernseys captured ribbons at the Piedmont Dairy Show, the State Fair, and shows in South Carolina. Hines Buttercup was declared the grand champion cow in North Carolina that year, having produced a record 18,069 pounds of milk containing nearly 820 pounds of butterfat. (The average annual butterfat production for cows on Durham farms was 500 pounds.)

In the fall of 1930, the local papers announced the arrival at Quail Roost of a prizewinning bull named High Point Prince Maxim, who was declared the most perfect specimen of his kind south of J. C. Penney's herds in New York. It was big news; Watts Hill announced he had paid $7,500 for the animal, an unbelievable sum considering the sorry state of farming at the time. While the price was high, a half brother of this bull had recently been sold for $16,400. John Sprunt Hill cautioned his son about such free spending, but Watts said the bull would double the value of his herd in two years. In ten years, he said, the majority of his herd would have been sired by High Point Prince Maxim, and the bull's offspring would raise the standards for dairying in central North Carolina.[27] He later claimed to have made $600,000 from the sale of Prince Maxim's services.[28]

In a few years' time, Quail Roost emerged as one of North Carolina's trophy farms, not unlike the farms that other gentleman farmers in the state had built. Pinehurst developer Leonard Tufts was raising Ayrshires on his farm in Moore County, while Guernseys were the pride of textile man Thurmond Chatham of Winston-Salem, whose herd grazed over the rolling foothills of the Blue Ridge Mountains on Klondike Farm near Elkin. In the summer of 1929, more than two hundred fifty dairymen gathered at Quail Roost for a barbecue picnic to see the transformation. Watts Hill called Quail Roost a demonstration farm for the county and even for the state, and he said that the improvements he had made showed that farmers could survive without growing cotton and tobacco.

ᵔᵔᵔᵔᵔᵔ

Born and raised in the city with nary a financial care, Watts Hill seemed an unlikely advocate or model for North Carolina farmers, whose plight had steadily worsened in the 1920s. But the young man's enthusiasm for agriculture and for improving the condition of North Carolina farmers was as deep and passionate as that of his father, who remained steadfast in his support for the expansion of rural credit unions.

The farm credit union movement had not regained momentum after the war, when both agriculture and textile prices fell. The price of cotton in 1923 would not be matched again in twenty years, and John Sprunt Hill watched as some of the hard-fought successes slipped away. Eleven credit unions closed in 1921 alone. In an effort to revive the program, John Sprunt Hill organized the North Carolina Credit Union Association, made himself the president, and personally paid the salary of Harriet Berry, whom he hired away from the road movement to evangelize for credit unions. Hill secured some outside support from a foundation created by Russell Sage, his streetside acquaintance from New York.

Berry's organizing produced renewed enthusiasm and attracted national attention to Lowe's Grove, which was featured in the July 1923 issue of *Collier's Weekly*. But Berry and Hill struggled against attitudes that discouraged the growth and development of credit unions from both sides—the lenders and the borrowers. Even when cotton prices were at their all-time high in November 1923, Leonard Tufts had rebuffed Berry's call for help in establishing a credit union in the Sandhills: "You start out, as I see it, on the basis that the world, and especially the money lender is a crook; that the farmer is an honest, hard-working, wonderful character, who is a prey to these crooks; your conclusions are correct but your premises are wrong. The average banker and capitalist is honest and you should devise a method to protect him if you want the farmer to have cheap money. The average farmer—no, more than that—practically every farmer is a crook and you should devise methods of protecting the money lender from him."[29]

The movement also suffered from the farmers' own independence. By the middle of the 1920s, the once-strong Farmers' Union had fallen into decline, and rural folk remained suspicious of cooperative efforts. "The name 'union' in North Carolina seems to be in bad repute," Hill told E. C. Branson in 1925. "Many of our people consider themselves 'outside the union.' At any rate the Farmers Union and the labor union organizations have given the name union a 'black eye' in North Carolina. As I believe that a 'rose by any other name smells as sweet' I am therefore willing to try the name savings and loan association, which name after all comes near emphasizing the fundamental ideas of the organization that we were to establish for farmers."[30]

Hill remained angry that the credit union movement had never received the support he thought it deserved from the state's Department of Agriculture. In 1927, Hill asked Governor Angus W. McLean, a Lumberton banker, to support the creation of a new state division to promote credit unions. McLean was cool to the idea, and enabling legislation died in the General Assembly. Legislators did make one change. The 1915 law was rewritten to substitute the term "savings and loan association" for "credit union."

Berry's organizing skill and John Sprunt Hill's money produced some growth. About sixty rural credit unions were operating throughout the state by the late 1920s, but the combined constituency amounted to only 3,000 members, merely a token number of those in need.[31] It was clear that credit unions were not going to save North Carolina's farmers, whose condition had grown desperate. Watts Hill saw it in his neighbors at Quail Roost, who were falling further and further behind in their obligations to lenders and suppliers. Even the early stock he had bought for his own farm had been the product of hard times.

❧❧❧

Farmers were begging for help from the federal and state governments by the fall of 1929. North Carolina governor O. Max Gardner remained hopeful that aid might come from Washington. When it failed to appear, local officials and farmers called on the state to unilaterally fix prices on cotton and tobacco, a move that Gardner knew was bootless. Just the year before, farmers in adjoining states had quadrupled production, further depressing prices.

In an effort to instill hope and perhaps turn the tide, Gardner announced his "Live-At-Home" campaign. With boundless enthusiasm, he declared the week of December 15, 1929, to be Live-At-Home Week. He encouraged North Carolinians to feed themselves on homegrown products in an effort to put some of the $250 million that Tar Heel families were spending on food imported from out of state into the pockets of local farmers. In the same spirit as Watts Hill's campaign to demonstrate the virtue of alternative farming such as dairying, Gardner declared, "One pure-bred bull is worth more than any county commission I ever saw."[32]

A little more than a month later, in January 1930, the Hills—father and son—helped convene a meeting of local officials and farm leaders with the governor to talk about opening a farmers' exchange for Durham County. It was not a new idea; about two dozen similar exchanges were in operation around the state. Durham's exchange was predicated on the same need as elsewhere. "I talked with many [farmers] and found that they were unable to sell chickens, hogs, hay, grain and so forth except at a surplus price which was below the cost of production," Watts Hill told the governor. "Therefore, for the past two years I have been talking with the Extension Service of the State, various County Agents, farmers and co-operative promoters and managers."[33]

The Hills offered a building to house the operations and money to pay the salary of the manager of the new Durham Farmers' Mutual Exchange (the term "mutual" was preferred over "cooperative" after the failure a few years earlier of a tobacco cooperative) as their part in building a "farm center" for the entire county. Included in the early plans were arrangements for the local sale of chickens, eggs, hogs, sweet potatoes, and other farm produce as well as subsequent shipment of surpluses to other markets where prices might be better. The hope was that farmers would no longer be captives of buyers in one area. Membership was set at a dollar a year; profits were to be distributed annually.

Watts Hill negotiated with other exchanges in the state for the Durham facility to clean, inoculate, and certify farmers' seed before it went on sale either in Durham or through the exchanges from which it came. He also arranged for the Durham exchange to serve as a clearinghouse for information and shipments of fertilizer and bulk supplies.[34] In years to come, this effort would lead to the formation of the Farmers Cooperative Exchange, or FCX, which grew into a multistate concern.

On March 13, 1930, hundreds of children filed out of the Durham city schools early and climbed aboard forty trucks for the ride to a former hosiery mill on Elizabeth Street that had been converted into the Exchange Building. They joined a crowd of more than twenty-five hundred adults for the dedication ceremonies and to hear speeches by Gardner and other dignitaries, including John Sprunt Hill.

In his speech, Hill recalled the plight of farmers fifty years earlier: "A six-pound hen sold for twenty-five cents, and glad was the able-bodied man who could sing, 'I am working on the railroad, forty cents a day.' Everybody was poor; many were ignorant, and the fires of discontent and prejudice burned on nearly every hearthstone." The town of Durham overcame those burdens, he said. "Today another crisis faces our state," Hill told his audience. "Our country people are disheartened; their crops are selling at low prices; their markets are disorganized, and more than one-half of our people are in a state of discontent and are crying aloud for help and leadership. This great assemblage today shows that history is repeating itself. Running true to form, the great spirit of Durham makes ready to lend a helping hand and shake from our shoulders some of the burdens of this great agricultural depression in this section of our state."

The doors of the exchange were no sooner open than Watts Hill announced that he would donate 300 acres of timberland on the eastern edge of Quail Roost for use by State College as a demonstration forest. Julius V. Hoffman, the dean of State's new School of Forestry, said the land included about three million board feet of pine, oak, maple, and cedar. Hill soon added more than 700 additional acres to the tract that was dedicated as the George Watts Hill Demonstration Forest. A year later, he added another 700 acres, which lay along the Flat River adjacent to the initial parcel, to the college demonstration farm.

∽∽∽

Problems on the farm foreshadowed an overall economic depression, which many simply hoped would pass. When Gardner took office as governor in January 1929, the state had recently published a promotional booklet that claimed that North Carolina, with its riches, resources, and able native workers, ranked as one of the top five states in the nation. Even John Sprunt Hill had believed that the troubles in the farm economy were temporary. When the Virginia-Carolina Chemical Company, a major producer of fertilizer, had failed and declared bankruptcy a few years earlier, he had remained optimistic. He told family members who held Virginia-Carolina bonds (the company was founded by George Watts and Eugene Morehead) that he would purchase the bond coupons; he hoped he could cash them in later after business improved.

Until the market crashed in October 1929, the excitement over rising stock prices hid the growing problems in the southern textile industry. The region's textile markets had fluctuated widely throughout the decade. In 1925, all of Durham's cotton plants had been put on reduced schedules for lack of orders. By the late 1920s, many mills across the state were enforcing virtually unattainable production quotas and "stretch-outs" in an effort to keep from operating at a loss. The grinding pressure on workers to meet demands played into the hands of union organizers. In April 1929, with eighteen hundred workers idled in Gastonia, trouble was brewing. Gardner ordered in the National Guard to keep order. The situation would grow far worse after the Gastonia police chief and, later, a striking worker named Ella May Wiggins were shot and killed.

༤༤༤

The changes taking place on the campus at Chapel Hill offered some hope in the midst of the gloom. After a decade of construction during which students had to navigate stacks of building materials, muddy streets, and a railroad track across the south lawn, the results were impressive. The university's new library—a building in which John Sprunt Hill had taken particular interest—was dedicated on October 19, 1929.

Hill's support of the library dated back more than two decades to the initial gift he had given to establish the North Carolina Collection. Over the years, Librarian Louis Round Wilson had turned to Hill when he needed money for various projects and acquisitions. In 1918, Hill had helped Wilson bring the 10,000 items of the Stephen Beauregard Weeks Collection to the university. It was the largest collection of North Carolina books, pamphlets, newspapers, maps, and printed colonial and state records known to exist. Weeks, an 1886 graduate of the university, had gathered the material during a lifetime as a government official, and he had left it to the State Historical Collection of Wisconsin at his death. It was argued that the collection, valued at $24,000, was too important to be housed out of the state. Hill helped raise the money for its purchase so it could be installed in Chapel Hill for use by researchers and others.

Hill also arranged with Wilson to hire Mary Lindsay Thornton as an assistant, and for a time he personally paid her salary. In the beginning, her duties included work on the North Carolina Collection and on the *University News Letter*, E. C. Branson's one-page weekly publication. Hill made his plans for Thornton and for the collection clear in a letter to Wilson. "I have never thought of the North Caroliniana as a collection of books but as a collection of all kinds of information pertaining to North Carolina and put to daily use," he wrote Wilson. "In other words, it was not my intention to establish a museum, but a workshop."[35] Thornton's salary and position were eventually made part of the university program, and she remained as curator of the collection until her retirement in 1958.

The North Carolina Collection was given a proper home in the grand new library building that anchored the university's new quadrangle. The building's impressive dome, which rose eighty-five feet over the second-floor reading room, was reminiscent of the Seth Low Library at Columbia University, which McKim, Mead, and White had also designed. The building was later named for the university's longtime librarian, Louis Round Wilson.

After the library dedication, Hill seemed determined to keep the campus building program alive even if he had to do so by sheer force of personality and with his own money. Four months after the library was dedicated, the trustees' building committee recommended that an auditorium be built to replace Memorial Hall, the aging wooden structure that had opened in 1885. The old building had clearly outlived its original purpose, and in recent years it had been used as a gymnasium. Some said the great soaring wooden arches were weakened by dry rot, but it took dynamite blasts to bring the building down. A year later, in 1931, a new Memorial Hall, complete with the commemorative plaques for Civil War dead from the old building, opened in midsummer, but not without a struggle.[36]

The $182,000 building was completed only with help from an emergency fund and a $7,000 gift from John Sprunt Hill. Even after the university took these extraordinary measures to raise funds, there still had not been enough money left over to pay for the 1,850 seats. When Hill presented the building to Governor Gardner at the October 10 dedication, guests sat on the moveable wooden benches brought from the old building.

John Sprunt and Annie Watts Hill had pledged $30,000 to purchase a new organ for the old Memorial Hall. After that building was declared unsafe, they increased their pledge to $70,000 on the condition that the university agree to renovate the old Carnegie Library and dedicate it to music studies. Plans called for an 800-seat auditorium with a stage large enough to accommodate the organ and an orchestra of sixty, as well as dressing rooms for performers. In January 1930, President Chase announced that the new building would be known as the Hill Music Hall, and it was dedicated the following November 14 with a concert by Edward Eigenschenck, soloist and associate organist of the Chicago Symphony Orchestra.[37] In recognition of Hill's generosity as well as his work in the building of the new campus, the class of 1932 dedicated the yearbook, the *Yackety Yack*, in his honor.

The concert was one of the last grand events on the campus. For all his wealth, there was nothing Hill alone could do to pull the university out of a desperate situation, although he never stopped trying. After he heard that students unable to pay their tuition were being forced to withdraw from the university, he joined a group of Durham alumni to raise a scholarship fund. Hill applauded efforts by university president Frank Porter Graham—recently named to succeed Harry Chase—to organize student aid and called the plan "the one bright spot on the horizon."[38]

∞ ∞ ∞

The state's economic situation was exceedingly grim. Even Governor Gardner had faced the prospect of bankruptcy when the First National Bank in his hometown of Shelby teetered at the edge of collapse. Gardner helped salvage the bank with help from his new political friend, former governor Cameron Morrison, the man who had defeated him in a rancorous campaign in 1920. Morrison deposited enough of his wife Sarah's money (part of the estate left her by George Watts) in the bank to keep it in business.[39]

Most of the early bank failures had occurred in the western part of the state. When Asheville's Central Bank and Trust Company collapsed in November 1930, local folks discovered that city officials had illegally deposited taxpayers' money in the bank to keep it solvent after the local real estate market had fallen apart in 1926. The mayor (who subsequently committed suicide) and others were indicted, and municipal finances were discredited.[40]

By the end of 1930, nearly a hundred banks in North Carolina holding deposits of more than $56 million had closed their doors. Bank runs—during which customers lined up along the street and waited to withdraw their deposits—had become commonplace in Raleigh and Charlotte, where scandals accompanied bank failures. After the First National Bank of Charlotte closed, John Sprunt Hill's friend Word Wood said that his competitor's business had collapsed because of extravagance and an "absurdly large investment which that bank made in its 21-story office building, which cost $1,818,000." That was the same amount of money that bank examiners had reported was on deposit at the First National Bank just ninety days earlier. An eighty-six-year-old Confederate veteran whose $2,700 was now gone was resolute. "I've gone through worse than this," he said.[41]

John Sprunt Hill had always been a conservative businessman, and during the height of the good times in the late 1920s some of his friends had criticized his tightfisted style. He now reminded a New York banker that his strategy had been the best after all: "For the past two and a half years I have insisted that all of the institutions with which I am actively connected should pay all of their debts and be prepared to stand a severe depression. Many of my New York friends criticized me very severely for my conservatism, but I am pleased to say that time has proven the wisdom of my country intelligence."[42]

Confidence in public institutions was shaken. When North Carolina was hit with the heaviest snowfall in years in mid-December 1930, the Durham Coal Fund for the poor was reduced to $200. In Raleigh, police arrested a man for tearing off the porch of a vacant house so he could have wood for his stove. Even local government needed a handout. In Asheville, city employees went home without paychecks after the city fathers paid money due on bonds rather than meet the payroll. All across the state, local officials had issued appeals to Governor Gardner for help in meeting their bond obligations. During the 1920s, North Carolina had piled up the highest per capita public debt of any state in the nation. North Carolinians owed more than $500 million. That included $115 million that fiscal conservatives like John Sprunt Hill had spent building roads. Governor Gardner wryly observed that citizens had "not only anticipated the future, they had actually spent it."[43]

When the General Assembly opened in early January 1931, Governor Gardner presented members with a plan for a complete overhaul of state government. Even before the session opened, he had asked state agencies to cut spending by 10 percent; he then raised that figure to 20 percent. The substantive changes he offered, however, were part of a plan prepared by the Brookings Institution in Washington, D.C. Gardner had appealed to the institution for help in streamlining the state government.

Among the Brookings recommendations were proposals to reduce the number of state agencies by consolidating programs. None of these changes was more controversial than what Gardner had in mind for the State Highway Commission, which the Brookings specialists recommended be centralized under a strong chairman. The report also recommended that the state take control of all of North Carolina's 45,000 miles of roads. Relieved of the cost of maintaining roads, counties would immediately have $6 million in local tax money to use for other purposes. Gardner made the road bill his top priority and a test for the rest of his package. The fight was bitter, and John Sprunt Hill, who had been reappointed for his current term on the commission by Gardner, stood steadfastly opposed to any change.

Hill took extraordinary pride in the state's road system. It was almost as if he felt responsible for the construction of every mile; certainly he did in his own district. And that was part of the problem, according to the Brookings study. The nine independent commissioners had created nine road systems, not one unified state system.

The governor outlined his program to legislators on a Friday, the day before the highway commissioners were scheduled to meet to distribute a special allotment of federal funds that President Herbert Hoover hoped would help local governments provide work for the unemployed. That business was dispatched quickly. Adjournment was expected immediately, but Hill turned the discussion to the governor's plan and kept the commissioners in debate over the changes for six hours. "The present plan is the bed rock of the highway law," Hill told a reporter afterward. "It assures a square deal to the counties, the allotments are given publicity and every county knows what it is going to get. Under the other plan there would be a lump sum appropriation and it would be a pork barrel proposition." He vowed to fight the governor "in every way possible."[44]

The 1931 General Assembly remained in session for a record 141 days, and it took nearly half that time to enact Gardner's road bill. Mass meetings, intense legislative maneuvering, and a radio appeal from the governor himself were required to push the bill through the legislature. Hill fought steadily and unceasingly. Midway through the debate, he provoked an investigation of the state prison system, which he said had reneged on a contract to provide crushed stone for state roads.

There was nothing Hill liked about Gardner's bill, least of all that it would relieve him of a position that had provided him with power, influence, and standing throughout a large portion of the state. The bill was an affront to the virtues of decentralized government that he held so dear. He urged legislators not to bend to what he called the Centralized State Highway Bureau. "I believe in the democracy of the State Road Law, and with the help of God, I will stand by the faith that is in me," he declared.[45]

The governor won, and overwhelmingly. But it took a floor debate in the state House that lasted well into the night before a final vote was called. Gardner's supporters delivered some well-placed shots at Hill, whose countermeasure was called "a millionaire's bill." Within ninety days, Hill was out of a job. On the first of July, the state took over local roads, and the governor appointed a new State Highway Commission.[46]

"Mr. Hill is the only Durham man who ever invited a state legislature to march over his dead body and got right up again right after they done it," a Durham newspaper columnist wrote that July. "He's better off now and thought more of than the legislature ever will be, because all of the leaders which opposed him are trying to make up with him now and are offering him anything he wants. I never seen a politician yet that wasn't mindful of a man that's got fighting courage."[47]

On the night of July 30, 350 men and women filled the ballroom of the Washington Duke Hotel for a testimonial dinner in Hill's honor. Associate Justice W. J. Brogden was toastmaster. U.S. senator Cameron Morrison (the former governor had been appointed to the senate to fill the unexpired term of the late Lee Overman) made a presentation, as did many of those who had served with Hill on the highway commission. Even Governor Gardner sent his carefully worded regards and thanked Hill for his years of service. He called Hill "one of the most useful citizens North Carolina has ever produced." Delegations from the University of North Carolina and Duke University attended. It was a lighthearted affair, with Brogden regulating each speaker's time by changing a stoplight from green to red.[48]

With the humor and high praise came a surprise. Two of Durham's most distinguished African Americans, Charles C. Spaulding and W. G. Pearson, leaders of the North Carolina Mutual Life Insurance Company, appeared at the hotel ballroom door and asked to make a special presentation. Neither had been invited to the dinner, which was for whites only. Nonetheless, they handed Hill a gold-topped, inscribed walking cane to symbolize, they said, the many times the black community had leaned on Hill.

∾∾∾

John Sprunt Hill's battle with the governor and the legislature over state government reorganization did not end with a fine dinner and splendid speeches. He did not like to lose, and he remained convinced that the governor and a majority of the legislators were simply dead wrong. Just over sixty days after the testimonial dinner at the Washington Duke, Hill announced that he was a candidate for the state Senate. His campaign, he said, would provide a platform for him to restore democracy and fight the centralization of power in Raleigh. Before he got to Raleigh, however, he would need the conviction and determination that fueled his political engine to deal with serious problems at home.

CHAPTER 9

No Axe to Grind

WATTS HILL TOLD A STORY—as if it were true—about one of his father's earliest visits to Durham. Just as John Sprunt Hill stepped from the train, he saw a large man beating up a fellow about half his size. Without hesitating, Hill stripped off his coat and top hat and jumped in on the side of the smaller of the two. Though small himself, Hill's training as a boxer and his tenacious spirit more than evened the fight. The bully limped off to tend his bruises.

There was no question that John Sprunt Hill was a fighter, and the point of his son's story was that his father had been taking sides all his life. He had upset the status quo when he opened his bank and started offering interest to depositors. A few years later, he risked going to jail when he stood with the Durham City Council in the fight with the railroad. He had also stood his ground against the popular Julian Carr in a dispute over the design of Durham County's new courthouse. In later years, some Durham merchants were not happy when the Hills—father and son—helped establish a cooperative farm supply company that was sure to dilute their business. John Sprunt Hill had clearly shown that he was comfortable and confident even when he was a minority of one.

"He'd rather scrap than eat," Hill's friend and frequent competitor J. L. Morehead had declared to the packed chambers of the Durham City Council in 1925 when he tried in vain to get Hill to allow for a wider street beside the new Washington Duke Hotel. The following day, the *Herald* editorial page showed the lineup—John Sprunt Hill versus the merchants' association, the hotel investors, the preceding city council, the newspaper, and the "majority of practically every commercial and civic organization in the city." Hill must have liked that. It was one of the newspaper clippings that went into a scrapbook kept by his wife, who would tell friends: "Well, he's always been in a fight with somebody. And if there's no fight, he'll go out and develop one."[1]

John Sprunt Hill did not have to go looking for a fight as the new year opened in 1932. One was right at his doorstep. The wave of bank failures that began in the western part of the state finally threatened Durham. The delay in its arrival was due in part to the work at Duke University's new west campus, where at one point more construction was under way than anywhere else in the South. The Durham textile mills were not operating at full tilt as John Sprunt Hill had hoped they would after the Durham Hosiery Mills installed new machinery early in 1929, but workers were not on picket lines. Operating profits had suffered in 1930, but there were signs of recovery in 1931.[2]

The city's economic base of tobacco and cigarette manufacturing remained a source of dividends and income for the Hills. During the crazy months prior to the collapse of the stock market in October 1929, American Tobacco Company's share price had jumped from $172 to $232. Even after the crash, American shares were selling for more than $200. The company's profits in 1930 were such that American's president, George W. Hill (no relation to the Durham Hills), drew a salary of more than $1 million.

There had been some local business failures, of course. John Sprunt Hill had purchased the Forest Hills golf course and clubhouse at an auction sale after J. O. Cobb's development company went bankrupt. Local troubles were not serious enough, however, to deter Annie Watts Hill, who embarked in the summer of 1931 on yet another trip to Paris and London accompanied by her cousin, Nell Watts Clark. Hill remained at home, where he advised an associate "to tighten up the business and [take] more strenuous efforts at less expenses, until this depression blows over."[3] His letter suggested that the depression might be short-term, but he knew from the people who came calling at his office that conditions were more serious than he let on. Hill disappointed retired general A. L. Cox, who had returned to a hero's welcome in Raleigh after World War I, when he could not help with a loan of $4,700 that Cox needed to prevent foreclosure on his Raleigh home. Hill loaned a state senator $200, writing, "I hope [it] will be sufficient to meet your present needs." Even Governor O. Max Gardner's close friend, N. A. Townsend, whom the governor had appointed to the state bench, asked for a loan from Hill. By the middle of 1931, John

Sprunt Hill had about $100,000 in personal funds on loan to family and friends.[4]

Few days passed that Hill did not receive some plea from a public institution, a church, a family member, or a friend. For those closest to him, he examined their personal finances closely—like a "financial doctor," he told one—and then passed judgment. "These securities are entirely worthless and you may as well forget that you have them," he told one friend who was unable to tap into accounts put out of reach because of the bank failures. On occasion, he guaranteed loans for homeowners who faced foreclosure, and he once told a real estate agent in Charlotte not to press a tenant for the rent. "He is working at the Ford plant where they are only working one day in the week," Hill told the agent. "I suggest that you allow him to continue to live in the house during the winter months, and do the best you can toward collecting the rent without eviction."[5]

Toward the end of 1931, John Sprunt Hill was upbeat in public. Determination and perseverance would overcome hard times, he said. Just before Thanksgiving, he declared that Durham was a "bright spot on the nation's economic map." He told a reporter for the *Durham Morning Herald* that the depression was on the wane and business on an upward trend. Unemployment in the city was not nearly as bad, he said, as the "many pessimists and calamity howlers have one believe." Hill was quoted as saying: "If you'll weed out the chronic drunkards, the drug addicts and loafers—types of men who won't work either in times of plenty or depression—I'll venture to estimate there aren't more than 200 men in Durham who want work and can't get it. The people in Durham, through reading conditions in the newspapers of conditions in other cities where unemployment and the general economic situation are deplorable, have become infected also with the depression and a certain type of hysteria. They have unconsciously applied to Durham the condition that exits elsewhere. The facts don't justify such feeling." With the cooperation of other businesses, he opened an employment service to help the unemployed find jobs.

John Sprunt Hill retreated to a romantic vision of the way life used to be and encouraged those who could not find work to return to the farm. "There are plenty of houses vacant," he wrote. "They could be assisted through the winter, and next spring let them be provided with a hog, a cow, chickens and otherwise be shown how to raise plenty to eat instead of attempting to produce only cotton and tobacco."[6]

Yet it was becoming harder for even Hill to discount the signs of trouble. In October 1931, Durham city employees voluntarily took a pay cut to balance the budget and avoid layoffs. Retailers were struggling, and Hill had to extend additional credit to A. P. Tilley to keep his department store running through the Christmas shopping season.

That fall, in Roxboro, a run on the People's Bank had been narrowly averted by a public plea from the bank's president and an emergency delivery of cash from Raleigh. Then, immediately after Christmas, six eastern North Carolina banks failed. One was the Bank of Goldsboro, which had been considered one of the healthiest in the region.[7] By the end of the year, the number of bank failures in 1931 had climbed forty-eight.[8]

∽∽∽

So far, no Durham bank had disappointed depositors, and John Sprunt Hill was determined to keep it that way—if not to avoid serious personal losses, then as a matter of pride. He had given his pledge when he recruited stockholders for Home Savings Bank and Durham Loan and Trust Company, and his commitment to investors was as firm as any he had ever extended. He wrote a depositor in late December to say that his money was as safe in Home Savings Bank as it would have been in any place in the world: "I am only too glad to guarantee it personally, and in this connection I wish to say that, as everyone knows, I am worth several million dollars and have no liabilities."[9]

The first day of 1932 was a Friday, and Durham banks were closed for the holiday. By mutual agreement, they remained closed until Monday, January 4, foregoing their normal Saturday operations. The local newspaper attempted to boost confidence. The lead editorial, "Don't Rock The Boat," said, "A survey reveals that the normal course in business in this city has increased bank deposits over the withdrawals needed for first-of-the-year business."[10]

The editorial was but the first round in a weeklong public relations campaign designed to ease the fears of depositors and build confidence in local institutions. The campaign carried the unmistakable imprint of John Sprunt Hill, although he was never publicly identified as having organized it. On January 2, a full-page newspaper ad signed by eight Durham companies, including Home Security Life Insurance Company and Tilley's Department Store, applauded the strength and reliability of the local banks. The ad read: "Durham banks are sound to the core, as can be attested by federal and state examiners, and by the banking departments of both the state and national governments. They must meet every test of good banking and sound policies of conduct. They deserve the confidence of the people." The ad advised depositors to withdraw no more money than they needed and to leave savings accounts undisturbed when the banks opened on Monday. "The matter is in the hands of the citizens," it concluded. "They can make or break their neighbors and their city. Which will they do?"[11]

On Sunday, January 3, the *Morning Herald*'s news columns may have raised some spirits. City Manager Robert W. Flack reported that the city had never defaulted on an obligation and that the year-end bond payments had been mailed on time. Tombstone ads, which did not solicit business and only reported a bank's statement of condition, were scattered about the interior of the paper. The Fidelity, Durham's largest bank, reported more than $12 million in assets. First National, Julian Carr's old bank, reported more than $7 million. Durham Loan and Trust and Home Savings had combined assets of about $3 million. The paper said that these statements showed that Durham's banks were "sound."

A full-page ad, signed by Hill alone, promised a reward of $100 for information leading to the arrest and conviction of any person violating a state law against spreading rumors about the soundness of a bank. It would be more than a year before President Franklin D. Roosevelt warned in a speech that "the only thing we have to fear is fear itself," but Durham's test was approaching. Hill feared panic.

Depositors remained anxious Monday morning, and the bank lobbies filled with customers clutching their passbooks and demanding cash. There was no hysteria, but the anxiety of depositors rose as the Merchants Bank closed after it ran out of cash. By noon, however, the lobbies had cleared, and "there came a feeling of confidence that was easily discernable on the streets," according to Tuesday's *Herald*. "The banks were taking deposits, while the frightened had departed."[12]

John Sprunt Hill had arranged to have extra cash available for his banks. Working with New York institutions, he had personally guaranteed a credit line of $225,000 by putting up 2,000 shares of American Tobacco Company stock and $100,000 in North Carolina bonds. The reserves served their purpose, although not in exactly the way that federal regulators must have intended. Years later, Watts Hill said his father used the money as part of a grand charade. Selected customers were secretly given cash that they boldly presented at the teller's window as a demonstration of faith in the bank. The money was then handed out the back door to someone else, who made the same trip to the window.[13] At the end of the day, the ruse helped the Durham bankers report that they took in $750,000 more than they paid out. Hill's strategy seemed to be working.

John Sprunt Hill's role in orchestrating the Monday openings was never revealed, at least not in public. Those who were close to the situation appreciated his hand in the affairs, however. At the end of Monday, Watts Carr, a Durham architect and Annie Watts Hill's first cousin, wrote a friend about the excitement he had seen on Main Street. "The Merchants Bank failed to open this morning. There was a run on the First National this morning but they were small depositors. Working class. This did not last long and I think by tomorrow things will move along as usual. John Hill was worth more to Durham today than Duke University will ever be."[14]

❧❧❧

In the midst of this turmoil, readers of the morning papers were shocked to learn on January 7 that state treasurer Nathan O'Berry had died of a sudden heart attack the day before. O'Berry had been under intense strain simply trying to find enough money for the state to pay its bills and meet bond payments due before the end of the month. Some in Durham recommended John Sprunt Hill as O'Berry's replacement. "Those who suggested the Durham man," a *Herald* writer reported, "realized it would be difficult to get him to accept, but they argued that if Mr. Hill were offered the post in an emergency, and it could be impressed upon him that he was needed to help the state through these trying times, he might be induced to accept."[15]

The governor did not make the offer to Hill, but instead appointed thirty-seven-year-old John P. Stedman to complete O'Berry's term. Stedman stepped in at perhaps the most critical point in the state's financial history. North Carolina had $2 million in short-term bonds due within a matter of days. The treasury was virtually empty, and default was a very real possibility. Acting with dispatch, Gardner imposed drastic cuts on state spending and marshaled support from the state's leading textile executive, Charles A. Cannon, who, along with John W. Hanes and George Gordon Battle, former Tar Heels at New York banks, convinced Wall Street lenders to renew the bonds.

ଔଔଔ

John Sprunt Hill's challenge in Durham was far from over. A few days later, he dispatched his son to the Federal Reserve Bank in Charlotte to pick up another delivery of cash. Traveling with his butler, Tommy Stroud, Watts Hill was on the return leg of the trip with $750,000 in the trunk of his car when he had a flat tire on the edge of Pittsboro in Chatham County. Hill was armed with a pistol, and he really did not expect trouble, but to be stranded in the dark on the side of the road with a disabled car loaded with money was frightening. He and Stroud repaired the flat and continued on without trouble. One of Watts Hill Jr.'s early memories was the sight of the cash stacked high on the dining room table. Over the next few days, John Sprunt Hill used the money to purchase mortgages and other negotiable securities from Durham banks that were struggling for liquidity to meet customer demands.

By the middle of the month, the crisis appeared to be over. Even the depositors from the Merchants Bank had met and arranged to reopen for business. Then, First National Bank, Durham's oldest and second largest financial institution, failed.

The First National failure demonstrated just how close the campaign to instill confidence that had been managed by Hill and others had come to succeeding. In its show of strength on January 3, when the banks had published their statements in the Sunday newspaper, First National had reported assets of more than $7 million, citing a September 30, 1931, examination report. In fact, by January 4, steady withdrawals over the previous weeks had drained First National's assets to about $3.5 million.[16]

At a shareholders' meeting that took place three days after the closing of First National, John Sprunt Hill announced a reorganization of Durham Loan and Trust Company that strengthened its position. He and his wife put another $187,600 in cash into the bank to raise the invested capital to $500,000. At the same meeting, Hill turned the presidency of the bank over to his son, Watts. John Sprunt Hill became chairman of the board, and the name of the institution was changed to Durham Bank and Trust Company.

The newspaper blamed Durham citizens for the First National failure. The *Durham Morning Herald* said the rush to pull money out of the strug-

gling bank had simply been too much for it to bear. The truth was different. First National and Merchants had been crippled by bad management.
Weeks before First National failed, John Sprunt Hill had warned Gurney P.
Hood, Governor Gardner's new reform-minded state banking commissioner, that these two banks were weakened by "the general tendency of officers and directors to borrow as much money as possible from their own
institutions, either directly or indirectly."[17]

State and federal banking authorities filed criminal charges against the
officers of the two banks. Some were convicted and drew active sentences.
The president of First National was acquitted, while two lesser officers
were sent to prison despite testimony that the president had funneled
money for stock purchases into a company that existed only on paper. At
the close of the trials, U.S. District Judge Johnson J. Hayes issued a stern re-
buke from the bench. "It is small wonder if the directors of the bank were
speculating on the stock market with the depositors' money that their subordinates tampered with the bank's funds," he said.[18]

◌◌◌

John Sprunt Hill knew many of the bankers across the state whose businesses were in ruins. He had served on the State Highway Commission
with J. Elwood Cox of High Point, whose Commercial National Bank
closed. Hill himself lost his investment in the Commercial National Bank
in Raleigh. The largest and only national bank in the capital city, Commercial had handed out nearly $500,000 in one day during a run before it was
forced to close. Hill and other stockholders were liable for the losses, and
Hill's share was $20,000. The bank's receiver offered him time to make the
payments, but Hill sent the full amount immediately, saying he hoped to
forget his "unfortunate experience with this bank."[19] He tried to help the
Bank of Faison in Duplin County with personal loans, but it too failed.
The North Carolina Bank and Trust Company, headed by former governor
Angus McLean, survived for two more years and failed even after $8 mil-
lion was pumped into it by the Reconstruction Finance Corporation.[20] In
addition to his losses in the Raleigh bank, a real estate deal in Charlotte
cost Hill $75,000.[21] Tilley's Department Store, into which he had poured
thousands of dollars in an effort to compete against "foreign interests," was
forced to close. Watts Hill took on the job of liquidating its assets.

At the same time, however, the woeful economic conditions offered opportunities. In March 1932, Hill's insurance company, Home Security Life Insurance, took over Greensboro Life Insurance Company, a $5 million firm that had fallen victim to the bank failures.

⮜⮜⮜

As winter gave way to spring in 1932, the world looked like a dangerous place. John Sprunt Hill had never seen such trouble in his beloved North Carolina, across the nation, or around the world. In Europe, a rising political leader in Germany declared that democracy was "doomed" in a speech to his countrymen, who had been economically driven to their knees by inflation and unemployment. Speaking to a hundred thousand people gathered at an outdoor rally, Adolf Hitler declared that voters in elections two days hence should "remove the rule of democracy and Marxism and its vassals from Germany, and restore a regime of discipline, national conscience, honor and power."[22]

In the United States, the newspapers were full of stories of strike violence. In March, four strikers were killed when hired police broke up a gathering of workers at the Ford Motor Company plant outside of Detroit. By the summer, about fifteen thousand workers around High Point, North Carolina, had shut down 150 textile mills and formed a strike organization. War veterans had descended on Washington to demand that Congress pay bonuses that had been promised but were not yet due. On the same day that the Durham newspaper reported Hitler's threatening speech, the president of the United States ordered troops to clear bonus marchers out of the makeshift shelters they had built on the Washington Mall.

Personal financial ruin was becoming commonplace. Conditions were acute across the state. Governor Gardner told a personal friend, "I have men offering to work for $2.50 a day who two years ago were worth a quarter of a million dollars, and a man who two years ago was president of one of the biggest banks now operating in the state, begged me for a $150-a-month job."[23] By the end of 1932, another twenty-seven banks would fail.

In addition, public violence and crime seemed to be out of control. Chicago gangster Al Capone had been sent to prison in the fall of 1931, but his absence had simply opened the city to public gun battles between warring factions. Police in New Jersey still did not know what had happened to Charles Lindbergh's infant son, who had been snatched from his bedroom in the middle of the night.

The kidnapping produced a spate of copycat abductions, some of them close to home. As a measure of caution, Watts Hill installed iron bars on the windows of the rooms of Harwood Hall where five-year-old Watts Jr. and his sister Dudley, who was then about two (she was born February 17, 1929), slept and played. The Hills' second son, John Sprunt Hill II, arrived at the height of these troubled days on April 30, 1932.

Just weeks after the banking crisis of January 1932, John Sprunt Hill told a friend that all his time was "taken in an effort to rescue people from the hands of receivers and collectors." That was the order of things, however, and he argued that "individual initiative and volunteer cooperation rather than paternalism and Socialism" would rescue the down-and-out.[24]

∽∽∽

If John Sprunt Hill had known he would be so preoccupied with financial matters, he might not have so boldly declared his intentions the year before to run for public office. He held true to his commitment, however, and launched his campaign for the state Senate about six weeks before the spring primary elections.

John Sprunt Hill had never displayed a hint of interest in running for state office prior to his battle with Governor Gardner. Local folks in Chatham County had urged him to run for governor in 1924, but he never encouraged such talk. Rather, Hill was one of those men that candidates counted on to support the local Democratic ticket. He encouraged gubernatorial prospects and delivered rousing patriotic speeches at the party's county conventions. Important members of the state political establishment knew him well; three governors had allowed him to keep his seat on the State Highway Commission.

This time, John Sprunt Hill was determined to go to Raleigh and return the state to sanity and its proper order. He believed Governor Gardner's consolidation of state departments was "one of the most dangerous principles known to man," he later wrote. "The history of consolidation shows a long story of selfishness, bureaucracy, dishonesty and human and financial wreckage. In all probability the greatest service that I have rendered to my State and to my family and to the institutions which I represent has been my eternal warfare upon consolidations."[25] "Bloodshed and rebellion" would be the result of the loss of the "people's right to local self government," Hill had declared at a hearing in Raleigh on Gardner's program.[26]

Hill faced no serious opposition in his first campaign. Democrats in the three other counties in the district—Orange, Alamance, and Caswell—did not field a candidate, since it was Durham's turn to hold the seat under a so-called gentleman's agreement. Certainly no one in Durham was going to oppose him.

It was a gentleman's campaign as well. At age sixty-three, the dignified John Sprunt Hill was not inclined to ask people for anything, including their vote. His campaign literature—a few posters and cards—described him as a "life-long Democrat" and promised "a square deal for a man of small means." Hill refused to declare his position on issues and took offense when he was asked to do so at public forums. He told voters he would make up his mind after he heard the debate on the floor of the Senate. Voters would just have to take him as he was and depend on his judgment.

For all practical purposes, Hill won election with his nomination in the June primary. Republicans did not stand a chance in the fall general election. For Hill, it had been an easy stroll to the General Assembly and the public platform that he would use for the next six years to expound on virtually anything and everything related to government, business, and public morals.

⁊⁊⁊

The state's biennial legislative session opened the first week of January in 1933. More than two-thirds of the members were newcomers like Hill, but few had his connections in state government. Hill took his oath in the same chamber where two of his brothers had served more than a half century earlier. The Senate membership included Representative Rufus A. Doughton of Sparta, a former lieutenant governor who served his first legislative term in 1887, when Hill was only eight years old. Among the forty-nine returning members were Robert M. Hanes of Winston-Salem, the head of Wachovia Bank and Trust Company, who was moving to the Senate after three terms in the house, and R. Gregg Cherry, an ambitious young representative from Gaston County who would later be elected governor. Of the fifty members of the Senate, only five had more seniority than Hill, so a committee chairmanship was assured. Lieutenant Governor A. H. "Sandy" Graham of Orange County put Hill in charge of the Committee on Banks and Currency, which was not among the long list of preferences he had submitted prior to the session.

Hill ignored the fine print in the Senate protocol that said a freshman should move slowly into the legislative process. The session was just a few days old when Hill pushed through a resolution requiring cities and counties that had defaulted on their public bonds to report their financial condition to the state. A howl arose in the provinces from local officials who were embarrassed enough about their situation without having to post it publicly in Raleigh. A few days later, Hill's picture was on the front page of the *News and Observer* with an account of the upbraiding he had given state officials who were asking for budget increases. Hill pointedly observed that the state-run mental hospital for African Americans in Goldsboro was operating on a per-patient cost of less than twenty-six cents a day and making a profit on its farm, while the farms at other state institutions were losing money and daily expenses were higher. Perhaps, Hill said, the record of the Goldsboro superintendent qualified him as the state's real efficiency expert; this comment was clearly a dig at the Brookings Institution study of efficiency in state government.[27]

Hill made it clear with his vigorous start that he was in Raleigh to "fix" things, and the sooner the better. "I had an idea that I could come down here and settle this thing right off the bat," he told a newspaper reporter near the end of his first legislative session. "Like other men who had not served in a legislature, I had lots of ideas I thought ought to be put right over. I had got up some facts and figures and I proposed to legislate."[28]

North Carolina voters had also elected a new governor in 1932. He was John Christoph Blucher Ehringhaus, whose friends called him Blucher (pronounced "Booker"). He was from Elizabeth City in the northeastern part of the state, where his family had lived since colonial days. Even though Ehringhaus had defended the Gardner administration during his campaign, he came from the conservative wing of the party that was deeply rooted in the state's bourbon tradition of land and power and was generally resistant to reform. There appeared to be nothing about Ehringhaus to cause Hill concern.

Under normal conditions, Ehringhaus might have been able to defend the virtues of limited government. The frightful condition of the state's finances and the struggle for simple economic survival were changing everything, however, from politics to business to social welfare. When Ehringhaus took office, the total state indebtedness of $532 million was equal to about 10 percent of the state's entire wealth. (Thanks to Hill, everyone in the state now knew that more than half of that debt was due to a spending spree by local governments.) Governor Gardner had been forced to borrow $7 million just to balance the budget for the current fiscal year; Ehringhaus was starting off with a bare-bones budget that was $12 million in the hole. There was little question that new taxes would be necessary if the government of North Carolina was to remain a going concern.

Like nearly every other member from out of town, John Sprunt Hill took up residence at the Sir Walter, the city's newest hotel. It was situated on Fayetteville Street, just two blocks north of Raleigh's new Memorial Auditorium, where Ehringhaus and other elected members of the council of state had been inaugurated. The hotel's wide, open lobby was furnished with large overstuffed leather chairs and sofas, ample ashtrays and cuspidors, and a surplus of political talk. Members often sat around until the late hours when the early edition of the *News and Observer* arrived, and then they ambled off to bed. Legislation was often conceived in the lobby of the Sir Walter to be born four blocks north in the Capitol.

Hill's housing arrangements were more spacious than those of most of his colleagues. He took adjoining rooms and used one as his personal apartment, equipping the other as an office for himself and his two assistants, whose salaries of $15 a week he paid out of his own pocket. It was quite an extravagance at the time. Even the legislative committees had to borrow meeting rooms on the upper floor of the state Revenue Building, which every two years was cleared for legislative work. Hill's two secretaries, Stanley S. Wohl and F. L. Morris, kept him supplied with facts and information that eventually became part of an extensive personal library of legislative research. The three often worked well into the night, munching on apples as they prepared for the next day's session.[29] It would be another fifty years before similar support staff were available to legislators at state expense.

∽∽∽

As the legislature opened in 1933, Durham was at rock bottom. One out of five families was on relief, and this time John Sprunt Hill said nothing about slackers, loafers, and drunkards. He tried not to add to the burden of public assistance by keeping his household staff and other personal retainers on the payroll, although at reduced wages. When he cut the pay of his caretaker at his Biltmore Forest House in Asheville from $125 to $100 a month, he reminded him that there were farm laborers in Durham County making only $1.00 a day. "Old General Depression still has us by the neck in this part of the country," he wrote one of his cousins in Canada, "but we are putting up an awful fight to beat him down, and little by little it looks like we are commencing to win out in the struggle."[30]

Durham banks had rebounded after the runs of 1932. As a measure of faith in the future, Durham's newest bank, Depositors National Bank, had risen from the ashes of First National and opened for business in January 1933 with a band playing "Happy Days Are Here Again." A clearinghouse for Durham banks had also been organized to coordinate transfers of paper.

Elsewhere in the state, however, many banks struggled still. Immediately after his inauguration on March 4, President Roosevelt declared a bank holiday in order to bring some order to the growing chaos. His order affected only national banks, but around the nation, state legislatures were following the president's order and closing state-chartered banks.

North Carolina held out to the very end. Governor Ehringhaus was still in Washington for Roosevelt's inauguration when North Carolina bankers filled the state Senate chamber for a meeting on Sunday, March 5. Ehringhaus prepared a statement in which he declared that there would be no moratorium in North Carolina, but state banking commissioner Hood was alarmed. He told the governor that if North Carolina did not follow the rest of the country, local banks would be drained of cash as out-of-staters rushed in to do business. He urged the governor to reconsider, and his concern was echoed by nearly every banker who rose to speak that afternoon.

Only one man opposed the idea. John Sprunt Hill was defiant in the face of the panic of his colleagues. He told the bankers that he would "'pay out every penny' of his own money and property, and that of his wife, son, and daughters, before he would ever restrict the withdrawals of a single depositor in any of his banks." Hill declared that in his thirty years of banking, he "had never known North Carolina banks to be in better condition."[31]

North Carolina legislators ignored Hill's warning and extended Roosevelt's order to cover state banks. Hill's banks, along with all the others, began a forced holiday on Monday. To underscore his own confidence, Hill remained in Raleigh for the three days of the bank holiday. He issued a statement expressing confidence in Durham banks, which he said had twice as much money on hand as they had a year before. "We have always come out of similar financial troubles and I am confident that in a few weeks we will emerge on a sounder moral and financial basis than has existed for the past few years," he told the Durham newspaper. "It is now up to us to face the situation calmly but firmly and be prepared to mobilize all of the moral and material forces of our city and county in order that we may prevent hunger, want and suffering and guarantee that business life in our city will be maintained."[32]

Hill claimed he did not even bother to call his son or others in his Durham office during the holiday. All of Durham's banks reopened promptly after three days with certification of their good health from the state examiners. But a week after the holiday began, 127 banks across the state—over half the total number—had not reopened. After two weeks, seventy of the state's counties still lacked adequate banking facilities.[33]

Hill thrived on the legislative give and take. Early in the session, he told his colleagues he would not oppose any bill unless he had an alternative plan in his pocket, a declaration that seemed to make his pen all the more prolific. When the senators got to the floor on days of debate on bills in which Hill had an interest, they often found their desks covered with charts and reports from Hill's office. Before the session was over, Hill and his assistants had prepared a local government finance bill, a lengthy beer bill, a thirty-six-page utility bill, an eight-month school bill, two measures relating to farming, and lesser bills, "all of which he [threatened] to introduce unless amendments satisfactory to him were adopted."[34]

Due to his age and his personal habits, Hill was something of a transition member. With his starched wing collars, his courtly demeanor, and his Old South traditions, he appeared to be a throwback to the legislative class of his brothers. Yet no member was more attentive or vocal on current affairs, according to veteran newsman Wade Lucas. Hill never missed the meeting of a committee at which one of his bills was being considered, and his favorite opening statement—"I have no axe to grind and I seek no office"—became a familiar refrain. In order to establish his credibility on a bill, he often prefaced his remarks by recounting his years of experience in the enterprise affected by it. As Hill had been a teacher, lawyer, soldier, banker, farmer, real estate developer, road builder, hotel owner, golfer, financier, textile executive, and city official, there seemed to be no limit to the number of topics he could discuss. One of Hill's colleagues, William Henry Joyner of Garysburg, noted Hill's repeated references to his experience and at the close of the session told magazine publisher Carl Goerch, "I've been keeping careful tab on what Mr. Hill has had to say during this session, and according to his own calculation he must be more than 300 years old."[35]

Even at the risk of his own reputation for dignity and decorum, Hill could not resist involving himself in a bit of legislative puffery, something that always colored legislative sessions. At one point, Hill defended the selection of the chickadee as the official state bird. During the course of the debate on the bill, Hill "hunched his venerable shoulders and sang out loud & clear, 'chickadee, chickadee, chickadee, dee, dee.'" The bill passed, but as *Time* magazine observed: "Then it was the state's turn to have fun. The chickadee is a member of the titmouse family. Editors [who] remembered 'little tommy titmouse' who 'lived in a little house' began to refer to the 'tomtit legislature.'"[36] Later, another bill was introduced, and quickly and quietly, without a voice of opposition, the legislature dethroned the chickadee. Some years later, the cardinal was named the state bird.

Liquor and taxes were the issues that most raised the temperature of the members in 1933. Wrangling over the end of Prohibition and the adoption of sales taxes extended the life of the session to 132 days. It was not the longest session on record (that was in 1931), but it wearied legislators who had not planned on being in Raleigh beyond the first of April. Wets were successful in winning approval for the sale of 3.2 beer in the state, but drys stifled approval of anything stronger and girded for a referendum in the fall on whether to call a constitutional convention to end Prohibition.

The question of how to find new sources of state revenue was more complicated. Ehringhaus had been greeted upon his arrival in Raleigh with a report from a tax study commission that argued against a state sales tax. He said nothing about sales taxes in his inaugural address, but a month later he declared himself in support of such a measure. It was the only way to keep the state's schools open, he said. Hill was one of the first members of the legislature to endorse the sales tax, and during the next several weeks he and his aides prepared no less than five different tax plans, complete with an accounting of potential revenue from each county. At one point an observer wrote, "If oratory could have balanced the budget of the state without resort to a sales tax, Senator T. L. Kirkpatrick [an ally of Hill from the Good Roads Association days] together with the aid of Senator John Sprunt Hill, of Durham, and a number of others, would have come very near accomplishing that feat."[37] The final bill, which imposed a 3 percent tax, passed on the eve of the legislature's adjournment. It included an exemption that Hill wrote to cover the purchase of up to $1,200 worth of basic food items such as meat, flour, and other staples. Merchants were required to keep track of individual shoppers' purchases.

Hill's performance in the session increased his visibility in state politics. Talk of his running for governor in 1936 surfaced immediately after the session ended, but Hill dismissed the idea in a letter to John A. Park, editor of the *Raleigh Times*. "Just watching the game from the side lines is all the interest that I expect to take in the present struggle for political control in the Old North State," Hill told Park.[38] He remained involved in politics, however, and in the months following the end of the session he supported the cost of printing a brochure defending the state's new sales tax and the benefits it brought to public schools.[39]

∾∾∾

During the legislative session, Hill was not as detached from his business affairs in Durham as he professed to be. At the height of the banking crisis in March, he was making plans to buy the Washington Duke Hotel, which he had been trying to save from bankruptcy for nearly a year. The hotel had never been as profitable as investors had hoped, and as Hill's friends and neighbors became desperate for cash he purchased their hotel bonds, sometimes at a discount of 40 percent. When he offered to buy the hotel in the spring of 1932, he held $447,000 of first mortgage bonds. He subsequently withdrew the offer as business continued to decline. By the summer, the hotel corporation was in the hands of a receiver. Revenue from rooms and meals was not even sufficient to meet its interest payments.

The Atlanta investors who had put up half of the cash needed for construction in 1925 were pushing for a public sale of the business. In March 1933, Homeland Investment Company, a company Hill had formed the year before, submitted the high bid for the property at $149,000. The Atlanta investors were unhappy with the results of what they thought was a fire sale, and they appealed to U.S. District Judge I. M. Meekins, who ordered a new sale. Four months later, Homeland Investment outbid Meyers Hotels of Atlanta with an offer of $275,000. By that time, John Sprunt Hill had acquired another $315,000 of first mortgage bonds.

Nothing encouraged John Sprunt Hill to open his checkbook faster than pride in his institutions and in his city. In pursuing his purchase of the hotel, he disdainfully referred to the Georgia bondholders as the "foreign" interests in his letters to Judge Meekins. He told the judge that Durham people did not need advice from Atlanta attorneys on how to revive the hotel. He took the same approach when the city's YMCA was faced with closure because it was in such disrepair that it needed $11,000 for basic improvements. Hill told a group of civic boosters at a meeting: "When the ship is sinking it is time to get out on deck and fight. Our city cannot afford to see this social enterprise bog down. Durham has never gone down in defeat and it will not go down now." He pledged $500 to the campaign, and a month later it had collected more than the required amount.[40]

There was more than money at stake for Hill. The failure of investments in which he had an interest was personally embarrassing. From time to time over the years, he and his wife had fulfilled their pledges to various institutions and charities by giving stocks and bonds rather than cash. When these investments failed to pay dividends, the gifts lost their value. Rather than leave favored schools like Union Theological Seminary in Richmond or the University of North Carolina in a lurch, Hill either sent a check to cover the amount that was due or substituted better securities for those in default.

◌◌◌

Nothing underscored Hill's independence as a legislator—and the pleasure he got from serving his first term in the General Assembly—more than his decision, after serving one term, to unilaterally declare null and void the gentleman's agreement that called for Durham County to pass the district's seat on to a candidate from Orange County. Two months before the 1934 primary elections, Hill announced that he believed the rotation agreement was unfair to Durham. He declared he would run for a second term. Hill complained that Durham County had three times the population of Orange, yet both were given equal standing in the seat rotation. Why, Hill asked, should Durham be penalized? He got a ruling from the state attorney general's office that said the agreement did not prevent him from running for reelection. With Durham County Democrats solidly behind him, Hill ignored the protests from adjoining counties and paid his filing fee.

Orange County fielded a candidate, and opposition also arose from Alamance and Caswell, the other two counties that counted on the rotation to put a member in the chamber. Hill depended on Durham's overwhelming numbers and campaigned as the champion of justice. "My candidacy for the State Senate is prompted entirely by my desire to prevent an unlawful and unjust political discrimination against Durham people," he told the Durham Voters League. Merchants around the state tried to gain commitments from legislative candidates to repeal the sales tax, but Hill would not bend. When the votes were counted, however, Durham's majority was more than enough to assure his renomination.

Hill was easily reelected in the general election despite an attempt by organized labor to muster votes against him. Two months before the election, thousands of Durham workers had joined in the national strike against textile mills. Durham mills were idle for nearly three weeks before negotiations returned workers to their jobs. In Durham, the walkouts were peaceful and mostly symbolic. Nothing changed in the Durham mills after the strike, and stirrings in the fall elections made no difference in the outcomes of local races.

❧❧❧

When John Sprunt Hill arrived in Raleigh in January 1935 for the opening of the General Assembly, the election had changed neither the issues nor the membership. Antitax organizations—most of them led by local merchants—were determined to repeal the sales tax. Hope was dim, however, as legislators knew of few other ways to raise the money to maintain basic services and give state employees a raise, as Ehringhaus planned to do. Prohibitionists were feeling particularly strong, having defeated a statewide referendum in the fall of 1933 that would have added North Carolina to the ranks of states calling for elimination of national Prohibition. (North Carolina remained dry after the repeal in 1933 of the Eighteenth Amendment to the U.S. Constitution.)

The session was barely two weeks old when a Durham newspaper reported that an unnamed legislator described as a "life-long dry" had prepared the draft of a bill to repeal the Turlington Act of 1909, the law that had outlawed liquor sales in North Carolina a full ten years before national Prohibition took effect. It was another two weeks before Hill was identified in print as the author of the bill after he began circulating copies to other members. Privately, Hill claimed that forty members of the Senate were in favor of his bill, but when he introduced it on February 8 he was the sole sponsor.

Hill put himself in the center of the biggest storm of the session. It was going to be a dandy legislative fight, and he seemed perfectly content with his position. Politically, he was safe. The sentiments in Durham County—measured by the vote in the 1933 referendum on the repeal of national Prohibition—showed he was with the people. Durham had been the only one of the state's larger counties to vote for repeal, though the winning margin was only ten votes. And his credentials with the Prohibition forces were impeccable. He had been a steady supporter of prohibitionists' cause ever since he had marched in the Durham antisaloon parades singing "Onward, Christian Soldiers" with his father-in-law. In addition, he was a practicing Presbyterian with a checkbook full of stubs to validate his regular monthly contributions to the state Anti-Saloon League.[41]

North Carolina had gained a reputation as a state that voted dry but lived wet. Until the 3.2 beer bill was passed in 1934, state law prohibited the transportation and sale of spirits of any kind for any reason, even medicinal spirits. As a result, the bootleggers' trade flourished, particularly in the border counties. Hill's personal accommodation of alcohol was a reflection of the state's dual system of dealing with it. Newsmen wrote that he was a "teetotaler," and Hill described himself as "a lifelong prohibitionist, both by precept and by example."[42] But in the privacy of Hill House and with very close friends, Hill enjoyed his bourbon with a little touch of honey.

Even before the days of national Prohibition, liquor sales had been curtailed in Durham, forcing John Sprunt Hill to import his supplies from a distributor in Baltimore. One shipment included six quarts of rye whiskey, four quarts of King William Scotch, four quarts of apple brandy, four quarts of peach brandy, two quarts of Jamaica rum, two quarts of Saint Julian claret, and a dozen bottles of domestic champagne. "You will find that for several years I have had an account with your house," he wrote the Acker, Merrall, and Condit Company.[43] Annie Watts Hill's cousin, Watts Carr Jr., recalled that when he was a boy and Hill visited his father at their home in Forest Hills, the old man could always be counted on for a good story after he had a drink or two. "He would entertain you gloriously and tell you the wildest tales of his days in New York."[44]

Durham Recorders Court judge J. R. Patton probably suspected Hill's private habits—or knew of them—when he began his campaign to expose the hypocrisy of the state's liquor laws. In the months leading up to the opening of the 1935 legislative session, Patton instructed juries hearing cases against bootleggers to acquit the defendants in his court.[45] A week before election day, Patton called the liquor laws "futile," and in the case of

Leroy A. Crotts he said, "If the roll were called as to who had possessed whiskey during the past 12 months, we would be here a long time listening to names. In cases of this sort, my judgment advises me to order a fine paid and the proceeds to go to the school fund." A week before Hill introduced his bill, Patton accused the liquor laws of being class legislation. "People pounce down on people like this, like a buzzard on a carcass," Patton told a jury, pointing to an accused bootlegger, "but if you take them over on Morehead Hill you couldn't get into a house with a machine gun, although they know and you know and I know that there is plenty of whiskey over there."[46] Patton's passion was clear, but his needling of Morehead Hill residents may also have been his response to John Sprunt Hill's efforts in the 1933 session to cut Patton's salary and that of the prosecuting attorney after they failed to take voluntary pay cuts along with other city employees.

A bill providing for outright repeal of the Turlington Act was introduced a few days before Hill released his proposed legislation. The first bill would have opened the state to liquor sales in commercial stores, while Hill's bill proposed to establish a tightly regulated system in which legal sales would be permitted only in state-operated stores. He estimated that the state stores would produce about $3.6 million a year in revenue for the state.

The terms of Hill's bill closely followed his personal attitudes about alcohol. He too disliked the hypocrisy that offended Judge Patton; Prohibition that did not prohibit was an affront to his sense of honor, as well as to the law. Based on his own investigation, he was convinced that bootleggers were selling up to three thousand gallons of illegal liquor in Durham County each week. "As I looked about me in this county and throughout this state," Hill later explained, "I observed that the prohibition law was thoroughly discredited in the eyes of the great majority of our people, and there had sprung up in our midst a widespread, unlawful traffic in liquor with its attendant debauchery."[47] "My opinion is that legalized sale of liquor, properly controlled by the state, would bring about a big improvement in existing conditions," he told the *State*'s Carl Goerch at the time he prepared his bill. He may also have tired of complaints from the out-of-state guests he saw at Pinehurst who questioned North Carolina's curious condition, shared at the time only by Kansas.

The state's dry forces, backed by leaders of every Christian denomination, rose up to oppose the bills. This time, the drys recruited former governor and senator Cameron Morrison to lead their campaign. Five years earlier, Morrison had campaigned as a prohibitionist when he lost his seat in the U.S. Senate to Asheville's Robert "Our Bob" Reynolds, who had campaigned for repeal.

The February 20 hearing on Hill's bill lasted more than three hours. The committee room was packed, and Morrison was at his oratorical best. At the conclusion of his prepared remarks, he promised retribution for any legislator who dared vote wet: "We drys are going to organize, we are going to elect dry sheriffs, dry judges, dry solicitors, dry congressmen, dry senators and dry governors." He told the crowd, "I don't know which I'm prouder of—being elected governor and appointed senator or being defeated because I refused to surrender my principles."[48]

Hill got the last word. He responded in measured phrases, using legal arguments and his own Bible quotations to distinguish between prohibition and temperance:

> We liberal drys are determined to hold to this distinction, and we vigorously oppose making adherence to the Turlington Act a test of our religious faith, or the final word in methods for the promotion of temperance. We are left here in North Carolina with legal liquor [from adjoining states] on all sides, trying to convince ourselves that we have prohibition, when in fact we know that we have an abundance of liquor with no control or money to enforce either prohibition or control. How much longer will you shut your eyes to the facts and conditions and, like ostriches with beautiful clerical plumes, hide your heads in the sands when danger appears imminent?[49]

When asked about Morrison's bluster, Hill said, "By the way, you know Cam is my stepfather-in-law, once removed, hence I do not get mad with him when he turns loose some of his hot shots. I just make allowances for him and go on about my business of trying to do something that will improve the present bad conditions in regard to liquor and make the cause of temperance attractive to young people."[50]

Mail began to pile up at Hill's hotel suite. Writers were vicious in their personal attacks. "If this bill is enacted into law," wrote one angry voter, "I hope the curse of God will rest on you and every other legislator who votes for the measure." An Asheville writer said, "You are evidently a very immoral man. I do not know you personally but I am convinced that only a drunkard and a degenerate would sponsor such a piece of legislation." It was said that Hill received more mail for a few weeks than any other member of the legislature.[51]

Hill answered many of the letters he received. He wrote the Reverend Gilbreath L. Kerr of Salisbury a lengthy and coolly reasoned response to what had been Kerr's third letter "wishing some calamity" upon him for introducing the bill. He said he had been a lifelong dry but had been persuaded to introduce the bill because he was convinced that outright prohibition "was more a breeder of crime, lying and hypocrisy than it was a method for controlling the use of liquor." Hill encouraged Kerr to look at his hometown of Salisbury, where "on election day, hundreds of people boasted of their 'political smartness in drinking wet and voting dry,' and big, high-powered bootlegger cars hauling dry voters to the polls were very much in evidence." Elsewhere, Hill reported, it was commonly known that dry forces cooperated with bootleggers to influence the outcome of the question of repeal. Hill concluded: "Now, my dear sir, instead of bothering yourself further about my welfare, do a little investigating on your own account and decide for yourself which plan will better safeguard the morals of your own community."[52]

Hill suffered through the hate mail. "These people don't mean any harm," he told Goerch.[53] He had a breaking point, however, which he reached on the day of the vote on his bill in the Senate. It was scheduled to be the first order of business after the session's opening prayer. The Reverend H. L. Arnold from Johnson Memorial Baptist Church began well enough, asking for God's guidance of the members. Then he said: "Hear, oh ye men of this legislature! God forbid that you should sell the character of our boys and girls for revenue, or debauch their souls by forcing intoxicants upon them. By such an act ye shall hear added hundreds of helpless babes crying in their mothers' arms for good, and behold emaciated children in tattered clothing while mothers wail under the drunken tyrant's hand."

Goerch was watching Hill as the minister prayed. He later wrote that Hill first turned pale, then his face became flushed. "His hands shook with nervous tension. It was plain to see that he was very much agitated." As soon as the preacher said his amen, Hill was on his feet. "Mr. President, I resent this," he said. "I resent it as deeply as anything that has ever happened in my life, and I cannot stand here and permit this Senate to be humiliated by a political speech offered under the guise of a prayer. I move you, sir, that it be recalled and stricken from the records." Lieutenant Governor Graham was momentarily dumbfounded. He called Hill out of order, and Hill looked back with surprise. "That prayer," Graham then said, "cannot be recalled; it probably is halfway to Heaven by now." After a moment of dead silence, the members broke into laughter, Hill included.[54]

In mid-April, Goerch had predicted that the Hill bill was dead. And so it was, along with others. After considerable buildup, it failed to pass the Senate by a vote of twenty-six to twenty-three. The legislative session appeared to be ready to close in May without any changes having been made to the liquor laws when a creative legislator from Wilmington introduced a local bill that exempted his county from the Turlington Act. Another bill followed for Pasquotank County, and then there were fifteen more, including one to exempt two municipalities, Southern Pines and Pinehurst. They all passed, but without Hill's vote. Elections were held within thirty days of adjournment, and in the first week of June, the first legal liquor store in North Carolina in more than twenty-five years opened in Wilson.

◌◌◌

If it was Gardner's reorganization of state government that had moved Hill to run for the Senate in 1932, then it was the same issue that kept him there, not the perennial fights over liquor and taxes. Hill and Kirkpatrick failed in their attempts to return to the good old days of district control of state highways. Hill also lost his battles to derail changes in the operation of other state departments. The best he could do was to try to stem the spending impulses of state government department heads, whom he claimed simply came back year after year looking for more and more money to improve their positions.

The highway reorganization was frustrating enough for Hill. What Gardner's program did to the University of North Carolina was even worse. As a trustee, Hill was among a number of campus partisans who in 1931 had opposed the governor's legislation to consolidate under one administration the three campuses located in Chapel Hill, Raleigh, and Greensboro. The governor argued that it was time to end the legislative logrolling for higher and higher appropriations at the three campuses, the result of which was duplication and confusion. For example, the School of Commerce at Chapel Hill and the School of Science and Business at Raleigh offered the same subjects at different tuition rates. Legislators in the mid-1920s were bothered that the Chapel Hill trustees had constructed a dormitory for women when the state's institution for educating women was clearly in Greensboro.

Hill mounted his initial opposition to consolidation on general principle. The proposed merger of the campuses appeared to be one that would maintain Chapel Hill as the leading institution, with the other two campuses feeding students to that campus for graduate study. From the outset, State College's president, E. C. Brooks, had opposed Gardner's bill for fear that his campus would be swallowed by Chapel Hill at the very time that State was enjoying its greatest expansion. The initial study of consolidation confirmed the fears of Brooks and other State supporters. A subsequent proposal, however, included plans in which State alumni saw an opportunity for their campus to become the place where engineers would be trained, thereby raising its stature in the academic community.

Hill was one of the 102 members of the new Board of Trustees for the consolidated university when it was created. At the board's first meeting, he was elected to the twelve-member executive committee, which was given extraordinary powers to make decisions affecting the three campuses. Only one other board member, Laura Cone of Greensboro, received more votes than Hill, and the two were the only members elected by a majority. The other carryover members included federal appeals court judge John J. Parker of Charlotte, newspaper publisher Josephus Daniels, the *Progressive Farmer*'s Clarence Poe, Haywood Parker of Asheville, and state insurance commissioner Charles W. Gold. Hill, John J. Parker, and Daniels were given eight-year terms, the longest possible.

The real battle lines on reorganization were drawn over whether State's engineering school would be closed and merged into the Chapel Hill program. Settlement of this question was delayed until virtually everything else had been arranged. In December 1934, Hill sounded the alarm for Chapel Hill alumni when he told a meeting of the Durham alumni that "enemies of the university [were] now plotting the removal of the engineering school" despite early recommendations to the contrary.[55]

Indeed, a special committee on engineering had voted six to five in September 1934 to concentrate engineering studies at State, but action on the committee's recommendation was postponed until June 1935, when President Graham was scheduled to make a report to the trustees. Graham's final plan adopted the report of the committee. When the executive committee met on June 5, Hill was ready with a counterproposal; he urged the trustees to retain the two schools. Professional engineers would earn degrees from Chapel Hill, while the State program would emphasize "practical and vocational training," he argued. In addition, State would retain its business school, which would offer courses to support the schools of Engineering, Agriculture, and Technology. The executive committee rejected Hill's plan, but he was given a chance to present it to the full board at its meeting six days later. With Daniels, John J. Parker, and others solidly behind Graham, the president's program was adopted overwhelmingly by a vote of fifty-eight to eleven.

Hill was not through. He privately told friends that Graham had been forced to sacrifice the engineering school to appease "the noisy opposition of some of the State alumni and a few important people in Raleigh."[56] By the fall, however, he was busy preparing for a rehearing of the proposed changes.

Hill threw himself into the campaign against the move of the engineering school to State with more fervor than he had for his own bid for reelection to the state Senate. In January 1936, he published a twenty-four-page pamphlet in which he set out detailed and specific reasons for his opposition. Moving the school to Raleigh would be expensive, he argued, and it would keep State from doing its primary job, which he considered to be turning out better-trained farmers and technicians for the state's textile mills. In letters to sympathetic alumni, he argued that the past few years had been a time of erosion of the power of the Board of Trustees and that Chapel Hill was threatened with becoming "an institution of secondary influence." Hill continued: "This is exactly what a small group of cunning politicians have planned from the beginning, and why some of the authorities at Chapel Hill will continue to allow themselves to be led around by the nose by this small group is a mystery to me."[57]

Hill argued that the changes cut to the heart of a man's relationship with his alma mater: "When a boy goes to College he is no transient. He enlists for life. He is no denatured, dehumanized, mollycoddle without loyalties, but becomes a red-blooded partisan, and for the rest of his life, after leaving College, he takes a day off every now and then and goes back to his beloved Alma Mater and lives over his old college days."[58]

There was no questioning Hill's loyalty or allegiance to Chapel Hill. He was more than a "red-blooded partisan" who gave a day or two a year. He counted his family's service on the university's Board of Trustees not in years, but in decades. Few had given more money to underwrite projects large and small. Through two terms in the General Assembly, he had defended the budgets of Chapel Hill and the other campuses against those in the legislature who had favored raising tuition to pay the bills of higher education. No matter what the men Hill called "educational politicians" might claim, he would always think of the Chapel Hill campus as the *real* University of North Carolina.

∾∾∾

Hill had a habit of making generous gifts to Durham at propitious times during his career in politics. Just as voters were preparing for the spring primaries in 1934, he announced that he was giving his Hillandale Golf Course to the city. Likewise, just as he was mounting his campaign against Graham's plan to move the engineering school in June 1935, Hill offered what was one of the most remarkable gifts ever given to the university community. In a letter to the governor, Hill presented the university with the Carolina Inn—from the building, furniture, and fixtures down to the blueprints—in the name of himself, his wife, and his children. He asked that the university hold the hotel in trust, with any profits from its operations going to support the collection of "books and papers known as the 'North Caroliniana'" at the library. Hill set the value of the inn at nearly three hundred thousand dollars.

The hotel had been a source of both personal pride and of financial disappointment. Hill had steadily cut the management's spending to the point that he was personally supervising minor details, such as the purchase of linens. In the summer of 1933, at the lowest point in the depression, when 20 percent of Durham was on relief, he had considered closing the inn altogether "until the dawn of a better day."[59] He had kept the inn open, but the spending restrictions he placed on manager Annie Martin had taken a toll. When the university officials took inventory in the summer of 1935, they found few financial records aside from records of money paid in salaries, and they reported that the equipment and supplies, including the linens, were in poor condition.[60]

Hill's campaign against the changes facing Chapel Hill was in full flower by February 1936, when a dinner celebrating the Hills and their gift to the university was scheduled in conjunction with the annual alumni meeting. Some thought the evening would be an awkward occasion for the Hills, assuming that the meeting would be "packed by pussy-footing Dr. Graham supporters." John Sprunt Hill said he was not concerned, and he explained, "Chapel Hill is my old stamping ground and I can imagine no circumstance that would cause me to hesitate one minute about attending any meeting of any kind of citizens on that hallowed soil."[61]

The weather and President Graham's persistent sinus ailments headed off any confrontation. Snow and rain limited the turnout to about a hundred. A severe cold kept Graham at home and relieved him of having to deal with political complications. In his place, Dean Robert House read a citation that had been presented to Hill two years earlier when the university awarded him his honorary doctor of laws degree. It described Hill as "a builder without vain glory, a fighter with abandon but without guile, a dreamer whose youthful dreams go daily into the making of a better university and a more beautiful state."[62]

If Graham had attended, he would have heard alumni speak as fervently as Hill in their opposition to plans for changing the university programs. Before the evening was over, the association went on record against the loss of the engineering school and in favor of Graham's proposal that academicians, not alumni, should run the school's athletic program. (Questions had arisen about the propriety of gifts and payments to college players.) Layered onto the opposition to Graham were complaints about his politics. Some trustees openly criticized the president for defending a former student and Socialist Party member who had been arrested the year before during an attempt by union laborers to shut down a High Point textile mill.

Hill's campaign to reverse the decision of the trustees proved to be an exercise in futility. The majority on the board remained quietly confident that the prior year's overwhelming vote would hold. Jonathan Daniels, who supported his father's decision in the pages of the *News and Observer*, countered Hill's pamphlet, but most papers were silent on the issue. Just before the alumni gathering at the Carolina Inn in February, Hill had all but begged Josephus Daniels to return from Mexico, where he was serving as the U.S. envoy, to defend the plan and offer worthy opposition. "Unfortunately for my discussion about the engineering school, I seem to find no opponent, like yourself, who is willing to stand up in meeting and speak for the New Plan. I trust, therefore, that you will hurry back to your home folks and carry the flag of the opposition. My own observation prompts me to say that nearly always great progress comes from great conflict."[63]

On May 30, 1936, the matter was settled once and for all. After nine months of mostly one-sided debate, and after rehashing the question of whether to close the Chapel Hill engineering school, the trustees voted fifty to twenty-four against Hill's motion to reconsider their earlier vote. University consolidation, an issue that had been on the table for five years, was finally settled. Ironically, the same issues that John Sprunt Hill raised in his pamphlet would be raised anew in the 1960s, when his son Watts Hill, who later succeeded his father on the executive committee of the Consolidated University of North Carolina Board of Trustees, and his grandson, Watts Hill Jr., who was then chairman of the state Board of Higher Education, fought legislative battles over whether to include the emerging campus in Greenville, the home of what later became East Carolina University, in the consolidated state system.

◌◌◌

Hill returned to the state Senate for the 1937 session, but the fire of earlier years was missing. Even before the session opened, he announced that he was through with liquor bills. By the end of the session, he had engaged himself in a handful of local measures and remained largely out of the spotlight.

John Sprunt Hill's political career was over. He was nearly seventy years old, and the world had changed, most especially in Chapel Hill, where old associates had died or been succeeded by a new liberal contingent led by Frank Graham, whose politics Hill simply could not abide. Hill still saw himself as a liberal agrarian reformer, the friend of the state's yeoman farmers, but the politics of Roosevelt, the New Deal, and questions that challenged the order of life were far from what he had known when he was a young man. He turned from politics back to business and to his home at Biltmore Forest, where he spent as much time as possible enjoying the cool summer season and playing golf.

◌◌◌

Hill still had the stuff for one last, grand gesture, however. During his last session in Raleigh, workmen were completing the Hill Building, a seventeen-story skyscraper in downtown Durham. Hill signed off on what he had planned to call the Home Bank Building in the summer of 1935 when he directed that his cousin, Watts Carr, be designated the architect. It was really his wife's decision. John Sprunt Hill had wanted a New York architect, but Annie insisted that Carr, a self-taught designer, be given the job even though he had never undertaken any building project of this size before. In fact, Carr was the supervising architect, while the design for the exterior and much of the interior came from the New York firm of Shreve, Lamb, and Harmon, which had gained international fame with its design of the Empire State Building.[64]

The west side of the new building stood inches away from the side of the Trust Building on the site of the old post office, which had moved into a new building a few blocks away. The construction of Hill's building provided Durham with desperately needed jobs. When work began in July 1936, it was virtually the only construction project in town.

The new building—estimated to have cost $900,000—was designed to allow sufficient space for Hill's two banks, two hundred offices for doctors and other professionals, the headquarters of the Home Security Life Insurance Company, and "a large commodious department store." The retail space was on the street level of a seven-story section that gave way to ten more stories in an office tower that stepped back in the fashion of New York skyscrapers.

The seventeen-story steel skeleton soon rose over downtown Durham. By the time Senator John Sprunt Hill was in Raleigh for the opening of the 1937 General Assembly, the Indiana limestone facing—later trimmed in aluminum—was being installed. The Hills chose the stone for the outer skin because it went up quickly and required less labor than brick. With the new building so close to the old, Hill and his son Watts could follow construction progress from their desks. Watts, who became the de facto construction superintendent, described the building as "modern, but not modernistic" and said it "emphasiz[ed] simplicity and straight lines."

The new building came with the latest conveniences and polished trim. The sixth floor had extra soundproofing to muffle the noise and clatter of the insurance company's tabulating machines. Four elevators carried passengers from Corcoran Street to the top of the building in sixteen seconds. Everything was first class, from the highly polished marble entrance on Corcoran Street to the dark teak paneling in the offices at the top. The bank offices were also paneled, and the floors were chipped marble and terrazzo. The door to the bank vault was two and a half feet thick and weighed more than thirteen tons.

The building opened in September 1937. The fifteenth floor was the Hills' inner sanctum. From John Sprunt Hill's new quarters in the northwest corner, he could see his dairy farm and the Hillandale Golf Course at the city's western edge. With him at the top were his son and their closest and most trusted associates—John Sprunt Hill's personal attorney, W. W. "Whit" Sledge, and Watts Hill's new personal business manager, B. W. "Bo" Harris Jr.

On paper, Watts Hill had succeeded his father at the bank and at the insurance company. He was president of the Durham Bank and Trust and had handled the expansion of the business through branch offices. Bank failures in the area opened business opportunities in nearby Creedmore, Wake Forest, Mebane, Hillsboro, and Apex. A branch was opened farther west in Cooleemee near the textile mill that George Watts and the Dukes had opened at the turn of the century. Watts was also chairman of the board of the Home Security Life Insurance Company and a director or officer in a half-dozen other businesses in which the family had substantial holdings.

Yet for all of Watts Hill's corporate titles, there was no question that control of the family businesses remained with his father. As a result, Watts largely focused his attention on other concerns, such as the management of Watts Hospital, his farming operations at Quail Roost, the construction of the Hill Building (for two years), and two terms of service on the Durham City Council.

All of these tasks had challenged his talents and presented their own opportunities, but his vision extended beyond the close environs of Durham. By the mid-1930s, Watts Hill was getting restless. In the next few years, he would find challenges far beyond anything he could imagine from his new office at the top of Durham's tallest building.

CHAPTER 10

In the Family Tradition

CONSTRUCTION OF THE HILL BUILDING was well under way early in the fall of 1936 when Watts Hill announced he was resigning from the Durham City Council. He offered little public explanation other than to say that eight years on the council was enough. He said he had stayed through the depression to keep the city's finances sound. Much to his father's satisfaction, Durham had never defaulted on its public debt, as a number of other municipalities had.

Watts Hill's seat had been handed to him in 1928, when he was appointed to fill the vacancy created by the death of Councilman Frank Ward. Hill was only twenty-seven, the youngest member to hold the office, but newspaper accounts suggest that he was a popular choice. A year later, when he ran for a full four-year term, he easily led the ticket. He campaigned hard for the job, and he enjoyed the give and take with the mill workers who made up much of Durham's Fourth Ward, which he represented. They voted heavily for him. When he ran again four years later, in 1933, the city was in the depths of the depression, and labor organizations were energizing local politics. Hill, the son of the city's leading capitalist, found himself in a three-way contest in the first primary, but he polled enough votes to discourage the number two man from calling a runoff.

Watts Hill's civic service honored a tradition that had started with his grandfather in the 1880s and had continued with his father, who had served two terms on the council before World War I. His uncle Isham Hill had also been a member of the council in the early years of the century. Throughout most of Watts Hill's time in city government, he chaired the council's finance committee. He proved to be a hard worker, and he was diligent about keeping Durham's finances in the black. When he took over the committee, the city manager handed him a copy of the municipal budget. Hill later said it appeared to have been designed more to confuse than to enlighten readers about the cost of municipal government. Hill hired an accountant to review the numbers and give him a report. The accountant's analysis showed that the city officials were using bond money for purposes for which it was not authorized. No money was unaccounted for, but it took more than five years to sort things out.

Hill's council record suggested that his political philosophy evolved while he was a councilman. At first, he talked like a conservative and favored limited government services, much like his father. He opposed early efforts by the city and county to build an airport, declaring that such a project was the province of private enterprise. By the mid-1930s, however, he was complaining that Durham was being shortchanged by the federal government's Works Progress Administration (WPA) when the WPA failed to come through with a grant to pay for a municipal airfield. Shortly before he announced his bid for reelection in 1933, he browbeat council members into approving a $1 million bond issue to build a municipal power system. Hill argued it was the only alternative, as the Durham Public Service Company refused to reduce its rates. The power company, which distributed electricity purchased from Duke Power, rallied enough support from John Wiley, the respected head of Fidelity Bank, and from officials of the companies that were major power users such as American Tobacco Company and Liggett and Myers, to persuade the mayor and a majority of the council members to withdraw their support for Hill's proposal. The approval for the bonds was rescinded.

Hill's politics could be described as progressive. He supported a study of the consolidation of city and county governments, and in 1936 he urged the merger of the two, something his father vigorously opposed just as he had before when the question arose. Consolidation did not succeed.

Watts Hill also persuaded the council to create summer recreational programs at the city parks and schools, and five centers were opened using Reconstruction Finance Corporation money.[1] During the time that their son was serving in city government, John Sprunt and Annie Watts Hill had been generous in their gifts of recreational facilities and land for city parks. On the last day of 1930, the couple donated thirty-three acres of the Forest Hills property—including the clubhouse and swimming pool—to the city for use as a public park. Two years later, they donated land on Holloway

Street for Long Meadow Park. With that land restricted to use by whites only, they gave additional property on Markham Avenue to create East End Park for African Americans. In the latter part of 1933, John Sprunt Hill gave the city $20,000 to buy the El Toro baseball park from his Homeland Investment Company, which had acquired the property after the owners fell deep into debt. The transaction was a bargain for the city, and it created a nice tax deduction for Hill. The Morris Street ballpark had been built in 1926 for $160,000, and it was considered to be one of the best fields in the minor leagues when the Durham Bulls won the Piedmont League pennant in 1930. The city accepted Hill's offer, renamed the property the Durham Athletic Park, and, agreeing to the Hills' condition, prohibited commercial ball games on Sundays.[2]

∽∽∽

Watts Hill's' seat on the council proved most useful in his campaign to improve the financial condition of Watts Hospital. When Hill joined the council, Durham's city and county governments provided only modest amounts of money to help offset the costs of indigent care, and local support was shrinking from year to year in proportion to what the hospital needed to pay for indigent care. The depression only aggravated the hospital's situation as patient counts declined. In 1932, fewer patients were admitted than had been annually admitted in the mid-1920s. Moreover, more than two-thirds of those admitted declared they were charity cases. The hospital hired a bill collector to satisfy delinquent accounts, but he often returned with only hams, beans, and other in-kind payments.[3] At one point, Hill became so impatient with the refusal of both his fellow council members and the county commissioners to increase annual stipends that he threatened to limit admissions of indigent county residents. The hospital administration never acted on the threat.

In the spring of 1934, Watts Hill persuaded fellow council members to pay for new X-ray equipment as well as to provide money to allow the hospital to catch up on bills due to local merchants. He told the council, "It is coming to the point where the hospital cannot do the impossible, or carry out in full the deed laid down in the gifts—that no person in Durham County in need of hospitalization should be turned away."[4] The municipal funds and a small amount remaining in George Watts's trust were just enough to pay for a $14,000 X-ray pavilion.

∽∽∽

The financial situation was even worse at the new hospital on the Duke University campus, where 90 percent of the patients were indigent. In the first year of the hospital's operation, the hospital subsidy amounted to $260,000. Duke officials appealed to the city and county for support similar to that given Watts Hospital. Hill opposed the request and defended Watts as "Durham's hospital." He said that while Duke did take charity patients from the surrounding area, it refused to allow local physicians to practice there.[5]

Both hospitals were struggling in the summer of 1933 when Dwight Snyder, a Raleigh insurance man, asked Watts Hill if Watts Hospital was interested in becoming part of a new group health plan called the Hospital Care Association. The nonprofit corporation that Snyder had created was remarkably similar to what Hill and Duke University's Dr. Wilburt Davison had attempted to create in 1929. New policyholders paid $1.50 a month and became eligible for up to nineteen days of hospital care a year. The length of the hospital stay for which policyholders were eligible expanded to thirty days a year after a policy had remained in force for a certain length of time. By the time Snyder and Hill met, Snyder had signed up Raleigh's Rex and Saint Mary's hospitals and was selling policies in Raleigh.

Hill discovered that Snyder's resources were so thin that his first policyholder had been the owner of a print shop who had taken coverage in lieu of cash for the cost of printing the company's certificates. Yet Hill was interested. He gave Snyder $250 to pay his back debts and offered free space in the Trust Building for Snyder to open a Durham sales office. Hill contacted Davison and told him about Hospital Care, and soon both Watts and Duke hospitals were part of the nation's first group health care organization with plans to offer statewide coverage.

By the end of 1933, Hospital Care had nearly 3,000 policyholders, most of them employees of either the *Herald-Sun* newspaper in Durham or Duke University. But while the numbers were impressive, the financial results were not. Hospital Care ended the year with a deficit of about $10,000, due in part to a greater use of hospital services by Duke University employees than had been anticipated. Snyder resigned, most of the staff was replaced, and the company's headquarters were moved from Raleigh to Durham. To ensure the association's continued operation, Duke and Watts hospitals each pledged up to $6,000 to cover the company's bills. Hill personally guaranteed Watts Hospital's share.

By August 1935, Hospital Care had 10,000 members, and it was under the management of Elisha A. Herndon, who had been hired to succeed Snyder. In the following year, Hospital Care expanded further afield and added clients in Fayetteville, Asheville, Greensboro, Charlotte, and Concord, where textile baron Charles A. Cannon had built a new hospital for employees of Cannon Mills.

At first, Hospital Care only sold coverage to white, middle-class working people with steady incomes. Near the end of 1936, the company expanded its offerings and created a certificate designed strictly for African Americans. Unlike white clients, most of whom had their premiums deducted from paychecks, few African Americans worked in factories or were paid from company payrolls. As a result, Hospital Care recruited field agents to collect the weekly payments in person. Six years after Snyder called on Watts Hill, Hospital Care had more than 62,000 members and had paid out more than $340,000 in benefits to hospitals across the state. The company also had an operating reserve of $11,000 and was qualified to carry the Blue Cross emblem of the American Hospital Association.[6] (By coincidence, the first Hospital Care membership certificates had also included a cross printed with blue ink.)

∾∾∾

During Watts Hill's first decade in Durham as the heir apparent to the Hill business empire, he seemed to be everywhere at once. In addition to his work on the city council and at the hospital, he was elected president of the North Carolina Dairyman's Association and the North Carolina Guernsey Breeders' Association. The state dairy association post included membership on the State Board of Agriculture, where he stayed for but a short time. After a very public spat with state Commissioner of Agriculture W. A. Graham, whom Hill thought was not giving enough attention to the dairy industry, Hill's appointment to the board was challenged by Graham. He said that a state prohibition of double office-holding prevented City Councilman Hill from serving on the state board. Hill resigned, but not before issuing a public challenge to Graham. Some suggested Hill should run against Graham. Alamance County dairyman Kerr Scott unseated Graham in 1936 and saved Hill the trouble.

Hill thoroughly invested himself in each new project. Most were outside the realm of the family business, where decisions were made by his father. His projects satisfied his eagerness to establish his own identity, but his preoccupation with these affairs left little time for his family. This was particularly hard on his wife, Ann, who found it a challenge to keep pace with a busy husband whose pursuits were so different from her own. She enjoyed art and literature and was a prolific writer. Her husband focused on cows and local affairs that grew from the family's extensive involvement in the county. He preferred to spend time with the mixture of people he found in his daily pursuits; she enjoyed quiet moments at home.

Though she had been an active person in her youth, Ann had not regained her health after the Cesarean birth of her third child, son John Sprunt II, in 1932. The family hired a governess, Doris "Dee-Dee" Castle, an Englishwoman whose father had been the captain of the port of Bermuda. Throughout their early years, the children saw more of her than they did of their parents. By the time Watts Jr. was ready for public school, he had adopted Castle's British accent.

Ann Hill's medical problems further isolated her from Durham, where she had never felt comfortable in the huge, three-story Harwood Hall. She discovered that she did not live in a home, but in a museum where the location of every piece of furniture and relic collected by the Wattses during their trips abroad was closely watched by her mother-in-law, Annie Watts Hill, who lived just a few steps away. Furthermore, the mansion was dark and hung with heavy, tasseled draperies, and it included a collection of oddities such as a full-sized stuffed bear. Even her husband made jokes about Harwood Hall, which he called the "pink elephant" in honor of both its pink granite exterior and its overwhelming size. Ann said later that she never even unpacked her wedding presents.

In 1932, the couple finally built an oceanfront home in Virginia Beach that offered some release for them both from the pressures of Durham. It gave Ann a place to escape from the watchful eye of the Hills and from Durham for several months of the year. Her husband came up on weekends and enjoyed boating and swimming in the surf. While she was at the beach, Ann reestablished social connections with family and friends from Maryland and New York.

The Hills' beach house stood near the fashionable Cavalier Hotel, and it easily accommodated all the family, a staff of servants, and a number of guests. It was designed by Watts Carr, who had done many of the homes in Durham's Forest Hills subdivision. Carr adapted the cottage style with gabled dormers on the second story and produced a large, rambling home with an open central room; it had high, vaulted ceilings of natural wood and a broad porch facing the ocean. The Hills called their beach home Quail Roost.

In addition to the house, the Hills also built stables on the edge of Crystal Lake behind the house to accommodate horses for Ann and the children that were brought from Quail Roost Farm each year. Riding had been a part of Ann's life since her childhood at Oldfields, and her horses were as important to her as the cows were to Watts. While her husband seldom rode, Ann spent much of her time with the horses at the farm.

Each spring when the steeplechase season opened at Pinehurst, the Hills usually had an entry. Their riders wore the registered Quail Roost silks—a white jacket with a maroon sash and a maroon cap with a yellow visor. Their horses also ran at Aiken and Camden, South Carolina. Then the family followed the circuit north into Virginia, Maryland, Connecticut, and Pennsylvania. The season closed in New York at Madison Square Garden with the National Horse Show. When they came of age, Dudley and Watts Jr. rode in the show competition at the Garden outfitted in shiny boots, red coats, and black caps. Ann's favorite confirmation jumper was a solid black horse named Inky who collected four championships and for two years was the highest money winner at the eastern shows. Another Hill horse, Balkonian, won three championships. At their peak, the Hill stables included nine thoroughbreds and eighteen foxhounds.

The family also spent time in Pinehurst, where John Sprunt Hill had acquired the Mid-Pines Country Club. The club had never succeeded as Pinehurst developer Leonard Tufts and his golf master, Donald Ross, had hoped. Only about a third of the 300 members that Tufts had projected had been recruited. As a result, the operation had lost money every year except one, when the total profit was less than $2,000. By 1931, bankers were threatening foreclosure. Watts and his father had helped Tufts by buying bonds that were sold in the hope that new cash would carry the resort through the hard times. By 1934, however, Mid-Pines was $294,000 in debt, and the Hills—father and son—were among the largest creditors. When the golf course and 250-room clubhouse were sold at auction, Hill's Homeland Investment Company bought them for $90,000.[7]

❦❦❦

The Hills' life—spring in Pinehurst, summer at the beach, trips to Biltmore Forest, and a mansion in Durham—was a distant dream for most of those who lived in Durham. The depression reduced mill workers to half their regular hours or none at all, and social tensions created by such disparity of wealth occasionally intruded a little too close for comfort. At a labor rally in early 1933, a Durham physician, Dr. Edwin H. Bowling, told a meeting of about six hundred unemployed workers—blacks and whites together—that the aid extended to those on relief was insufficient: "What they are giving us is just enough to keep our mouths shut. I am opposed to revolution, but before I would see my family suffer I would be willing to follow a mob or lead one." At the same meeting, someone complained about "too many Hills."[8]

Durham had changed since Watts Hill was a youngster who walked to school with his grandfather. By the time Watts Jr. was ready for school, Morehead Elementary School was a different place from when his father had attended classes there. Students in the Durham system followed established tracks. The route from Morehead Elementary did not lead to education beyond high school. As a result, talented youngsters like Watts Jr., who had been exposed to books and homeschooling, were in the minority. Most of Watts Jr.'s classmates were the sons and daughters of mill workers, and they had fun with Watts Jr.'s accent. After his boy's first year at Morehead, Watts Hill discovered that his son had learned to cuss, but little else.

The Hills had the option of paying an extra fee to allow their children to attend another school in the city. It was located near Duke University, and many children from the homes of Duke faculty were enrolled there. Instead, however, Ann Hill found the answer within her family of educators. For some years, the Calvert School in Baltimore had been marketing a homeschooling instruction program created by school founder Virgil Mores Hillyer, a Harvard-trained educator. Hillyer's program was designed for the children of Americans living abroad—missionaries, engineers, or diplomats—who were posted far from a major city and either English-speaking neighbors or teachers. By the late 1920s, Hillyer was shipping his course outlines, books, and supplies to 3,000 pupils around the world.

Hillyer's curriculum included rigorous exercises designed to teach basic skills with an emphasis on language and reading that included an understanding of the Latin or Greek origins of words. He had also created a distinctive system of cursive writing that students carried into adulthood. The texts were well illustrated and covered the worlds of art, literature, music, and history, with an emphasis on the classics. He supplied everything students required, including a hinged nine-by-twelve-inch blue box in which to keep their work. Teachers, who were most often parents, followed his explicit instructions and returned the completed assignments at the end of each term for certification.

In the summer of 1933, Ann Hill and the mothers of six other youngsters arranged for the use of the Forest Hills clubhouse for their school. That September, classes began at what was loosely called the Calvert Method School. Since Hillyer had designed his program to be taught by nonprofessionals or even self-taught in higher grades, parents and governesses like Castle composed the Durham "faculty." Each morning after breakfast with the children, Castle loaded Watts Jr. into a Model A Ford and drove him down the hill to "school." Classes began promptly at 8:30 A.M. At the end of a school day that included rest periods with milk and cookies brought from home, students left to complete their homework.

"Hillyer was the author of at least two wonderful books," Watts Hill Jr. later recalled, "*A Child's History of the World* and *A Child's History of Art*. Both had copious illustrations, both placed heavy emphasis on the classics. We were steeped in the origins of government and its debt to the Greek tradition."[9] Hillyer's selection of episodes in Greek history was carefully edited to suit "our young psyches," Watts said, as was the selection of artworks. But, he remembered, "art, music, history and literature became incorporated into our lives as a normal, everyday occurrence and so deeply ingrained that they continue as such today, more than six decades later."

After the school's first year, another grade was added, and Watts Jr. was joined by his sister and later by his brother Sprunt. By the time Sprunt enrolled, the school had outgrown the clubhouse and had moved into George Watts's original house at 815 S. Duke Street where John Sprunt Hill first lived when he came to Durham in 1903. Watts Hill arranged a $15,000 mortgage on the house for the Calvert Method School—as it was now legally called—and paid for $9,000 in renovations to accommodate the nineteen students then attending in six grades.

Watts Hill became a member of the school's first Board of Trustees, and his assistant, B. W. Harris Jr., kept the school's books. Harris had already become familiar with private school management from another Hill assignment. In 1935, Watts Hill had hired him part-time to overhaul the financial records at Oldfields when declining enrollment had threatened the school's future. Hill also loaned money to Oldfields and helped Ann's brother, Duncan McCulloch Jr., who had succeeded their father as head-master in 1932, to restore buildings and revive the school's working farm. Watts Hill remained on the school's Board of Trustees for more than twen-ty years, until the McCulloch family sold its interest in Oldfields in the ear-ly 1960s.

∾∾∾

Within a year after Watts Hill left the Durham City Council, he began making plans to move his family out of Durham altogether. Work had not yet begun on a 13,000-square-foot home the Hills planned to build at Quail Roost Farm when Annie Watts Hill suffered a severe heart attack in the late winter of 1938. She was hospitalized for more than two months. When she returned home, she convalesced in her rooms on the second floor of Hill House, where John Sprunt Hill had installed a new air-condi-tioning system—one of the first in the city—to cool the upstairs bedrooms and make his wife more comfortable. Her husband also altered the Bilt-more Forest house to accommodate the construction of an elevator for Annie Watts's use. She spent only one summer in the mountains before suffering another heart attack in November 1939. She died about four months later on March 26, 1940, at the age of sixty-three.

Annie Watts Hill had lived a storybook life of castles and princes that was not so far removed from the lives of the members of the European royalty whom she passed at the spas she had visited with regularity. She had enjoyed comfort and pampered elegance steeped in the formal Victo-rian tradition. Like her father, she was deeply committed to a spiritual life, and she had been a devoted worker in Durham's First Presbyterian Church. Twenty years after her father's death, she still supported the insti-tutions and missionaries he had been benefactor for, including even those missionaries who had gone into retirement. Like her mother, she loved her garden. During her life, she chose flowers for bouquets and arrangements for the sick and invalid. She was a generous supporter of Watts Hospital, she helped the Young Women's Christian Association, and she organized the Durham chapter of the American Red Cross. Until shortly before her death, she had also presided over the Needlework Guild, which quietly aid-ed those in need.

She left a world that was changing rapidly. The old order was overturned by World War I, and another revolution was underway in Europe. Poland had already come under Nazi domination by the time of her death. Britain and France would soon face the wrath of Adolf Hitler's drive to the west. Many in the United States—including North Carolina's own Senator Robert R. Reynolds—argued the case for isolation. Her son, Watts, had already taken sides. He had missed the first war. He would not miss this one.

CHAPTER 11

The Way to War

DURHAM AND THE REST OF NORTH CAROLINA were still struggling with the burdens of the depression in January 1939 when Watts Hill boarded a train and headed south for a conference in Atlanta organized by a group called the Southern Policy Committee (SPC). The invitation came from Francis Pickens Miller of Virginia, Kentucky newspaperman Mark Ethridge, and a small group of southern political moderates concerned about the future of the region. President Franklin Roosevelt had called the South the nation's number one problem, and the delegates to the conference were eager to do what they could to remove that distinction.

Hill himself would later joke that as a banker and businessman he was often the odd man out in this crowd of social thinkers, journalists, and do-gooders. How his name came to be on Miller's invitation list along with the names of the leader of the Southern Tenant Farmers Union and of labor organizers, writers, New Dealers, and preachers remains the subject of speculation. Hill may have come to know Miller through the dairy business. Miller's wife, Helen, raised Guernseys on their farm near Fairfax, Virginia. It is more likely that Miller learned of Hill through their mutual connections at the University of North Carolina at Chapel Hill, the home of several players in the growing debate over race, poverty, illiteracy, and other ills of southern society. At the center of this discussion were Chapel Hill sociologist Howard W. Odum, the leading proponent of the creation of a regional research and planning council; W. T. Couch, the combative director of the university's press, which had published some of Miller's work; and, of course, university president Frank Porter Graham, the South's best-known liberal.

Hill was just the kind of new recruit that Miller was seeking. He was a bright, energetic businessman with boardroom credentials who could lend credibility to the Southern Policy Committee, whose membership was thin on capitalists. Regardless of who was responsible for his invitation, the Atlanta meeting was the first in a series of conferences and conversations Hill attended that would lead eventually to his involvement in organizations increasingly concerned over the fate of the world as well as of the South. It also would lead to Hill's recruitment as an early member of the Office of Strategic Services, or OSS, and to what would be one of the most exciting and liberating experiences of his life.

❧❧❧

When Miller called the Atlanta meeting, he was a freshman member of the Virginia House of Delegates, but he had already become an irritant to status quo politicians under the control of the state's controlling conservative interests, who were led by U.S. senator Harry Byrd. Miller lived with his wife and family on their farm on the outskirts of Washington. Helen Hill Miller was the daughter of a wealthy northeastern family, but she worked as a journalist in the city when she was not tending cows. Her husband had recently joined the staff of the Council on Foreign Relations as a field secretary in the South. Nearly five years older than Watts Hill, Miller was a Presbyterian minister's son and a graduate of Washington and Lee University. He had served in the army in World War I and remained in Europe following the armistice, where he worked with the international YMCA and then later studied at Oxford as a Rhodes Scholar. He returned to the states in 1930 to lecture at Yale University, where he helped found the magazine *Christianity and Crisis* with Reinhold Niebuhr and others. In the summer of 1936, he was instrumental in the formation of the Southern Policy Committee at a meeting at the Lookout Mountain Hotel in Chattanooga, Tennessee. As a roving ambassador for the Council on Foreign Relations, Miller engaged civic, political, academic, and social leaders in a discussion about regional and national issues.

The Lookout Mountain meeting was the first of a series proposed by Miller and Raymond Leslie Buell, an editor at *Fortune* magazine, as a truly democratic approach to solving the nation's problems. The idea was to bring together men and women of goodwill and competing points of view—management and labor, for example—who could develop rational answers to difficult questions. Miller was inspired by the "committee of correspondents" who during the nation's earliest days had engaged one another in a debate about national issues. As Miller and Buell envisioned their program, ideas would rise from regional meetings and go forward to a National Policy Committee, which would see them through to implementation. By the time the Atlanta meeting took place, a new land planning law had come from one subgroup of the Lookout Mountain gathering. The New Deal's Farm Security Administration had been modeled on a plan devised by another.[1]

The SPC was but one of a number of such organizations at the middle and, in varying degrees, to the left of the political center that sent representatives to Birmingham, Alabama, in November 1938 for a summit meeting of southerners. They arrived from thirteen states and encompassed representatives of religious groups (including Jews and Catholics) and organized labor as well as New Dealers from posts both in Washington and across the South, a few elected officials, journalists who edited the most influential newspapers, socialists, academics like Odum, and even a few communists. Most of the fifteen hundred or so who gathered for the opening session of the Southern Conference on Human Welfare (SCHW) in Birmingham's Municipal Auditorium were white, but a significant minority was black. As the crowd moved into the cavernous hall where segregated seating had been arranged as was required by law, whites and blacks mingled freely and finally just took seats where they were available. There had been nothing like it before, and it would be remembered by some as a "singular moment of Southern hope and promise." Others would call the SCHW a haven for radicals, leftists, communists, and worse.[2]

After three days of speeches, committee meetings, and debate over such topics as child labor laws, discriminatory freight rates, poll taxes, Jim Crow, and antilynching laws, the meeting closed on Tuesday with a speech by First Lady Eleanor Roosevelt. Despite all the talk, what most delegates would remember after they headed home was the racially mixed seating at the meetings and the fact that a piddling handful of those who attended were communists. This was a politically fatal combination that would haunt the SCHW into extinction. It would also tarnish Frank Graham, who emerged as the chair of this polyglot union, when he sought reelection to the U.S. Senate in 1950.

Miller left Birmingham bothered by the leftist tilt of the delegates and the agenda. He declined a vice presidency of SCHW, saying he could not belong to any organization that included avowed communists.[3] He immediately set about convening another session to consider an agenda that could somehow avoid the dominating influence of such a hot-button issue as racial segregation. Most of those invited to Atlanta by Miller and Ethridge were middle-aged white men like themselves, such as U.S. senator John Sparkman of Alabama, J. Hadden Alldredge from the Tennessee Valley Authority, Louisville newspaper publisher Barry Bingham, editors Virginius Dabney from Richmond and Jonathan Daniels from Raleigh, academicians Odum and Graham from North Carolina, and Chancellor Oliver Carmichael from Vanderbilt University. SCHW field secretary H. Clarence Nixon was on hand, as was the regional director of the Textile Workers Organizing Committee. Four in the group of about forty were women, and two were black. Of those who would sign a resulting report, Hill was the only one identified as a "businessman," although the group included a couple of lawyers.

The report from the Atlanta meeting, called "A Working Economic Plan for the South," received some attention in southern newspapers due largely to the number of editors present at the meeting. It dealt with issues that would have been familiar to Hill's father and the progressives of an earlier generation. It focused attention on the burden of one-crop farming, discriminatory freight rates that discouraged industrial development in the South, and the need for improvements—financial and otherwise—of public health and schools. The group stepped lightly around anything that hinted of a challenge to racial segregation, although it endorsed new state laws to eliminate the poll tax (a device used in many southern states to disenfranchise poor whites and African Americans) and called for stronger tenants' rights laws. Also included in the report was a vaguely worded section supporting the rights of organized labor.

❧❧❧

The Atlanta meeting lifted Hill's attention from the parochial issues of Durham and the social chatter of Pinehurst and Virginia Beach and introduced him to a company of people who were growing increasingly concerned about the state of the world as well as the state of the South. In the spring of 1939, New York writer Dorothy Thompson spent three days at the Hill's home in Durham while she was a visiting lecturer on the campus at

Chapel Hill. Other guests included writer William Alexander Percy (*Lanterns on the Levee*) and artist Eleanor Beckham, who was a close friend of Ann Hill.

The depression had shaken America loose from its financial moorings and upset traditional political values. Conservatives like John Sprunt Hill were alarmed over the growing influence of socialists and convinced that social planners involved in Roosevelt's New Deal, as well as those in Raleigh, were destroying democracy. Meanwhile, many liberals were alarmed about the isolationist attitudes of Americans, some of whom seemed to accept without question the propaganda of the increasingly belligerent Fascist governments that threatened Europe.

At the close of the Atlanta meeting, Hill agreed to Miller's request that he organize a North Carolina committee for the SPC. A few weeks later, Hill joined yet another policy discussion group. This one met in New York and was organized by Buell and *Fortune* editor-in-chief Russell Davenport, whose wife Marcia Zimbalist Davenport was Ann Hill's close friend. While Miller's bunch had a decided preference for the Democratic Party, the *Fortune* crowd gave Hill a seat close to some of the nation's top moderate Republicans. Davenport and Henry R. Luce, the owner and creator of *Fortune* and *Time* magazines, were already making plans for Wendell Willkie to capture the GOP presidential nomination in 1940.

By the end of 1939, Hill was preparing to host a SPC meeting at the Mid-Pines Country Club in Pinehurst, where the agenda was far less ambitious than what had been attempted in Atlanta. From the perspective of the present, the resulting resolution, which focused on the split within organized labor, appears to have been more an effort to mark the occasion than to resolve substantive regional concerns. In fairness, however, the attention of those on hand was divided between problems at home and a world headed toward war. Four months earlier, the Nazis had invaded Poland, and declarations of war had swept the European continent. With so much attention focused abroad, the committee's call for a presidential effort to negotiate a peace between the feuding factions of organized labor was largely overlooked.

Hill's own attention had begun to shift to the conflict in Europe. In the days leading up to the Pinehurst session, he worked with a group of North Carolinians, including W. T. Couch and writer Struthers Burt, one of Hill's friends in Southern Pines, to raise money to aid the government of Finland, which in December had come under attack from Russia. With their own western border presumably secured by a nonaggression pact with Nazi Germany, Russian troops won early victories in Finland and forced the capitulation of the Finnish government within months. In a short time, Hill and others raised $7,100 for the Fighting Funds for Finland, a group that drew more support in the Midwest than in the South.[4]

The Finnish invasion was a diversion from what many were calling "the phony war." After Adolf Hitler's army overran Poland, the front in the west fell quiet. It was not until April 1940 that the German army began to move again, and then it exploded with surprising speed to overtake Norway, the Netherlands, and Belgium before it headed into France in a sweeping movement around the "impregnable" Maginot Line. In late May, more than two hundred thousand British, French, and Belgian soldiers were faced with capture or annihilation before they were miraculously rescued from the shores of Dunkirk by a hastily organized armada that sailed from England. From the perspective of the United States, the end of a free Europe appeared to be close at hand. France was considered to be gone, and Britain was expected to fall as well. Fewer than two out of ten Americans believed the Allies could stand against Hitler.[5]

Allied soldiers were heading to the beaches at Dunkirk when Richard Cleveland, the son of former president Grover Cleveland and the chair of the National Policy Committee, called Francis Miller and asked him to convene a meeting to consider the implications for the United States of a German victory in Europe. Cleveland, the Millers, and a few others were gathered at Miller's home outside Washington planning the meeting on the day that the armada carried the remnants of the defeated Allied armies across the English Channel. The conversation that afternoon took an urgent turn. Who would speak for Britain in America? Miller asked. It was time, he felt, to say something to awaken Americans to the threat they would face if Europe fell. He turned to Whitney Shephardson of New York, a man experienced in international business, to draft a statement. The result was a document they titled "A Summons to Speak Out."[6] The next day, the Millers gathered names, reproduced the statement, and mailed it along with an urgent letter asking for endorsements to more than a hundred people around the country.

Shephardson's statement was a call to Americans to recognize the futility of neutrality in the face of events in Europe. If the United States remained out of the war and allowed France and England to fall to Nazism, it reasoned, then it was only a matter of time before the United States would stand alone against Hitler. The statement recommended that America should act now and act decisively to aid the Allies with all "disposable air, naval, military and material resources." Because there were standing neutrality laws, the only way for America to legally support the Allies would be for it to declare "that a state of war exist[ed] between [America] and Germany."[7]

Watts Hill wired his endorsement of the statement from Virginia Beach with a note asking Miller to advise him if he could provide further help and suggesting that congressmen be pressured to support the statement.[8] Stories appeared on June 10 in the *New York Times* and New York's *Herald-Tribune* about the group of influential Americans who were calling for war on Germany. Hill's name was included in these stories along with about thirty others. The only other North Carolinian in the group was Calvin Hoover, a Duke University economist and specialist on the totalitarian regimes of Russia and Germany.

Only about a fourth of those who received the appeal endorsed the statement. Some declined because they held government positions. Others, like Jonathan Daniels and Clarence Poe in North Carolina, wired vigorous dissent. "If we should go precipitately into a war which might be lost in Europe almost as we entered it," Daniels wrote Miller, "whatever power and prestige we might have in the limiting of a victorious German peace would be lost."[9] Miller later told Hill that half of the most negative replies came from North Carolina, but none was as resentful as the reply that arrived from Robert E. Wood, chairman of the huge Sears Roebuck retail operation and a leader in the America First movement. "I regard such steps as you proposed as unwise, unpatriotic and hysterical in the extreme," Wood said.[10]

∽∽∽

In Watts Hill, Miller found a willing and able ally and a knowledgeable foot soldier for the cause. The nations of Europe were not simply places on the globe for Hill, but lands that he had visited more than once since he was a youngster. He had flown the Channel in an open plane, had traveled by train across France, and had spent time in Rome, London, Paris, and cities in Germany. Immediately, Miller asked Hill to enroll other North

Carolinians in support of the statement, and Hill responded with a mailing to friends around the state. His endorsement of war was not regarded highly by some who got his letter, and he was forced to defend his position.

Hill told W. Hays Godwin of Goldsboro that Europe needed equipment and materiel, not American soldiers, and that he did not believe it would be necessary to send troops to Europe. However, Hill wrote, it was imperative that the United States do everything possible to prepare "to defend from the madmen of Europe all that we hold dear." He continued: "It is only through a definite organization of this country—possibly temporary organization along very dictatorial lines—can we meet the great dangers that hang over us."[11] In a note to Frank Graham, Hill blamed the newspapers for overplaying the call for a declaration of war. At the same time, however, he told Graham, "Universal conscription—men, materials and wealth, to me is a fundamental and immediate necessity."[12]

Generally speaking, by tradition and by heritage, southerners held a more sympathetic attitude toward affairs in Europe than other Americans did. Isolationism was strongest in the West and the Midwest, where the American Nazi Party had been building in strength since the early 1930s. Yet Hill found no sympathy for a declaration of war among the state's congressional delegation, particularly not from Senator Robert Reynolds, who was becoming increasingly vocal in opposition to aiding the Allies. Others were not as outspoken as Reynolds, but they were as firm in their opinion to remain clear of the war abroad.

∾∾∾

On the same day that the report of the "Summons" was published in the *New York Times*, advertisements sympathetic to the Allies appeared in that newspaper and in others across the United States. They had been placed by a new organization with a cumbersome title: the Committee to Defend America by Aiding the Allies, or CDAAA. The group's honorary chair was William Allen White, the legendary editor of the *Emporia Gazette* (Kansas) and a lifelong Republican. The organization's membership included leading figures in the political, social, and economic elite of the Northeast. Among its early supporters were Harvard University president James B. Conant, Frank Graham, Louisville's Barry Bingham, financier J. P. Morgan, and former governors and future cabinet secretaries. The CDAAA official position stopped short of calling for a declaration of war, but the ads urged

President Roosevelt to do everything legally possible to lend aid to France and England, including offering humanitarian relief to civilians in the conquered nations.

Begun with the endorsement of just a handful of persons, the CDAAA gathered support rapidly. The 53 original endorsers were joined by 350 others within a month. Membership would grow to more than 750,000 within the year.[13] Just days before the CDAAA's advertisements appeared, Joseph J. Spengler of the Duke economics department had asked Hill to head the North Carolina chapter. Because of his involvement with Miller, however, Hill referred Spengler to Couch, who had been on the phone with him the same day that Spengler's letter arrived at Hill's office.[14]

Pressure from CDAAA put President Roosevelt in a difficult position. His sympathies lay with those who urged American support for the Allies, and he had already opened a connection to British prime minister Winston Churchill outside of normal diplomatic channels through a Canadian named William Stevenson. He also began receiving confidential reports from William J. Donovan, a New York lawyer and World War I hero who was traveling the world gathering information on his behalf. At the same time, playwright Robert Sherwood, a Roosevelt speechwriter and White House insider, worked closely with the CDAAA. But Roosevelt was hamstrung by neutrality laws passed in the mid-1930s that prohibited shipments of arms or supplies to any belligerent in an international conflict. At the same time, he was weighing a decision on whether to seek an unprecedented third term. Any tilt toward the Allies would be sure to draw a strong response from isolationists.

❧❧❧

As the summer of 1940 began, Ann Hill and the children headed to Virginia Beach. Watts joined them when he could break away from Durham, usually on weekends. At the same time, he was making weekly trips to New York. The Hills enjoyed the city (Ann had many friends there), and a year earlier Ann had taken an apartment on East Fifty-fourth Street just off Fifth Avenue. Hill's attention was rapidly shifting from problems in the rural South—Graham had enlisted him to work on a ten-year agricultural planning group—to the alarming developments abroad. He seemed fully energized by the excitement in his circle of friends. In addition to spiking his patriotic fever, this new work offered Hill a chance to become part of a new national conversation.

In mid-July, Hill received a telegram from Lewis W. Douglas, the president of the Mutual Life Insurance Company, urging him to attend a July 11 meeting at New York's Columbia Club. "In view implications for United States of possible British defeat," the telegram from Douglas read, "I am asking a dozen carefully selected men of wide influence to confer." Hill could not make this meeting, but he was present two weeks later at New York's Century Club when the group that would later be called the Miller Group, or the Century Group, convened again.

Francis Miller had prepared the guest list for Douglas's meeting, and it included some of the leading figures in the interventionists's camp. Included were magazine publisher Henry R. Luce, retired admiral William H. Standley, theologian Henry Sloane Coffin, Dartmouth College president Ernest M. Hopkins, and Whitney Shephardson. In the following weeks, the group doubled in size to include future secretary of state Dean Acheson, columnists Joseph Alsop and Robert S. Allen, future CIA chief Allen W. Dulles, news commentator Elmer Davis, Barry Bingham, *Herald-Tribune* editor Geoffrey Parsons, New York manufacturer Ward Cheney, writer William Agar, Harvard's Conant, Robert Sherwood, and others.[15]

Ann Hill joked with her husband about his "boys' club,"[16] but at the same time she encouraged his participation in an effort in which her more progressive and liberal political attitudes actually merged with those of her husband. While it was not apparent at the time, this group would produce the leadership cadre of the wartime intelligence and spy operation known as the Office of Strategic Services and establish a network whose influence in the media and in Washington would shape public opinion and public policy for years to come. Miller later called his work with the Century Group "the most satisfying experience in my life." He wrote, "It was thrilling that summer to realize what it meant to be an American and to have some part in turning the tide against tyranny."[17] The OSS would be rated as one of the pivotal forces in the shaping of U.S. policy in the months prior to American entry in World War II.

Douglas's June 11 meeting ended without a decision on a clear course of action but with a consensus that the United States was as threatened by Nazi Germany as were France and England. The British fleet was all that stood between the United States and the Nazis, and it was a thin line indeed. There was work to be done, and Miller asked for a release from his duties at the Council on Foreign Relations to organize a campaign. He rented an office on the twenty-ninth floor of the Albee Building on Forty-second Street in New York, just a few blocks away from the offices of William Stevenson, Churchill's man in America, whose quarters were on the thirty-fifth floor of Rockefeller Center. Ironically, Miller found that among his neighbors in the Albee Building were officials of the German Fellowship Forum, a front group for German intelligence. Over the following months, he kept an eye on the Germans and forwarded details of their activities to the Federal Bureau of Investigation.[18]

By the time members of the Century Group gathered for a meeting on July 25, a plan was beginning to take shape. Miller had gathered information from the British, who badly wanted flying boats—the patrol bombers, or PBYs, in service as part of the American coastal defense—as well as ships, particularly destroyers, which were needed to patrol the English Channel. At the meeting's end, the group agreed to work to influence public opinion in such a way that it would become safe for Roosevelt to release more than a hundred out-of-date American destroyers to the British without crippling his political influence. "The naval situation is more desperate than anyone realizes," Hill wrote in the minutes of the meeting that he later transcribed and circulated to the members. In addition, England was running short of airplane pilots. The British were outnumbered two to one in fighter planes and twelve to one in bombers.[19]

President Roosevelt had already stretched the limits of the neutrality laws in June, when he used a provision in the law that allowed the War Department to sell "surplus" planes, guns, ammunition, and tanks to private concerns. Working with Stevenson, Roosevelt ordered the sale to a corporation that in turn sold the materiel to the British. Ships were being loaded at East Coast ports within days. Army chief of staff George Marshall later said he would need divine forgiveness for declaring a significant portion of America's bomber squadrons and valuable munitions to be surplus. Ships of the line, such as the mothballed destroyers, were another matter. It was going to be difficult to pull them under the surplus tent.

In late July, Miller and members of the Century Group along with the CDAAA launched an advertising and public relations campaign that they hoped would pave the way for the destroyer sale. A major coup for Miller was gaining public endorsement of the sale from General John J. Pershing, perhaps the nation's best-known warrior, who made a radio appeal on behalf of the transfer. Other broadcasts followed by Admiral Standley,

William J. Donovan, and Sherwood. Congressmen found their offices flooded with letters.

Hill did his part at home and organized a group in Rocky Mount, North Carolina, that bought an ad in the local newspaper in support of the destroyer deal. He was less successful with North Carolinians in Washington. Senator Reynolds told him that he believed he had gone as far as he could in approving the sale of surplus material; "I cannot see by any stretch of the imagination how we can say that destroyers are surplus material," he told Hill.[20] Representative John H. Kerr wrote Hill to say that while he hoped the British Empire could be saved, the sale would be "such a war-like act that Germany and its allies would immediately . . . declare war against the United States."[21]

Hill's blood was up. He responded to Kerr on August 24, just as the campaign reached its peak with the radio broadcasts orchestrated by Miller. The letter was characteristic of a style that would become more pronounced in Hill's later writing; he argued his case boldly and without reserve. "I feel that we should do whatever we do openly and above board, straight from the shoulder, and not give a whoop what Germany may think," he wrote. "Why should we worry about the feelings of a totalitarian state when their actions prove that they do not worry in the slightest about the feelings of any one other than themselves. They are opportunists of the first water. Germany will attack the United States when she pleases, if she pleases, and no declaration, or lack of one will have the slightest effect on her actions."[22]

Given the opportunity, Roosevelt was determined to answer Churchill's urgent plea for help. At a midsummer cabinet meeting, he embraced the notion of exchanging the ships for leases to British bases in Newfoundland and the West Indies, an idea offered by Secretary of War Frank Knox. (Miller is credited with having conceived the plan, which he forwarded to Knox, who was in close touch with Donovan and others in the Century Group.) The exchange plan was bolstered in mid-August after a supporting legal brief written by Dean Acheson, another Century Group member, was published. What Roosevelt was looking for was political safety, and finally, in late August, Douglas and Davenport received assurances that Wendell Willkie, the Republican presidential nominee, would not turn the destroyer sale into a campaign issue. This news was forwarded to Roosevelt, who announced the destroyers-for-bases exchange at an impromptu news conference in his railroad car on September 3. Roosevelt called it the "most important event in the defense of the U.S. since Thomas Jefferson's Louisiana Purchase."[23]

❧❧❧

Hill had become as preoccupied with events in Europe in the fall of 1940 as he was at Quail Roost, where he and Ann were awaiting the completion of their new 13,000-square-foot house at the farm. E. Bradford Tazewell of Norfolk, Virginia, an architect who later participated in the restoration of Colonial Williamsburg, designed a large two-story brick home in the Williamsburg style that he tailored to the Hills' special tastes. Despite its size, the house was not imposing, and it sat on the edge of the woods facing west, with its back side a virtual wall of windows. The Hills had a commanding view of the green pastures and post and rail fences below. After more than fifteen years of marriage, it was the first home the Hills could call their own. While Watts focused on the architectural details, Ann outfitted the interior and landscaped the grounds.

The house was the latest addition to a farm that had grown well beyond even Watts Hill's early estimates. The entire operation was under the watchful eye of manager W. W. Fitzpatrick, who supervised a staff of thirty that worked fifteen hundred acres planted in oats, corn, alfalfa, lespedeza, and pasture. Among the outbuildings were the main barn with individual drinking fountains for eighty cows, a test barn with box stalls for thirty more, two calf barns, a milk house, and a feed mill. The grave of High Point Prince Maxim, the prize bull Watts Hill had bought for $7,500, was on the grounds in the center of this complex of buildings. Hill had sold more than $50,000 worth of Prince Maxim's progeny by the time of the bull's death. There were nine thoroughbreds in the horse stable, and the farm kept eighteen foxhounds. The Quail Roost dairy herd included two hundred seventy-five registered cattle. On an average day in 1940, each one of Quail Roost's "Golden Guernseys" produced a little more than three gallons of milk.

Watts and Ann Hill hoped the move to the farm would be the balm she had not found in medications prescribed for her chronic ailments, which produced a serious strain on the entire family. Her physical limitations made it almost impossible for her to keep pace with an active and headstrong husband who often followed his passions without particular regard for where others were in their own lives. She often found that her husband had invited unexpected guests for dinner. After more than fifteen years of marriage, the couple's relationship was not so much a partnership as an arrangement where each stayed within the narrow corridors of their own lives. Ann was finally about to become mistress of her own house; Watts was in charge of everything else.

☙☙☙

Building the new house and working with the Century Group were welcome releases for Watts Hill from the routine of his duties at the bank offices on Corcoran Street. Although Hill had seen a lot of the world in his lifetime, Francis Miller introduced him to a part of America that was not readily apparent in central North Carolina. The South had not seen the huge America First rallies that elsewhere drew tens of thousands to hear Charles Lindbergh, U.S. senator Burton Wheeler, and other isolationists who preached that aid to the Allied cause was a waste of precious resources. And nothing in Durham was as provocative as what Hill witnessed one evening in September 1940 at a small theater in New York's Yorkville section, a German-American neighborhood on the city's Upper East Side. For two and a half hours, he watched German newsreels, a short film entitled "The Parade" that showed Hitler reviewing his troops, and a feature-length film about the German invasion of Poland.

"I hope that you and every member of Congress may be able to see this picture," he wrote to North Carolina's Senator Josiah Bailey a few days later, "as I believe any American who stops to think will develop as much cold hate as I did during that two and a half hours." He continued: "It was also quite a shock to me to hear the tremendous cheering whenever Hitler's picture came on the screen, as well as the cheers when some statement derogatory to America appeared."[24]

By the end of 1940, by which time President Roosevelt had been reelected, there was evidence of a shift in public sentiment; more Americans now favored the idea of providing aid to the Allies. For some Americans, the fall of France in the summer had underscored the urgency of the situation in Europe. In Chapel Hill, the CDAAA chapter had enrolled 350 members, while in Asheville a CDAAA organizer recruited more than 3,200 supporters. In mid-December, with Watts Hill acting as secretary, the SPC's North Carolina chapter gathered again at Mid-Pines and issued a statement endorsing Roosevelt's foreign policy.

Hill did not stop there. Shortly after the first of the year, he began working with Couch, Graham, Duke's Calvin Hoover, and Ralph McDonald, a liberal college professor and unsuccessful Democratic gubernatorial candidate, on yet another effort to raise public outrage over events in Europe. On January 10, 1941, Hill announced the names of nearly three dozen people prominent in business and politics who had responded favorably to a resolution that stopped short of advocating a declaration of war but called for the mobilization of North Carolina "for defense by backing up President Roosevelt's foreign policy for defense, including the fullest aid to Britain." The group, described as a "spontaneous movement," would later become the foundation for a new organization, the Southern Committee to Defend America, or Defend America Now.[25]

Those on Hill's list were a cross section of North Carolina life. They had been recruited one afternoon by Hill, Couch, and McDonald, who gathered in Hill's Durham office. By telephone and with telegrams (all paid for by Hill), the three won the endorsements of former governors Clyde Hoey and J. C. B. Ehringhaus; textile manufacturers Stuart Cramer of Charlotte, Thurmond Chatham of Elkin, and Kemp Lewis of Durham; bankers Word Wood of Charlotte and Robert Hanes of Winston-Salem; and newspaper editors Julian Miller of Charlotte, D. Hiden Ramsey of Asheville, Louis Graves of Chapel Hill, and John Marshall of Wilmington. The list also included Hervey Evans of Laurinburg, one of the largest cotton growers in the Carolinas; Duke University president R. L. Flowers; and William D. Carmichael Jr., Hill's boyhood friend who had left his business in New York to become the business manager of the University of North Carolina. Hill even got his father's endorsement.

While the statement did not go so far as to advocate a declaration of war against the Fascist governments of Germany and Italy, it was apparently as strongly worded a statement as the group could sell. Stuart Cramer, a former West Pointer, told Hill he would allow his name to be used but that Hill should know he was leaning toward isolation. "I am not in the slightest interested in trying to impose our philosophical system on anybody except ourselves," he wrote, "any more than I am willing to have Hitler and Stalin dictate our philosophy of government."[26] Even the Chapel Hill CDAAA chapter was reluctant to go too far. At the group's January 10 meeting, where Hill made his announcement, chapter president Dr. Archibald Henderson argued that a resolution that called for both an end to neutrality and the use of American ships to transport war supplies was too drastic. It was sent to a committee for study.

Hill planned for the new group to be the first in a southern alliance that would generate vocal and vigorous support for the Lend-Lease Bill, which was currently before Congress. Local chairs were to be selected, and they in turn were to contact civic clubs, churches, lodges, and women's clubs in both the black and white communities to help turn out crowds for mass rallies. Local committees would be encouraged to sponsor radio "round table discussions on aid to Britain at least 30 minutes once a week." A planning memo advised, "Let the opposition speak in these discussions because only when the opposition is allowed to speak can interest be built up."[27] It was every bit a political campaign, but one built around a cause, not a candidate.

At the end of January, Hill was on the phone to Hollywood movie producer Walter Wanger, a member of the Century Group, asking for help in arranging for movie stars to enliven rallies around the state. He told Couch that he hoped to get actress Joan Bennett, who was Wanger's wife, but that he would settle for actor Douglas Fairbanks Jr., who had endorsed the CDAAA.[28] Meanwhile, Couch dispatched the woman who had registered the CDAAA members in Asheville to Atlanta to open a regional office, and he began making arrangements to bring actress Tallulah Bankhead to a rally in Atlanta.

The regional network never developed into the popular movement that Hill and Couch had envisioned, but it did stir some comment across the South. Their failure was not for lack of trying nor for lack of money. Once again, Hill personally paid the expenses of field-workers who periodically traveled around the South to maintain contact with the committees established in other states. The group simply got overrun by events.

∾∾∾

Even as the southern committees were being organized, Hill remained busy in New York with Fight For Freedom (FFF), which was sponsored by the Century Group. This effort was closely linked to the growing cooperation between British intelligence agents operating in the United States and the White House. One historian even credited William Stevenson with orchestrating the creation of FFF to mobilize America on behalf of the Allies. That was a bit of an exaggeration, but there is no doubt that the members of the Century Group who launched FFF were in regular contact with Stevenson.[29] Clearly, FFF fit neatly into the British strategy to bring the United States into the war.

In late April 1941, James P. Warburg, editor of *Foreign Affairs* and one of the original Century Group members, explained the FFF mission in a nationwide radio broadcast: "The Fight For Freedom Committee believes that the time for half-measures has passed, that we no longer have a choice between war and peace, but only a choice between total war now, with victory reasonably assured, or total war later, when victory will be infinitely more difficult to attain." It was a call to arms more strongly worded than anything heard before. Warburg continued: "This is our Fight for Freedom. This is no 'foreign war,' nor is it a fight to save any other nation. It is our fight—for us to win, or for us to lose. The longer we wait the harder will be our battle."[30]

FFF attracted support from nearly every corner of American society. Most of its members lived and worked in the Northeast, but money poured in from Hollywood moguls Darryl Zanuck and the Warner brothers. David K. E. Bruce of Virginia, whom Hill had come to know socially on the horse circuit, contributed $10,000 to the cause, an amount matched by the Rockefellers.[31] Hill contributed his name and his bank account when he agreed to raise $300,000 in sponsorships for the FFF newspaper advertisements, billboards, and radio broadcasts.[32]

The FFF logo featured a large V crossed by a lightning bolt, with the dot-dot-dot-dash Morse code sign for "V" underneath. Its newspaper ads carried endorsements from men and women from across the nation. In September 1941, Hill's picture appeared with the pictures of eleven other national business leaders in a full-page ad in the *New York Herald-Tribune.* The page was topped by a headline that asked the question, "Business With Hitler?" It was intended to be an antidote to the claim of isolationists like Lindbergh that American businessmen had nothing to fear from a Nazi-dominated Europe. In the statement that appeared beside Hill's photograph was the quotation, "We know that it is either Hitler's way or ours, and that unless we act fast, there'll be no free business here or elsewhere in the world."

During the summer of 1941, before the ad appeared, Hill heard firsthand reports of the war from officers of the British carrier *Formidable*, which was in the yards at Norfolk for repairs. Officers from the ship visited the Hills's beach house. Later, Hill and others learned of the Battle of Britain and heard the German bombs that were pounding London; radio broadcasts brought the war home to all Americans, who for the first time heard the rolling thunder of explosions, the steady firing of anti-aircraft guns, and the footsteps of Londoners headed to underground shelters. That fall, Hill was in New York's Madison Square Garden for a rally sponsored by FFF's stage, screen, radio, and arts division. The crowd listened to addresses from Burgess Meredith and Helen Hayes and enjoyed a variety show that included popular screen and radio personalities Jack Benny, Eddie Cantor, Carmen Miranda, and Eddy Duchin. War was just around the corner.

The surprise attack at Pearl Harbor by the Japanese on December 7, 1941, left Hill struggling with questions about his own future. Even before the attack, he was convinced America would eventually join the war, and he had inquired about a commission in the navy. The navy told him he was too old. He talked with Couch in Chapel Hill about keeping alive the southern committees, which in the fall had been merged into the FFF organization. Then, just before Christmas, Hill learned that FFF was being shut down. Some of those with whom he had shared long hours in the battle for public opinion were already in uniform. The New York offices were empty.

Hill felt he was going to be left behind as his country headed to war. He had been too young to serve in 1918, and now at age forty it appeared he was too old. In an desperate plea to FFF's Ulric Bell, he wrote, "If you know of any way that I can be of more assistance in any capacity. Army, Navy, New York, Washington, or what not—than I am in the present job of draft board chairman and head of various industrial organizations, I would appreciate your letting me know."[33]

෴෴෴

It was hard to keep the Christmas holidays in perspective. The old standards no longer seemed to apply, and the impossible seemed to have come true. The war was far away, yet as close as the morning paper. The *Durham Morning Herald* published silhouettes of German and Japanese fighter planes. Guards were posted around Erwin Mills and the Wright Automatic Machine Company, both of which had defense contracts. The offices of the Depositors National Bank were turned into a recruiting office for white volunteers; black volunteers were advised to report to the post office. A leader of the "home guard" urged folks to be on the lookout for saboteurs, particularly Germans. He was not as worried about hostile Asians. "There are hardly any Japanese in this area, anyhow," he said. "You can spot a Japanese a mile away."[34]

Fear of a possible Japanese attack on the West Coast threatened to cause the cancellation of the popular Rose Bowl football game until officials decided to move the 1942 game to—of all places—Durham. Before the December 7 attack, the Duke team had been scheduled to meet Oregon State on New Year's Day in Pasadena, California, for the nation's most popular holiday sporting event. After some quick negotiation, Duke and Durham prepared to welcome 50,000 football fans, which was almost as many people as there were residents of the city.

At Quail Roost, Watts Jr. was due home from Millbrook, the private school in upstate New York where he was midway through his third year of classes. Ann Hill was expected home soon too. She had been away since October at Silver Hill, a private hospital in Connecticut. Dudley and Sprunt were at home and finished with their classes at the Calvert School. One tradition did not change; the family headed to Southern Pines with Grandfather Hill for golf and foxhunting.

Watts Hill was restless but hopeful that he would find some way to serve in the military soon. On December 16, President Roosevelt endorsed a War Department request that American men between the ages of nineteen and forty-four be made eligible for the draft. In the midst of the holiday celebration, Watts wrote his wife's doctors to ask their advice about whether he should reapply for a commission in the navy. He was told that there should be no problem as long as he made arrangements for the care of Ann and the children.

On New Year's Day, 56,000 people turned out for the Rose Bowl game at the Duke football stadium, a horseshoe of seats built to hold half that many spectators. It was rainy and cold, but even bad weather could not dissuade the faithful from attending the most exciting athletic contest in years. Julian Price of Greensboro, the head of Jefferson Standard Life Insurance Company, showed up in waterproof overalls. Before the kickoff, the stadium fell silent in a tribute to Army Second Lieutenant Foy Roberson Jr., the son of Watts Hill's close friend who was medical director at Watts Hospital. The flier had been killed in a midair collision while on sea patrol off San Diego, California.

Duke was favored to win, but Oregon State beat them with a passing game, twenty to sixteen. The game was an exciting end to the bewildering holiday season. Shortly afterward, the Hills put Watts Jr. on a train for the trip back to Millbrook and then drove to the Charleston Navy Yard, where Watts volunteered for active duty and took a physical examination. The navy doctors pronounced him fit, and Watts and Ann returned to Quail Roost, where he awaited word about his future.

The decision to join the navy had not come easily. In addition to his wife's health problems, Watts Hill was concerned about his absence from the family businesses. He confided to his wife's doctor that he was constantly on call from John Sprunt Hill's subordinates, who came to him with questions about instructions they had received from his father, who was approaching his seventy-third birthday. "He issues orders on incorrect information, and it has been my job to try to straighten out the mess," he wrote just before Christmas.[35] At the same time, however, Watts Hill was confident that B. W. Harris Jr., his accountant and trusted personal assistant, now treasurer of the bank, could handle his affairs and even act as a stand-in until he could deal personally with pressing issues.

Harris occupied a desk just outside the door to Watts Hill's office, where he had been since the Hill Building opened. His first full-time assignment was to pay the bills for the construction of the Hill Building. By 1942, he was handling virtually all of Watts Hill's personal finances and preparing tax returns for both father and son. The Hills relied on both his judgment and his discretion.

As the days passed in February, Watts Hill became impatient to receive his orders from the navy. Even though his commission had not come through, he had already ordered a uniform from his New York tailor. He answered the navy's request that he chair the Navy Relief Society campaign in North Carolina, and he even put in a few days of work at the society's New York office. On March 11, he finally reported to Admiral William H. Allen, commandant of the Sixth Naval District, in Charleston, and Allen told Hill that he was to be the navy procurement officer who dealt with applicants for commissions from North Carolina. His office would be in Raleigh. Then Hill got a telegram from Francis Miller.

⟳ ⟳ ⟳

Since the first of the year, Miller had been working with William J. Donovan, who had been running something called the Coordinating Office of Information (COI) for President Roosevelt. Americans had never been keen on the spy business, and as the nation stumbled toward war in the summer of 1941 Roosevelt asked Donovan to begin gathering all manner of intelligence on affairs abroad. One columnist called the COI "a somewhat mysterious ideological and political Scotland Yard, studying the origins and technics of Nazi power." In the fall of 1941, Donovan added David Bruce to his staff along with Duke's Calvin Hoover, whose studies of totalitarian regimes included two recent books on the Third Reich.

Miller wired Hill to say that Bruce wanted to see him in Washington as soon as possible. "This is important. Let me know when I can make appointment for you and see me before you see him," Miller's telegram read.[36] Hill left for Washington immediately aboard the overnight train he called the "Rattler" for a meeting with Bruce on the nineteenth.

"He talked to me for about an hour," Hill later recalled, "and I said, 'Well, what do you want me to do?' He said, 'Come up here and help me.' And that's the only instructions I had for about two years. I came on home, got my stuff together, went back to Washington. My wife was ga-ga. She didn't know why I was moving so fast, but he said he wanted me so I went on up."[37]

On Monday, March 23, Hill reported for duty as the executive officer in the SA/B (Special Activities/Bruce), the secret intelligence section of COI. He was number twenty-three on the employment roster in an organization that would expand to employ more than thirteen thousand employees by war's end, when it would be known as the Office of Strategic Services.

Cloaked in secrecy, staffed by eccentrics, and run by the indomitable Donovan, the staff of the COI was mushrooming like nearly every government agency in Washington. When Hill arrived, he knew a few of those working at COI's temporary headquarters at Twenty-fifth and E streets, an old building that had once been part of the National Health Institute. Hill's taxi driver recognized it by the distinctive red flagpole that stood out front. Most of the familiar faces were from his prewar campaigns. In time, more than two dozen of those who were active in the Century Group became part of OSS.

Of all those with whom Hill would work during the next four years, Bruce certainly epitomized the side of OSS that would earn it the nickname of "Oh So Social," which referred to its ties to Eastern Establishment money and power. Handsome, cultured, and wealthy, Bruce was the Princeton-educated son of former U.S. senator William C. Bruce of Maryland. He had served with the field artillery in World War I before earning a law degree at the University of Virginia. In 1926, he married Ailsa Mellon, the daughter of Secretary of the Treasury Andrew Mellon and heiress to a vast fortune. They spent their honeymoon en route to his assignment with the State Department in Rome. In 1936, the Bruces returned to the States and settled at Staunton Hall near Brookneal in Southside Virginia. Bruce was representing the American Red Cross in London when Donovan asked him to come to Washington to organize COI's intelligence-gathering operations.

Bruce joined COI in October 1941. Donovan told him he wanted information from any source, including underground operations in Europe. Bruce connected with the experienced British intelligence operation, and in February he brought Francis Miller on board to oversee affairs in England. Bruce wanted Hill in Washington to bring order to the administrative chaos in his corner of COI. Hill took little convincing; Bruce's offer was eminently more challenging and exciting than the prospect of processing applications for navy commissions in Raleigh.

There remained the sticky question of Hill's obligation to the navy. Some high-ranking officials had gone out of their way to make a place for him in the service, and orders had already been issued for his assignment to Raleigh. Since Hill's commission was in the pipeline, Bruce asked the navy to simply reassign him to COI. In a letter to navy commander Francis P. Old, he said, "Lt. Hill has been employed as an executive in this office for some time and possesses qualifications, special training and contacts which make him literally indispensable for certain confidential special duty assignments under our direction."[38] Bruce was told that the transfer would not work, however, and three days later Hill resigned the commission he had worked so hard to get. The same day, Donovan wrote Secretary of War Frank Knox on Hill's behalf, asking Knox to put a notation in Hill's file explaining that Hill had resigned for good reasons. "I feel that in justice to his patriotic motives there should be some record in the Navy files as to the real reason for his declination of the proffered commission, so that if he applies at a later date for commissioning there will be no misapprehension regarding his case," Donovan wrote.[39]

The onrush of war preparations that Hill discovered in Washington compounded the dramatic changes that the once sleepy southern city had undergone in the previous decade. Washington's population had nearly doubled in the 1930s, and one observer said that with the expansion of New Deal agencies, government was spreading throughout the district "like warm axle grease."[40] Government agencies occupied more than three hundred fifty buildings, many of which had not been built to last long or to suit their requisitioned use. When COI moved into the Health Institute building, caged animals still remained in the laboratory on the upper floor. The government was busy building a colossus across the river that would later be called the Pentagon. Meanwhile, military offices were scattered about the city.

Hill was only one of about seventy thousand new residents who arrived in 1942. Everything was in short supply, particularly housing. Rooms were so scarce that hotels limited guests to a three-day stay. Hill and others from the COI found quarters on the outskirts of town at the Congressional Country Club, which had been commandeered as a training camp for Donovan's growing staff. Though a fashionable address, the accommodations were spare. A late-season snowstorm hit one weekend shortly after Hill arrived, and the club lost electrical power, effectively shutting off water to the bathrooms. Hill rose early in the morning to siphon a personal supply from a spigot in the basement. Later, he had to bum a ride into town because his car was short on antifreeze.

Lifestyle aside, Hill knew he was embarking on an exciting and challenging phase of his life that promised to give him more freedom to demonstrate his talents in a way impossible within the confines of the family-owned businesses back home. At the same time, the COI was the ultimate "boys' club," as Ann Hill had called the Century Group. The stakes were higher than they had been before the war, but Hill believed he would adapt easily. In fact, he excelled in his work for the COI, demonstrating alacrity and finesse. He had finally found his war.

Hill reported to work at Q Building, a "temporary" building on Constitution Avenue that was left over from the First World War. For the time being, he was an unpaid civilian, working for $10 a day to cover expenses. ("I can live on my $10 subsistence," he wrote Harris in Durham, "but it won't be much fun.") He was called a "consultant," but he leveraged Bruce's authority to make things happen. His first assignment was to outfit the section's offices. That meant finding desks, chairs, file cabinets, and typewriters for a staff that was growing daily. Not long after Hill arrived, the government said it was short six hundred thousand typewriters; Chester

Bowles of the Office of Price Administration sent a team through empty offices at night to liberate one out of every seven machines that they found. Hill cajoled phone installers into putting his office at the top of the list. At the same time, he told his father he had to "steal" three desks before he even found one for himself. But by the time Bruce returned from a trip to England in the summer of 1942, he found the place in good order and his own desk flanked by British and American flags.

Much of Hill's time was spent interviewing prospective employees. He met all kinds. Some wanted to be spies, others just secretaries and assistants to spies. One was a German musician who had known Ernst Roehm, a top Hitler aide who had been killed in a prewar purge. Another was, like Hill, a former Hotchkiss student; he offered to handle the OSS public relations. Hill hired the office personnel, fixed their salaries, and settled their disputes in the course of meeting an exhausting daily schedule that began with breakfast at 8 A.M. in the Q building cafeteria and often ended after 7 P.M. The work was absolutely exhilarating, he told Harris. "Folks have been most cooperative, the work is tremendously interesting and I have a great boss. If I live thro it I think I can really show Durham how to get the work out of people."[41]

Hill was impressed most with the people he found around him. There were the socially prominent, like Bruce and Bruce's in-laws the Mellons. A Vanderbilt was working in special operations, a Du Pont headed French operations, and in time two of J. P. Morgan's sons would become part of the organization. Hollywood director John Ford was in charge of the OSS photographic operations. Rhodes Scholars and academics with advanced degrees were commonplace. "I am one of the real outcasts," Hill wrote his father, "but because I get the work done in spite of the red tape, they have tolerated me so far."[42] Hill put a former auto mechanic and a Brooklyn motorman behind a desk. One of his best scavengers for unattached equipment was Francis Miller's street-savvy assistant from New York City. "We were working with an unusual type of individual," an OSS employee named R. Harris Smith wrote. "Many had natures that fed on danger and excitement."[43] David Bruce later recalled: "All were fish in [Donovan's] net. Ornithologists, anthropologists, college professors of every category, safe-crackers, paroled convicts, remittance men, professional wrestlers and boxers, circus stars, code experts, military characters, night club frequenters, and a miscellany of others, including the majority ordinary citizens, jumbled together in what, organizationally, appeared to be chaos."[44]

Donovan liked his odd-lot collection of lawyers, businessmen, and bankers; he said it was easier to train an honest man to be shady than to surround himself with thieves. After columnist Drew Pearson complained that OSS was made up of too many "Wall Street bankers," Donovan said, "You know, these bankers and corporation lawyers make wonderful second-story men."[45]

Hill wrote his father: "It does seem queer that me with no particular technical experience should have been pitched into a job to hold a bunch of prima donnas in line and make the wheels go around in the right direction. Maybe it is a good thing that I worked with so many and varied jobs in Durham; the experience has certainly stood me in good stead."[46]

Donovan's freewheeling manner was infuriating to many, but Hill liked his boss's style. It was not entirely unlike his own. Throughout his life, if Watts Hill wanted to do something, he usually found a way to satisfy the urge. Donovan, too, was not put off by inconveniences. When the OSS needed extra money or equipment, he simply called the White House, and his wishes were fulfilled. Both Hill and Donovan were men of action, eager to see results and impatient with lengthy preparations. Francis Miller would eventually leave the OSS, frustrated by Donovan's contempt for the virtue of well-laid plans. Hill stayed to the end.

From time to time, Hill found himself representing Bruce's section in Donovan's weekly sessions, meetings at which all manner of ideas might arise. "He ran OSS like a country editor," Bruce later wrote of Donovan. "Woe to the officer who turned down a project because, on its face, it seemed ridiculous, or at least unusual."[47] One day, before the initial allied offensive in North Africa in the fall of 1942, Donovan turned to Hill and told him to get him everything he could on North Africa. Three weeks later, Hill returned with details from the Library of Congress on electric power, airports, seaports, highways, and even a warning to avoid the swamps around Dakar, which he personally had seen during his honeymoon trip fifteen years before. In fact, Hill discovered that many of the photographs from his trip around the world with Ann were useful to the OSS. Hill's snapshots of Tokyo and other locations in Korea and Asia were as current as anything that the government had on hand. After all, the map in the president's war room had come from the National Geographic Society.

All the while that Hill was filling an exhausting schedule in Washington, he was monitoring affairs three hundred miles away at Quail Roost through phone calls, letters, and weekly financial reports from Harris. Ann Hill was at home with Dudley, Sprunt, and the household servants. Life had become more difficult in Durham than it had been even during the height of the depression. For example, gasoline rations for the city had been calculated on the basis of Durham's prewar usage, which did not account for the gasoline needed by the 20,000 workers who were building Camp Butner ten miles north of the city. The federal encampment covered portions of Durham, Granville, and Person counties, and the same bus that carried Sprunt to school was filled each day with workers shuttling to and from Butner.[48]

Hill bunked at the country club until June, when he finally found a house to rent, no small accomplishment in a city where men and women stood outside the newspaper offices at press time to grab the first editions of the classifieds. After real estate agents failed to turn up anything, he finally started knocking on doors himself. The house he found was near the Wardham Park Hotel at 2701 Thirty-first Street NW, and it was furnished except that it lacked linens and silver, which Hill had someone send up from Quail Roost. With Ann and the children at Virginia Beach for the summer, he invited another COI couple, Arthur Roseborough and his wife, to share the house with him. Like Hill, Roseborough was an early recruit; he was Donovan's fourth pick when he set up COI. When Watts could break away, he joined Ann at the beach, often hopping a navy flight from Washington to Norfolk.

In Virginia Beach, the war was uncomfortably close at the edge of the Atlantic. German U-boats used the Atlantic seaboard for a shooting gallery throughout much of 1942. With the U.S. Navy short of ships for convoy duty, hundreds of lone merchant vessels went to the bottom that year. Lifeboats leaving burning hulks were often visible from shore, and the beaches were closed due to the contamination from oil and refuse that came in with the tide. Ann wrote that the explosion of torpedoes against steel hulls could be felt as well as seen from the beach. Watts Jr. spent part of the summer on the dunes spotting airplanes with an older family friend.

In June, the COI was disbanded. The agency's propaganda function was given to a new Office of War Information headed by newsman Elmer Davis. The balance of the group was reorganized into the Office of Strategic Services and placed under the operational control of the Joint Chiefs of

Staff. Donovan remained in charge, and the military tried to impose controls on his unorthodox methods and style.

The overhaul put Hill's own future with the OSS in doubt. As an "unvouchered" consultant, he was really working off the books, and there was no official record of his service, duties, or responsibilities. It was a common practice for Donovan to hire such unvouchered consultants in the early days when he ran COI out of his hip pocket. Hill's uncertain situation coupled with the secret nature of his work caused him to feel moments of regret that he had given up his commission. Describing his feelings about giving up the commission, he told a friend: "This was one of the toughest decisions I had to make in a great many years. You know enough about the job to know that I cannot describe it or discuss it with anybody, and folks at home will never understand, and will think and say that I ducked active duty for a desk job in Washington."[49] He confided that he was considering trying to rejoin the navy, although he had been told that once he had turned down a commission, the service was not likely to offer it again. Whatever happened, he hoped that he could remain with OSS in some capacity.

Bruce was not about to let Hill get away. Hill had turned Bruce's operation into an island of efficiency in an agency where that word was seldom mentioned. "Standard operation procedures were almost taboo in OSS," one observer later wrote. "Effective action was the sole objective."[50] One of Hill's supervisors told Bruce: "Seldom have I seen a business man, accustomed to operating his own affairs, make the adjustment to the radically different field of government with such superb tact and judgment as has Watts Hill. Business men as a rule do not make good government administrators. If this opinion is accurate, Mr. Hill's ability to adjust himself, not only to work connected with broad-gauge policy affairs but also to the very simple details of office arrangement, etc., is all the more outstanding."[51]

After a few weeks of uncertainty, Hill's situation improved. Bruce asked him to make a scouting trip to England, where the OSS planned to open a London office. For a hush-hush agency like the OSS, it was unusual for news of an overseas trip to reach the papers, but the *Durham Sun* carried a short story about Hill's upcoming departure. News may have leaked from the draft board, which had to approve Hill's trip out of the country because he was still technically eligible for the draft.

Hill traveled on the same open-ended orders that Bruce had issued the day he offered Hill the job. His only portfolio was a memorandum from Bruce introducing him to contacts in London and oral instructions to take a measure of the place. On July 27, Hill left Washington on the train bound for New York. He held a seat on one of Pan American's Clippers; the company had initiated transatlantic service just three years before. A berth on a Clipper was hard to come by. Crossing by air was much preferred to ship crossing, which took longer and was vulnerable to Nazi submarine attack.

The Clipper was a huge lumbering bird whose four fourteen-cylinder engines mounted on a 152-foot wingspan carried the plane at a top speed of 190 miles per hour. It carried a crew of nine, including two stewards. Five passenger compartments, each of which contained ten seats by day and six berths at night, were on the lower deck. The lounge, dressing rooms, lavatory, and galley were on the upper deck. At 2:20 A.M. on the twenty-ninth, Hill's aircraft pushed off from the marine terminal near the New York airport and taxied out on the waters of the bay. Twenty-three hours and twenty-five minutes later, after a stopover in Ireland, Hill reached England.

The OSS had moved into its London quarters in the code room at 1 Grosvenor Square about ten days before Hill's arrival. He reported in to Whitney Shephardson, who had joined COI in April and had recently been assigned to London. Hill had less than a week to complete his work for Bruce, which included checking the logistics of the London office and completing details for a communications network between London and the States. Bruce had also asked him to take a look at the operation of one of the British commando schools. After Hill finished his administrative duties in the city, he was escorted north to Scotland for an orientation tour of a training camp. The instructors told him he was too old for a practice parachute jump, but they did put him through the paces in a survival course in which Hill had to make his way overland on his own. Tucked in his kit when he boarded the Clipper at Bristol for the return trip home was a copy of the school's training manual, which would be put to use when the OSS opened similar schools in the States.

On his return, Hill filed his report with Bruce, and the two later presented it to Allen Dulles at a special meeting in New York City. Most of the particulars involved streamlining communications and keeping overseas cables short and to the point. Hill also brought a request for $50,000 to build a communications center as a backup to one run by the British. And he put in a bid for ultraviolet lights and the establishment of a laboratory to produce special inks and papers for secret communications.

Another proposal had intriguing possibilities. Hill recommended to Dulles that as refugees arrived in the United States, OSS agents should "pinch" their clothing, identification papers, and passports and stockpile them for use by OSS and other agents who were being secreted into occupied territory. Within a few months, the OSS "closet," housed in the storage area of a former brewery across the Potomac from Washington on the Virginia end of Key Bridge, began to fill with clothing.[52]

❧❧❧

Hill did many jobs before he left the OSS in 1945, but nearly all of them involved locating all manner of devices—large and small, explosive and benign, mobile and stationary—and getting them into the hands of OSS agents. For a time in the latter part of 1943, he was director of the Division of Special Services, and he arranged supplies and logistics for both the intelligence and the special operations agents of OSS.

On February 10, 1943, Hill finally received the commission he had been seeking for more than a year. He was sworn in as a major in the army. He was not in the navy, as he had hoped, but he found the uniform to his liking nonetheless, and it fit him well. Unlike some of his peers at OSS who disdained military proper dress, Hill enjoyed the spit and polish and the sharp creases in his trousers. After receiving his commission, he was appointed as the requirements and transportation officer for special operations and put in charge of coordinating the delivery of all manner of war materials, from basic quartermaster supplies such as clothing and toilet paper to weapons, medical and engineering supplies, and chemical ordnance.

At one point, Hill helped Donovan obtain the first three planes in a modest OSS air force. Transportation had been a problem from the start, as the organization's bureaucrats and agents had to rely on available seats in navy and army aircraft to get around. Hill prepared a detailed analysis of the various types of aircraft available, taking into account their load capacities and ranges, and then drafted the paperwork for both the purchase of three medium-range transports and the appointment of an air officer from the army. He won high marks from his superiors for his work. "He got results," wrote one of his bosses in the spring of 1943.

The job was all consuming, but not without its quirky moments. As one of the few on the staff with an automobile, Hill was often called on to drive visitors to evening events. One night, Hill's fancy Lincoln Zephyr convertible died just as Donovan pushed in the cigar lighter. Apparently, the lighter shorted out the car's electrical circuits. Hill never forgot another encounter that occurred when Donovan was recuperating from a leg injury at his favorite New York hotel, the St. Regis. When Hill arrived at Donovan's room, he found Donovan soaking in a large St. Regis bathtub that was of a size to fit his considerable girth. Donovan had one woman at his head and another at his feet giving him a massage. "What are you doing here, Hill?" Donovan barked. Hill told him he had papers for his eyes only. "Girls, scram," Donovan ordered. Hill recalled: "The girls went out, I gave him the papers, he told me what to do and he said, 'Girls, come back.'" Hill headed back to Washington.[53]

Near the end of 1943, Hill arranged for a portion of the Oldfields School property just north of Baltimore that belonged to Ann Hill's family to become an OSS training outpost and way station. Filston, a large residence with nearly a dozen bedrooms, and two other country estates fell under strict government control. Hill's nephew, Duncan McCulloch III, was a youngster at the time, and he recalled seeing strangers on the narrow country road that led from the school to the small Glencoe train station. "Nobody dared go near them," he said many years later. Many of those assigned to train at Filston did not speak English, and their uniforms suggested that their homes were in nations far away. Access to the property was restricted; an armed guard escorted even the Oldfields farm manager to and from his fields when he went to cut hay.

The houses were turned into classrooms for courses in hand-to-hand combat, picking locks and blowing up safes, Morse code, ciphers, and other skills. OSS trainers erected pillboxes and bunkers along the nearby Gunpowder River and used them for demolition training. Agents tested explosive devices disguised as baseballs, explosives with delayed ignition, flashless guns, and tiny cameras disguised as matchboxes.[54]

"The neighborhood sometimes rattled with small arms fire and sometimes shook with explosions," McCulloch said. "At night, tracers and star shells illuminated the dark neighborhood with a strange eerie light." After the war, a model of the Normandy beaches and cliffs that had been scaled by American rangers on D-day was found in the basement of the house.

❧❧❧

Opportunities to take assignments overseas were offered to Hill, but he remained in Washington, largely because of his ongoing responsibilities in Durham. In the early months of his duty, he occasionally broke away to spend a weekend in the country at Quail Roost with Bruce or others from the office. As his workload grew larger, however, these trips became less frequent, and he relied on weekly reports and regular phone calls from Harris, who handled virtually everything, to keep his business affairs in order. Harris even found the Hills a suitable cook for their Washington house. With the family spread about the country, Hill had rented a more comfortable house in Washington. This one was on McGill Terrace, a short, tree-lined street near the fashionable Shoreham Hotel on Connecticut Avenue. It became the wartime base of Watts Jr., who entered his final year at Millbrook in 1943 after spending a summer working at the Wright-Patterson Air Force Base in Dayton, Ohio, as well as for Dudley and Sprunt, who both spent the summer at camp before returning to boarding schools near Washington.

Watts Hill's father, John Sprunt Hill, kept the family supplied with produce from his garden, hams, and fresh peaches when they were in season. The elder Hill planted a second garden in the back of Harwood Hall to add to the supply of vegetables for himself and other members of the family. In letters to his son, John Sprunt Hill offered news on the businesses and passed along his own view of the world. "I am not much disturbed about the country people here," he wrote in 1943, "but, believe me, I think some of the millions that are huddled together in big cities are going to catch the devil sure enough."[55]

Dudley probably saw more of her father than her brothers did in this period, and she found the times exciting. She was a student at Madeira, a private school in northern Virginia, and from time to time she spent weekends in Washington. She was in awe of a father who spent his time with men who had their homes checked for wiretaps and bombs, who made explosive gadgets disguised as camel dung or writing pens that exploded in gas tanks. One night, she arrived home with her date to find her father standing in the hallway of the house with a .50-caliber machine gun cradled in his arms. "He was trying to see if captured German and Italian bullets could be adjusted so they could be used in this gun," she said.

"You'd go to get a stamp and there'd be a grenade rolling around in the drawer," Dudley said. "Or the next door neighbor would lock himself out of the house and come over to use our phone and dad would say, 'Wait a minute.' And he'd go around and pick the lock, which isn't a skill a lot of bankers have."[56]

Watts Hill was indeed resourceful. He could parlay a tube of lipstick—a valuable commodity in wartime—into an appointment with people OSS agents needed to see. First, he sent the outer cover to a secretary with a promise that the lipstick would arrive when the appointment was confirmed. He also negotiated for a shipment of silk to be delivered to the family's hosiery mill in Durham—guaranteeing payment personally when brokers balked at taking an OSS voucher—that was to be woven into a special order of stockings for OSS agents to use in exchange for favors. Agents were instructed to supply one leg of the pair when a request was made; the second was delivered when the favor was done.

∾∾∾

Toward the end of 1943, Hill took an assignment that would be his for the balance of the war. The stockpiling of refugee clothing and the organization of its use by agents traveling behind the lines had become a fulltime job. For the record, he was the special equipment officer of the secret intelligence side of the agency. What that meant, among other things, was that he was in charge of expanding the agency's collection of clothing, documents, and other paraphernalia from abroad, as well as of designing reproductions that were carefully matched almost fiber by fiber with the originals. The used clothing collected from refugees was not even laundered in the States; the OSS wished to avoid introducing the telltale residues of cleaning fluids not used abroad. By the time the Allies landed at Normandy in June 1944, the warehouse in the States was full, and Bruce was ready to open additional collection and distribution centers in London and in the Far East. Hill began preparing to return to London as the chief of the OSS camouflage division.

Before he left for London, Hill delivered the commencement address at the Millbrook graduation ceremony of his son Watts Jr. No record of his speech survives, and his son only recalled the broad strokes of his father's message, which dealt with the global responsibilities of the United States. Watts Jr. had been accepted by both Stanford and Princeton, but he was headed to the navy. He had enlisted in 1943—as soon as he was eligible—in the navy's V-5 flight training program, and he was awaiting assignment. Before Watts Jr. left for active duty, he saw his father in New York, where the elder Hill was about to board the Clipper for the trip to England.

Watts Hill would later joke that he was the OSS "Fuller brush man," comparing himself to the popular door-to-door salesmen of the same name.[57] Indeed, when Hill arrived in London, his catalog of disguises included more than used coats, sweaters, pants, dresses, and hats. The agency had an inventory of personal articles such as toothbrushes and combs, toilet items like soap and shaving gear, tattered currency, ladies' handbags, men's wallets, and doctored passports and official papers. In addition, Hill brought along a makeup artist from Hollywood who had developed a training manual on how to adopt disguises. Hill's offerings also included the innocent-looking lethal devices developed by Stanley Lovell, the inventive creator and head of OSS research and development.

The OSS camouflage warehouse at 70 Brook Street in London was under the care of Major T. B. Pitman, who ran a complete tailor shop and a photographic studio. Pitman's rack of German uniforms, recently gathered from prisoner-of-war camps in France, was growing larger as the Allies pressed inward from the Normandy beachhead. On September 2, 1944, Hill reported in to Bruce, who was running the OSS operations in Europe. Hill's plans to present the OSS disguises to agents in the field were thrown into disarray, however, because the situation at the front changed from day to day. It was not going to be easy to get his collection into action. On October 2, while others in the operation flew to Italy, Hill started making arrangements to get to Paris.

Seats were hard to find on planes headed to the Continent. He finally found space on a crowded airplane that took off into an overcast English sky. Hill was perched on a wooden bench in the back with other officers when he heard the pilot call back to the cabin for help in finding the French capital. As the junior officer on board, Hill sat quietly until he heard the pilot's third call for help. When it was obvious that no one was going to respond, Hill moved into the cockpit, took the empty copilot's seat, and offered to do what he could.

Hill peered out the window at the land below. Just ahead, he saw the familiar outline of the ruins of Mont Saint Michel, a popular tourist site that he had visited years before. "I was just lucky," he recalled. "I said, 'Yeah, just follow the damn railroad and we'll go to Paris.'" We followed the railroad just above the tracks on into Paris. I knew my way. That was just one of those luck—hell, I had good luck everywhere I went."[58]

Hill spent about a week in Paris meeting with intelligence officers before he packed seventy-five pounds of supplies into a jeep and headed off toward Belgium. He found the OSS detachment of the Twelfth Army Group quartered in two houses outside of Verdun. They placed an order for briefcases, belts, shaving gear, toothbrushes, and other toilet articles. Down the road in Etain, agents wanted hairbrushes with secret compartments, belts, ladies' handbags, and German cigarette lighters with compartments for messages.

As Hill moved around the region, he discovered the brutal reality of war. He passed bombed-out homes as his jeep maneuvered along beside thousands of displaced civilians and soldiers weary from the long fight. He also learned of the very real risks that remained for the men and women assigned to OSS detachments along the line. In Luxembourg, the team had been sending agents behind German lines for short-term missions; a fourth of them did not return. In Eindhoven, he met with members of the Dutch underground who had been in occupied Holland and were preparing to go back. They gave Hill samples to add to the London inventory of German wallets and flat cigarette tins that German workmen used to carry their papers. American and French cigarettes would come in handy, he discovered; "1000 cigarettes worth far more than 1000 marks," he wrote in his report.[59] After making his rounds, he headed back to Paris, then on to London, and finally back to the States, where he arrived in late October.

Before he left the Continent, Hill went up in a small reconnaissance airplane, a fabric-covered Piper Cub type of plane that flew over the German lines. He later told his son Watts Jr. that at one point he heard a shot; a bullet penetrated the parachute he was sitting on and gave him a very small flesh wound.[60]

Less than two months later, the German army made a final dramatic effort to blunt the Allied offensive in Europe in what came to be known as the Battle of the Bulge. Watts Hill followed the progress of the Allied forces, who mounted their resistance in the same countryside and towns that he had just left a few weeks before. In the early months of 1945, the Allies crossed the Rhine River into Germany. In a matter of weeks, Hitler was dead and the German government had capitulated. The war in Europe ended on May 7.

☙☙☙

The fighting continued in the Pacific, but for the OSS, the war was over. General Douglas MacArthur had never approved of OSS operations in the Far East, so with the fall of Germany the agency's mission was complete. Two days after VE-day, Watts Hill was a civilian again. Just over six months later, the OSS was formally decommissioned on orders from the nation's new president, Harry Truman, who had never been a supporter of the agency. It never really disappeared, however. As America faced the hard realities of the growing Cold War, the Central Intelligence Agency was created, and it included among its early members many with OSS records, such as its director, Allen Dulles.

The war was a liberating experience for Hill. As he explained to Francis Miller in a letter that he wrote as he prepared to return to Durham, "I had both a lot of fun, received invaluable experience, made a few close friends, [and] learned much about human nature." Ironically, it also was the only time in his professional life when he was on a regular payroll or under the direct orders of any superior other than his father. He responded well and built a record of meritorious service that brought him the Cross of War Merit from the Italian government and the Legion of Merit award from the French government. David Bruce recommended him for promotion to lieutenant colonel early in 1944, but the papers got lost in the rush of events.

Hill had also been offered a medal from the Finnish government during the war, but he turned it down after the Finns sided with the Nazis following the so-called Winter War with the Soviet Union in 1941. Hill said he could not accept recognition from a government that was "an ally of the Axis Powers, an enemy against the Soviet Republic, and therefore, an active enemy of the British Empire and the United States of America." Finland should have resisted the Nazis, Hill lectured the head of the Finnish legation in Washington. "It would have been in the tradition of Finland, which we all cherished, to have resisted the infiltration of German influence to the utmost; instead the Republic sold its heritage for a 'mess of pottage.'"[61]

When he was released from the army, Hill knew that his responsibilities were at home. Before he returned to Durham, however, he headed off for one last brief adventure in Italy with OSS veteran Earl Brennan, who had lived there before the war. Hill never explained why he made the trip with Brennan, a colorful character who would remain involved in various types of intrigue for the rest of his life. Hill returned from Italy in time to spend a few weeks in Durham before heading to Cape Cod for a summer vacation with Ann.

There was some talk of a position in the State Department. David Bruce later won an appointment to London as ambassador to Great Britain. By the time Japan fell in August, however, Hill was looking toward Quail Roost. "I have had all I want of Washington, government, hot air and armchair strategists," he wrote Miller, "and will be glad to return to a position where I may be of some value to the community."[62]

CHAPTER 12

A Most Important Time

AS THE WAR CAME TO A CLOSE, Watts Hill heard the rumors in Durham that he was not returning home, or that he was bringing people with him to "turn everything upside down." Talk like that unsettled folks involved closely with the Hill enterprises, so when Watts finished a weeklong visit to Durham in the early summer of 1945, he drafted a confidential seven-page report to his father to clearly state his plans and offer some ideas about the state of the family's various businesses.

When John Sprunt Hill received his son's report, he was at his mansion at Biltmore Forest outside of Asheville, where golf, not business, was his favorite pastime. In the years after his wife's death, the elder Hill usually retired to the mountains for the summer and left his day-to-day affairs in the hands of the steady and reliable managers in Durham. Before writing his father, Watts Hill had met with W. W. "Whit" Sledge, the elder Hill's attorney and closest advisor; Ben Roberts, the executive vice president at the bank; and Bascom Baynes, the president of Home Security Life Insurance Company. These three and other senior managers were the men whose futures would be most affected by Watts Hill's appraisal of the family businesses.

"I want to return to Durham, full-time as soon as possible," Watts wrote his father. He told him that nothing had changed since the two had met in Washington in April 1945 before the Germans surrendered. It would probably be fall before he would be back, he said; "In all fairness and honesty," Watts wrote, "I cannot walk out on the OSS job I have been doing for three and a half years until I clean up the loose ends." At the same time, he assured his father: "I have no idea of running away from Durham and shirking my responsibilities and opportunities. Why should I? The work in Durham was my life, and will be to an even greater extent."[1]

While Watts Hill's declaration was a comfort to his father, reassuring him that his succession was secure, Watts had no intention of involving himself in the day-to-day affairs of business. No doubt he hoped to return to the life he had enjoyed before the war, when he could pick and choose his pursuits, acting as a gentleman farmer, hospital director, architect, and builder at different times. The routine of banking and insurance work was dull compared to the satisfaction he received from working with doctors at the hospital or from visiting a construction site. The urgency in Watts Hill's letter was the result of his own questions about how the family would find successors to the able caretakers like Roberts and Baynes who had served his father.

Preparing for John Sprunt Hill's succession would require a delicate touch. Watts was challenged with balancing his personal interests with those of his father and his two sisters, neither of whom was expected to come into the business. Frances had the best head for numbers and business in the family, but she had her career in medicine. She had graduated from Duke and gone on to medical school at the University of Pennsylvania. At the end of her residency in Cleveland, during which she had married Dr. Herbert Fox, she and her husband had returned to Durham before being uprooted by the war. They would be returning. Meanwhile, Valinda and her husband, David St. Pierre DuBose, had lives of their own. They lived at Meadowmont, a large Georgian Revival residence on the edge of Chapel Hill that they built in 1933. Watts was content for DuBose to remain in the executive offices of the family-owned Durham Hosiery Mills. The two men were not close.

What Watts Hill found in Durham left him impatient, even anxious, about the future. His review sounded much like John Sprunt Hill's own assessment of the safe, inbred business atmosphere he had found in Durham in 1903. Watts Hill told his father that the top management at the bank had to become more promotion minded and seek new opportunities. When customers came in to borrow money, Watts Hill argued, then the loan officers should be asking about establishing checking accounts as well. He said the bank needed fresh investors and directors, even if that meant the Hills had to put some of their own stock on the market. "We have been asleep at the switch for years," he wrote his father, "and it's time we did something about it." He recommended that his father also enlarge the bank's loan policy. "Our present loan policy is so ultra-conservative that we are threatening to drive business away from the bank."

Moving on to the insurance company, Watts argued that it needed an advertising campaign and that the home office needed to be reorganized. Rather than let weak men go, he observed, Baynes had created jobs for them. "We badly need better type men in the company. We have enough scrubs. Get in some good youngsters who can be developed during the next few years," Watts recommended. There was a commonly held belief in Durham that a job with the Hills was virtually a lifetime appointment. Nobody ever seemed to get fired. Watts wanted to do something about it.

Watts Hill also had suggestions for the hospital, which remained a burden for the family. During the war years, the hospital management had reduced indebtedness from $102,000 in 1939 to $18,000 in 1944, but the quality of service had been sacrificed in the process. The hospital was operating at full capacity, and expansion would certainly be needed soon. Watts did not dwell on it, but he knew it was only a matter of time before the hospital's needs would outstrip the family's ability to meet them. Soon, it would be difficult for the Hills to continue to support this critical public charity that the community seemed content to leave in their hands.

Finally, there was the matter of the new dairy cooperative that was just getting organized. During the war, Watts and his father had severed ties with the Durham Dairy Products Company. Neither man had been comfortable as a minority shareholder, so when differences with the owners came to a head, John Sprunt Hill offered to either buy out the majority interests or be bought out himself. To his surprise, the company's managers rounded up sufficient credit and cash to take him up on his second offer.[2] In 1945, as he prepared to return home, Watts Hill began to organize a dairy cooperative to handle milk from his cows at Quail Roost, from his father's farm, and from the herds of any others who would join. The base of the new dairy would be the former Long Meadow Dairy Company plant and equipment, including a dozen trucks available for home delivery. The Hills put up half of the $60,000 needed to pay for new buildings and production facilities; the rest was expected to come from the other farmer-members.

Watts Hill's letter was perhaps the first critique of the family businesses that John Sprunt Hill had seen in years. Of course, only Watts would be so bold as to suggest that the elder Hill sell some of their bank stock in order to bring in new directors. Watts knew that ideas such as this would disturb the safe, conservative operation of the bank that prevailed locally, but he was nonetheless ready to move. "Durham is not the sleepy town it once was," he wrote in the concluding paragraphs of his report. "Many changes have taken place in both people and their approach to business, it is far more competitive than before the war, and unless we get out and fight for business we will not get it."[3]

John Sprunt Hill may have seen a bit of himself in his son's letter, but a half-century had passed since he had arrived in Durham eager to shake things up. In his prime, the elder Hill had built banks, acquired thousands of acres of property, erected Durham's tallest office buildings, and become the city's wealthiest and perhaps best-known citizen. He had been a generous benefactor to the city, and he had shouldered more than his share of civic duties. In 1944, when he was well past seventy years of age, he led the drive to authorize Durham's first legal liquor stores in thirty years. However, along with his power and wealth had come resentment and jealousy from those whose losses had been his gain during the depression. For some, the Hill-owned Washington Duke Hotel in the center of Durham remained a monument to Hill's opportunistic grab for property during hard times. Few knew that in purchasing the bonds and debts of the bankrupt hotel corporation out of an abundance of local pride, Hill had taken on annual losses just to keep the hotel open. That made little difference to one former stockholder in the hotel, A. J. Pollard, who often stood outside of the Hill Building and railed, "I love the mountains of North Carolina, but I don't give a damn for these Hills."[4]

John Sprunt Hill was approaching eighty in the summer of 1945, but he was not ready to retire. A staff of seven servants attended his home on Duke Street, where his housekeeper, Effie Cotton, was the senior employee. She had been with the family since 1913. Chauffeur John Torian had come to work for the Hills in 1926. Each weekday when he was in Durham, Hill finished his breakfast in a small nook off to the side of the enormous kitchen. When Hill was ready, Torian buttoned his black uniform and brought the Cadillac to the south entry to pick up his boss for the ride to the Hill Building. Hill liked to be in the office by nine, and he usually spent the day there, napping briefly in the afternoon. He was often chipper and in good humor. Each morning, he ribbed his old friend Whit Sledge, who was a lifelong bachelor, about Sledge's lady friends. One morning, B. W. Harris heard Sledge confess to Hill, "That nurse out at Duke wants me to buy her an automobile." Hill asked Sledge if he was going to do it. "Hell no," Sledge replied. "I'll pay her $75 cash and that's going to be it." Hill said, "Mr. Sledge, I think you're a smarter man than I thought you were."[5]

John Sprunt Hill seemed more occupied with the past than with the future. He had become fascinated with his family's history when he was a young lawyer in New York, and over the years he had maintained a steady correspondence with genealogists around the South and in Europe as he pursued his passion for family history. Now, his files were filled with the reports of researchers whom he had hired to confirm relations that included French Huguenot settlers of Virginia and a fifteenth-century English baron.

John Sprunt Hill remained a trustee of the university, but his relations with President Frank Porter Graham had cooled in the wake of their battle over consolidation in the mid-1930s. Hill still responded to individual requests for help, however. He had financed Albert Coates in his struggle to get his Institute of Government on firm footing. His favorite recipient of benefaction was the North Carolina Collection, which was under the care of curator Mary L. Thornton, and he was intensely interested in the postwar expansion of Wilson Library, which included plans to give additional space to the collection. Over the years, the library had become, as Hill had hoped it would, the "historical center for the campus."[6]

John Sprunt Hill and "Miss Thornton," as he always referred to her, worked together on the collection for thirty years. Their long and abiding relationship prompted whispers of a love affair after his wife's death, as Miss Thornton enjoyed deliveries of floral bouquets handpicked in Hill's gardens. Such talk was unfounded, but Hill's daughters kept a close eye on their father nonetheless, mindful of how surprised the family had been when George W. Watts had remarried after the death of his wife. When the library's new wings were opened in 1952, the collection's reading room was furnished with a $5,000 set of handsome mahogany tables and Chippendale chairs that Hill had selected personally and donated. He had already underscored his support for the collection by giving the university, over the course of a number of years, the Carolina Inn as well as commercial buildings at 138, 140, 142, and 144 East Franklin Street that were valued at nearly $100,000. Hill had stipulated that any income from these holdings, which included Julian's men's store and the Carolina Coffee Shop, was to be used exclusively for the support of the collection.

At the time Hill donated the Franklin Street buildings, he joined two former classmates—William R. Kenan Jr. and John M. Morehead III—for a reunion that produced a photograph of "three of the university's greatest benefactors," as they were called. The occasion was the laying of the cornerstone for the Morehead Building and Planetarium, which had been given by Morehead and his family. The three old men looked ill at ease in the photograph; none offered a smile to the photographer. Competition for recognition on campus remained a point of contention among them, particularly for Kenan, who believed his part in the discovery of calcium carbide that led to Morehead's financial success had never been fully appreciated.[7]

⤳⤳⤳

Watts Hill was mindful of his father's conservative bent and his confidence in his dependable, longtime subordinates. While Watts might have been eager to make changes, he assured his father before returning home from the war that he would work with constraint. "You need not worry that I am expecting to do everything in a minute. It will take time, it can't be rushed and it's best that changes be made slowly," he wrote. At the same time, he declared that he was operating under "a higher head of steam than some of the boys in Durham" and was eager to get started. "Let's work out our plans, talk them over, select the best men we can find within our price range, and then go to work," he wrote.[8]

Durham had grown during the war, like most of the state's urban areas. By the late 1940s, the city's population was 70,000, up from 60,000 a decade earlier. Another 30,000 people lived in the county. Business was booming. Textile mills and cigarette factories were running full shifts. Twenty percent of the nation's cigarettes, including popular brands such as Chesterfield, Lucky Strike, Pall Mall, and Tareyton, rolled out of the Durham plants. Even the farm economy was strong. The Farmers' Mutual Exchange that the Hills had organized in 1931 had more than 12,000 members. It was not long before the Long Meadow Dairy co-op was processing the Hills' favored "golden Guernsey" milk from Quail Roost, Hillandale, and a hundred other area farms. Durham Bank and Trust Company was not the leading bank in town. Fidelity Bank, the old Duke bank, had more deposits. Yet bank deposits for all banks had nearly tripled during the war years, and all of Durham's banks were strong and profitable.

John Sprunt Hill adopted some of his son's recommendations. In 1946, he approved a four-for-one exchange of the bank's stock, which dropped the share price to a level such that he could extend ownership within the community. Even after the split, however, the family still controlled 70 percent of the stock, and the Board of Directors included John Sprunt Hill, his son Watts, his daughter Frances, and his son-in-law David St. Pierre Du-Bose. Three years later, in 1949, John Sprunt Hill retired as chairman of the board in favor of Watts, and Ben Roberts became president of the bank. Then, in April 1950, the Home Savings Bank was merged into Durham Bank and Trust.

At the same time, the elder Hill heeded another bit of his son's advice and moved an $850,000 trust fund for his grandchildren from a New York bank to Durham Bank and Trust, a move that was intended to renew confidence at home. The bank's trust department under Frank Bozarth was considered one of the best in the state. Bozarth had been brought in by Watts Hill and given the freedom to roam the state looking for estates to manage. One of the most important was the estate of Ceasar H. Cone, one of the founders of the Cone Mills operations in Greensboro.

As Watts Hill promised, he turned his attention to his hometown and his family responsibilities. He joined the Board of Trustees at Union Theological Seminary, where his grandfather had been such an influential presence. Each year following the war, he chaired a subdivision of the local Community Chest (later the United Way) campaign, and in 1950 he led a campaign to raise $225,000 from the local community for Duke University. At the time, it was the largest donation ever raised by non–Duke alumni and one of the largest local fund-raising campaigns ever to be organized for any project. Duke used the money to expand the Union, Administration, and Page buildings and to create a student activities center on the West Campus. In 1951, the Durham Chamber of Commerce named Watts Hill "man of the year" in recognition of his civic work.

Watts Hill gave George W. Watts's mansion, Harwood Hall, to the Durham arts community after his efforts to find a suitable alternative use failed. The home had largely remained empty in the years after Watts and Ann Hill moved to Quail Roost. During the war, Watts Hospital had used it as a temporary nurses' home, but it was too far from the hospital campus for continued use to be practical. In 1949, Watts Hill tried to lure a hotel management company to Durham to turn it into a stylish downtown hotel. He came up with the idea during a vacation trip to St. Simons Island, Georgia, where he had seen a house that had been similarly converted. Hill suggested to one hotel management company that the large rooms on the first floor could be converted to a dining room and living space, while the six bedrooms on the second floor could be "used for high-priced accommodations." He recommended building another twenty to fifty rooms in a modern annex at the rear of the property. To sweeten the deal, Hill even offered to raise local money and provide construction loans through his bank.[9] Nothing came of the proposal, and Hill turned the rambling old house over to Allied Arts of Durham, which used it until 1961, when the mansion was demolished to make way for a Hospital Care Association office building.

None of his civic work—and his continued leadership of the Hospital Care Association fit that category—occupied more of his time than Watts Hospital. In the spring of 1942, John Sprunt Hill turned down a request from the hospital to build space for more beds because it was unable to pay its way at its current size. He had never been comfortable with the burden of responsibility for the hospital left to him by his father-in-law, and Hill was discouraged about the institution's future. "I can see the day, not far ahead," John Sprunt Hill said at the time, "when the hospital will be closed for lack of funds."[10] Reflecting on that period some years later, Watts Hill recalled: "The hospital was losing its shirt because one of the requirements was that no one be turned away because of lack of funds. And the hardest thing in the world was to get Watts Hospital to sue patients that could afford to pay and [were] just riding on the damn hospital."[11]

Fortunately for the community and the family, the hospital was in the hands of Sample Forbus, an able administrator who had remained in close touch with Watts Hill during Hill's years in Washington. As the war in Europe came to a close, Forbus began compiling a report on the hospital's future needs. Watts Hill personally paid half the cost of the yearlong study that, when completed, would be used as a blueprint for the expansion of both Watts and Lincoln hospitals.

Even with their problems, Watts and Lincoln hospitals, along with the hospital at Duke University, made Durham a virtual oasis of health care in central North Carolina. In Durham, anyone could find a hospital bed. If you were poor, black, or both, there was still money to pay for your care. More than a third of the state's counties had no beds at all, and North Carolina ranked forty-fifth in the nation in the number of physicians who practiced there. Nothing underscored the distressing state of health care in North Carolina more than the demands of the war had. Forty percent of the state's white draftees and 60 percent of the black draftees had been determined to be unfit for military service because they were either functionally illiterate or in poor physical condition. In 1946, numbers like these provided the data that fueled a comprehensive campaign for the public good that equaled Governor Charles Aycock's efforts on behalf of public schools and Governor Cameron Morrison's road-building program of the 1920s.

<p style="text-align:center">~~~</p>

The good health campaign began with University of North Carolina president Frank Porter Graham, who cleverly combined his concern over the woeful condition of health care in the state with the university's desire to expand the medical school at Chapel Hill. The university's two-year medical program had been operating on borrowed time since the late 1930s, when the accrediting arm of the American Medical Association (AMA) had threatened to revoke the accreditation of all two-year medical schools. Graham kept the AMA at bay, but he knew that eventually the university would lose its accreditation unless the state underwrote the expense of opening a four-year school. Late in 1943, he took to Governor J. Melville Broughton a report prepared by medical school alumni and leading doctors in the North Carolina Medical Society. It called for an expanded, four-year medical school and a new teaching hospital at the university in Chapel Hill, as well as for public funds to be made available to build and improve hospitals and clinics around the state.[12]

The governor, looking for an initiative to define his administration, immediately endorsed Graham's proposal. When he presented Graham's plan to the university Board of Trustees in January 1944, he declared, "The ultimate purpose of this program should be that no person in North Carolina shall lack adequate hospital care or medical treatment by reason of poverty or low income."[13] The governor named a fifty-member commission chaired by Clarence Poe to study health conditions and report to him by year's end. Among the commission members was Watts Hill's sister, Dr.

Frances Hill Fox, who was teaching at Chapel Hill, and whose students used Watts Hospital for their clinical training.

The Poe commission returned its report late in 1944, just as Broughton was leaving office. Declaring that "the common health is the foundation of the commonwealth," the commission cited three "supremely needed" factors that would promote better health care in the state: "more doctors, more hospitals, and more non-profit health service insurance."[14] The cornerstone of a comprehensive good-health program, the commission said, should be the development of a four-year medical school and the construction of a five- to seven-hundred-bed teaching hospital to serve the entire state.

Early in 1945, Graham visited Broughton's successor, the recently inaugurated Governor R. Gregg Cherry, to remind Cherry of the support he had given the Poe commission during his election campaign. At this meeting, Cherry balked at endorsing all of the commission's recommendations, and he told Graham he would support the medical school if Graham would drop the other parts of the commission's health program. Cherry's backpedaling worried Graham. It was clear the governor had heard from doctors around the state whom Graham knew were suspicious of government intervention in medical care. The new medical school was also being discouraged by Dr. Watson S. Rankin of the Duke Endowment, who believed that the medical schools at Duke and Wake Forest were sufficient to supply the state's needs. Cherry was also wary of the total cost of such an ambitious program.[15] Moreover, the location of the medical school was a politically charged issue, and the commission's recommendation that the state provide money for the training of black doctors was sure to raise a howl.

Graham held his ground and said he wanted it all, however, and the governor almost lived up to his word. Cherry delivered a special legislative address on health care and included an endorsement of all the commission's recommendations, but he did not put the full weight of his office behind broader improvements. As a result, legislators failed to provide all the money requested. A two-year appropriation of $500,000 was approved to pay for indigent care in hospitals, but legislators bypassed a request for $5 million to assist cities and counties with hospital construction. The expansion to a four-year medical school at the University of North Carolina was approved, and the North Carolina Medical Care Commission was created to recommend a site for the teaching hospital and make recommendations about the future of state aid for local hospitals and clinics.

The Medical Care Commission was completing its study of where the medical school should be sited in the early months of 1946 when Graham decided to build a fire for medical care. He contacted newspaper editors, civic leaders, politicians from both parties, businessmen, and others to lay the foundation for a grassroots movement to improve health care. His strategy was reminiscent of the one he had taken when he organized the campaign in the early 1920s to rally alumni behind the university's plans to expand the Chapel Hill campus.

No one was left off Graham's roster of contacts. He enlisted the support of former governors J. Melville Broughton and Clyde Hoey, the state chairs of the Republican and Democratic parties, the leaders of the American Legion, labor unions, farm groups, women's clubs, chambers of commerce, and civic clubs of every stripe. D. Hiden Ramsey, a university trustee and the general manager of the *Asheville Citizen-Times*, took a leading role, and Graham's efforts also drew the attention of the *News and Observer*.

Graham created the North Carolina Good Health Association and introduced it on March 14, 1946, in the furniture-manufacturing town of Thomasville, the so-called Chair City, where an oversize chair sat on a pedestal beside the north-south rail line that cut the town in half. Graham chose Thomasville because it was centrally located and because it was not a competitor for the medical school. It also was the home of Thompson Orphanage, a Baptist institution run by Graham's friend Isaac Greer, a 1905 graduate of the university.

Graham wanted Greer to head the association largely because he had a compelling story to tell. Young men from the orphanage and others like it in the state had not experienced the high rejection rate for the military draft that was reported elsewhere. Of the 1,138 boys from state orphanages examined to determine their fitness for military service, only 16 were turned down for health reasons. "The boys of our North Carolina orphanages are not coddled. They are not given luxuries," Greer said, "but they do receive nutritious food and reasonable and adequate medical and hospital care."[16]

Graham's ambitions, particularly the construction of a teaching hospital at Chapel Hill, had important implications for Watts Hospital and for

Watts Hill, who still awaited the results of the study of Durham's hospital needs. Hill had not returned to Durham from military service when Graham launched the Good Health Association, but he had followed the developments that led to its creation. His sister was a member of the Poe commission, and he talked often with the university's chief financial officer, Billy Carmichael Jr., whom Hill considered one of his closest friends.

If Graham was the university's spiritual leader, dreamer, and sometimes impractical visionary, Carmichael was the man who made the place run. He paid the bills on time, prepared the budgets for the legislature, and mollified conservative businessmen and trustees, such as John Sprunt Hill, who were uncomfortable with Graham's liberal politics. Carmichael brought to Chapel Hill the integrity and success of Wall Street and the savvy of Madison Avenue. Like Graham, he knew how to cultivate the old-school ties of graduates, and reconnecting with Watts Hill, whom he had known since childhood, was as natural for him as the sunrise.

The Good Health Association enjoyed a rousing start, but it was almost dormant in the summer when Carmichael introduced the association's chairman to popular bandleader Kay Kyser, who was one of Carolina's best-known graduates. A native of Rocky Mount, Kyser had turned his antics as a Carolina cheerleader of the late 1920s into a career. By the 1940s, he was hosting a weekly radio show—the "Kollege of Musical Knowledge"—and appearing in motion pictures. Three of his records made the top ten in 1942. In the summer of 1946, Kyser was showing his new bride, Georgia, around the state when he saw Carmichael and Greer at lunch in Chapel Hill. They told him about the health care campaign.

Did the general public know about the Good Health Association? Kyser is said to have asked Greer. Greer responded that it probably did not, and he told Kyser that he believed it would take a tremendous effort to bring the campaign to public attention. Whereupon Georgia Kyser challenged her husband to make good his claim that he could sell anything. Kyser is said to have responded that it was "time to start a bonfire at the grass-roots."[17]

A few weeks later, Kyser was the featured speaker at an association luncheon at the Sir Walter Hotel in Raleigh. Watts Hill was among a crowd that included most of those who had been in Thomasville as well as Governor Cherry. Kyser played to the hometown crowd just as if they held tickets for one of his Saturday night radio shows. His comedy routine was as good as any he put on the air. This time, however, he wanted to do more than entertain.

"Did you know that we had the highest percentage of draft rejections because of physical unfitness?" Kyser asked the Raleigh audience. "The highest of any state in our entire union? We can't even say 'Thank God for South Carolina.' They were rejected because they couldn't do a day's work for Uncle Sam. Why were they sick? They were sick because there is no place for them to grow up healthy and sound, because they had nobody to take care of them. They just weren't given proper treatment and care as to their health."

Kyser talked about people that he and Greer had visited in thirty-four counties across the state. The two had talked to country doctors and corporate leaders such as insurance executive Julian Price of Greensboro and textile magnate Charles A. Cannon of Concord. "I talked to Herman Cone and Ben Cone and Ceasar Cone and Ice Cream Cone and all the others," he joked at the expense of Greensboro's textile family. Turning serious, he related disturbing stories of citizens who lived miles from health-care providers and of the striking contrasts he had seen across the state. He spoke of "God's nature and our negligence of medical care being side by side" at Blowing Rock, a popular mountain resort. If he had fallen sick or suffered an injury there, the closest medical care he could have found was fifteen miles away in a four-room clinic in Boone.

The lack of proper health care ignored racial lines, he said. Kyser told the group that it was a matter of self-interest for the white majority in North Carolina to improve health care conditions for the state's African American community. "Now, if you think I am going to discuss the matter of social equality between the two races then you are crazy," he said. But he argued that African American neighborhoods with their dilapidated houses, poor sanitation, and overcrowding were simply breeding disease that spread throughout the state's cities. "What good is [health care for whites] if you don't care what the condition is of those who are fixing your food in the kitchen?" Kyser asked. "What good is it to take such care of your children and then turn them over to a nurse, not knowing what sort of disease, if any, that nurse has got?" He continued: "Let's go to Manteo and let's go to Murphy, and let's go everywhere between them and ferret out ignorance, complacency, lethargy from every nook and corner in our state.

Let's everybody get a Flit gun and spray the state with intelligence and enlightenment as to what good health means and as to why we must have it."[18]

Eight days later, the Good Health Association was reborn when it was formally incorporated at a meeting in Watts Hill's office in Durham. Afterward, Carmichael wrote a friend to say that the association was in "good hands—Watts Hill, Ben Cone, and Hyman Battle are the coordinators." All had a vested interest in improving health care. The Cone family had long hoped that the university would put a new medical school in Greensboro, where the family would eventually build Moses H. Cone Memorial Hospital, one of the finest in the state. Battle, a Rocky Mount textile man, had worked with Hill in the 1930s during the formative years of the Hospital Care Association. Hill remained hopeful that the campaign would improve the situation at Watts Hospital.

The Good Health Association's Board of Directors included virtually every leading business and civic leader in the state. Among them were Clarence Poe, Julian Price, and Charles A. Cannon, who were members of the study commission; farm leader Ralph Scott of Alamance County; Charles C. Spaulding, the head of North Carolina Mutual Life Insurance Company; James E. Broyhill of Lenoir, a Taft Republican and founder of the state's largest furniture manufacturing concern; Charles R. Jonas, a Lincolnton attorney and leading Republican; the *News and Observer's* Jonathan Daniels; and Greensboro lawyer and Democratic Party leader L. P. McLendon. Greer was elected as the association's president, but most of the work in the following weeks would flow from Watts Hill's office in Durham.

Kyser was designated the honorary vice president of the association, but he devoted more than his name and reputation to the campaign. One friend later said that in the good health campaign, Kyser finally found a cause of his own after years of supporting those of his Hollywood friends. He issued orders from Hollywood just as if he was sitting in Hill's office in Durham. "We must merchandise health to the people and we must employ the same techniques a major manufacturer would use in marketing a new product," he wrote in a marketing proposal that covered a dozen pages. If America can sell a five-cent candy bar, he argued, then good health should receive no less attention.[19]

Watts Hill committed himself and his personal resources to the campaign and put aside calls from Francis and Helen Miller, who wanted Hill to help revive the National Policy Committee of which he had been a part in the 1930s. Watts had attended some NPC functions during the war years in Washington, and he had stayed close enough to the Millers for them to include him on the NPC Board of Directors. He did some spade work toward establishing an NPC committee in North Carolina, but the old organization never regained its steam, and it was on its last legs by the time the good health campaign was underway.

Now more than ever before, Hill was completely focused on his home state. Two weeks after the Good Health Association was formed, he opened free office space for the campaign headquarters in the Hill Building. Carmichael, with Hill and Durham public relations man John Moorhead in tow, convinced H. C. Cranford of Durham to forsake his journalism studies at Chapel Hill and join the campaign as publicity director. Hill rented an apartment in Durham for Cranford and his wife, and he ordered up a Nash automobile for Cranford's use. The young couple was dazzled by the attention. When the Cranfords got word about the car, they searched the parking spaces on streets in Chapel Hill for a Nash so they would know what their new automobile would look like.[20]

Kyser laid out a campaign that would take advantage of every conceivable advertising medium, and he called in markers from friends. He arranged for the production of one- to two-minute filmed appeals featuring movie stars Randolph Scott, who was a Charlotte native, and Ava Gardner, who grew up near Smithfield in Johnston County. These films were distributed free to theaters across the state, where they were shown as trailers to the main features. Kyser's lineup of stars also recorded radio spots that the Durham office distributed to the state's forty-seven radio stations.

The campaign asked local preachers to turn their pulpits over to community leaders for Sunday morning testimonials about the importance of good health. Cranford organized a speakers' bureau for civic clubs and chambers of commerce. Local schools prepared essay contests for children to write about health, and newspapers were supplied with ideas for feature stories. The public was asked for help in picking a campaign slogan. Kyser suggested more than a dozen, including "Come on chillun, let's live!" and "Get Hep—Help Yourself to Health." The campaign settled on something more sedate: "North Carolina's No. 1 Need is Good Health." The campaign kickoff was set for November 9, when a special edition of Kyser's weekly radio show would be broadcast to all North Carolina stations.

In the days leading up to the broadcast, Kyser prodded Carmichael to do more and more. Carmichael, who had no shortage of duties at the university, sarcastically responded to one Kyser message, saying: "I apologize for spending only 22 hours a day on program. Also for not being quintuplets. Remember I was born in North Carolina [where] four out of five don't survive."[21]

Meetings of the leadership of the Good Health Association became weekly entries on Watts Hill's work schedule. His first job was to raise money, and he rounded up a $1,000 contribution from his father and another from his sister Frances. His first personal contribution was $2,500, and he soon matched that. In addition to providing free office space to the association, Hill arranged for his accountant, B. W. Harris, to keep the association's books at no charge.

Watts Hill's fund-raising skills were effective. He tapped large hometown companies Liggett and Myers, American Tobacco Company, and Erwin Mills, where he had influence. He called on the heads of other North Carolina businesses and contacted executives at New York–based corporations that had plants or did business in the state. Hill had no patience for those who contributed less than he thought they should. He told Julian Price that the contributions of Jefferson Standard Life Insurance Company were half what they ought to be and that they came in at less than a third of what Hill gave personally. At the first accounting in November, fully 10 percent of the more than $40,000 raised for the campaign had come from the Hills or their companies.

On Saturday November 9, Kyser's special North Carolina show went on the air from KFWB's Studio Three in Hollywood. Woven throughout his script of gags, music, and comedy were public appeals from movie stars. Bandleader John Scott Trotter, a Charlotte native, and Anne Jeffreys, an actress who hailed from Goldsboro, made personal appearances. Messages from the governor and Good Health Association president Isaac Greer—speaking from WPTF studios in Raleigh—were patched in between the comic antics of Red Skelton's "Mean Widdle Kid" and the introduction of a Sammy Cahn and Jule Styne tune titled "It's All up to You (To Make North Carolina Number One in Good Health)."

Ironically, Durham station WDNC did not broadcast the entire show.

When the show went on the air, the station's engineers were technically on strike. The station manager pulled the plug on the last four minutes when WPTF in Raleigh notified him that if he continued to broadcast with the "on strike" engineers, the entire network would go off the air.[22]

The song, "It's All up to You," was Kyser's idea. He reasoned that a catchy tune would reach more people than newspaper articles, billboards, or even slogans. Cahn and Styne, one of America's best-known songwriting teams, created the tune as a favor to Kyser, who then asked Dinah Shore and Frank Sinatra to record it with his orchestra. Ten thousand copies of the song were shipped east for distribution by radio stations. It also showed up on jukeboxes across the state.

The public campaign continued through the winter and into spring. Promotions crept into nationally syndicated comic strips such as "Moon Mullins," "Ripley's Believe It or Not," and "Bringing Up Father." When Watts Hill, Carmichael, and others discovered that billboard space had been reserved months in advance by major advertisers, they prevailed on the oil companies, breweries, department stores, and banks to free a percentage of their billboards to the campaign. During November and December, more than a thousand billboards carried the campaign slogan. Meanwhile, Hill enlisted the state's dairymen, who hung paper collars carrying the campaign slogan on milk bottles delivered daily to thousands of North Carolina homes.

The payoff came March 28, 1947, when the state Senate approved a health bill without a dissenting vote. Some last-minute wrangling took place over where the new medical school would be located, but the General Assembly funded the school and a $5.3 million teaching hospital for Chapel Hill. Legislators also gave the Medical Care Commission another $6.25 million to build local hospitals, clinics, and health centers. In addition, the legislature increased aid to state hospitals for the treatment of chronic diseases and mental and tubercular patients. It was one of the largest appropriations ever for health care. The timing of the campaign and the legislative appropriations put North Carolina at the head of the line for federal hospital construction funds that were just coming available through the Hill-Burton Act. The first Hill-Burton check written was for a North Carolina hospital.

The campaign proved to be a homecoming for Kyser, who a few years later retired to Chapel Hill. One of the ironies of the Good Health Association campaign, which jump-started the improvement of medical care in North Carolina, was that Kyser eventually became a devoted Christian Scientist.

Watts Hill's work with the association did not end with the legislative victory. He helped finance the Good Health Association for another two years and continued to guide its program. During that time, it assisted dozens of local communities with public campaigns to raise money so that they could receive their share of the federal and state matching money used for new hospitals. By December 1948, the Medical Care Commission had approved twenty-one new hospitals—eight were already under construction—and plans for the new medical school. Six months later, when the association was out of money, Hill put up another $1,000 to clear the debts. Then he hired Cranford to become the public relations director of the Hospital Care Association. When the Good Health Association finally closed its books, the Hills had contributed more to its operation than any other family—or institution—in the state.

ᗡᗡᗡ

By 1950, half of Watts Hospital's main buildings were more than forty years old and in need of renovation. At the same time, rising labor costs threatened the institution's solvency. In the comprehensive study that Hill and others had been awaiting, Dr. Claude Munger, a leader in the American Hospital Association, said that Watts Hospital would not only need new facilities but also broader community support if it was to remain in service.

Watts administrator Sample Forbus was among the first members of the new Medical Care Commission, and he waited for the right opportunity to submit applications for new construction funds for both Watts and Lincoln hospitals. In January 1950, the commission approved a $2.8 million hospital building program for Durham. Of that amount, more than $900,000 came from federal funds, with the balance to come from local bonds. After a vigorous campaign, voters approved the bonds by a two-to-one margin in an April referendum.

The funds from the bond issue would help the hospitals keep pace with demand. More importantly for the Hill family, the approval of the bonds marked the beginning of the end of Watts Hospital as a private charity. In order to qualify for public money, the trustees of Watts and Lincoln hospitals were required to transfer ownership of the hospital properties to the county. With the exchange, Watts Hospital finally became a "community business," as Forbus announced in the 1950 annual report, and a burden was lifted from the Hill family.[23] The change did not end Watts Hill's participation in the administration of the hospital, however. He remained as president of the hospital board for another decade.

❧❧❧

The campaign broadened the horizons of Watts Hill, according to John Moorhead. By participating in the campaign, "Watts Hill grew up," Moorhead said some years later.[24] What Moorhead meant was that the campaign gave many in the state's business community their first look at Hill as one of the state's new, postwar leaders. His service on behalf of the Good Health Association demonstrated a leadership style that Hill had refined in the OSS, where prima donnas were as common as khaki, and that he would perfect in years to come. As he once told a reporter: "When you persuade people, you've sold them. And that's more important than if you had the actual authority."[25]

By the early 1950s, Watts Hill seemed comfortable with the place he was creating for himself in Durham. He was less imposing than his father and less formal. While few called him Watts, he liked the sound of "major." He owned a big car, a Cadillac like his father's, but he drove himself and made no show of his wealth. His suits were well tailored, but he often appeared with his shirtsleeves unbuttoned, a habit he would continue for years. From time to time, he would drop in at the offices of the family-owned Durham Realty and Insurance Company on Market Street to chat or use the telephone rather than ride the elevator to his own office on the fifteenth floor at 111 Corcoran Street. He often asked the men in the office to join him for lunch at the Washington Duke Hotel, where his favorite meal was a bacon, lettuce, and tomato sandwich with a glass of buttermilk or orange juice. The boss's moods were easy to read: "He would come into the office in the morning with a gray hat on," said one who knew him. "If he came in with his brim turned up, he was in up spirits. If he came in with his brim down, why, you went about your business and didn't bother anyone. Once, someone pointed this out to him. He enjoyed turning the brim up or down as his mood went."[26]

Watts Hill showed a decided preference for working behind the scenes, unlike his father, who loved public attention. Even in his later years, John Sprunt Hill wrote annual epistles on the state of the nation and the world and had them printed as pamphlets. The *Durham Morning Herald* often published them verbatim. Advancing age did not quench the old man's fire when his political passions were aroused. In 1949, he and former lieutenant governor A. H. "Sandy" Graham appeared before a legislative committee to oppose Governor Kerr Scott's plan to pave rural roads. When John Sprunt Hill declared to a legislative committee, "You build roads to travel on, not to pay political debts," he stood the ridicule of a host of farmers, who booed him and dismissed his opposition as selfishness. "Sit down," one shouted, "You live on a hard-surface road."[27] Scott's request for $200 million in road bonds passed the legislature and won voter approval in a statewide referendum.

Hill also resisted change in Durham. In 1949, when zoning laws were proposed for Durham County, he vigorously opposed them as a threat to individual freedom. The county commissioners then tabled a proposal they had asked the county manager to prepare. He fought efforts to consolidate the Durham city and county school systems and mounted a modest campaign against the closing of his old high school in Duplin County. He wrote a cousin that the Faison school had been good enough for him and should remain open, even though she offered to promote the idea of naming a new consolidated school in his honor.

A few months later, Hill declared himself against efforts to add sodium fluoride—which had been found to reduce tooth decay, particularly in youngsters—to Durham's drinking water. Most of the public statements against fluoridation came from one of Hill's close friends, Mayor Pro Tem E. C. Brown, and from attorney Robert M. Gantt. Fluoridation was "mass medication," Gantt told the council, and he argued that it "violate[d] definite Constitutional rights to force people who think otherwise to conform."[28] Gantt threatened to sue the city for damages and found a ready ally in Hill, who paid for the creation of the Fluoridation Education Society of the Carolinas. Hill believed—as did many others—that the fluoridation campaign had originated with an English communist and had been promoted by socialists in the United States.[29]

Any change in racial segregation was out of the question. In 1951, John Sprunt Hill dismissed out of hand the proposition that African Americans should be able to attend the University of North Carolina Medical School. With the support of trustees like Hill, the university had gone to court rather than admit African Americans to the law school. After four African

Americans applied for admission to the medical school, Hill told a reporter for the Durham newspaper, "There are over 50 better qualified white boys who have their applications in." He further said that "lack of money," if nothing else, would prevent the black students from enrolling.[30]

Durham's *Carolina Times*, a black-owned paper, answered Hill: "Old man John Sprunt Hill, 80-year-old tycoon, who controls or dictates the policy of about everything in Durham, with the exception of the B. C. Remedy Company and this newspaper, needs to be pitied rather than condemned for his vituperative utterances against the attempt of Negroes to enter the University of North Carolina. John Sprunt has about as much business out on the main avenue of the world's affairs today as an oxcart or an old fashioned water closet with its bucket of corncobs in one corner and an old Sears-Roebuck catalog in the other."[31]

As the newspaper said, John Sprunt Hill's opinions were important to local officials. Before Hill weighed in against fluoridation, it appeared that Durham would join more than one hundred fifty other cities across the nation in treating their water. The medical community was supportive, public health agencies were eager, dentists were in agreement about its beneficial effects, and the city council voted eight to two in July to purchase the equipment to make the changes for Durham. A month later, however, the council was in retreat, and its members voted seven to five against fluoridation. A young councilman, Watts Carr Jr., was angry and upset as he left the August meeting at which the fluoridation vote failed. "If I didn't fear for the city," he told a reporter, "I'd resign from the council."[32]

The morning that quotation appeared in the Durham paper, John Sprunt Hill arrived at his office and demanded that his son immediately fire Carr, whom Watts had hired a few years before at the Durham Realty and Insurance Company. It made no difference to Hill that Carr was the son of one of his late wife's favorite cousins, the architect of the Hill Building. Watts cooled his father's temper. Carr remained in the family's employ and eventually became president of the company.

Watts Carr Jr. was the kind of person that Watts Hill had in mind when he had suggested to his father that the Hill companies needed to recruit new blood. Having graduated from the university in Chapel Hill just before the war began, Carr had volunteered for the Marine Corps and come home a major. When he talked to C. W. Toms, the head of Liggett and Myers, about a job, Toms offered him a spot similar to the low-paying position he had held between graduation and his induction in the Marine Corps. Carr turned him down. When Hill learned that Carr was looking for work, he asked him to come see him. Hill gave him a job at Durham Realty and Insurance Company, where Carr handled insurance matters, including policies for many of the Hill enterprises.

Another of Watts Hill's family recruits was Arthur Clark, who was the son of his grandmother's favorite cousin, Nell Watts Clark. She had met her husband while doing Red Cross work during World War I. After the war, they returned to the States, where they were married at Hill House in Durham. They headed west, where Clark's father, a Yale graduate, got a law degree. The family settled in the state of Washington near what is now Mount Clark, which carries the family name. As a youngster, Arthur Clark visited in Durham during the holidays; later, he came east for his education. He graduated from the university in Chapel Hill in 1939 and joined the army Air Corps. During the war, Watts Hill had tried to get Clark assigned to the OSS, but Clark served out his duty in the Far East. Shortly after the war's end, Hill wrote Clark's mother and told her that he and his father saw her son as the kind of man who in time could run their Home Security Life Insurance Company.

After his release from the army, Clark entered graduate school at the University of California at Berkeley. He was recuperating from a bout with pneumonia at Quail Roost in 1948 when he agreed to come to work for the Hills. "[Watts Hill] wanted a manager that he could trust and rely on and he knew that I knew how to keep my mouth shut," Clark later recalled.[33] Clark was recalled to active duty for service in Korea (he would eventually earn the rank of major general in Air Force), but he was back in Durham by 1952 as director of planning at Home Security, a job that allowed enough flexibility for Hill to use him on special assignments. In time, Clark became one of Watts Hill's closest confidants.

Hill also brought in Arthur Roseborough, whom he had come to know during the war. Roseborough had been a Rhodes Scholar, and before the war he ran the Paris office of the influential New York law firm of Sullivan and Cromwell. Watts had met him in Washington, where Roseborough ran the western European section of the OSS. For a time, the Roseboroughs had lived with Hill in his rented house. During the latter years of the war, Roseborough served as a liaison between the Ninth Air Force and the French underground. When Roseborough arrived in Durham, he joined the bank's trust department and became a gentleman farmer on land on a farm about a mile south of Quail Roost. Hill hoped that Roseborough would bring a vision to the bank that saw beyond the local economy.

ᘛᘛᘛ

The future of the bank caused Watts Hill great concern, because the bank was the cornerstone of all the family's businesses. Problems there could create ripples in all directions. While his father had adopted some of his suggestions about improving services, there remained much to be done. If anything, the merger of Durham Bank and Trust and Home Savings Bank, which should have created a more efficient institution, only compounded the pervasive featherbedding. Home Savings employees were absorbed without a single layoff. As a result, the bank had more employees than there was work for them to do. Some regularly ended their workday at three in the afternoon and headed home.[34]

The Durham banks enjoyed a comfortable noncompetitive relationship. It was a condition that mitigated against change. The unspoken rule was "You stay away from my customers and I'll stay away from yours."[35] Leadership was stagnant. Ben Roberts, a banker of the old school who had become president when Watts Hill became chairman, was coasting toward the end of his career. He had been a demon in his earlier days when John Sprunt Hill hired him in 1932 as credit manager to collect overdue loans that Hill himself was reluctant to call. Roberts had done a good job; Durham Bank's loan losses "were phenomenally low."[36] At the same time, however, the bank's lending had become so cautious that only loans with low risk were approved. Roberts's aversion to delegating authority had also left the bank short of middle managers. With no incentive to move up, low-level employees had little reason to take on new tasks.

The banking business had grown over the years. During the depression, Durham Bank and Trust Company had expanded to nearby communities, largely to replace other banks that did not survive the hard times. The war brought this expansion to a halt. Yet in the boom times of the postwar years, Durham Bank and Trust remained in the same familiar locations. In 1951, Watts Hill opened the bank's first new office since the depression when he put a branch office on Broad Street in Durham.

In addition to Frank Bozarth's trust operation, another bright spot in the bank was R. Bailey Reade's installment loan department, which provided short-term loans for customers furnishing their homes or buying cars.

While it produced nice profits, Watts had to soft-pedal the department's services because his father questioned the soundness of consumer lending. He also had to fend off complaints from a car dealer who was a bank director, because the bank's lending rates were cheaper than the dealer's. Burdened with such concerns, Watts assigned Reade's department to space in the old Trust Building, which his father seldom visited.[37]

For all its faults, Durham Bank and Trust was not that different from other banks in the state. The depression had taught bankers a painful lesson, and the men who survived the worst were determined not to see a repeat. What Durham Bank and Trust needed was not new financial science, but different attitudes and simple ideas that could be found in any issue of *American Banker* magazine, recalled Watts Hill Jr., who, like his father, had returned to Durham to assume his responsibilities to the family businesses.

∾∾∾

Watts Jr. and his wife, the former Mary Lamberton of Chicago, received a rude awakening on their arrival in the late spring of 1950. Mary was pregnant with their son, George Watts Hill III, and had developed serious complications on the trip to Durham. She required immediate hospitalization on arrival, and Watts Jr. moved in with his grandfather at Hill House. He watched in amazement and disappointment as John Sprunt Hill marshaled all his resources to help defeat U.S. senator Frank Porter Graham. In a bitter, racially charged contest with Raleigh lawyer Willis Smith, Graham fought to serve the balance of the Senate term he had been appointed to fill in 1949 after the death of J. Melville Broughton.

Durham may as well have been the dark side of the moon when Watts Jr. arrived to become an assistant vice president at the bank. For all practical purposes, he had not lived there since he left for Millbrook, a college preparatory school in New York, at the age of twelve. Upon graduation, he went straight into a navy flight training program, first at Hampden-Sydney College in Virginia and then at Princeton. Family visits during prep school years had been to Quail Roost in the country; most summers had been spent at Virginia Beach. He met Mary in Washington at a holiday party arranged for the children of OSS employees. They became sweethearts immediately and married after the war, before Watts was twenty-one. They moved to Chapel Hill, where Watts finished his undergraduate studies and earned a degree in economics. Upon graduation, his parents pressed him to take up his family duties in Durham, but Watts and Mary left for Geneva, Switzerland, where he did graduate work at the Institute of Higher International Studies.

Watts Jr. was interested in many things—the foreign service, teaching, further studies—but he was not interested in the family businesses in Durham. In Europe, he wrote more than one letter questioning how he might fit into the various enterprises at home. It was a situation not all that different from his father's a generation before, but Watts Sr. had the hospital and Quail Roost to absorb his creative energy. Nothing like that awaited his son. Nevertheless, family considerations—plus a low bank balance—finally forced Watts Jr. to return to the States and take a job in New York at Bankers Trust. He hoped for an assignment in the bank's foreign operations area, but the Hills' long-standing relationship with the bank guaranteed him a slot calling on Bankers Trust's correspondent banks in the South. After a little more than a year in New York, Watts and Mary moved to Durham.

Father and son could not have been more different. The elder Watts Hill was private, a man with few close friends. His son was open and gregarious. The father liked cows and farming, while the son turned down the offer of Wakefield, John Sprunt Hill's farm in northern Wake County. Watts Jr. liked airplanes and photography; his father had few interests outside of his work. Watts Jr. preferred small nimble European sports cars, while his father drove a Cadillac that allowed plenty of headroom for his hat. The two shared a fascination with architecture, but the elder's tastes ran to traditional architecture in the Williamsburg style, while the younger preferred modern design. After Watts Jr. gave Durham one of the first homes of contemporary design, his grandfather worried that the building would collapse in a storm. He was also astonished that anyone would build a house with the bedrooms on the first floor.

Dealing with the actual mechanics of banking was not in Watts Jr.'s future, and he knew that when he returned to Durham. He took on duties at the bank that corresponded better with his interests, such as the bank's advertising and promotion campaigns. It was clear to Watts Jr., as it was to his father, that he was not the one to succeed Watts Sr. at the bank. When a seasoned banker from Richmond named Paul Wright Jr. was recruited into senior management in 1953, Watts Jr. assured Wright that he supported him as Ben Roberts's successor.

Wright was a Duke graduate and no stranger in North Carolina banking circles. He first met Watts Hill in 1934, when he applied for a job at the old Durham Loan and Trust Company. "He told me, 'Some day,' but they didn't need me then," Wright later recalled.[38] Wright began his career as a bank examiner and was subsequently hired by Wachovia Bank and Trust Company to work in its Salisbury office before he moved on to Richmond.

Wright's arrival eased Watts Hill's concern about the bank's future management, but it did not immediately cure the overall problems. Competition would do that. Durham's comfortable banking club dissolved in the summer of 1956 when the state's largest bank, Wachovia Bank and Trust Company of Winston-Salem, acquired Durham's largest bank, Fidelity. With nearly half a billion dollars in assets, Wachovia was more than ten times larger than the Hills' bank. Durham banking would never be the same.

∽∽∽

Wachovia's entry into the Durham market came at a time when central North Carolina was beginning to learn about the most challenging and creative idea in industrial development since Charlotte's D. A. Tompkins began building textile mills along the railroad tracks of the Piedmont Crescent in the late nineteenth century. In the last days of 1953, a Greensboro builder with the unlikely name of Romeo Guest had talked to Governor Luther Hodges about developing the area between the cities of Raleigh, Durham, and Chapel Hill into a home for corporate and industrial research. Guest knew from experience that modern industry preferred to locate plants in proximity to major universities. Certainly there was not another location in the South better situated than the piney woods in the heart of a triangle formed by the campuses of North Carolina State College in Raleigh, the University of North Carolina in Chapel Hill, and Duke University in Durham. Guest was not the first to recognize the potential for synergy that would eventually transform the rural crossroads communities of Nelson and Lowe's Grove, but he was the first to put a name on it. In the early months of 1954, when he mailed a promotional letter and brochure to a host of top industrial prospects, he called his planned development the Research Triangle Park.

At the time, Durham's textile mills and cigarette factories remained a firm foundation for the city's economy, and it looked like nothing was going to change that. Of the twelve hundred new industries that had located in the state since 1950, not one of them had come to Durham County. A group of local boosters called the Committee of 100 had been organized to compete with similar organizations across the region in an effort that would be known as the "selling of the South." Under the auspices of the Durham Chamber of Commerce, the group raised $84,000 and optioned land on the city's southeastern perimeter that it offered for sale to new industrial citizens. In February 1955, the Durham City Council earmarked more than $70,000 in tax money to extend water and sewer connections to the proposed industrial park. Watts Hill was an active member of the committee, but it would be Guest's vision of a research park that would capture his attention and ultimately shape Durham's future.

Guest did not have Watts Hill at the top of his list of contacts when he set out to attract attention to his new project. Rather, Guest was closer to Raleigh insiders such as State Treasurer Brandon Hodges, who campaigned for office in 1948 with the pledge to bring new industry to the state, and Robert M. Hanes, the legendary leader at Wachovia, which had become a commanding presence in the state in terms of both deposits and influence. In the mid-1950s, Hanes was nearing the end of an illustrious career that included holding the presidencies of both the American Bankers Association and the prestigious Association of Reserve City Bankers.

It was only a matter of time, however, before Guest would end up in Watts Hill's office in Durham. There were few laymen in North Carolina with stronger ties to the state's leading universities. Hill had worked with North Carolina State since the 1920s, when he had set out to become a dairyman. His gift of more than a thousand acres of Quail Roost forestland had given an important boost to the school's forestry department. His relations with Duke dated to the 1930s, when he became associated with Dr. Wilburt Davison and the Hospital Care Association. As for the university at Chapel Hill, no North Carolina family claimed more years of service on its Board of Trustees. John Sprunt Hill ended nearly fifty years on the Board of Trustees in 1953 when the General Assembly declined to reappoint him. John Sprunt Hill's father had been a trustee for twenty-three years in the nineteenth century. Watts Hill would soon join the board to begin more than two decades of service.

There also were not many men in the region who enjoyed designing and executing projects, great and small, as much as Watts Hill did. He had built hotels and office buildings, classrooms and dormitories, dairy barns,

John Sprunt Hill's love of golf continued well into his later years.

Watts Hill Jr. and his father cochaired a division of the Durham United Way campaign in the 1950s.

Three generations: Watts Hill Jr., John Sprunt Hill, and George Watts Hill at the groundbreaking for the Home Security Life Insurance Company building in the late 1950s.

Early planners of the Research Triangle Park. From left are Akers Moore of Raleigh, Archie Davis of Winston-Salem, Watts Hill, and Elizabeth Aycock.

Durham Interim Committee, created in 1963 at the height of civil rights demonstrations. From left are Floyd Fletcher, James R. Nelson, Asa Spaulding, Watts Hill Jr., Mayor Wensell Grabarek, Watts Carr Jr., Watts Hill, Harvey Rape, the Reverend Warren Carr, E. L. Phillips, and John Wheeler.

Watts Hill, Governor Luther Hodges, and Robert Hanes at a press conference in 1960 announcing plans for the Research Triangle Park.

Watts Hill in the 1960s.

Durham banker John Wheeler and Watts Hill with campaign posters in 1964.

The dramatic sloping eastern face of the Blue Cross Blue Shield building on October 19, 1973, when the building was dedicated.

The members of the first Board of Governors of the University of North Carolina with Governor Robert W. Scott, far left in the door, in the Executive Mansion in Raleigh. Watts Hill is on the far right. Watts Hill Jr. is in the middle of the group.

Watts Hill enjoyed his largely ceremonial post as chairman of the board of the Durham and Southern Railway Company. He christened the line's Bull Durham engine in 1973.

Research Triangle Institute president George Herbert (far left) and Watts Hill with (from left) North Carolina governors Luther Hodges, Dan Moore, Robert Scott, and Terry Sanford.

Outstanding contributors to the future of the University of North Carolina.
From left, Watts Hill, bandleader Kay Kyser, university president William
Friday, and Frank Kenan.

Watts Hill and his second wife, Anne Hutchinson Hill.

Watts Hill Jr., Dudley Hill Sargent, Watts Hill, and John Sprunt Hill II at Watts Hill's seventieth birthday party.

CCB president William L. Burns Jr., Watts Hill, and retired CCB president Paul Wright Jr.

Dr. Frances Hill Fox, David St. Pierre DuBose, Valinda Hill DuBose, and Watts Hill at the dedication of the Hillandale Golf Course, which John Sprunt Hill built to bring golf to Durham before World War I.

The George Watts Hill Alumni Center at The University of North Carolina at Chapel Hill.

Watts Jr. and Mary Hill.

Watts Hill Jr. in his garden.

department stores, and more than one hospital building, as well as his home at Quail Roost. At the time the park idea was first floated, Hill was supervising construction of Durham's first shopping center, which was located south of his father's home near the Forest Hills subdivision.

The financial resources that Hill could bring to the table were considerable, and the family's reputation for supporting civic projects reached back to the turn of the century. In addition, Hill was president of the Durham and Southern Railway Company, whose tracks passed by the western boundary of the property Guest hoped to acquire for the new park.

But what the early boosters of the Research Triangle needed most from Durham was water. If Guest's dream was to be realized, the city of Durham would have to be able to supply more than two million gallons a day to a site that was not only located beyond the city limits, but part of which was in Wake County. The group needed someone who would help Durham officials and others overcome objections to such a novel project. Watts Hill could probably deliver.

The Research Triangle Park was little more than a brochure in Guest's sales portfolio when he called on Watts Hill. He had yet to purchase the first acre of land, and less than $40,000 had been raised to support the work of George L. Simpson Jr., a sociologist and Howard Odum protégé at Chapel Hill who had just been hired as the executive director of the fledgling Research Triangle Committee Incorporated. Governor Hodges appointed Wachovia's Hanes to chair the committee, which he directed to prepare plans for a research institute and help recruit tenants for the park.

The Durham representative on the committee was William Ruffin, the head of Erwin Mills and one of Durham's largest employers. But when George Simpson had his first meeting with Durham businessmen, it was Watts Hill who spoke for the city's leaders. Simpson was new on the job when he got a call from Hanes, who asked him to meet him for a luncheon at the Washington Duke Hotel to explain the Research Triangle to a group of Durham businessmen. After lunch, Simpson gave his pitch, and then Hanes explained the need for seed money necessary to get the project rolling. The distinguished banker was met with silence. Finally, Simpson saw Hill rise in the back of the room. Durham would do its share, Hill said. "Clearly he was ready to make a response," Simpson later recalled. "He brought Durham into it."[39]

❧ ❧ ❧

Watts Hill was ready to take on a project of substance. His interest in farming was beginning to wane. Changes in tax laws had made the operation of Quail Roost a most expensive hobby, and the efficiency of artificial insemination had reduced the value of maintaining bulls for breeding. After World War II, dairy farmers had become less interested in buying bulls with a distinguished lineage to enhance their herds, because at a lower cost and for a greater return they could use science to fill a pasture with registered animals. In 1956, Hill resigned from his position on the board of the American Guernsey Cattle Club, where he had served for twenty years.

The Hills' personal situation was also changing. Ann Hill's health was a tremendous burden on them both. Watts sold the beach house in 1952, keeping only the pine-paneled cottage that had once been a stable on a back-channel lake. Ann broke a hip and was immobilized for months in 1953. That injury plus other medical problems left her isolated at Quail Roost Farm. In 1956, the Hills began to divide their time between Quail Roost Farm, where they often entertained guests for dinner, and a large, white-shingled, gabled house in Chapel Hill at the end of a steep drive called The Glen. Located just off Franklin Street on the east side of town, the Chapel Hill house and an accompanying twenty acres backed up to the university's Battle Park. Watts exchanged his morning walk around the farm for laps in the pool, where he swam in the nude.

By the time of the move, Watts Hill had increased his investment in affairs in Chapel Hill. He had been appointed to the university's Board of Trustees in 1955 and was devoting considerable time to projects at the University of North Carolina. He had an interest in the University National Bank, which he had started in 1954 to offer competition to the Bank of Chapel Hill. And in April 1954, he purchased Chapel Hill's local newspaper, the *Chapel Hill Weekly*, from founder Louis Graves after it appeared that its ownership might go to outside interests upon Graves's retirement.

The newspaper business had been a fascination of Hill's for some time. During the war, he had talked with army friends about starting what he called "an honest-to-God newspaper" in Durham.[40] That never came to pass, but when the Chapel Hill paper came available, he bought it and then sold a majority of the stock to others, including William D. Carmichael III, a Durham advertising account executive; William Muirhead, a Durham construction company executive; J. A. Branch, director of the university's purchasing department; Collier Cobb III, son of the chair of the university's building committee; and Durham lawyer Victor S. Bryant Jr. The Hill interests were divided among Watts Sr., Ann, Watts Jr., and Bo Harris. It was Watts Hill's plan that no individual, including himself, would have a controlling interest in the newspaper. He became the perfect newspaper owner for General Manager Orville Campbell, who was left to run the weekly without interference. Graves, an institution in the town, remained on to write occasional pieces.

Newspapers around the state acknowledged Orville Campbell's desire to retain the local flavor of the paper, which had developed over the years into Graves's personal journal of reflection about and for the community, but they nonetheless lamented Graves's retirement. The *News and Observer* said that the *Weekly* without Graves was like Walden Pond without Thoreau.

From time to time Hill put his money behind other Campbell projects, including a recording of "Wabash Cannonball" by Dizzy Dean on Campbell's Colonial Records label. Another Campbell promotion was "What It Was Was Football," a recording by a young comic named Andy Griffith.

Hill remained faithful to his pledge to keep the newspaper based in the community. In 1961, he declined an offer to sell his family's stake to Mark Ethridge and Barry Bingham of the *Louisville Courier-Journal*. The paper flourished under Campbell, who converted it to a daily. From its offices came a number of outstanding journalists, including Editor Jim Shumaker, who later taught in the University of North Carolina School of Journalism, and Jeff McNelly, who first began drawing editorial cartoons for Shumaker and later won two Pulitzer Prizes for his work as a syndicated artist.

Hill remained first and foremost a banker and booster of the Chapel Hill and Durham communities. From his home in Chapel Hill, he commuted daily to his office in Durham on a route that took him by the future home of the Research Triangle Park. Hill had enough sense of business and awareness of the changes taking place in the South to grasp Guest's vision for the property. Certainly the park presented an important opportunity, and Guest was sure that all who participated in its development would be winners. He believed that the 4,000 acres optioned for $135 an acre would eventually sell for $2,000 an acre and produce a handsome profit for the developers. Meanwhile, the state stood to gain blue-chip corporate citizens that would bring high-paying jobs to the region. Guest was not the only one bubbling with enthusiasm. Wachovia's George Geoghegan, who ran the bank's Raleigh office, told Guest, "The governor told me once he did not see how any investor in the acreage could ever lose, nor can I, unless we are all going completely busted and I see nothing like that on the horizon."[41]

Despite this early enthusiasm, the project soon stalled for lack of a backer with sufficient resources to underwrite the purchase of the land. "What nobody knew was whether there would be a park," Simpson later recalled.[42] At one point, Guest suggested that Governor Hodges approach John Motley Morehead III or John Sprunt Hill for a donation of $1 million to acquire the land. Watts Hill asked the governor if state property at Butner north of Durham or land inside the newly dedicated Umstead State Park between Raleigh and Durham was available. Still others suggested that the cities of Durham, Raleigh, and Chapel Hill pool money and buy the property. In late spring 1957, however, the governor, George Simpson, and William Saunders, the state director of conservation and development, met for breakfast at the Executive Mansion with Karl Robbins, a wealthy New Yorker and former Tar Heel textile man. After listening to a short presentation, Robbins agreed to invest $1 million.[43]

Robbins's commitment revived the project. Guest took Robbins's down payment of $55,000, and by the summer of 1957 he had secured options on hundreds of acres of land in the name of the Pinelands Company, a for-profit business whose Board of Directors included Robbins and his son, Romeo Guest, Watts Hill, George Geoghegan, and Collier Cobb Jr., the president of the Bank of Chapel Hill. The last three were the nominal representatives of Durham, Raleigh, and Chapel Hill.

Watts Hill became an active partner in the land purchases. The Pinelands land agent worked out of the Hill-owned Durham Realty and Insurance Company, whose president, Worth Lutz, searched titles and located owners. William Maughan, a Duke University forestry professor, took Lutz's research and negotiated the purchases. Pinelands's big break came in the summer of 1957, when Maughan optioned a 1,000-acre tract for $105,000.

The early success was promising, but the project remained a bit awkward. On the one side were the interests of the three campuses. The academic community had been attracted by the promise of a world-class research institute that would bring national and international research projects to use the intellectual horsepower of the three campuses. On the other side were the for-profit venture capitalists, who stood to get rich from land sales and construction contracts. At one meeting, the University of North Carolina's Billy Carmichael told Guest: "Let me see, Romeo, if I really understand what it is we are talking about here. You want the professors here and all of us to be the prostitutes and you're going to be the pimp."[44]

Watts Hill moved easily between the competing interests. As a university trustee, he understood the concerns of the academics. At the same time, he was a pragmatic businessman, and he did what he could to assist Guest, Robbins, and others, even though he did not own a single share of stock in Pinelands or stand to profit from land sales. If Hill had any vested interest, it was to protect the franchise of the Durham Bank and Trust Company and other family enterprises and to see that they were not overtaken by Wachovia or other competitors. Like his father, Watts Hill was also proud of Durham, and he wanted his city to share in whatever benefits lay ahead.

∾ ∾ ∾

As he had for the Good Health Association, Watts Hill became one of the Triangle project's most enthusiastic pitchmen. With Simpson and a large map of the proposed park in tow, he hosted prime rib luncheons at the Sheraton Astor Hotel in New York, where he outlined the project to prospective tenants. He was persuasive, precise, and creative. "North Carolina banks must realize the old collateral of cotton and corn must be replaced with more dynamic collateral of brains," he told one group.[45] No job was too big or too small. One day, he turned out in shirtsleeves to help volunteer firemen contain a woods fire on Pinelands property that threatened nearby houses. Hill's vitality impressed Guest, who told Simpson, "Watts is our strongest supporter and a very keen person who is going to help us all more than anybody."[46]

The project had all the features necessary to attract Watts Hill. It was big: by the first of January, 1958, park planners were looking at a need for 7,000 acres, not the 4,000 Guest first proposed. It was innovative: no new facilities such as this had been designed or opened in more than a decade. Hill fussed over every detail, sometimes to the irritation of others. Early on, he recommended that Guest begin the paperwork with the U.S. Postmaster General to obtain a postmark that would read "Research Triangle," rather than "Nelson," which was the city where the closest post office was located. The project also needed a logo, he told Guest, "possibly a combination of statistics, pharmacy, chemistry and electronics. Certainly not sputnik."[47] At a time when telephone prefixes were names, not numbers, he spent eighteen months working with the telephone company to get "Triangle" as the prefix for park phone numbers.[48]

Hill's enthusiasm rubbed some the wrong way. Raleigh interests were not happy with Hill's constant pushing and aggressive nature. They became jealous when they discovered that the park's first development sites would be closer to Durham than to Raleigh. Some saw Hill as an "urbane know-it-all." That was the first impression that Pearson Stewart, the park's first land planner, had of Watts Hill. Stewart spent hours with Hill, who was full of questions about the layout of streets, utilities services, and details of the park's overall plan.[49] Hill could be presumptuous. For example, he addressed his letters to the governor "Dear Luther" even though the two did not know one another well at the time. What was important, however, was that he could deliver. Years later, Hill said he was simply "bull-headed."[50]

For the first eighteen months that Hill worked on behalf of the park, he was nothing more than an enthusiastic volunteer. However, upon the death of Brandon Hodges in 1957, the governor named Hill to replace Hodges as secretary of the Research Triangle Committee and chairman of the Research Institute Committee. The assignment of the latter group was to create the Research Triangle Institute, which would become the focal point of the park. George Simpson had urged the governor to name Hill to both jobs: "As you know, Watts Hill has become greatly interested in the Research Triangle and has done as much work as most of us with regard to it."[51]

Hill's appointment was timely, perhaps even critical. Of all the businessmen involved in the project, Hill had more resources, access, and time at his disposal than the others. His peers were tied to day-to-day corporate responsibilities, while Hill happily broke loose from the routine at the bank. His personal situation was helped by the governor's recent appointment of Durham Bank and Trust president Ben Roberts to the post of state banking commissioner. Roberts's departure from the bank opened the presidency to Paul Wright Jr., the Hills's handpicked successor. Hill not only filled the void left by Brandon Hodges's death but also became a substitute in critical meetings for Robert Hanes; by the spring of 1958 Hanes was seriously ill, and his illness prevented him from spending time on the project.

With urgent nudging from Hill, Durham city officials delivered on the water. At first, Durham city manager Robert W. Flack, who had been welcomed to town by Hill and his father a decade earlier, was cool to the idea of the park because it would not be sited within the city limits. Yet once Watts Hill began walking the paperwork through the various city departments under Flack's control, things began to happen.

"There was a good deal of opposition to putting the water out there," recalled Watts Carr Jr., who was a member of the council in the late 1950s. "[Council members] tended to think in terms of a tax base and not the residual benefits that would flow to the city. [Hill] went around and talked to members of the council. It would not have been built except for his influence."[52] In late January 1958, Durham's Mayor E. J. "Mutt" Evans informally endorsed the park's water needs, and a final commitment was affirmed in April 1958 when the council endorsed a water supply of two million gallons per day.[53] The resulting deal, which required the park to build a $400,000 water line, irked members of the park committee, but they accepted it.

∽∽∽

Despite all the work, the park remained without a tenant. While many of the leading companies in American industry had shown interest in the project, none was willing to make an investment on what was clearly a speculative venture. There were other concerns. By 1958, the nation's economy had gone soft, and some companies were concerned about relocating plants and facilities in the racially segregated South. One prime candidate, Sperry Gyroscope, a division of the huge Sperry Rand Corporation, passed on the park because of the growing resistance to school desegregation in the South. "Since the South has the integration problem," Pearson Stewart reported in 1957, "it may well be unwise, Mr. Ackerson [a Sperry executive] said, to complicate the problem further by adding a wide variety of creeds and colors. Sperry wants complete freedom to hire scientists of whatever garb. To be able to have this freedom, it must be able to guarantee the existence of communities where people of odd garbs and creeds may live normal community lives."[54]

Watts Hill helped land the first tenant, ASTRA Corporation. The company was a small outfit that conducted nuclear research from offices over a grocery store in Milford, Connecticut, when George Simpson called on them. Yes, they would like to move to the Research Triangle, company officials said, but they would need a $50,000 line of credit to cover relocation expenses. When ASTRA executives were next in Raleigh, Simpson took them to Wachovia Bank to talk terms. Simpson's guests emerged "white-faced" after an hour's visit with a Wachovia loan officer who told them AS-TRA did not qualify for a loan, not even one secured by a $250,000 research contract with General Electric.

The next morning, before his ASTRA guests headed back to Milford, Simpson called Watts Hill at his home and asked if he could come by. "I told him about these people," Simpson recalled. "He was eating breakfast and I said I sure hate for them to go back without something. He said, 'How much do they want?' I told him, 'Fifty thousand.' And he said, 'I'll sign the note.'" ASTRA began making plans to move south.[55] Hill later gave ASTRA a letter of introduction to his old OSS boss, David Bruce, who was the U.S. envoy in West Germany when ASTRA went to Europe in search of new customers.

At about this same time, Hill also gave a needed boost to the Research Triangle Institute. The institute was a critical component in plans for the Research Triangle Park because it would unite the academic power of the campuses and help to establish a comfortable environment for corresponding corporate research. The North Carolinians used the Stanford Research Institute as their model and reported that Stanford had attracted about $15 million in research contracts. They also looked at the Armour Research Institute in Chicago, where annual contracts were even larger. A few days after Watts Hill chaired his first meeting of the institute planning committee, he informed Simpson that his father would donate 1,000 shares of Wachovia stock—proceeds from the Wachovia-Fidelity merger of 1956—to cover the $15,000 in planning costs that Gertrude Cox of North Carolina State College projected would be necessary to launch the institute.[56]

Cox was the first woman to become a full professor and department chair on the Raleigh campus. She also successfully tapped into the anxiety over America's second-place position in the space race and attracted substantial research grants. Her experience in statistical research was just what the institute needed: statistical work did not require expensive laboratories or buildings, and Cox's early experience could jump-start the process of attracting grants to the institute. With her Survey Operations Unit running short of space, the institute appeared to be a perfect new home.

Hill was impressed with Cox's record, but he thought she was pretentious and told her so. He later told University of North Carolina president William Friday: "She would not be worth a darn if she wasn't a prima donna. She seemed to like it. I understand it's the first time anybody has called her a prima donna to her face."[57]

The progress on the institute and the ASTRA signing were the sort of demonstrations that park organizers badly needed to shore up the confidence of Karl Robbins, whose enthusiasm for the project had begun to wane. At the beginning of 1958, Robbins invested another $275,000, which was used to purchase 2,000 acres and acquire options on another 2,000, but he was anxious about the future. Robbins told Watts Hill and the governor at a February 1958 meeting in Durham that he expected North Carolina investors to come up with half of the $1 million he had committed to; he also expected them to raise the $1,125,000 needed to start the research institute.[58] As the economy began to slip into a recession, Robbins grew more reticent about investing additional funds, but at an April meeting in New York he gave Hill a commitment to pay $100,000 of the $600,000 cost of the institute's first building.

Other problems loomed. Governor Hodges was beginning to have second thoughts about the propriety of the state's top official promoting a struggling for-profit venture. The park was a tough sell, particularly in the competitive environment that existed between cities outside the Triangle. Charlotte banker Addison Reece shocked one state industry hunter when he angrily rejected a request to support the project. "We've got the greatest industry complex in the state," Reece was reported to have said, referring to Charlotte. "Why should we turn around and try to help the east? Your people in Raleigh cut us to ribbons every legislative session."[59]

In late summer 1958, Governor Hodges and Robert Hanes prevailed on Archie K. Davis, who was due to become Hanes's successor at Wachovia, to try his hand at recruiting investors. Davis turned the proposal back on the two and suggested that rather than sell stock he preferred to solicit donations for a nonprofit foundation that would buy out the Pinelands investors altogether. He told Hill that the institute would be his principal selling point. "With that in hand, I feel certain that the rest would be relatively easy after landing two or three corporate contributions in the neighborhood of $100,000 each," Davis said. Durham's goal was to raise $100,000, and businessmen in Raleigh were asked to raise a like amount. "Too much hard work and good judgment have gone into this undertaking for it to fail for want of money, and we simply have to find it some place, somewhere," Davis wrote Hill.[60]

Davis set year's end as the deadline for raising the money. Certain options on park land were due to expire in January 1959, and Davis was going to be occupied in the spring with the General Assembly, where he was a member of the state Senate. Hill used a "Salute to Industry" dinner organized by local businesses and chaired by Paul Wright to corner Southern Railway officials for a donation. In a report to Davis, he said that he told them he "did not think Southern Railroad could afford to be sitting out in the cold and letting other people do their job for them."[61]

When Hodges announced the creation of the foundation in January 1959, the fund-raisers had surpassed their $1 million goal and secured commitments for $1,425,000. That amount later grew to $2 million. Park boosters cut it close, however. When it appeared that some land purchase options might expire, Watts Hill personally covered the amount due.[62]

Later in 1969, Durham's business community recognized Watts Hill's work on behalf of the park by presenting him with the Durham Committee of 100's "Industry Bowl." Governor Hodges made the presentation. In fact, Watts Hill's work on behalf of the Research Triangle Institute and the park had just begun. It would come to occupy more and more of his time over the next twenty-five years.

௯ ௯ ௯

The Research Triangle was a welcome venture for Hill because it was one where he was not subject to a veto on his decisions by his father. Though John Sprunt Hill was approaching ninety years of age and was removed from many daily decisions, he could still second-guess his son, and he exercised his authority without hesitation. In 1957, for example, the Board of Directors of the insurance company had gathered to review the final plans for a new building planned for the edge of downtown. The building featured modern lines and lots of glass. As John Sprunt Hill looked over the plans, he observed that the building needed columns. He also commented wryly that his 57 percent of the stock believed that the building stood too close the street and needed steps. The final plans reflected his changes.

The elder Hill remained up for a fight. In 1957, he renewed his crusade against the fluoridation of the Durham water system when a second effort was initiated. He published a pamphlet replete with quotations from selected medical authorities that supported his position. The Durham papers also made much of the difference of opinion between Hill and his grandson, Watts Jr., who was a member of the county's legislative delegation and who favored the water treatment. The elder Hill declared that he would draw his water from a private well if the city added what some called "rat poison" to it. The city's heath director said if Hill did install a well, then it would have to be tested for purity, and he would close it down if it did not meet specifications. When the city council voted in April 1957, fluoridation was postponed again. Durham's water system was not fluoridated until 1962, a year after John Sprunt Hill's death.

A few years before the fluoride battle, John Sprunt Hill mounted an aggressive legal campaign to keep the control of Erwin Mills out of the hands of a South Carolina textile company. The Hills owned about 20 percent of the company, and they objected to changes that were made in the mill's operations after the death of the company's longtime president, Kemp Plummer Lewis. The Hills made a bid for stock owned by Ben Duke's daughter, Mary Duke Biddle, but lost out to Abney Mills of Greenwood, South Carolina. A protracted court battle ensued, and John Sprunt Hill sat through the entire proceedings, usually dressed in a light linen suit and wearing a green eyeshade. At one point, after hours of testimony, the judge thought he saw Hill nodding with fatigue. "Mr. Hill is tired," the judge said. "We'll recess." Hill waved to the judge to show he was attentive and replied, "On no, carry on."[63] The Hills lost their bid for control.

John Sprunt Hill's stubborn opposition to fluoridation, and even the Erwin fight, tended to create a public image of a crusty, ill-tempered old man. Those who knew him said that the reputation was far from reality. He remained a courteous, well-mannered, and good-humored Southern gentleman who enjoyed writing romantic poetry, reading the classics, and playing an afternoon game of checkers with his great-grandson, Watts Hill III, who often stopped in on his way home from school. When artist Ernie Barnes recalled his childhood in Durham in his book *From Pads to Palette*, he remembered being in the Hill home, where his mother worked as a maid. He found a kindly old man there who allowed him to wander at will through his collection of art books. "I enjoyed this room of polished mahogany walls with leather chairs, shelves of leather-bound books and the sound of classical music. He would tell me about the various schools of art, his favorite painters, the museums he visited and other things my mind couldn't quite comprehend at age seven. But he seemed to enjoy educating me as much as I enjoyed his books," Barnes wrote.[64]

Hill took life as it came. One day, he left his desk in his office in the Hill Building to check on papers in the vault downstairs. He was on his way back to the office when he stopped in a lavatory, where the door to the stall locked behind him. Hill called for help, but it was two hours before a bank officer found him and set him free. When he emerged, he said, "You know, it's clear to me that everybody around here is working hard because I have been locked in here for two hours and not anybody has been down here."[65]

Durham continued to enjoy gifts from the Hill family. In June 1955, John Sprunt Hill donated nine acres of land for two new holes at Hillandale Golf Course. Two years later, he donated lots in the new Bellevue subdivision that were sold to pay for a rebuilding program at the course. In 1959, his daughter Frances and her husband donated fourteen acres for additional changes at Hillandale. Many of Hill's good deeds, however, were private. A black physician who had completed his education with a loan from John Sprunt Hill finished his training and came to repay the loan. "Don't pay me back," Hill told the doctor. "When you can, do the same for someone else." The physician said later that he turned the money over nine times.[66]

Hill took great pride in the growth of the credit union movement, which by 1960 included thirty state-chartered credit unions serving more than twelve thousand members. Along with nearly two hundred federally chartered credit unions, cooperative banking in North Carolina had assets of more than $33 million and a membership of over one hundred thousand. While Hill's vision had been to serve rural customers—farmers struggling against crop liens and high rates—most of the latter-day credit unions served customers in cities.[67]

In 1959, the General Assembly named John Sprunt Hill and John Motley Morehead III lifetime trustees of the university. At the time, it was estimated that during Hill's lifetime his contributions had amounted to more than $6 million. Some of his most important gifts continued to produce income to support his beloved North Carolina Collection. In 2002, $711,000 was distributed to the library for use by the collection.

⌒⌒⌒

The Hill interests remained closely interwoven with the affairs of Durham, but the family was not always united, as became clear when a proposal to consolidate Durham's city and county governments was float-ed in 1961. Watts Hill Jr. had succeeded in getting enabling legislation passed in the 1959 General Assembly that would allow the city and county governments to merge. His father, who saw the merger as a way of boost-ing Durham's economic future, became vice chairman of a study commis-sion that subsequently recommended a merger plan to voters. As the cam-paign for the approval of a new charter entered its closing days in December 1960, Watts Hill found himself publicly opposed by his sister Frances Fox and his father. John Sprunt Hill's argument against consolida-tion was contained in a lengthy legal document that was too complicated and involved for an aging man with sight and hearing problems to have prepared, yet it appeared in the *Durham Herald* as Hill's gospel on the sub-ject. Voters turned down the merger proposal by a three-to-one margin. The loss was more than disappointing for Watts Hill, who had staked him-self out clearly in favor of the change.

The merger vote came only weeks before a pending merger of Durham Bank and Trust Company with University National Bank in Chapel Hill. Bank mergers were becoming almost commonplace, as larger North Car-olina banks began to expand their franchises across the state. North Car-olina National Bank, created in a 1960 merger of Charlotte and Greens-boro banks, now had a Durham address. Two years earlier, Watts Hill had consolidated Durham Bank and Trust's position through a merger with Citizens National Bank in Durham. (Citizens National Bank traced its roots to the bank Gerard Watts owned with Eugene Morehead.)

The Chapel Hill expansion offered considerable promise; the college town was growing. Watts Hill had launched University National in 1954 as a competitor to the stuffy Bank of Chapel Hill, which controlled virtually all the local business. In the early days of the new bank, Watts Hill owned a large share of the stock, but by the time of the merger he controlled less than 5 percent. The merger was under final consideration by the boards of directors when Hill decided that Durham Bank and Trust Company need-ed a new name if it was to have any standing in the regional banking com-petition. Moreover, Hill later said, he felt that it would not do for a loyal Carolina man to open a "Durham" bank in Chapel Hill.

With merger votes pending in early May, Hill and B. W. Harris Jr., who had handled negotiations with the Chapel Hill stockholders, left their offices at 111 Corcoran Street and headed for a meeting with John Sprunt Hill to talk about changing the name of the bank the elder Hill had started nearly sixty years earlier. Watts Hill was nervous. His father did not take well to change, and Watts had not found a name he really liked even as he left his office for the meeting. Just as Harris turned the car off Chapel Hill Street and headed toward Hill's house, Watts Hill said, "I've got it." "What is it?" Harris replied. "Central Carolina Bank and Trust Company," Hill said, and he wrote the name on the back of an envelope. The inspiration for the name came from his recollection of the history of the Farmers' Mutual Exchange that he and his father had helped found during the depression. It had since been renamed Central Carolina Farmers' Exchange.

"The nurse got Mr. John Sprunt," Harris later recalled. "So we told him about the merger and that we were supposed to change names and Mr. Hill said, 'We think Central Carolina Bank and Trust Company.' And Mr. John Sprunt said, 'That sounds all right to me.'" Watts Hill turned to Harris, rose to leave, and said, "Boy, let's go. We've got what we want."[68]

∾ ∾ ∾

John Sprunt Hill died a few weeks later on July 29, 1961, at the age of ninety-two. Leaders from across the state offered their praises of his productive life. Governor Hodges called him "one of the greatest citizens the state has ever produced." Frank Porter Graham said: "He was one of the great North Carolinians of our time and one of the best graduates the University of North Carolina ever had. He promoted the building of our state industrially, agriculturally, educationally and spiritually."[69] On Monday August 1, a simple service was conducted at First Presbyterian Church with Dr. Benjamin Rice Lacy, the former president of Union Theological Seminary of Richmond, officiating. Hill was buried at Maplewood Cemetery beside his wife Annie Watts and his father-in-law George Watts.

John Sprunt Hill's way of life had largely been consigned to history by the time he died. Just months before, the South had begun to observe the centennial of the Civil War, which had ended only a few years before John Sprunt Hill was born in Duplin County. He had known men who had served in that conflict, and he had shared membership on the university's Board of Trustees with former soldiers who still referred to one another by their military ranks. North Carolina was a far different place from what he had found on his return from New York City in the early years of the century. The solid, two-lane highways that Hill had built forty years earlier to connect county seats were being replaced with wider, multi-lane interstate highways that connected state capitals. Few of the yeoman farmers he had valued for their independence and attachment to the land survived the depression or returned to the farm after World War II. Those that remained soon saw their farms consolidated and mechanized. Lowe's Grove, the site of Hill's first credit union, would soon become important for its proximity to the Research Triangle Park, not for its historical value.

He left his mark during a busy, vigorous life, especially in Chapel Hill on the campus of the university. While only one campus building carried the Hill name—the music hall named for his late wife, Annie Watts—the shape of the campus between South Building and Wilson Library was the result of his service as a trustee. The Carolina Inn had become one of the most important institutions in campus life. Perhaps his most valuable, unique, and lasting legacy, however, was the North Carolina Collection, which was endowed by the income from property he left for its support.

Hill's death came on a Saturday. The *Durham Morning Herald*'s weekend reporter, Jake Phelps, had been working at the paper for about a year and knew little of Durham's history when he drew the assignment to write John Sprunt Hill's obituary. Phelps was at his desk in the newsroom when he saw Watts Hill walking his way. Hill sat down across from Phelps and talked for an hour with love and affection about his father and the great fun they had had together. "I thought, 'God almighty of all places to be,'" Phelps remembered. "And then for him to spend so much time. I didn't want to cut it off. I was so grateful to hear all this. He was so proud of his father," Phelps said. "He said he had done well by doing good."[70]

∽·∽·∽

John Sprunt Hill's death marked an important turning point in his son's life. Although their relationship had not been one of particular warmth or affection, Watts Hill would later name his father as one of his closest friends. There was much to admire in the independence, strength, and determination of John Sprunt Hill, who rose from meager circumstances on a Duplin County farm to command the attention of those of wealth and influence across the state. Yet the same qualities that Watts Hill admired in his father and which he inherited had also bred frustration as John Sprunt Hill refused to relinquish power and authority to his son, who as a man of sixty years was still required to seek his father's approval for important decisions. On more than one occasion, Watts Hill had laid his stock on his father's desk and offered to step aside. All the years of being under the strong influence of his father weighed heavily on Watts Hill as his father's funeral services concluded. Standing at the graveside, Watts Jr. was beside his father when he heard him say in a quiet yet determined voice, "Never again will anyone tell me what to do."

CHAPTER 13

On His Own Terms

EXCEPT DURING HIS YEARS with the OSS, Watts Hill had always been in his father's shadow. Even in John Sprunt Hill's later years, when age had slowed mind and limb, he refused to pass the mantle to his son. As a result, the words Watts Hill spoke over his father's grave came not from anger but from relief that he was finally, at nearly sixty years of age, on his own.

Watts had never shared his father's entrepreneurial zeal. Watts once said his efforts on behalf of rural cooperatives, not-for-profit ventures such as the farmers' exchange, and the Hospital Care Association marked him as unworthy of the title of capitalist that his father enjoyed. "I think my father was very much interested in public service in many ways," Watts Hill said. "But he was interested in making money too."[1]

Watts saw his duty on a much grander scale. He envisioned his role as similar to that played by his grandfather, George W. Watts, with whom he had spent countless hours as a youngster. In his lifetime, Watts Hill would leave his mark on educational institutions such as the University of North Carolina at Chapel Hill, on medical care and the needs of hospitals in North Carolina generally, and especially on the nurturing and development of the Research Triangle Institute. Durham Academy, the private school his wife had helped launch during the depression as the Calvert Method School, also occupied much of his attention.

Certainly it was easy for Watts Hill to take a more casual attitude toward financial affairs than his father had. He had enjoyed the benefits of great wealth throughout his life. He had never wanted for anything, and he placed full confidence in those he hired to manage the bank, the insurance company, and even his own personal finances. That did not make him a spendthrift. Rather, he took his good fortune seriously, and, like his father, he was a conservative guardian of the Hill financial empire. At the same time, he was mindful of the examples set by his mother and grandfather, who had taught him that along with great wealth came a special responsibility to the community.

Hill's longtime friend, William C. Friday, the president of the University of North Carolina, once described him this way: "[Watts Hill] wanted to know what you could do that was important, what you could do to change things. I know that Watts felt that when you have great wealth, your job is to pay back. You are a custodian of that wealth for the benefit of the people."[2]

∽∽∽

According to the Durham newspaper, John Sprunt Hill's estate was valued at more than $17 million. In truth, the amount was a great deal more, although the total was never publicly disclosed. It was sufficiently large to cause the wags on Capitol Square in Raleigh to suggest, when the annual figures were reported the following year, that the settling of Hill's estate was responsible for the doubling of state revenue from inheritance taxes. The state and federal taxes on his estate were large enough that the family had to make a public stock offering in the Home Security Life Insurance Company to raise the $14 million needed to cover them. Despite the lessons he had learned in settling estates for his father-in-law and his wife, John Sprunt Hill had failed to find tax shelters for many of his assets.

John Sprunt Hill left most of his wealth to his son and to his two daughters, Frances Hill Fox, whose home was set into the crest of a hill on Croasdale Farm northwest of Durham, and Valinda Hill DuBose of Chapel Hill. Into his children's hands passed control of the two primary institutions, Central Carolina Bank and Home Security Life Insurance Company. They also took control of the Homeland Investment Corporation, whose principal asset was the Washington Duke Hotel in downtown Durham, and Durham Realty and Insurance Company, a prosperous business that was run by Watts Carr Jr. The estate also included substantial holdings in Durham Hosiery Mills and Erwin Mills.

The balance of the estate was used to establish a charitable trust that included 5,000 shares of stock in Erwin Mills, 10,000 shares in Wachovia Bank and Trust, 4,000 shares in American Tobacco Company, and 100 shares in Security Savings and Loan Company. Hill gave 1,500 shares of

Wachovia stock to the First Presbyterian Church and 2,000 to the university to support the North Carolina Collection and supplement the salaries of librarians Mary Lindsay Thornton and her assistant, Elizabeth Cotten.[3] The servants in his Duke Street home were also remembered with bequests roughly equal to a year's pay.

The Hill mansion on Duke Street was given to the women of Durham to be used for meetings and events as a memorial to Hill's wife, Annie, who had organized a number of civic endeavors from those very rooms. The gift drew comment from the *Carolina Times*, Durham's black-owned newspaper, which observed in an editorial that before Hill's death in 1961 he had changed his will to provide for use of the mansion by all women, not just "white women," as he had earlier specified. "Thus, at the age of 91," the *Carolina Times* noted, "Hill was able to discern the shadow of coming events that will disregard the color of one's skin, race or creed and accept a person for his or her real worth."[4] The paper did not report that about a year before the will was changed Hill's grandson Watts Hill Jr. had also arranged for a friendly lawsuit to remove racial references in trusts that had restricted the use of the public parks that John Sprunt and Annie Watts Hill had given the city.

ᦂᦂᦂ

John Sprunt Hill's death in 1961 came at a time when Durham was beginning to fall behind other cities of comparable size in the state. Just weeks before Hill's death, the *Morning Herald* published a weeklong series of articles on the noticeable deterioration of the city's central business district. Shoppers were being drawn to suburban stores where they did not have to contend with narrow thoroughfares and limited parking. In addition, manufacturing jobs—the lifeblood of Durham's economy—were also disappearing. City leaders had taken notice of the robust growth in Greensboro, Charlotte, and Raleigh and had checked Durham's economic pulse. It was weak. "The big boys had better get together," a Durham officeholder warned.[5]

Yet in the same edition with the newspaper's report on Durham's slide into negative economic numbers, there appeared a front-page photograph and story announcing a $160,000 investment by the U.S. Atomic Energy Commission in an isotope laboratory for the newly organized Research Triangle Institute. Standing with the government officials signing the agreement were Watts Hill and the institute's first director, George Herbert. The story noted that Hill and Herbert had already been to the legislature to ask for $200,000 in state money for other equipment for the institute.

Tobacco and textile stocks—representatives of the passing economy—were the underpinnings of the Hill fortune. Yet Watts Hill was as excited about the future of the Research Triangle and its implications for Durham as he had ever been about any enterprise. Almost from their first meeting, he and George Herbert had bonded like brothers despite a generation's difference in their ages. (Herbert was thirty-six when he arrived in Durham.) They made a formidable pair, and Hill would remain as chair of the institute's Board of Governors throughout most of Herbert's career.

Herbert had been trained as an electrical engineer at the United States Naval Academy and was involved in the early days of the Stanford Research Institute in California. When he was contacted by the Research Triangle Institute committee about coming to North Carolina, he was an executive at the American and Foreign Power Company in New York City, a holding company that could offer him plum assignments virtually anywhere in the world. In the early fall of 1958, Watts Hill invited Herbert to Quail Roost for dinner and an evening with the institute's planning committee. Herbert was not a "scientist of high scholarly nature," a standard the committee had set in its search for a chief executive, but he impressed the group nevertheless. The committee met a man of "modest demeanor" and "quiet self-confidence" who had experience in managing people, programs, and money.[6] Hill liked Herbert's stamina; the two sat up late that night talking about the institute. "You can learn a lot about a man just sitting around the swimming pool," Hill once said of his early meeting with Herbert. "If he can hold his liquor, for one thing."[7]

Herbert was impressed too, especially with the commitment to the project demonstrated by Hill, the University of North Carolina's President William C. Friday, and George Simpson, the director of the Research Triangle Park. "It was clear to me that this wasn't their project of this week and they were going to move on to something else next week," Herbert later said. "I have no recollection of Bill Friday, or Watts Hill or George Simpson ever having any doubt as to the ultimate success [of the institute]."[8] Wachovia Bank and Trust Company president Archie K. Davis urged caution in hiring Herbert and suggested that Herbert be brought on as a consultant, but the committee knew they had their man.[9] Herbert was equally excited. He wrote his first research grant proposal even before he went on the payroll on December 1, 1958.

It was a leap of faith for Herbert. When he accepted the job, Hill, Davis, and others had yet to raise the money needed to buy out the interests of Karl Robbins and other for-profit investors and turn the park project into a nonprofit enterprise. Yet Davis saw opportunities in the plan, and a few days after the creation of the nonprofit Research Triangle Foundation was announced in January 1959 Herbert moved into temporary quarters in the Home Security Life Insurance Company building in downtown Durham, where Hill made offices available free of charge.

The free office space was more than a gesture. It helped the project survive in the early days. Even with the impressive response to the fundraising effort, the foundation's operating funds were limited. There was barely enough money for the construction of the institute's first building, which was to be named in honor of Robert Hanes, and little for the land purchases needed to keep the park boundaries intact. On two occasions, Hill acquired property and held it until the foundation's financial condition improved, at which point he sold it to the foundation for the original purchase price. One tract that was purchased in this way was a critical 191 acres that straddled the Raleigh–Chapel Hill highway in the heart of the park, while another later became the site of the U.S. Environmental Protection Agency research facility.[10]

Once the Hanes Building opened, Hill became a frequent visitor to Herbert's offices. As secretary-treasurer of the foundation and chairman of the institute board, Hill proved to be an important link between the institute, which conducted research for a wide range of private and public clients and generated needed operating revenue, and the foundation, whose principal function was to develop the property and manage the growth of the park. He often arrived at Herbert's office with blueprints under his arm. He was constantly tinkering with plans for the institute's campus, guided by a vision that went well beyond what others thought practical. He dreamed of research buildings sited around a forty-acre lake, with several guesthouses and a museum for the display of products developed by companies in the park. When construction began on each new building, he monitored the progress. He personally presented the plans for the institute's second building, the Camille Dreyfus Laboratory, to Dreyfus's widow for her approval.[11] When the last tract in the park was deeded in 1972, the institute's campus included 158 acres. It was less than what Hill had wanted; the guesthouses and museum never did materialize.

Neither did he get his lake, but his name was put on the tenth building in the Research Triangle Institute complex, which was dedicated in his honor. Originally the building was to be only five stories, and like the others on the campus it was designed within the limitations of a tight budget. From the outset, Hill had pressed George Herbert to pay more attention to appearances, and he was appalled that the director's office remained uncarpeted because Herbert had put the money to what he considered a better use. When Hill was told about the building that would carry his name, he volunteered to pay for the addition of another story if he was allowed to outfit it in the style he believed was required.

At the dedication ceremonies of the Hill Building on October 21, 1977, Herbert rang a brass cowbell not unlike one that Hill had hung on one of his Guernseys at Quail Roost Farm. Herbert called Hill "my counselor, my consoler and my critic." He continued: "But any time and all the time I know that he is, first and foremost, my friend. He is RTI's first and foremost friend, too, as his long, long hours of care and concern have shown so amply and so often."[12] Hill remained chairman of Herbert's board until 1992.

∾ ∾ ∾

One of the reasons the Research Triangle Park attracted notice in the 1950s from companies interested in building research facilities in the South was North Carolina's reputation for moderation in race relations. The state had escaped the violent confrontations that by 1960 were occurring elsewhere in the Deep South. Students had remained in North Carolina classrooms, where a modest degree of desegregation had taken place, while less than a hundred miles away in Farmville, Virginia, whites had closed the public schools rather than admit African Americans.

North Carolina did not fully join the civil rights movement until 1960, when four students from North Carolina Agricultural and Technical State College (North Carolina A&T) in Greensboro sat down at the lunch counter at the F. W. Woolworth store and asked to be served just as white customers were. When their request was refused, they remained at the counter until the store was closed for the day. The next day, others joined the four, and within the week the sit-down in Greensboro—later called a "sit-in" and credited with founding a movement—had spread to cities all across the South. It arrived directly at Watts Hill's front door both in

Chapel Hill where he lived and in Durham where he worked. For a man accustomed to proper order in his personal and social life, the picketing and street marches were troubling, even maddening, because they threatened his way of life.

Watts Hill's racial attitudes had been shaped by the segregated society in which he was raised. His father firmly believed that segregation was ordained by God and had written a tract explaining his convictions. "The slogan, 'one blood, one world, one people,' probably had its origin in the efforts of certain Northern politicians to influence the vote of millions of foreign-born citizens living in northern cities," Hill wrote.[13] The African Americans Watts Hill had known best were the servants in his home and the field hands at his farm. Watts Hill's African American butler, Tommy Stroud, was as loyal and steady a retainer as any who had served a master in the Old South.

At the same time, Watts Hill's experience in Durham had brought him closer to more black businessmen, doctors, and educators than most southerners of his social and professional station ever encountered. When he arrived at the Hill Building on Corcoran Street each morning, he was only steps away from the home of Mechanics and Farmers Bank and the North Carolina Mutual Life Insurance Company, two strong and successful black-owned institutions. Over the years, he had come to know administrators and doctors at Durham's Lincoln Hospital, which the Dukes had established for the care of African Americans.

The Hill family's relationship with the founders of these outstanding black institutions dated back half a century. During the banking crisis of the depression, John Sprunt Hill gave Mechanics and Farmers Bank the same assistance that he offered to the owners of white-owned banks. After the war, Watts Hill recruited the top executives at North Carolina Mutual to participate in the statewide good health campaign. Later, he and John Wheeler, the president of Mechanics and Farmers Bank, campaigned together for public support of a bond issue to pay for the expansion of facilities at Watts and Lincoln hospitals. Watts Hill Jr. had worked with Wheeler in a friendly lawsuit that voided the racial restrictions on the use of the public parks given to the city by his grandparents.

The older generation of leaders at these institutions respected the racial separation that traditionally defined life in Durham. North Carolina Mutual had never been in the forefront of the civil rights movement. Company executives had worked quietly for modest changes without raising any dust or public notice. In the postwar years, Asa Spaulding, who had followed William J. Kennedy as head of the company, organized dinners in a private room at the Washington Duke Hotel for black and white guests to honor visiting speakers whom his company brought to Durham for appearances at North Carolina Mutual, Durham's North Carolina College, or Shaw University in Raleigh.

By the 1960s, the most influential member of Durham's black community was John Wheeler, the tough-minded chief executive at Mechanics and Farmers. He was the undisputed leader of the Durham Committee on Negro Affairs, one of the state's oldest and strongest local political organizations, and he had long been impatient with the slow pace of change accommodated by the North Carolina Mutual leadership. The civil rights of black Americans had Wheeler's undivided attention. In the early months of 1961, just as Governor Terry Sanford was settling into office, Wheeler wrote the governor and demanded the immediate integration of state jobs, the National Guard, and state-owned parks and institutions. He told Sanford that it was time for a modern-day Emancipation Proclamation. It was a proposition that he would raise over and over again with the young progressive governor. Wheeler reinforced his calls for change by giving his determined support to the black students who were picketing on Durham streets, and he opened the lobby of his bank as a haven for demonstrators who carried signs in the rain and cold. He personally paid for their meals, and along with other black businessmen he raised the money to pay bail bonds when police took young people into custody. All this he managed in the face of intimidation from influential whites including Watts Hill, who pressured Wheeler to use his influence to get the students off the streets. In response, Wheeler simply became more steadfast; he kept one of Hill's threatening letters in his desk drawer as a reminder of the challenges that blacks faced in Durham.[14]

⌣⌣⌣

By the spring of 1963, the movement had made modest progress in removing racial barriers in Durham. Eleven of sixteen downtown retailers, including the large Belk and Thalhimer department stores, had integrated their sales staffs and eliminated discriminatory restrictions and customs. But downtown restaurants, the Hill-owned Washington Duke Hotel, and popular tourist stops such as the Howard Johnson's and Holiday Inn motels refused to accommodate African Americans.

The tension building in Durham came to a head on municipal election day, May 18, 1963, the day after the ninth anniversary of the Supreme Court's *Brown* decision, which had desegregated public schools. When students from the campus of North Carolina College marched into downtown Durham to challenge the resolve of segregationists, they were met by a large group of angry whites. Police officers moved in to keep the sides apart. The following day, a Sunday, demonstrations resumed at the Howard Johnson's restaurant and motel on the Durham–Chapel Hill boulevard. Four thousand protesters—most of them students—blocked the entrance to the restaurant. Five hundred people marched around the building singing, "We're going to eat at Howard Johnson's one of these days." By the end of the day, police had packed 700 demonstrators into a jail designed to hold 120.

Durham's newly elected mayor was Wensell Grabarek, a former city councilman who had defeated Watts Carr Jr., the preferred choice of business leaders like Watts Hill. Grabarek had won with the help of the city's more liberal voter networks and with overwhelming support from black voters. A transplanted Pennsylvanian who had come south during World War II, Grabarek was tall, with an angular face and a salt-and-pepper crew cut. He was partial to two-tone wingtips and often wore a white carnation in his lapel. He was a senior partner in a Durham accounting firm, and he had made his reputation in city government by sorting through the tangle of municipal finance, just as Watts Hill had done thirty years earlier.

Grabarek's first day in office could not have been more exhausting. The jails were full. Anger, not reason, seemed to prevail when a student was injured while being ejected from the Howard Johnson's restaurant. Blacks responded by throwing stones at cars. Members of the Fruit of Islam, the paramilitary arm of the Nation of Islam, lined the railroad tracks near downtown Durham. The men stood in silent formation to guard the home of civil rights leader and attorney Floyd B. McKissick, whose office was the headquarters of the demonstrators. On Tuesday, Grabarek appeared before an overflow crowd at Saint Joseph's AME Zion Church and declared, "The demonstrations have accomplished their intended purpose to the extent of alerting the entire city of the seriousness and sincerity which the Negro attaches to them."[15] The following day, he began putting together an interracial group called the Durham Interim Committee; he appointed Watts Carr Jr. as the chairman and Asa Spaulding as vice chairman. He asked Carr to work fast and not become entangled in the city government bureaucracy. A week after the election, the committee members divided into subgroups and began to hear complaints.

Earlier efforts at dialogue about racial issues had produced little action. This time, Grabarek picked a committee membership that guaranteed results. In addition to Spaulding and Carr, he enlisted the help of Watts Hill and Watts Hill Jr. as well as Harvey Rape, who with a shotgun cradled in his arms had barred blacks from entering his cafeteria. Rape made no pretense about his segregationist beliefs, but Grabarek later said, "I knew that Harvey Rape had to be on my committee for this town to be successful."[16] The same could have been said for John Wheeler, who was joined by former city councilman Floyd Fletcher, the general manager of WTVD television; the Reverend Warren Carr, pastor of Watts Street Baptist Church; James R. Nelson, a drugstore manager; insurance man James R. Hawkins; and E. L. Phillips, an assistant superintendent of the Durham city schools.

Committee members were asked to make recommendations for the integration of employment, schools, and public accommodations and to consider other miscellaneous issues, including seating in movie theaters. Watts Hill Jr. was assigned to the education subcommittee with Spaulding. Carr asked the elder Hill to take on public accommodations, where public pressure was most intense. Just three days earlier, the Durham Restaurant Association had reaffirmed its opposition to integrated service just after some of its members had agreed to serve all customers regardless of race. Among those opposing change was Frank Sherrill, the owner of the S&W Cafeteria chain, which had one of its restaurants in the Home Security Life Insurance building.

Watts Hill Sr. approached his meetings like the "captain of a destroyer."[17] He was determined to remain in control even though the meetings often disintegrated into angry venting sessions for various groups seeking one goal: desegregation. "He went in with the assumption that it was going to happen," Carr said. "He was very persuasive and very domineering."[18]

Asa Spaulding remembered telling Hill before one meeting: "Durham likes to call itself the friendly city. Do you want to put a premium on violence? Or do we want to be smart and provide leadership? If we keep letting violence force us to do things, we're putting a premium on it. Because people get to think that the only way you're going to make any progress, or bring about change, is through violence. But if we want to be smart, we'll take the leadership and bring about change without this having to happen. And we all ought to do it."

Later, Spaulding said, "Watts Hill, you know, once he decides to do anything, he rolls up his sleeves and goes at it. And you see, he owned the hotel, he and his family. So he rolled up his sleeves. And he curses a lot, you know. He said, 'Goddamit, we can't let these things happen here that happened in these other cities. We've got to straighten this thing out.' And so we went to work on it. And within a matter of weeks, we had all the public accommodations open except the theaters. It was the last stronghold; we had to break through. And we broke that through."[19]

After a week of work, Watts Sr. preceded the announcement of the subcommittee's recommendations on June 4 by saying that the Washington Duke Hotel would be open to all, as would eleven other motels in the city. His group also recommended the desegregation of eating facilities and said that about half of the restaurants in the county—55 of 103—had dropped barriers to blacks. Among the converted was Rape, who held out to the end before appearing at the new mayor's house on Sunday night to say that he was ready to admit blacks even though he knew it would mean the end of his business downtown.[20]

There were other changes. Criminal charges against those arrested during the demonstrations were dropped. Grabarek arranged for integration of the movie theaters and obtained pledges from more than thirty businesses to hire new employees without regard to race. Job training for blacks who were interested in retail jobs was arranged at the Durham Industrial Center, and the city council opened the swimming pools to all. "The number of businesses simultaneously opening their doors to prospective black customers and employees was unprecedented in Durham's history," one later study declared.[21]

There were holdouts. One was the Palms Restaurant, a popular downtown eatery that served the courthouse crowd from across the street. The owner of the Palms, Otis Kapsalis, finally agreed to serve all customers after he got a call from Watts Sr., whose bank held a mortgage on his building. Kapsalis later said that Hill made it clear to him he could integrate or go out of business.[22] Hill described their conversation differently. "All I had to do was quietly suggest this and suggest that," Hill said.[23]

The owner of the S&W Cafeteria chain was another matter. Frank Sherrill was steadfast in his decision not to integrate his cafeterias, which were located in the downtown business districts of every major city in the state. Just a few weeks before the demonstrations in Durham, the manager of his Raleigh cafeteria had ejected the Liberian ambassador to the United States when she had attempted to be served. Pickets were marching in front of Sherrill's establishments in Greensboro, Charlotte, and Asheville. The situation in Greensboro had become particularly tense; thousands of students from North Carolina A&T led by a promising young leader named Jesse Jackson had brought downtown business to a standstill. In Durham, Watts Jr. had begun working with Newton Angier, an old family friend and Sherrill's son-in-law, to integrate the S&W in the Home Security Life Insurance building even before the street demonstrations began.

"Now, Mr. Sherrill was a Christian, with a capital C," Watts Jr. recalled. "He was a very, very strong church person, and also very conservative. He was not very happy about Newt and me putting pressure on him. We had gotten other restaurants to desegregate by then, but not S&W. It was getting to be damn embarrassing."

Watts Jr. said that Sherrill was close to changing his policy in May when he got a call from U.S. Attorney General Robert F. Kennedy, who had begun his own campaign to pressure men like Sherrill to desegregate their businesses. "That stopped it. Mr. Sherrill wasn't going to have anybody pressure him," Watts Jr. recalled. "No Catholic in Washington was going to tell him what to do."[24] It took several more weeks and a visit to Sherrill by Governor Sanford before S&W opened its serving lines to black customers late in the summer of 1963.

The entire process was an unpleasant exercise for Watts Sr. Like Sherrill, he did not enjoy being forced into change. A few months after Durham's affairs had settled into a routine, he declared, "We still believe the managers of these places have their right to refuse undesirable guests regardless of who the guest might be."[25] Hill had complied with—and even orchestrated—desegregation in Durham nonetheless, probably because the continuing demonstrations were costing Durham businesses money and North Carolina its reputation as the island of racial moderation in the South.

⚬⚬⚬

As the demonstrations built to their peak in the early summer of 1963, the import of the protests and the constant picketing of public establishments was not lost on the conservative leaders of the state General Assembly. Throughout the spring, segregationists in the legislature had sponsored reactionary measures, including resolutions condemning the U.S. Supreme Court. Most of the bills were killed. In the session's final hours, however, both chambers ignored protocol and approved a law prohibiting communists or those who advocated the overthrow of the government from speaking on the campuses of state-supported universities and colleges. The bill became law upon passage—it did not have to go to the governor for a signature—before either Governor Sanford or University of North Carolina president Friday could respond.

Moreover, Democratic Party conservatives were fed up with the progressive politics of Governor Sanford, who had refused to move aggressively against demonstrators whose counterparts were being met by police dogs and fire hoses in other southern states. The party's conservative wing was already urging segregationist I. Beverly Lake, who had lost to Sanford in 1960, to run again, and the mood of the voters suggested he might win in 1964. As the talk continued, a few of those in search of a conservative candidate as an alternative to Lake wrote Watts Hill Sr. and encouraged him to consider the race.

Watts Sr. had always been a Democrat, but he had never demonstrated much interest in partisan politics, and he could occasionally stray from the fold in presidential campaigns. A photograph that ran in a Durham newspaper in 1952 showed Hill with a button on his lapel that read, "I Like Ike." His wife Ann was decidedly more liberal than he was, and she probably kept her husband from growing even more conservative over the years. During one family discussion late in their lives, Watts Sr. defended what he believed to be his progressive political philosophy by declaring that he had voted for Franklin D. Roosevelt in every one of his three presidential elections. Ann went him one better, however. Much to her husband's surprise, she told him she had once voted for Norman Thomas, Roosevelt's socialist opponent.[26]

Ever since he had served on the Durham City Council during the depression, Watts Sr. had limited his political participation to making financial contributions to candidates. He helped his old law school roommate

Claude Currie win election to the state Senate from Durham County, and he heartily supported governors William Umstead and Luther Hodges in the 1950s. In 1960, he issued a rare public endorsement of Terry Sanford in Sanford's second runoff election against Lake.

Watts Sr. had never given much notice to those who suggested that he seek public office, and he shrugged off the idea when one of his biggest fans, Dr. Lenox D. Baker, the head of Duke Medical Center's orthopedics division, began a modest letter-writing campaign on Hill's behalf in the spring of 1963. Baker told his friends that Hill was an attractive candidate. "He has everything going for him," Baker wrote a friend. "There is no group to which he will not have some direct appeal. With his fast gait, smile and ability to wave and say hello to everyone, he would make quite a candidate walking down the street. He has a good platform appearance and delivery. He is photogenic. He looks like a Governor."[27]

Hill was flattered. He had been told that once before, in the early fall of 1959, by Orville Campbell, his publisher of the *Chapel Hill Weekly*. Then, Hill told Campbell: "I don't think I could win, but the fundamental reason is that I just am not interested in being governor. I would far rather work quietly behind the scenes and not have the full-time responsibility that goes with the job. Luther Hodges appears to eat up the job—he loves it. I'm not a politician and that's what is required in this particular job."[28]

Hill discounted Baker's suggestion in 1963 as quickly as he had dismissed Campbell's four years before. "I have no delusions of grandeur and would rather be a little dog in a small puddle and work behind the scenes than to get into that particular rat race, regardless of the honor and publicity," he wrote Baker. He told Baker to put his efforts behind Thomas Pearsall of Rocky Mount.

Hill knew Pearsall well. The two had served together for nearly ten years on the executive committee of the university's Board of Trustees. Highly regarded by the state's business and political establishment, Pearsall was a lawyer by training, but during the depression he had assumed the management of his wife's family's vast farming operation in Nash and Edgecombe counties. He had served in the legislature and handled a number of difficult chores for governors Umstead and Hodges, including the shaping of the state's response to the *Brown* decision. "I think if enough of us put pressure on Tom he might be willing to run for Governor," Hill told Baker.

"Tom is so well known in the state . . . and a fine man of great integrity that I believe even the Republicans would tend to rally around him."[29]

Another candidate whose name was being circulated as an alternative to Lake was Dan K. Moore of Canton, a former superior court judge who had left the bench to become legal counsel for Champion Paper Company. Moore was a tall, broad-shouldered man with a ready smile, an affable manner, and a solid reputation in the state's legal community. One of those most interested in his candidacy was John McDevitt, a savvy politician from western North Carolina whom Watts Jr. had hired as the personnel director of Home Security Life Insurance Company.

McDevitt had remained close to Moore after joining the insurance company. He encouraged Moore's political ambitions and talked to Watts Sr. about him. As Arthur Clark, Hill's cousin who was the chief operating officer at the insurance company, later recalled, McDevitt said, "If we could get a couple of people together, we could make us a governor in this state."[30]

Watts Sr. was intrigued with McDevitt's suggestion. He asked Clark, an accomplished pilot who held the rank of colonel in the Air Force, to fly him to Asheville to meet Moore. One day in early August, Clark banked a small plane into a landing pattern above the Asheville airport and picked his way through the morning fog onto the runway. He taxied to the side of the terminal, where Hill got out and had a conversation with Moore while standing up. "They didn't even go into the terminal to talk," Clark recalled. Hill got back in the plane and returned to Durham. A few days later, Clark flew Hill to the coast for another meeting, this time with Pearsall.

Following these separate meetings, Hill asked Moore and Pearsall to join him at his home in Chapel Hill. McDevitt sat in on the meeting, as did William Friday. The group spent a few hours talking politics before Pearsall and Moore parted "on the nicest of terms." McDevitt recalled years later, "They were sort of deferring to each other."[31]

Clearly both men were interested in becoming a candidate, but Moore was the more eager of the two. If he was going to run, this was his time. He was approaching retirement age, and he did not want to wait another four years for an opening. On the other hand, Pearsall was better known and would have less trouble putting together a campaign. If Pearsall entered the race, he thought that he might even be able to draw the support of

Governor Sanford, who had put Pearsall on his list of potential successors after learning that his first choice, state party chairman Bert Bennett of Winston-Salem, would not run.[32]

After the meeting at Hill's home, one week passed, and then a second, and Moore heard nothing from Pearsall, who had left the state on vacation. Finally, after making several unsuccessful attempts to reach Pearsall, Moore called Hill and told him he was going to run regardless. "A decision had to be made, so he made it," McDevitt said. The next day, Moore paid a visit to the editor of the *Asheville Citizen*, who helped him shape an announcement statement. It appeared in the following day's paper. Sanford's candidate, Richardson Preyer of Greensboro, announced a few weeks later. By Thanksgiving, Lake had declared his intention to run, giving the Democrats a three-way contest.

ᴖᴗ ᴖᴗ ᴖᴗ

The Moore campaign united the Hills—father and son—like no effort before or later. In fact, it was the first time and the last that the two collaborated on much of anything, as they turned virtually all the family's resources to promoting Moore's election. Watts Sr. attended early fund-raising meetings for Moore, while Watts Jr. produced position papers on higher education and wrote speeches for him. Arthur Clark often ferried the candidate around the state to campaign appearances in airplanes borrowed or leased from others. John McDevitt devoted much of his time and energy to the campaign. Lake was eliminated in the first primary, leaving Moore and Preyer to a runoff. In the closing days of the second campaign, staff members at Hill's *Chapel Hill Weekly* handled press chores for Moore. When Preyer attempted to make Moore's solid support from the state's business community an issue in the second primary, he singled out Duke Power lobbyist Wade Barber of Pittsboro, banker Lewis Holding of Smithfield, and road builder J. A. Jones of Charlotte as examples of business interests who had a hold on Moore. The Hills, who had contributed as much if not more than these three to Moore's campaign, escaped any mention at all.

Moore won the nomination and was virtually assured of success in the fall general election. The victory invigorated Watts Sr., who sat in on strategy sessions and joined the Business and Professional Men and Women for Kennedy/Johnson, an effort led by former governor Luther Hodges. Hill also helped to organize a welcome to Durham for Lady Bird Johnson when the first lady's campaign train stopped in town. A crowd of 7,000 turned out on a chilly Wednesday morning in mid-October to see Johnson, Moore, Governor Sanford, and others. A photographer caught the Hill Building in the background of the crowd, where the CCB logo atop the building had been replaced with a banner carrying the letters "LBJ." Hill had personally arranged for the sign to be hung over the objections of his top bank officers; Lyndon Johnson later invited Hill to Washington for a White House visit and photograph session.

❧❧❧

Moore's election provided the relief sought by those like Watts Sr. who had become anxious about the energetic Sanford administration and were eager to slow the pace at which new government programs were being created. For example, Hill urged Moore to take a look at state money used in a "recent proliferation of various related but not state-controlled programs such as performing arts, LINC, North Carolina Fund, etc." LINC (the Learning Institute of North Carolina), the North Carolina Fund, and state support of the arts had all been special projects favored by Sanford. Such programs would struggle for support in the years to come.

The new governor approached his office with the same sort of judicial restraint he had demonstrated on the bench. Matters came to him, he dealt with them, and then he moved on. There would be no bold initiatives. At the same time, his first legislative term was far from placid, and nothing more overshadowed the new governor's first months in office than the issue of free speech and the speaker ban law.

The speaker ban controversy was unlike anything that University of North Carolina president William Friday had encountered before. He had always been comforted by the political influence of the university's Board of Trustees, who had held off uprisings against the school. Diverse and strong, the group included the governor and leading figures such as federal appeals court judge John J. Parker of Charlotte, state representative John W. Umstead Jr. of Chapel Hill (the brother of the former governor), former House Speaker Frank Taylor of Goldsboro, Durham lawyer Victor S. Bryant Jr., Thomas Pearsall, Wade Barber, and journalist and Woman's College alumna Virginia Lathrop. "That's raw power," Friday later observed. "And they took this place dead serious and they were tough. They lived and breathed the university and Watts was right in the middle of it."[33]

Watts Sr. approached the speaker ban issue with his customary pragmatism. He favored the philosophy of Frank Porter Graham, who encouraged open debate. "Hell, let 'em talk," Hill told an interviewer some years later. "I believe in the Hyde Park approach. Give 'em a place; let them talk their fool selves to death. And people, students, get tired of it."[34] After the 1963 law was passed, Watts Sr. had been a member of a trustee committee that had worked out a resolution that did not advocate outright repeal but that placed the control of speakers in the hands of trustees. According to the resolution, the change would "remove this legislative impairment of intellectual freedom and preemption of the authority and prerogatives of the Board of Trustees." Hill, Barber, and Bryant won its adoption by the full Board of Trustees, which gave Friday the freedom to work for a change in the law but little else. The legislature remained the problem, and Hill was named chair of a trustee committee to monitor the situation in Raleigh.

∽∽∽

Hill had first hoped to be appointed to the board after his father's term expired in 1953. The General Assembly, which named the trustees, passed over his name in picking members of the board. He was on the list in 1955, however, and he immediately joined the executive committee, just in time to join the debate over the selection of Friday as the successor to retiring president Gordon Gray. Friday, then only thirty-six years old, was considered too young and untrained for the job by some, including Hill, who told the governor, "Unless there is a strong and outstanding educator as president, the unit chancellors cannot expect to obtain the needed understanding of education from the president." Hill was finally persuaded by his old friend Victor Bryant Jr. that what the university needed most was an able administrator as chief executive. Friday's commitment to the university, plus an agreement to hire an experienced educator as a deputy, soothed concerns. "I am happy to go along," Hill wrote Bryant.[35]

The executive committee, along with the administration, effectively ran the university. As a matter of economy, members were expected to deal with issues that arose in their particular areas of interest and to keep other board members informed. Bryant had written the board's early statement on academic freedom and watched over university governance. He had chaired committees that had selected two presidents. Virginia Lathrop and Laura Cone of Greensboro looked after the Greensboro campus. Taylor, Barber, Pearsall, and Umstead were the university's unofficial team of lobbyists in Raleigh. Watts Sr. became the "non-licensed architect," as Friday put it. "He watched over all building projects. You never saw him without a sheath of blue prints. It was either for a water system or a building."

Hill's experience in health care and the management of Watts Hospital also naturally led him to become the trustees' one-man oversight committee on the growing health affairs program at Chapel Hill.[36] The university had laid the cornerstone for Memorial Hospital in 1948, and it did not stop building for more than a decade. During the 1950s, more than $53 million was appropriated for health affairs buildings, an amount that would be equaled during the next decade.

Hill's support went beyond bricks and mortar. He understood the challenges of running a hospital, recruiting faculty, and attracting the top names in medicine to a campus that was relatively isolated in tiny Chapel Hill from the major centers of the medical community. Hill readily assisted medical school dean Reece Berryhill in this endeavor, often entertaining faculty prospects at Quail Roost. When a new person accepted a position, Hill helped the family find a home and financed it with a low-interest loan from his bank. (It was a practice he would continue at the Research Triangle Institute.)[37]

"He didn't care about policy," Friday remembered. "He wanted to know who put the nut and the bolt in the engine. He wanted to know what we were doing, what difference were we going to make this year in running this program or that program. He realized and always operated on the principle that the chief executive is the person that trustees look to. Not the chancellor, not the department head. He didn't engage in the business of the institution. Power to him was not that all-consuming. Knowledge was his big drive."[38]

Like his father, Hill was a stickler for details, and he took complete notes at any meeting he attended. While still a junior member of the executive committee, he scolded the leadership over the content of the minutes of board sessions. After one meeting of the executive committee, he submitted three pages of amendments to the minutes that were distributed for review, and he asked for corrections. "Perhaps I don't understand just what should be in the minutes of the executive committee meeting," he wrote board secretary Arch T. Allen of Raleigh. "Since you have been on the board a long time, I am sure you could be helpful to me."[39]

Hill had not been on the Board of Trustees long when he wrote his friend Billy Carmichael—who was probably largely responsible for his appointment to the board—to complain about the vulnerability of university blueprints he found stored in an unprotected building. "Billy, I'm dead serious about this," read a note penned at the bottom of the letter. Carmichael calmed Hill's fears and told him the original plans were safely stored in vaults of the state archives in Raleigh. On another occasion, Hill offered advice on where and how trees should be planted on campus. In yet another letter, he told Carmichael that Duke University had the right idea in calling its medical complex the "Medical Center" rather than "health affairs," a name that Hill said was vague and would not be understood by the public it was supposed to serve. In later years, he spent more than $25,000 of his own money to analyze the propriety of the sale of the public utilities by the university in Chapel Hill. (Hill was opposed to the university's selling of its electric power and telephone systems, but the sales proceeded nonetheless.)

Though he watched operations with a critical eye, Hill never retreated from his unyielding devotion to the "university," which always meant Chapel Hill. That was the campus, he believed, that was at the "center of leadership in the state."[40] In 1968, the university returned the favor and paid tribute to Hill's dedication by awarding him an honorary degree. (It was not Hill's first honorary degree. Duke University had conferred one on him two years earlier.)

❧ ❧ ❧

Hill quickly became one of Friday's most steadfast allies, and he admired what he called Friday's "quiet approach to university activity." He said of Friday, "There was a mailed fist underneath, but he didn't let it show." At the same time, Hill would challenge the young president. During the heat of Friday's first serious crisis, an investigation of point-shaving in a basketball tournament in 1961, Hill cautioned Friday about going too far. "We must be practical about athletics. You and I both know that Frank Graham and Gordon Gray had the devil beat out of them and the same thing will happen to you and [Chancellor] Bill Aycock if the administration attempts to eliminate football or basketball scholarships and by so doing break up that particular sport at either Chapel Hill or State. I think the general public, the legislature and the alumni will insist that these sports be continued. You know I'm an idealist, but I hope, a practical idealist. I also believe these groups will also back the administration as you do your best to run a taut ship."[41] He told Friday: "I for one will back you and the administration, right or wrong, but still reserve the right to argue with you about anything at any time."[42]

Hill admired Friday's talent as a consensus builder, which was a skill he felt he had mastered himself. Friday was "never hurried, always friendly." Describing his relationship with Friday, Hill said, "Both of us are good listeners and both shoot straight from the shoulder."[43] Likewise, Friday valued Hill's support and knew how to handle Hill's challenges and blustery behavior. Hill would often burst into the president's office without so much as a knock on the door. "He would roll [blueprints] out and say, 'Look here, we've got to do something,'" Friday recalled. "And I'd say, 'What have we got to do?' And he'd go back and I'd listen to him and we worked it out. There was no harshness, but always the right challenge."[44]

Friday saw warmth in Hill that was not readily apparent to others. When Hill learned one afternoon that Friday and his wife Ida were celebrating their twenty-fifth wedding anniversary that evening, he had an engraved silver platter delivered by sundown. On another occasion, Hill arranged for an airplane to fly Friday and his staff to the funeral of the mother of a colleague. Hill annually provided Friday with a modest cash account on which he could draw for entertainment expenses that could not be covered in the state budget. "Sometimes he would be a little too harsh," Friday recalled, "but he and I had that relationship that where he'd get into one of these states of mind, he would come over and we'd sit down and talk and I'd listen to him. We'd diagram the problem and by the time we got through, he'd get an answer and out he'd go. Over the years there became a very deep affection between us. I really admired the man and he was very generous to me in word, deed, kindness, energy and whatever. I never called on him once that he didn't respond. I was very careful when I did, but I did it when I needed him."[45]

☙☙☙

As involved as he was in university affairs, Hill never let his attention stray far from the growing needs of health care in Durham. In 1962, he resigned from the board of Watts Hospital with the hope that a total separation from the institution would convince the community that his family was no longer involved in its operation. In 1963, Hill's work in hospital administration was recognized by the American College of Hospital Administrators, which presented him with an honorary fellowship in the college for his work at Chapel Hill, at Watts Hospital, and in the good health campaign.[46]

Hill was not through, however. In 1963, he financed the organizational work that led to the creation of a health planning council for Durham, Orange, and Wake counties, the first such regional agency to be created in the state. Later, he brought five nationally recognized experts in to meet with sixty persons from Durham, Orange, and Wake counties as they began work on a coordinated health program for central North Carolina.

Durham's hospital needs were becoming acute. Watts Hospital was overloaded, and the aging facilities at Lincoln Hospital, which had never received as much financial support as Watts, were even more pressing. The new Health Planning Council for Central North Carolina subsequently endorsed a bond program to provide nearly $14 million for Watts and a little more than $1 million for Lincoln. However, on Election Day in November 1966, the bond proposal was defeated by a two-to-one margin. The opposition included a curious coalition of the segregationists from the White Citizens Council, who used the vote to protest the integration of Watts Hospital, and the powerful Durham Committee on Negro Affairs. This time, banker John Wheeler opposed the bonds because he believed the money allotted for Lincoln, the black community's most important institution, was not sufficient to prevent its closure.

The results were a crushing disappointment to Hill. Some voters had opposed the bond issue in the belief that additional tax support was unnecessary because the Hill family would not let the hospital fail. "In the public eye," one historian reported, "Hill still ran Watts Hospital because he had aligned himself with its expansion proposals." Even memories of the Washington Duke Hotel purchase by John Sprunt Hill turned voters away. "Some people thought that if Watts Hospital failed, the Hill family would acquire it and make a profit of what had been a tax-supported institution."[47]

Hill avoided any public participation in a subsequent referendum in 1968. This time the bonds were approved, but it was eight years before the new Durham County General Hospital opened on county land north of the city. Watts Hospital was closed, and the campus stood empty until the buildings were turned over to the new North Carolina School of Science and Mathematics, a state-supported residential high school for gifted students that opened in 1980.

∾∾∾

Hill was more successful in merging the state's competing Blue Cross Blue Shield programs. One was the older Hospital Care Association, which he had helped launch in 1933. The other was the Chapel Hill–based Hospital Savings Association, which had been founded two years later with help from the Duke Endowment and the North Carolina Medical Society. The programs had remained apart largely because of the underlying tensions between hospital administrators and practicing physicians. Hospital Savings' founding father was Dr. Isaac Manning, the dean of the University of North Carolina Medical School, who had earlier discounted the plans of Hill and Duke University School of Medicine Dean Dr. Wilburt Davison when they started the Hospital Care Association. Over the years, both programs had become part of the nationwide Blue Cross Blue Shield program.

Since the two organizations operated from headquarters located less than ten miles apart, merger was often discussed. One round of talks began immediately after World War II, but the boards of directors could not reach agreement even under pressure from the national Blue Cross Blue Shield organization. Hill actively opposed merger because he believed that Hospital Care was the stronger of the two associations and the proposed merger terms were not equitable. Finally, with the arrival in the mid-1960s of Medicare, the new federal health care plan, the merger became a more urgent issue. In January 1968, with the top managers at both companies ready for retirement, Blue Cross Blue Shield of North Carolina was created under a new chief executive, J. Alexander McMahon.

McMahon was a Harvard-trained lawyer who had worked first at the Institute of Government at Chapel Hill, where he specialized in local government. He had later become executive director of the North Carolina Association of County Commissioners. Hill knew him through his service as the chair of the Health Planning Council.

McMahon's first task was to bring the two organizations together under one roof. Hospital Care's Durham offices were in a relatively new building on Duke Street on the site of Harwood Hall, which had been razed in the early 1960s after being used for a decade by Durham arts organizations. The Chapel Hill offices of Hospital Savings were in a cramped and dated space downtown. The Durham building was modern enough to justify its continued use, but it was not large enough for a combined operation. New headquarters were needed, and a site was chosen on the border between Durham and Orange counties on U.S. 15-501, the major thoroughfare between Durham and Chapel Hill.

The merger gave Watts Hill his greatest opportunity to work as an amateur architect as well as a chance to collaborate with architect A. G. "Goulie" Odell of Charlotte, who was then at the height of his career. Odell was a creative designer whose buildings were as useful as they were innovative. "Architecture is 90 percent business and 10 per cent art," he once said, adding that he preferred the art but understood the importance of the business side.[48] He was the first architect from the South to be elected president of the American Institute of Architects.

The Blue Cross Blue Shield Board of Directors asked Odell for a ten-story building that would sit on the crest of a hill on the wooded thirty-nine-acre tract. The first drawings "looked like a fortress," recalled Alex McMahon, and they were rejected by all. Odell's subsequent offering became the basis for one of Hill's favorite buildings. The final design was for a structure 500 feet long and 100 feet wide in the shape of a rhomboid, or three-dimensional parallelogram. Odell put four stories above the crest of the hill and another below ground. The exposed exterior walls were glass that sloped forty-five degrees to the south and west. Virtually all the workspace was free of columns, which offered flexibility and the optimum capacity for future expansion.

The building had not been imagined in that shape when planning began. "Goulie and myself got to laughing about it," Hill recalled, "and I said, 'Just lay the damn building down.' We just laid it down. Then it was Goulie's idea to have it so the sun didn't hit it but just the absolute minimum." Hill helped Odell sell the design of the $10 million building to the Board of Directors, stressing the environmental features that would save money. "It was done that way to protect it from sunlight so that the north side opened to the sky—that's the one you see from Chapel Hill Boulevard. The sun doesn't warm up [the south side] because it never gets to the point where it's beating down on it," McMahon said.[49]

∾∾∾

Frank DePasquale of Durham worked more closely with Hill than any other architect. The two had become acquainted when DePasquale was a student at the North Carolina State College School of Design in the years after World War II. He was working with a Durham firm when Hill showed up at his office and asked him to design a kidney-shaped swimming pool for Quail Roost Farm. Hill's direct style and his sense of design impressed the young architect, whose client eventually became his mentor.

"I remember a conversation one day when he came down and was discussing a plan he didn't like," DePasquale recalled. "I jumped in and started giving him quick answers, and he said, 'Frank, you don't have to impress me on how smart you are. What I really want you to do is to stop and think, listen and think.' Boy that hit me like a ton of bricks. And he was right. You do a lot of listening before you say anything, and you analyze what's going on and then you come up with some good ideas."

DePasquale said Hill was particularly adept at siting a building on a piece of land. "He didn't like ditches; he would talk about swells. He wanted land to flow and be shaped in such a way that the water could run into these swells and these valleys and run off without affecting anything else." After a few experiences, DePasquale also learned not to bring finished drawings in to Hill when a project was in its early stages. Instead, he would make rough drawings and bring in four or five site plans for Hill to review. "He'd go through those things and analyze every one of them. Then he would take the good parts of each and try to get them into one plan."[50] Hill said he just liked to design a building from the inside out "and put a cover on it."

Over the years, DePasquale designed new interiors for Central Carolina Bank offices, but before making each major change he and Hill conducted an investigation. At one point in the 1960s, the two visited other bank offices, making a close inspection of teller windows at banks in New York. Hill usually called ahead to arrange for access to areas behind the teller counters, but one day in New York the message had not reached the guard on the floor. Hill and DePasquale, who had arrived at the bank wearing soggy raincoats, were detained as suspected bank robbers preparing a holdup.

Hill loved to gather details. He talked to tellers to learn how they would improve their workspaces, for example. Hill and DePasquale learned that tellers everywhere believed the counters were too small. Checking further, they discovered that the uniform five-foot width of the teller's work area was designed as a convenient measurement for architects rather than as a space that was actually best for the work required. "So we came back and every teller station was five-foot, six-inches wide, because he sensed that's what it had to be," DePasquale said. "He hated offices where the banker sat down at a desk and the two chairs were on the other side of the desk," De-Pasquale further recalled. "He felt that was a very unfriendly approach to banking and just would not have it." Under Hill's orders, every CCB office was designed with the customer's chair at the end of the desk so the bank officer and customer "could touch each other." Hill said: "You can't separate yourself from people. I mean, you are asking this guy to put his money in your bank, how can you separate yourself from him?"[51]

Hill personally selected paint colors, furniture, pencil holders, even the ashtrays. "Everything that related to the appearance of the bank, he picked it out," DePasquale recalled. Hill instructed DePasquale to see that necessary but unsightly attachments, such as gutter downspouts, were painted the same color as the exterior brick. "I mean even down to electrical outlets on walls," DePasquale marveled. "He wanted them painted out." De-Pasquale successfully proposed Hill as an honorary member in the American Institute of Architects. "He was looking forward into the twenty-first century," DePasquale said of Hill, "and he wanted something that was going to be here for a long time."[52]

Hill extended his design tastes to include art, which had long been a passion of his wife Ann. Through the bank, Hill began collecting the work of regional artists; he subsequently accumulated more than two thousand pieces, many of which were displayed in the branches and offices of CCB. He chose traditional pieces at first, but Durham artist Nancy Tuttle-May helped him gain an appreciation of abstract works. Tuttle-May later said that Hill told someone, referring to her, "This young woman has loosened my bones."[53] Hill later financed Tuttle-May's first show in New York City.

Hill persisted in a losing battle to revive Durham's downtown, and he paid for redevelopment studies and conceptual designs for a new central business district out of his own pocket. Yet even he was unable to salvage the Washington Duke Hotel, which was imploded and reduced to rubble in thirteen seconds on December 14, 1975. "There she went," Hill said as he watched from an office building. "The old lady is gone." Before the hotel was demolished, Frank DePasquale had told Hill that the building was structurally sound but that the cost of renovations would be prohibitive.[54]

A new hotel and office complex and the Durham Civic Center were eventually built adjacent to the site.

❧❧❧

Throughout his life, Hill had faced few situations that he could not shape to his satisfaction through either his influence or his determination and sheer energy. As Hill entered the early 1970s, when he was in his seventies, many of the institutions that had meant so much to him and the family no longer operated under conditions that had once readily responded to the will of a Hill.

In 1971, he found himself at odds with his son Watts Hill Jr., who was negotiating the sale of Home Security Life Insurance Company to Capital Holding Company. The sale was good for the shareholders, according to Arthur Clark, but Watts Sr. saw it differently. He told his son that he had sold his birthright. What he meant was that Watts Jr. had lost a base from which to operate effectively as a Hill, something Durham had known for three-quarters of a century.

Even the farm had become a burden. In the summer of 1973, Watts Hill Sr. turned most of his Quail Roost Farm over to his children—his son, John Sprunt II, had moved his family, and they had made their home in the enlarged stable cottage since 1969—and sold the last of his famous Quail Roost Guernseys. He parted with a herd of 267 cows—"my guys and gals," as he called them—in a sale that netted $182,520, which was only a fraction of what he made from the sale of offspring of the famous bull he had bought for $7,500.

The management of the farm had become problematic since the death in 1962 of W. W. Fitzpatrick, the Quail Roost manager who had been with Hill since 1936. During his tenure, Fitzpatrick had become one of the leading proponents of the North Carolina dairy industry. After Fitzpatrick's death, Hill had told Friday that he wanted to give the farm to the university, but Hill and the university could never come to the terms by which North Carolina State College would take over the farming operation. In 1962, Hill had transferred the title for the house and about ninety acres of land to the university for its use as a conference center. He hoped it would be used by all the universities in the area as well as by the Research Triangle tenants. Ironically, in the late 1960s it became for a time the home of the Learning Institute of North Carolina, one of the Sanford educational programs that Hill had asked Governor Moore to abolish. The home never worked out as a conference center, and the university eventually sold the house and adjoining land to a private owner.

Hill did leave a lasting mark on the American Guernsey world during his career as a dairyman. The year before he sold his herd, he received the Distinguished Service Award of the American Guernsey Cattle Club (later called the American Guernsey Association), which created an annual award named the Quail Roost Maxim Trophy. A photograph taken in 1939 of High Point Prince Maxim and one of his sisters at Quail Roost Farm became one of the best-known images of prize Guernseys in the world.

Perhaps most indicative of Hill's growing uncertainty about the future was a decision he pondered in 1974 following Paul Wright Jr.'s retirement as president of Central Carolina Bank. To the astonishment of Wright's successor, William L. Burns Jr., Hill suggested that the bank be put on the market. Burns urged Hill to proceed slowly. He argued that financial stocks were depressed and that a sale would not bring a price equal to the bank's real value. While CCB was not the largest bank in the state, it was among the top tier, Burns said, and it had a commanding presence in its market. CCB had added nearly fifty offices in twenty-seven communities, and new markets had been opened in Greensboro and towns west of Winston-Salem. The impulse to sell passed.

❧❧❧

The most troubling change was occurring within the family. The estrangement of Watts Sr. and his eldest son was all the more striking because of the proximity of their homes in Chapel Hill. Watts Jr.'s home at the end of Greenwood Lane on the north side of Raleigh Road in Chapel Hill was only minutes away from Quail Hill, a new home in Chapel Hill that the elder Hill built on a wooded ridge on the south side of Raleigh Road. Watts Sr.'s new house was reminiscent of the family's first home on the farm. Three rooms—the living room, dining room, and library—were the same dimensions as companion rooms in the home at Quail Roost Farm had been. Furnishings moved from Rougemont found familiar spots in the new house.

As close as they were, father and son communicated most often through messages delivered by Maceo Bullock, who had replaced the aging Tommy Stroud as the Hill family butler. Bullock had grown up near Quail Roost

Farm, and his father had helped lay the water line to the house. When Bullock was a boy, he and his brother would stop Watts Sr. as he left Quail Roost for Durham and ask for a nickel. "And he'd say," Bullock recalled, "'Who do you think I am? George Watts Hill or somebody?'" A job at Quail Roost was good work. "The people at Quail Roost lived better than anyone else in the community," Bullock recalled. "They had everything. I mean they had a job, they had food, they had milk, they had houses. A lot of them lived right there on the place, and they lived good."[55]

Bullock had retired from the Air Force and was working at a drug store in Durham when, in 1969, the phone rang and he heard a voice say, "This is George Watts Hill." "I was a comedian," Bullock recalled, "and I said, 'Well, this is Napoleon.'" When Bullock realized he really was talking to Watts Hill, he heard him say, "I have a position I want you to take." He invited Bullock for an interview. Bullock ignored Hill's offer, but when Hill called a second time, he agreed to hear him out. Hill told him he wanted a successor for Stroud, who was ill and would soon retire. He explained the job, which sounded like something from another age, to Bullock. While the Hills provided generously—salary, living accommodations, health care, and a wardrobe of blue blazers and gray slacks for Bullock—they required full-time service. When the cook was off, Bullock would be expected to prepare meals. He took the job.

"We just hit it off," Bullock recalled. "He had been in the military, and I had been in the military. One time, he told me, 'If you stayed in the military any length of time, you have a sense of discipline and respect.' He was of the kind of mind that he was your best buddy, but it wasn't any question who the boss was. And I learned to respect that. I had some disagreements, but I was smart enough to keep it to my damn self. He would listen to you. He told me, 'Maceo, you take care of me and I'll take care of you.' And I said, 'You can't beat a deal like that.'"[56]

While the military had prepared Bullock for Watts Sr., it had done little to satisfy Ann Hill, who instructed him on the proper placement of flatware for a dinner table and introduced him to foods he had never before seen on a plate. While Bullock handled occasional chores for Watts Sr. and later became his driver, he found that even George Watts Hill deferred to his wife's priorities for the servants. "That was the rule," Bullock said, "You do what Mrs. Ann says." Ann Hill always remained "the 'lady of the house,'" Bullock recalled, "and you know the definition of a lady in those days. I mean she was a refined lady. She knew everything that she was supposed to know in the position she was in. Yes, she was a fine lady."[57]

☙☙☙

On October 3, 1974, just three days after the couple's fiftieth wedding anniversary, Ann Hill died. Her death was not unexpected; she had been diagnosed with lung cancer several months before. Life had been a constant struggle for Ann, who had entered what she believed was storybook marriage in 1926 to a millionaire's son. The yearlong honeymoon around the world soon gave way to a lifetime of difficulty, first with medical problems brought on by the births of her children and later with a husband whose pace and personal style was very different from what she had known as the daughter of the headmaster of a private girls' school. Shortly before her death, Ann made a rare public appearance at the dedication of the library in the lower school of Durham Academy—formerly the Calvert Method School that she had helped start in 1933—when it was named in her honor.

☙☙☙

Less than a year after his wife's death, Watts Sr. announced plans to remarry. His bride was Anne Gibson Hutchinson, a history teacher at Durham Academy's middle school. She was forty-seven; he was seventy-four. Despite his age, he remained quite a catch, with thinning silver hair and striking good looks enhanced by strong facial lines and the remnant of a dimpled chin. He was trim and fit from his daily swimming regimen.

The two were married June 14, 1975. Nothing in Hill's experience—except perhaps his service with the OSS—more profoundly changed his life. After remaining close to home for much of the past twenty years, the Hills left for an extended trip abroad shortly after their wedding. The newlyweds visited many of the places that Hill had seen during World War II, including the site of the commando school he had visited in Scotland. They traveled on to Italy's Lake Como and to Moscow, where Hill stood in Red Square, a spot he had thought he would never see. A decade earlier, Watts Sr. had told his son he did not think he could ever safely travel to the Soviet Union because of his wartime service with the OSS.

"We were gone forever," Anne Hill recalled. "By the time we got to Spain, I said, 'Are you broad-minded?' And I said, 'I want to go home.' Actually our honeymoon was so long I got homesick, because I had three children and a poodle." Watts Sr.'s new family included his wife's two daughters and a son. They joined their mother when she and Watts Sr. returned to Chapel Hill, where Anne Hill taught her husband some limited domestic chores—he learned how to load a dishwasher.

In 1981, Watts Sr. became interested in the education of his wife's eldest daughter, Anne, who was struggling at boarding schools in New England. Her problem was not that she was unintelligent, he discovered, but that she had a learning disability called dyslexia, which causes words and numbers to become reversed in the mind. She was studying with a tutor, Cathy Harkey of Chapel Hill, when Watts Sr. decided to find a solution that would allow Anne to attend school closer to home.

What Watts Sr. learned was that a range of neurological disorders—dyslexia, dyscalculia, and dysgraphia—caused children to have problems with language, symbols, reading, writing, spelling, and math despite their normal to above average intelligence. Three to 5 percent of all children had some degree of disability, and the public schools were not prepared to teach them. Working with Harkey and Lucy Davis of Duke University's psychology department, Hill gave $100,000 to finance the first three years of a new program for learning disabled students. He bought an old house on Picket Road in Durham on the edge of Durham Academy's upper school campus for the first classes.

Jean H. Neville was one of the program's original faculty of three. She had trained under Davis and was teaching in the Chapel Hill schools, where she was one of only three teachers of learning-disabled students in the entire system. Students like Anne Hill joined Neville and the other two teachers for a half day of concentrated attention in a program designed to stimulate learning in three areas—reading, written language, and math. After classes at the center, students returned to their regular schools. In 1977, there were 11 students enrolled. When the school outgrew the small yellow farmhouse, Watts Sr. bought a new building, which opened in 1986. In the 2000–2001 school year, the Hill Center, as it was then called, had 154 students attending classes in a newly opened building with classrooms tailored for small-group and one-on-one instruction. More than half of the center's students arrived daily from public schools; the others were either in private school or in homeschools.

The school not only changed the course of learning for students from kindergarten through high school, it also became a center for the training of educators of learning-disabled students. Watts Sr. said that creating the school was one of the most satisfying investments he ever made.[58]

CHAPTER 14

The Last Generation

PLAYWRIGHT PAUL GREEN was flush with his early success when he bought a large tract of land along a wooded ridge at the eastern edge of Chapel Hill. There, in the 1930s, at the end of a narrow, winding road, he built a modest two-story home reminiscent of a country farmhouse. Over the years, the unpainted interior paneling in the living room aged to a blend of warm, red tones that complemented a large stone fireplace. The wide planks in the floor creaked underfoot. In time, Green added a wing to accommodate his large library, and the porch across the back was enclosed with glass to offer a view of deep lawn that spilled down a hill into the woods. He did much of his writing in a small office he built to the side.

Watts Hill Jr., his wife Mary, and their two teenage children, Watts III and Deborah, were beginning to outgrow their home in Durham when Green's house went on the market in 1965. Once Watts Jr. walked through the house, he was as sold on the purchase as Mary was. Green liked the idea of having a family with a long Chapel Hill connection move into his home, and he rejected a higher offer from an out-of-town bidder in favor of the Hills'. It was not long before Mary revived the flower garden and, along with Watts Jr., filled the shelves in the library with all manner of books reflecting their broad range of interests. Also stored close at hand were recordings of jazz and other musical favorites. Though Watts Jr. was not the technophile that his brother John Sprunt II had become, he enjoyed fiddling with recording equipment and gadgets. "We're both hi-fi buffs," he told a reporter as he and Mary were unpacking in 1965. "I suppose our musical taste is catholic . . . everything from Albeniz to Zampa."[1]

Even more impressive was the collection of books, reports, and research tracts that surrounded Watts Jr. in the snug office, where available wall space was accented with black and white photographs. The collection included images from early European photographers as well as contemporary shots by North Carolina's Billy Barnes, who documented the civil rights movement and the short-lived activities of the North Carolina Fund, for which Watts Jr. was a board member. Watts Jr. consumed knowledge from any manner of sources. He was much like his father in that respect. But the subjects that interested Watts Jr. were often esoteric, and they touched on the literary and artistic dimensions of life that had interested his mother. It was a characteristic that completely exasperated the elder Hill, who was more prone to action than reflection. Watts Sr. often said he liked to start something and then "run like hell." Meanwhile, his wife Ann would worry a subject into submission by writing letters that went on for pages and then were never mailed.

For nearly forty years, Chapel Hill would be the warm, comfortable home that Watts Jr. had never really known as a child. Born in Baltimore, Maryland, where his mother had gone when complications arose during her pregnancy, Watts Jr. had spent his childhood at Harwood Hall in Durham before leaving in 1938 when he was twelve for boarding school at Millbrook in New York. Millbrook was filled with the talented sons of the wealthy, and being educated there proved an intellectually challenging experience for Watts Jr. He learned to appreciate both the discipline of learning and lively, intelligent verbal exchanges. One of his classmates was William F. Buckley Jr., with whom he debated the virtue of American support for Britain against the Nazis. (Even in his early years, Buckley, the father of modern conservative thought, argued that communists were the greater evil.)

Watts Jr. dreamed of becoming a pilot, and upon graduation from Millbrook in 1944 he immediately joined the navy's V-5 program, an accelerated college education that took him first to Hampden-Sydney College in Virginia and later to Princeton. As a cadet, Watts Jr. met men from all walks of life, including sailors the navy had plucked from combat assignments in the Pacific to be trained as officers. For the first time in his life, Watts Jr. was exposed to those who could only imagine the advantages of wealth that for him were commonplace. Tutoring sessions that he provided for fellow sailors struggling in their classes left him with an understanding of the value of education that remained with him throughout his adulthood.

The war came to an end before Watts Jr. completed the V-5 program. He was a bit at loose ends and one year short of his degree in economics when he and Mary became engaged and were married. Since neither Princeton, where Watts Jr. was enrolled, nor Vassar, where Mary was a student, permitted married couples to attend, they moved to Chapel Hill for Watts Jr.'s final year. The Hills—Watts Sr. and Ann—were irritated with their son's decision to marry. He was young, only twenty, and unsettled about his future. The parents, of course, were eager for their son to join the family business in Durham just as Watts Sr. had done twenty years earlier. Watts Jr. stubbornly refused, and the young couple headed to Europe, where Watts Jr. planned to concentrate on graduate work in international studies and perhaps to find a job.

When he returned home in 1950, Watts Jr. assumed the role of rising young businessman. He joined the Junior Chamber of Commerce and helped lead a portion of Durham's community fund drive with his father. But it was politics, not business, that offered the greatest personal satisfaction. He ran uncontested for a seat on the Durham City Council in 1955. A year later, he became a candidate for one of Durham's two seats in the state House of Representatives. It was a tense race filled with racial overtones. Hill won the Democratic Party nomination, beating a segregationist candidate with the help of the influential Committee on Negro Affairs and the union-sponsored Voters for Better Government. He commuted to legislative sessions in Raleigh in his low-slung sports car, which along with his pronounced patrician accent set him apart from his peers, many of whom had served with his grandfather.

Watts Jr. remained relatively quiet during the 1957 session until he got his teeth into a bill that he believed favored banks that held state funds. His opposition to the measure surprised many, considering his family's holdings, but Watts Sr. complimented his son's position when Jesse Helms, then the executive director of the state bankers' association, skewered Watts Jr. in the columns of the *Tar Heel Banker*, a trade journal that Helms edited. Helms wrote Watts Sr. to "state our resentment" of Watts Jr.'s opposition to the bill, which Helms said Watts Jr. had undertaken without having had the benefit of hearing the association's point of view.[2] The elder Hill responded, telling Helms that he had never talked to his son about the bill but that if he had, he would have given him his support. "It seemed to me," Watts Sr. told Helms, "that you were expressing anger and resentment rather than valid arguments against the stand Watts took."[3]

Watts Jr. easily won reelection to the House in 1958, and during the 1959 legislative session he was named to chair the higher education committee and to cochair an appropriations subcommittee on education. He was as thorough in his study of issues as his grandfather had been twenty years earlier. Before Watts Jr. joined in supporting a bill that required the certification of teachers through a national examination, he took the test himself. Near the end of the session, he gained statewide attention when he led a revolt in the House over Governor Luther Hodges's request to give teachers only a modest pay increase. Watts Jr.'s exposure in Raleigh provoked talk that he was a young man with potential, even a possible candidate for governor or a higher office. One of his mentors was his father's old friend Francis Pickens Miller, who invited him to join other young politicians in the South for weekends spent discussing pressing issues. In 1961, Watts Jr. was chosen as one of fifty-two southerners who were "foremost in the South's new leadership."[4]

Watts Jr. never encouraged talk of his ambition for higher office, knowing it was not practical. Frankly, he had neither the temperament nor the personality for campaigning. His polished upbringing along with his accent suggested an elitism that in truth occasionally rose to the fore. In 1961, he told a newspaper reporter, "I probably have too big an ego." Like his father, he had little use for those whom he considered to be just dead wrong in their opinions. "One of the Hill traits," according to a Charlotte newspaper account, "is that they're awfully sure of themselves. When they pounce onto an issue and find out they're right, they get impatient with anybody who bucks them."[5]

Talk of a political career became moot after Watts Jr. withdrew from elective politics in 1960 in favor of the family business. It was not what he wanted to do, but it was necessary. While he enjoyed a modest inheritance, he needed a paycheck to support his family. In 1959, he became an assistant to President Bascom Baynes at Home Security Life Insurance Company, and in 1961 he succeeded Baynes. It was a real job that required full-time attention.

Baynes was a generous, outgoing man who like Ben Roberts at the bank had been left on his own by John Sprunt Hill and his son Watts Sr. Over the years, the company had produced steady profits, but like the bank it had not responded to the changes in the insurance market. For example, Home Security relied heavily for a major portion of its income on the sale of debit life insurance, or industrial insurance as it was also known, that policyholders paid for in weekly installments. Watts Jr. realized that for the company to survive, it would need to offer more and better lines of coverage (group health insurance was coming into the market) and a sales force trained to sell these more sophisticated lines. There were other fundamental problems. Home Security's rate book was based on an insured's race, not his occupation. And while nearly half of the policyholders were African American, the entire Home Security sales force was white. Both conditions were becoming untenable as the civil rights movement challenged prevailing attitudes about race.

Watts Jr. tackled the changes with the help of John McDevitt, the former state personnel director whom he recruited away from state government to handle personnel matters at Home Security. He also leaned heavily on his father's cousin, Arthur Clark, whom Watts Jr. promoted to top management shortly after he succeeded Baynes. The rate book was overhauled to reflect the hazards of individual occupations, and the integration of the sales staff was set in motion. While some companies took a half step, creating separate white and black sales forces, Watts Jr. brought Home Security's sales force together as one sales team, which required a delicate period of transition that was completed with help from executives at North Carolina Mutual. The changes were not made without difficulty. At one point, the company's salesmen threatened to quit en masse.

Watts Jr. did not fully withdraw from public affairs. In 1963, he was part of the interim committee on desegregation that defused the tense racial situation in Durham, and he stayed on to chair the permanent Mayor's Committee on Community Relations, a job he held until 1966. He became a director of the North Carolina Fund, the antipoverty agency created by Governor Terry Sanford, and he was a founding director of Outward Bound, a wilderness leadership program based in the North Carolina mountains. Dan Moore's campaign for governor in 1964 and Watts Jr.'s assumption of an advisory role after the election provided him with an even more substantial opportunity to participate in the political process. Once engaged in the reorganization of the state's system of higher education, which would occupy the state legislature in the second half of the sixties, Watts Jr.'s attention would never fully return to business, which he left in the hands of Arthur Clark.

✆✆✆

Midway through Governor Dan Moore's first legislative session in early 1965, the burden of the speaker ban law was taking its toll. Faculty members at Chapel Hill and on other campuses talked openly of their dissatisfaction. Some threatened to leave if the law was not repealed. Nonetheless, legislators were in no mood to change the 1963 law, and there was talk of further interference in the management of the state's institutions of higher learning.

Watts Jr. weighed in as a member of the governor's unofficial task force to resolve the situation. He worked with the governor's legislative team long enough to become convinced that there were insufficient votes for an outright repeal of the law. At the same time, Watts Jr. tried to tone down the rhetoric of faculty members in Chapel Hill. One of his close friends was Arnold Nash, president of the Faculty Senate. "He and his colleagues were sure the thing to do was to go to Raleigh and tell the members of the General Assembly what a bunch of damn fools they were," Watts Jr. recalled. "I probably spent as much time with Arnold and cohorts as I did elsewhere with some success in getting them to understand that compromise was as much a victory as [was] possible."[6]

Watts Jr. and others could not find enough support even to amend the 1963 law, much less to repeal it outright. A major hurdle was the opposition of Thomas J. White, an iron-willed senator from Kinston who chaired the Senate appropriations committee. White vowed his allegiance to the university, but his support for the speaker ban law ran just as strong. "To put it bluntly, the proponents of [changing] the law were faced with a terrible choice," Watts Jr. later reported. "Should they push for repeal of the law and see their appropriations shot down, or should they obtain their appropriations and then attempt to secure repeal or amendment of the law? Then, as to Senator White, it should be said that he is not the kind to make such a threat."[7]

The governor was in a difficult spot. He had won election partially on the basis of his support of the speaker ban law. He later modified his position to support the idea that the invitation to visiting speakers should be left to the boards of trustees at individual universities. But his intent was clear, and he was not about to perform an about-face on the issue. Since taking office, he believed, he had been steadfast in supporting the university, yet he remained an object of derision for determined opponents to the speaker ban who wanted his support for repeal. "There appeared to be just one fire after another," Watts Sr. wrote in a memo after meeting with the governor in early May 1965, "and all of the fires were being dropped in [Moore's] lap." Hill continued: "[Moore] was carrying the burden and he was tired of it."[8]

As the issue came to a head, Watts Sr. attended a two-hour meeting at the mansion that was called after Moore received word that the accrediting committee of Southern Association of Colleges and Schools (SACS) had the North Carolina situation under review. There appeared to be a very real threat that if the legislature did not act, SACS would send a letter advising that North Carolina institutions had been given probationary status and that their accreditation might be withdrawn. The SACS plans immediately raised the stakes for the state.

Supporters of the law scoffed at the threat from SACS and said that sanctions would have no effect. Some even suggested that SACS itself should be investigated. Friday assured Watts Sr. that the threat was genuine. At one strategy session, he told Hill, "Such a consequence . . . would be a national humiliation for us, a strong deterrent to recruiting good faculty members, and the first time in the long history of the university that such a question has ever been raised about its status in higher education."[9]

The legislature adjourned without making a change in the speaker ban law, but Moore won approval for a study commission whose assignment was to return with recommendations about the future of the law. In July, Moore named Watts Jr. chairman of the state Board of Higher Education, a politically charged and troubled agency that had been created a decade before in an effort to remove political interference from the state's campuses. It was a job in which Hill would fully invest himself, and it would lead to the reorganization of higher education in North Carolina. It was also an assignment that would produce differences between the Hills, junior and senior, that would never be resolved.

ॐ ॐ ॐ

The state Board of Higher Education was a political stepchild when Watts Jr. assumed the chairmanship in the summer of 1965. It had been created in the mid-1950s by the legislature at the urging of Governor

Luther Hodges in an effort to coordinate the growing demand for state funds from nearly a dozen institutions, especially the consolidated university with its campuses at Chapel Hill, Raleigh, and Greensboro. Hodges had hoped to achieve a balance between the needs of the consolidated university and the increasing legislative attention that was being given to the state's smaller four-year colleges at Cullowhee, Boone, Greenville, Durham, Winston-Salem, Fayetteville, Pembroke, and Elizabeth City.

By the time Moore became governor in 1965, the board had been sidelined by institutions that went directly to the legislature for state dollars. The competition was accelerated with the addition to the consolidated university of a campus at Charlotte and the growing ambitions of President Leo Jenkins at East Carolina Teachers College in Greenville. Another sign of the board's impotence came when Governor Terry Sanford, Dan Moore's predecessor, created a separate commission to study education beyond high school rather than ask the board for its help. Its recommendations had little impact on the legislature, where in 1965 the board's recommendation against giving seed money for a medical school at East Carolina was roundly ignored. In fact, some members of the 1965 General Assembly were eager to disband the board altogether until Hill and state senator Robert Morgan, East Carolina's champion, patched together changes that saved it from extinction. Such was the playing field that Watts Jr. found in the summer of 1965.

∾∾∾

First was the matter of the speaker ban law. Upon his appointment, Watts Jr. was thrust into the center of efforts to forestall the revocation of accreditation for the state's schools by the SACS. Governor Moore was wary of the Chapel Hill establishment, many members of which had not supported him in his campaign, and he turned the management of the issue over to Watts Jr. and stood behind his efforts to find a resolution. "Dan knew that [SACS was on our side]," Watts Jr. said some years later. "He, in effect, worked with them and quietly welcomed their involvement. My impression is that Dan had mixed feelings personally. Part of him was sympathetic to both sides—disgust at communism and especially with the war—while he was also deeply concerned about the law and its impact on the university and on the state's reputation. He, as a jurist, must have seen that the long-term outcome was inevitable, that the issue was one that would take care of itself in time."[10]

Hill coordinated the state's response to SACS and appeared as the board's spokesman when a legislative study commission began meeting in September 1965. The atmosphere was as politically charged as it had been on the day the bill was hastily passed in 1963. Charlotte attorney Ralph Clontz consumed much of a morning session with an account of his experiences as an undercover agent for the Federal Bureau of Investigation during its investigation of communists in North Carolina in the years following World War II. The Veterans of Foreign Wars sent a spokesman, as did the Presbyterian Church, the League of Women Voters, the North Carolina Alliance of Conservative Republicans, and the College Young Democrats. State senator Tom White, representing the archconservatives who had rammed the speaker ban bill through in 1963, told the commission that the state should thumb its nose at sanctions and take the SACS to court if it tried to remove accreditation.

Watts Jr. delivered a spirited defense of academic freedom. In his typically thorough fashion—he was not one for short answers—he presented a detailed review that made it clear that the issue was not whether North Carolina institutions would lose accreditation but whether the state could stand to lose academic integrity if the ban law remained in place. His remarks drew praise from many corners and boosted the governor's marks among the cautious Chapel Hill crowd. Even Richardson Preyer, whom Moore had defeated in the 1964 campaign, sent Watts Jr. a congratulatory note.

University of North Carolina president William Friday's testimony was called "the longest and most impressive."[11] He offered a compromise and urged the commission to recommend the return of control over speakers' appearances to trustees, who would see that visits included full and open discussion and participation by a faculty member. When the commission released its recommendations, the plan was strikingly similar to Friday's proposal.

Moore was eager to settle the matter as soon as possible because he feared that a federal court ruling expected in mid-November could invalidate the current seating of the General Assembly, thus effectively sidelining the issue until a reapportioned legislature was elected. Immediately upon receiving the study commission report on November 5, Moore called a special legislative session to convene in ten days. The two-day session was as carefully choreographed as possible, but die-hard defenders of the law were undeterred. Ultimately, the legislators amended the law to reflect the commission's recommendations, granting campus trustees the power to approve outside speakers. In equally short order, trustees at each of the institutions adopted policies that permitted appearances of controversial speakers if they "served the advantage of education."

Watts Hill Sr. applauded the governor for his role in what he believed was the end of the matter. He told Moore that the university community had "closed ranks behind [him]." He continued: "They are proud to have you as their governor. The faculties, students and administration, as well as the townspeople, were proud of the position you took immediately before and during the special session—I haven't heard a word of criticism but I have personally heard many highly complimentary statements."[12]

In late November, as it appeared the drama was drawing to a close, Watts Jr. appeared before the SACS on behalf of the presidents of North Carolina colleges and universities to report on the legislative action and urge the commission to end its inquiry into the matter. Hill said he was disappointed that the law had not been repealed outright, but he explained that what he called the progressive forces in the state had "banded together to emasculate the Speaker Ban law and to eliminate it as a threat to independence of action by the trustees of the state-supported institutions of higher education."[13] The SACS recommendation to continue accreditation of the North Carolina campuses followed within a few days.

Watts Jr.'s appearance before the SACS drew the ire of Jesse Helms, who by 1965 had become the editorial spokesman for WRAL-TV in Raleigh. Why, Helms asked in his nightly commentary, had the proud state of North Carolina been reduced to pleading for relief from the SACS? "It is not merely a matter of our State's having sent a boy to do a man's job," Helms argued. "If any emissary was to have been sent at all, it should have been a man of sufficient backbone to tell the Southern Association of Colleges and Schools where to head in, a man who would have read to these arrogant educators the provisions of their own charter, and certainly a man who would have said—speaking for the honorable people of a proud state—that North Carolina does not intend to submit further to intimidation and blackmail."[14] Helms's belittling comments cut deep. Watts Jr. complained to the Federal Communications Commission, and his letter was added to a growing file of complaints from others stung by Helms's commentaries over the years.

Indeed, the issue was not thoroughly exhausted. On January 3, 1966, the Chapel Hill chapter of Students for a Democratic Society (SDS) issued an invitation to two speakers whose names and reputations were sure to force a showdown. One was Frank Wilkinson, who had spent a month in prison for refusing to answer questions about his Communist Party membership. The other was Herbert Aptheker, a longtime communist who had recently led a delegation to Vietnam. It was not Aptheker's first appearance on campus, as Clontz's testimony made clear, but Aptheker's appearance a dozen years earlier had been wholly unremarkable.

A faculty advisory committee recommended the speakers be allowed to appear, and Friday took the matter to the trustee executive committee. By the time it came to a vote in February 1966, Governor Moore and a majority of the members were dead set against approving the appearance of the two. A motion permanently barring Wilkinson and Aptheker from speaking carried seven to four. Standing with Friday in favor of open debate were Watts Sr., Victor Bryant Jr., Virginia Lathrop, and Mebane Burgwyn.

"[Watts Sr.] was the one member of the board that stood with me all the way through the Speaker Ban thing," Friday recalled. "The rest of them, they got pressured and they would buckle. But not Watts. He stood there like a rock and nobody pushed him anywhere, not even the most vigorous arguments that we had in there. You know, here's a man with no solid academic depth about him in the sense of a professor or anything else. But he was up there and he said, 'No, we're not going to do this.'"[15]

Friday lost the round, and the exclusion of the speakers created an even more embarrassing spectacle for the university. Wilkinson came to Chapel Hill as scheduled and spoke from the public sidewalk on Franklin Street to students seated across the low stone wall on university property. The issue was finally made moot two years later when a federal appeals court ruled the law unconstitutional after hearing arguments in a student-initiated lawsuit that Friday had encouraged.

∾∾∾

The responsibilities of the Board of Higher Education occupied Watts Jr. almost daily for six years, and he devoted between thirty and forty hours a week to this unpaid assignment. He thrived on the details of the work and set about to rebuild public confidence in the board and its mission to chart a course for higher education in North Carolina. He hired Cameron West to replace the board's executive director, William Archie, who had performed valuable service but whose personality had created sufficient political turbulence to cost him his job. Hill lobbied Moore for more operating money to replace that stripped away by the General Assembly, and the governor responded with special appropriations from his contingency and emergency accounts.

At the top of the board's list of missions was a long-range plan for higher education, and no aspect of the state's institutions required more pressing attention than the woeful condition of its traditionally black institutions.[16] North Carolina had five colleges that served African Americans. North Carolina College in Durham, with its liberal arts curriculum, was counted as one of the top black schools in the country, as was North Carolina A&T in Greensboro, although neither received the resources the state devoted to white schools. These two institutions were well ahead of the colleges at Elizabeth City, Fayetteville, and Winston-Salem whose mission over the years had been to produce teachers for a segregated school system.

As Watts Jr. assumed the chairmanship of the board, Archie outlined the problems that lay ahead. The traditionally black schools had neither the trained faculty nor the facilities to qualify as institutions of higher learning. Entering students from segregated, underfunded public school systems arrived unprepared, with little more than a rudimentary education to serve them. More than three-fourths of the graduates—the state's next crop of African American teachers—failed to qualify for certification in their first attempts at the national teachers' examination, Archie told Hill.[17] The schools had survived not because of their contribution to higher education but rather through the neglect of the white establishment. Meanwhile, the institutions were regarded as important assets by the African American communities they served. Closing them would create deep resentment among African Americans, Archie told Hill, but upgrading these campuses to a status equal to that of white institutions would entail an expense the legislature would never approve.[18]

Watts Jr. and the board staff compiled evidence of the staggering inequities—from facilities to faculty qualifications—and when the board's long-range planning document for all campuses was released in 1968 (a document largely written by Hill), it called for radical changes and increased investment in the traditionally black institutions.

The board's report was released at a time when the political logrolling in support of the ambitions of white institutions was about to reach its peak. In 1967, the legislature had elevated the white teachers' colleges at Greenville, Boone, and Cullowhee, as well as the largest black institution, North Carolina A&T, to the status of "regional universities." In 1969, Governor Robert W. Scott endorsed the addition of existing junior college campuses at Asheville and Wilmington to the consolidated university system, and the legislature in turn anointed as universities the remaining four-year institutions, including Pembroke State, a school founded for Native Americans; North Carolina College in Durham; and the black teachers' colleges, despite the fact that these campuses had none of the requisites for credible graduate programs. The legislature dealt a second blow to Chapel Hill's prestige by making an appropriation to pay for the first stages of a medical school at East Carolina University in Greenville.

The legislative interference in higher education and especially the bold political maneuvering on the part of President Leo Jenkins at East Carolina University played havoc with not only the future of the consolidated university but also the plans for higher education as laid out by the Board of Higher Education. When it appeared that these plans were about to collapse in 1969, the board's director, Cameron West, along with Watts Jr. and others, convinced Governor Scott that the board needed more political clout. With Scott's help, the legislature revamped the board's membership to include the governor as well as the chairs of the legislature's money committees—taxation and appropriations. Scott then set in motion plans for an overhaul of the system.

∾∾∾

Watts Hill Sr. remained unwavering in his support of the consolidated university, although he had his differences with the University of North Carolina's president, Bill Friday, over the growing divisions between the university and the board. Hill opposed the addition of the campuses in Charlotte, Wilmington, and Asheville, which were thrust upon the board for political rather than academic reasons. Adding Charlotte helped expand the university's sphere of influence to the growing financial center of the state, while the addition of Wilmington and Asheville fulfilled campaign promises that had been made by Governor Scott. "I fought [Charlotte] until they agreed it was a political move," Hill recalled. "The same thing applied to Wilmington and Asheville. I fought it just as hard as I could fight it until they agreed it was a political move."[19] At the same time, he complained to Friday about what he considered Friday's intransigence to work with the state's other institutions. After one encounter, Friday made a note to his file that said: "[Watts Sr.] then shifted to the necessity for the university and the BHE [Board of Higher Education] to pull together arguing that West and I were butting heads. I told him the university had lived within the law. He accused the university of failure of leadership, citing the medical school particularly, and implied we were the cause of the present conflict. I asked him to note an instance where we were responsible. I made it clear to him that I intended to stand, and that I will deal factually with the BHE actions."[20]

The future of the governance of the state's system of higher education came to a head in 1971, when Governor Scott initiated a plan for reorganization that would combine all sixteen state-funded campuses in one system. The Hills found themselves facing off from opposing sides of the issue. Watts Jr. stood with the governor. Watts Sr. backed Friday and the Board of Trustees, which wanted to leave the consolidated university as it was. Throughout a protracted legislative fight that required a special session of the General Assembly, father and son seldom spoke to one another. It was during this period that Watts Sr.'s personal assistant, Maceo Bullock, became the conduit for messages between them.

In October 1971, the future of higher education was settled with the creation of a new consolidated university and the appointment of a Board of Governors. At the board's first meeting in January 1972, two Hills answered the roll. Watts Sr.'s appointment had come through his tenure on the Board of Trustees; Watts Jr. was made a member by virtue of his service on the now disbanded Board of Higher Education. Any differences between the two were tucked carefully away. Watts Sr. spoke to a reporter about his son: "[Watts Jr.] is a lot like his mother with a very inquiring mind, and he goes right down the road digging out information. I don't anticipate any problems. We'll just handle each other as individuals as we've always done." He said he would work to make the new board successful. "Men of good will can make any damn program work. All I want is an opportunity to be heard. If I can't convince anybody, that's my fault."[21] Watts Jr. served one two-year term. His father remained on the board until 1981.

∞∞∞

During the last fifteen years of his life, Watts Sr. saw little of his son Watts Jr. or his daughter Dudley, who was married to Orville Campbell, the publisher of the *Chapel Hill Weekly*. He was closer to his youngest son,

John Sprunt Hill II, who had launched several successful business ventures. John Sprunt II had carefully steered clear of family businesses throughout his life and pursued his interest in electronics. His home was at Quail Roost, where he and his wife Irmgard raised horses. Ironically, he had been the least interested in horses when he was a child. When John Sprunt II died from cancer in October 1991, the loss devastated his father.

When Watts Sr. was well on in years, he acknowledged that his children had always been secondary to his other interests. "In the daytime I was in the office, and the [children were in bed] at night."[22] He said that his home life had not been that different from what he had known from his own father. "My father was there," he said, "but I had gone to school and would see him at suppertime. The family always gathered at supper and he would tell us about this, that, and the other thing. We learned a lot, but my mother was the guiding influence. . . . [She] represented the family to me."[23]

Watts Jr. said that while his father could develop close friendships with those outside his family—people with whom he could have a relationship limited in time—he remained distant with his immediate family. "He was the stern figure to his children, the one who wanted us to be what he visualized we ought to be, the one who could not understand that each of us was sufficiently different to be different from him, to be our own person. The one exception to this was the youngest of the three of us, my brother John, who was so completely different from anyone in the family in his interest in electronics that he was treated as an exception."

Dudley said her father never quite understood that his children's circumstances could be different from his own. She said that when her father paid his first visit to her home in Chapel Hill, he was surprised that she and her husband could not afford servants. Watts Sr., moreover, never approved of Mary Hill's career in retailing. For years, Mary managed the Montaldo's department store in Durham, and she later ran her own retail business in Chapel Hill.

"I think a lot of my father's relationship difficulties go back to the way he was raised and the way his mother was raised," Watts Jr. said. "That 'Puritan Ethic,' with all of its wonderful aspects, also carried with it a certitude that one was right and that anyone who thought differently, or did not share the same priorities, was somehow lesser, either ethically or intellectually."[24]

Most of the family's differences remained private. In 1981, however,

Watts Sr. was in his final year of service to the state's university system—one of the longest in University of North Carolina history—when his son appeared as a witness for the federal government in its action to force greater integration of the university system. Watts Jr.'s testimony at an administrative hearing, which grew out of his long-standing interest in uplifting the state's black institutions, was interpreted as having encouraged the federal lawsuit that bedeviled the university for a decade. The *Raleigh News and Observer* said, "Hill's testimony may have been discomfiting to North Carolina officials and may not have offered a final solution to the impasse. But by spotlighting the black campuses, which remain poor cousins, Hill addressed the crucial issue on which the outcome of the government's hearings may ride." Following Watts Jr.'s appearance at the hearings, his father wrote members of the Board of Governors to apologize for his son's testimony. He did not send a copy of the letter to his son.

∾∾∾

After the one lapse in 1974, Watts Hill Sr. never discussed the sale of CCB. He jealously held to his title and prerogatives as chairman of the CCB Board of Directors. While North Carolina banks began expanding across state lines to new markets in the South, Hill and CCB stayed in familiar territory in central North Carolina. Hill drew his greatest pleasure from scouting trips to locate new sites for branch offices. Hill called himself the "unofficial, unregistered, unlicensed architect of Central Carolina Bank. Doin' what I want to do."[25]

Roaming about the region in his 1963 Cadillac, whose odometer had passed beyond 130,000 miles, Hill often made unannounced visits to CCB branches to see how things were running. One day, when he arrived at the Northgate branch in Durham, he found the manager's desk littered with paperwork. The disorderly appearance offended Hill, who called the manager to the carpet and told him it was a disgrace. On another occasion, he heard a customer complain about having to wait in line behind business customers whose complicated deposits took longer to process. A sign soon went up in CCB branches directing business deposits to a special lane.[26]

In 1986, CCB negotiated a merger with Republic National Bank in Charlotte, giving CCB a stake in the state's largest market. By that time, CCB had assets of more than $1.2 billion and was operating in more than thirty communities. The state's largest financial institutions—Wachovia, NCNB (formerly North Carolina National Bank), and First Union—had begun to crowd CCB's core market in the 1980s as they completed an expansion across the state. During the merger frenzy of the period, there were opportunities for Hill to sell the bank either to one of these competitors or to out-of-state banks looking for an entry into the booming market around the Research Triangle. He discouraged all these overtures even though a merger would certainly have enlarged his personal bank account.

Watts Sr. was "Mr. Central Carolina Bank," and he defied anyone to remove his title. With more than 12 percent of the bank stock under his personal control, no one did. "He didn't want to see it go down," his personal lawyer Jack Walker said. "He'd rather have control than the money."[27]

∾∾∾

By the 1990s, Watts Sr.'s pace had slowed considerably, but with the help of a cane he continued to be active. Then, in late December 1992, he suffered a severe stroke; he died a few weeks later on January 20, 1993, a Wednesday, at his home in Chapel Hill. His death brought tributes from those who had worked with him over the years. His longtime friend and coworker, the Research Triangle Institute's George Herbert, said, "We all love Mr. Hill for what he is, not what he's done. He's been a man of tremendous generosity—not only in terms of money, but in his enormous energy." During their years together, the institute had grown from a small concern that occupied borrowed space in Home Security Life Insurance offices to a world-renowned research facility that employed more than fifteen hundred persons and handled $118 million in projects. "I don't think anyone was more important to the endeavor and keeping it together than Mr. Hill," Herbert said.

The chancellor of the university's Chapel Hill campus, Paul Hardin, said, "We have lost one of the most distinguished, indeed one of the most majestic leaders in the twentieth century." Another significant benefactor of the university, Frank H. Kenan, said that Watts Hill and his father, John Sprunt Hill, "did more for the general public in education and philanthropy than any family other than the Dukes." He noted, "That's about as high praise as I can give."

Hill's funeral service was conducted at First Presbyterian Church. Hill had asked for a "brief and dignified service" with "no eulogies." His wishes were obeyed; the Reverend Joseph S. Harvard offered a homily on faith. Harvard said Hill was raised on the Westminster Confession, which includes questions such as "What is the chief end of man? And what is God?"

The minister said, "Such questions and answers provide us with a foundation that leads us to the center of life." Hill's body was cremated, and the urn was buried in Maplewood Cemetery in front of the remains of his grandfather, George W. Watts. Only the family attended the graveside services.

⟡⟡⟡

Watts Sr. did not live to see the completion of the new Hill Alumni Center on the Chapel Hill campus; it was only weeks from opening when he died. The new home of the Alumni Association was built with the help of a $3.5 million challenge gift from Hill that grew out of a 1985 visit from Bill Friday, who was about to retire after more than thirty years as president of the university. Friday told Hill: "I don't want to leave the university administration without there being a building on this campus that has your name on it." Hill had been in this position before, and he knew the next question. "How much?" he asked bluntly. "Three million," Friday said. "You got it," Hill replied.

After Friday left, Hill called Jack Walker of Durham, the lawyer who had helped him plan his estate. When he told Walker what he had done, Walker applauded Hill's generosity but told him that not a single nickel was tax deductible. Hill was stunned. "The hell you say," he told Walker. "Why's that?" Walker explained that Hill had already given his limit for the year. Even his tax carryover was pushing the limit. "Well, I'll be goddamned. Such is life," Hill said.

Hill's challenge gift was designed to cover one-half of the $7 million estimated cost of the new building, which campus planners had originally planned to site on a hill near the Kenan Center. Subsequent changes pushed the alumni building off the hill, however. Finally, a site was chosen at the east end of Kenan Stadium, and Hill attended the groundbreaking in 1989. The 65,000-square-foot building that eventually cost $12 million to complete was designed to nestle into the hill.

As he did with most buildings with which he was involved, especially one that would carry his name, Hill fussed over the plans for the alumni center and pushed for a more traditional design than the one first proposed. He tinkered with some elements on the exterior such as the choice of the brick, and designers followed Hill's advice and did all the exterior trim in muted tones to match the color of the mortar. Anne Hill donated photographs of Watts Sr. and other memorabilia, including the decoration

Hill had received from the Italian government for his service in World War II and his 1988 honor from the university, the William R. Davie Award.

∽∽∽

Watts Sr. was as private in death as he was in life. He did his best to conceal the value of his estate—which may have been as great as $45 million—by creating a trust managed by CCB. He made some specific bequests, including $500,000 to the First Presbyterian Church and $2 million to the endowment fund for the Learning Development Center. He also added $2.5 million to the George Watts Hill Foundation, which he had established in 1982 and contributed to in the intervening years. The foundation supported the Research Triangle Institute, the University of North Carolina, and Durham Academy. The university also received Hill's Chapel Hill home and the surrounding 19 acres. The house later became the residence of the chancellor of the Chapel Hill campus.

The home was among several properties that Hill family members donated to the university as other members of Watts Sr.'s generation passed away. In 1988, the family of Laura Valinda Hill and David St. Pierre DuBose provided the family's Georgian Revival residence, Meadowmont, to the university along with 28 acres of their farm on the edge of Chapel Hill. After David St. Pierre DuBose's death in 1994, the home and grounds became the dining and social center for the Kenan-Flagler Business School. Another 435 acres was later developed into a mixed-use community called Meadowmont that included office space, a retail center, and high-end residential condominiums.

∽∽∽

Watts Sr.'s death provoked speculation that CCB would become a merger target, and the bank's stock price jumped 10 percent. There was some pressure on CCB president William L. Burns Jr. from Hill's heirs to sell, but six months after Hill's death the bank purchased $16.5 million of Hill's CCB stock—450,000 shares—from his estate to keep them off the market.

The bank remained independent until the spring of 2000, when Ernest C. Roessler, who succeeded Burns as CCB's chairman and chief executive officer, announced a merger with the smaller National Commerce Bancorp (NCB) of Memphis, Tennessee. At the time, CCB Financial Corporation, the bank holding company, had assets of $8.2 billion. The merger created a $15 billion corporation that gave NCB a foothold in North Carolina and an entrance into a more traditional banking operation. (Most of its business was conducted through supermarket offices.) NCB won a majority of the board control, but Roessler reassured Durham that the CCB initials would remain the most visible landmark in the city skyline. "That tall building in downtown Durham will still be there," he told reporters. At the same time, he said that the headquarters for the new company would be located in Memphis.

This blow to Durham's pride was followed just a few months later by the announcement by Liggett and Myers Tobacco Company, the maker of what had been Watts Sr.'s favorite Chesterfield brand, that it was moving its cigarette production—mostly generic brands—to a plant in Mebane in neighboring Alamance County. A small cigarette manufacturing operation would open about a year later in Durham, but for a time cigarette production disappeared from the city. Flush with the economic expansion stimulated by the growth of the Research Triangle Park, Durham's citizens paid little attention to the passing of the city's old enterprises.

Certainly neither John Sprunt Hill nor Watts Hill Sr. ever imagined either Durham without tobacco or a Hill without a bank. The city's growth had been fueled by the fortune that George W. Watts helped create with the Dukes and by the financial institutions that John Sprunt Hill had created and passed on to his children. In good times, the family had amassed tremendous wealth that was enriched by Durham's mills and factories. In hard times, the Hills had salvaged civic projects and enlarged the public domain with gifts of parkland and recreational areas. The Hills raised grand buildings, churches, and hospitals that had changed more than the city's skyline. Hills managed the schools, financed public improvements, created jobs, shouldered public office, expanded the opportunities of rural life, and bolstered the farm economy.

They left their mark on North Carolina as well. The state became a different place in the twentieth century in part because three generations of Hill men enjoyed the freedom and resources to pursue a vision unencumbered by modern corporate and political boundaries. They were inspired by old-fashioned patriotism, a competitive spirit, enlightened self-interest, and a sense of noblesse oblige in state-building enterprises that produced results even they could not have imagined. In the early years of the century, John Sprunt Hill had championed rural credits in pursuit of a nineteenth-century notion of improving the lot of the yeoman farmer. His work on behalf of credit unions did not save the family farm, but the movement he supported with his time, his talent, and his money became the foundation for low-cost banking in credit unions, which later served millions of twenty-first-century suburbanites. Watts Sr. spent years trying to find a way to improve the financial condition of Watts Hospital before he embraced a cooperative health care program that eventually led to both the creation of Blue Cross Blue Shield of North Carolina, one of the largest nonprofit health care operations in the state, and to advances in the planning of health care facilities.

No family devoted more time to the raising of the University of North Carolina. Four generations of Hills were either trustees of the university and the consolidated university or were members of the Board of Governors of the new consolidated university created in 1972. The record of service that began with Edward Hill in the years after the Civil War continued virtually without temporal interruption with his son, his grandson, and finally with his great-grandson, George Watts Hill Jr. It is a record that in all likelihood will never be surpassed. It is also a record that could pass largely unnoticed, given that only two campus buildings carry the family name.

Indeed, one of the most lasting monuments to the Hill family is called the North Carolina Collection, whose archives include the stuff of both the important and the mundane. The collection records the passing of everyday life, from the earliest settlement of North Carolina to the present day. Born of John Sprunt Hill's devotion to his state, its history, and the university's library, the collection, supported by the income from the Carolina Inn and the Franklin Street property that Hill left to the university, continues to serve scholars and laymen. In November 2001, Watts Hill Jr. happily reported to friends and family that with the Carolina Inn finally operating profitably after a $13 million renovation, $100,000 would be distributed to the library from the inn in 2001 and more than $700,000 was available for future needs. Future annual income would amount to an estimated $250,000. "What is important," Watts Jr. wrote, "is that Mr. John Sprunt Hill's wishes are finally being carried out in a fashion I believe would meet with his full approval."

❧ ❧ ❧

On March 15, 2002, Watts Hill Jr. was walking in his garden, where the grounds were prepared for a spring garden tour, when he suffered a heart attack and died. He was a sturdy seventy-five years of age, and his death stunned his friends and family. Only weeks before, he had been in Palm

Beach, Florida, where he had taken his 1964 Ferrari, a 250 GT Berlinetta Lusso that had been restored to prizewinning appearance and performance. Hill had enjoyed a lifelong fascination with sports cars and the people who drove them. Some of his favorite photographs were those that he had taken at racetracks around the world. Like everything in which he became interested, he invested himself fully in the sport. Dilettantes were not asked to chair the professional competition board of the Sports Car Club of America; the owners of showcase automobiles did not become stewards of the Ferrari Club of America. He had devoted the same enthusiasm to the building of the North Carolina Center for Public Policy Research, of which he was a director in its formative years, and later to the marine sciences programs at both Duke University and the University of North Carolina.

The sanctuary of Durham's First Presbyterian Church filled to capacity the day of Hill's memorial service as the clergy prepared to preside over the passing of a representative of the fourth generation of a family that had laid the foundation for modern Durham. Like the services for George W. Watts, John Sprunt Hill, and George Watts Hill, the observance for George Watts Hill Jr. was unpretentious, simple, Presbyterian. The Reverend Joseph Harvard was preceded to the pulpit by civil rights attorney Julius Chambers, who read scripture. Chambers was the recently retired chancellor of North Carolina Central University, where Hill had received an honorary degree some years earlier to mark his support for civil rights and the cause of black institutions. The congregation sang the "Navy Hymn."

Before his death, Watts Hill Jr. had pondered the prospect of being the last of a dynamic line of men who had involved themselves in the life of North Carolina for more than a century. The interests of his own son and namesake, Watts III, led him in a different direction than his father. In a sense, it had been that way almost from the start. John Sprunt Hill had helped bring Durham and central North Carolina into the economic fullness of the twentieth century. His son had set aside his own ambitions to continue working for the financial growth of the family and the region, but with a different vision than his father's. And Watts Hill Jr. had been one more step removed from his own father. At the same time, all three generations produced bold soldiers in a corps of civic entrepreneurs whose interest in the public good expanded opportunities and enhanced life for North Carolinians during its greatest century.

ABBREVIATIONS

CIP   Carolina Inn Papers, University Archives, University of North Carolina, Chapel Hill, N.C.

DKMP   Official Papers of Governor Dan K. Moore, North Carolina Department of Archives and History, Raleigh, N.C.

ECBP   E. C. Branson Papers, Southern Historical Collection, University of North Carolina, Chapel Hill, N.C.

EMP   Eugene Morehead Papers, Manuscripts Department, Duke University, Durham, N.C.

EPP   Early Presidents' Papers, University Archives, University of North Carolina, Chapel Hill, N.C.

FPGP   Frank Porter Graham Papers, Southern Historical Collection, University of North Carolina, Chapel Hill, N.C.

FPMP   Francis P. Miller Papers, Manuscripts Department, University of Virginia, Charlottesville, Va.

GWH   George Watts Hill

HFP   Hill Family Papers, private collection.

HMBP   Harriet Morehead Berry Papers, Southern Historical Collection, University of North Carolina, Chapel Hill, N.C.

HSL   Health Sciences Library, University of North Carolina, Chapel Hill, N.C.

JBDP   James B. Duke Papers, Manuscripts Department, Duke University, Durham, N.C.

JSH   John Sprunt Hill

JSHL   John Sprunt Hill Letterbooks, Hill Family Papers, private collection.

JSHP   John Sprunt Hill Papers, Hill Family Papers, private collection.

LHP   Official Papers of Governor Luther H. Hodges, North Carolina Department of Archives and History, Raleigh, N.C.

MTL   Mary Thornton Letterbooks, North Carolina Collection, University of North Carolina, Chapel Hill, N.C.

NCC   North Carolina Collection, University of North Carolina, Chapel Hill, N.C.

OSSA   OSS Archives, National Archives, Washington, D.C.

RGP   Romeo Guest Papers, Manuscripts Department, Duke University, Durham, N.C.

SHC   Southern Historical Collection, University of North Carolina, Chapel Hill, N.C.

SOHP   Southern Oral History Program, University of North Carolina, Chapel Hill, N.C.

WCDP   Wilburt C. Davison Papers, Medical School Archives, Duke University, Durham, N.C.

WCFP   William C. Friday Papers, Southern Historical Collection, University of North Carolina, Chapel Hill, N.C.

NOTES

Chapter One

1. Evans, *Ballots and Fence Rails*, p. 77.
2. Allcott, *Campus at Chapel Hill*, p. 53.
3. JSH, "Triumphs over the Shades of Night," HFP.
4. Love, *'Tis Sixty Years Since*, p. 4.
5. Ibid.
6. Battle, *History of the University*, p. 348.
7. Ibid., p. 338.
8. Hill, "Triumphs," HFP.
9. Battle, *History of the University*, p. 399.
10. Ibid.
11. Ibid., p. 317.
12. Ibid.
13. Love, *'Tis Sixty Years Since*, p. 48.
14. Hill's school in Faison continued to operate from the same building until the middle of the twentieth century, when it closed and classes were consolidated with a school in the nearby town of Calypso. Hill was eighty-five years old when his old school was closed, and he argued against consolidation even though local folk offered to name the new school in his honor.
15. Hill, "Triumphs," p. 3, HFP.
16. H. G. Jones, "Son of Duplin," (remarks prepared for delivery to the Duplin County Historical Society, February 2, 1985), NCC.

Chapter Two

1. Morris, *Incredible New York*, p. 274.
2. Classified advertisement, *New York Times*, June 5, 1892.
3. JSH, "Triumphs over the Shades of Night," HFP.
4. "Staley A. Cook, Distinguished Carolinian," news clipping, n.d., JSHP.
5. George Lougee, "A Doughty Multimillionaire with a Twinkle in His Eye," *Durham Morning Herald*, September 18, 1961.
6. JSH to Edward J. Saunders, July 3, 1895, JSHL.
7. Ibid.

8. JSH to Wednesday Cotillion Committee, n.d., Annie W. Hill Scrapbooks, HFP.

9. Hobart Nichols, "With the Cavalry," *Washington Evening Star*, clipping, n.d., Annie W. Hill Scrapbooks, HFP.

10. JSH to Kemp P. Battle, April 25, 1898, University Archives, University of North Carolina.

11. Barry, *Squadron A*, p. 43.

12. Alger, *Spanish-American War*, p. 316.

13. Morris, *Incredible New York*, p. 200.

14. JSH to Dr. Charles Baskerville, September 22, 1899, JSHL.

15. "Deed, Key to Watts Home Turned over to Allied Arts," *Durham Sun*, July 17, 1954.

16. "Miss Watts to Wed," *Charlotte Observer*, clipping, n.d., HFP.

17. "Crowning Social Event," *Durham Sun*, November 30, 1899.

18. Connable and Silberfarb, *Tigers of Tammany*, p. 209.

19. Ibid.

20. "Croker Rejected His Young Men," news clipping, October 4, 1900, HFP.

21. Ibid.

22. John DeWitt Warner to S. E. Moffett, October 20, 1899, JSHP.

23. JSH campaign brochure, HFP.

24. "A Sound-Money Candidate," *New York World*, October 25, 1900.

25. "Can't Stand Absalom, Fourteenth District Wants a Man in Congress," *New York Sun*, November 1, 1900.

26. "Gave up House," *New York News*, October 27, 1900.

27. "Sound Money March," *New York Times*, November 4, 1900.

28. Connable and Silberfarb, *Tigers of Tammany*, p. 226.

29. "Low, the 'Reformer,' Lo," *Louisville Courier-Journal*, clipping, n.d., HFP.

30. JSH to Lewis Nixon, January 14, 1902, JSHP.

31. Lewis Nixon to JSH, January 16, 1902, JSHP.

Chapter Three

1. There are a variety of spellings for G. S. Watts's first name. The one used here is found in S. A. Ashe's biography of George W. Watts.

2. Webb, *Jule Carr*, p. 60.

3. Ibid., pp. 61, 67.

4. Ibid., p. 88.

5. GWH, interview by Reynolds, August 16, 1984.

6. G. W. Watts to Eugene Morehead, July 31, 1879, EMP.

7. Boyd, *Story of Durham*, p. 210.

8. Reynolds, "Watts Hospital," p. 36.

9. Eugene Morehead to Lucy Morehead, December 31, 1882, EMP.

10. Ashe, *Biographical History*, p. 475.

11. Anderson, *Durham County*, p. 184.

12. George Watts to Eugene Morehead, November 11, 1888, EMP.

13. Ibid., November 7, 1888, EMP.

14. Valinda Watts to Lucy Morehead, July 3, [n.d.], EMP.

15. George W. Watts to Valinda Watts, February 4, 1889, private collection of Dr. J. McNeely DuBose.

16. Dr. H. P. C. Wilson to George Watts, February 28, 1889, private collection of Dr. J. Mc-Neely DuBose.

17. "The Morehead Banking Company," *Daily Tobacco Plant*, March 4, 1889.

18. George W. Watts to Valinda Watts, April 20, 1889, private collection of Dr. J. McNeely DuBose.

19. Winkler, *Tobacco Tycoon*, p. 72.

20. Chernow, *Titan*, p. 298.

21. J. B. Duke testimony, *U.S. v. American Tobacco Co.*, JBDP.

22. Tilley, *Bright-Tobacco Industry*, p. 637.

23. "Duke Is a Winner," *Durham Globe*, November 2, 1893.

24. Anderson, *Durham County*, p. 188.

25. Durden, *Dukes of Durham*, p. 158.

26. Daniels, *Editor in Politics*, p. 209.

27. Durden, *Dukes of Durham*, p. 159.

28. Porter, *Trinity and Duke*, p. 49.

29. "Watts Hospital, Its Inauguration Last Night," *Durham Sun*, February 22, 1895.

30. Reynolds, *Watts Hospital*.

31. Ibid.

32. Josephus Daniels, Untitled editorial, *Raleigh News and Observer*, March 17, 1896.

33. Peter Fish, "History of First Presbyterian Church," Collections of the First Presbyterian Church.

34. Ibid.

35. Leyburn, *The Way We Lived*, p. 27.

36. "Pearl Cotton Mills," *Durham Globe*, December 19, 1895.

37. Chernow, *Titan*, p. 191.

38. JSH, interview.

Chapter Four

1. JSH, interview.

2. Ibid.

3. JSH, Proposal to George W. Watts, n.d., HFP.

4. Ibid.

5. Ibid.

6. JSH, Draft proposal to George W. Watts, January 1903, HFP.

7. "Durham Loan and Trust Company," *Durham Sun*, August 30, 1904.

8. GWH, interview by Leutze, January 30, 1986.

9. Transcribed notes from meeting of Board of Directors, Durham Bank and Trust Company, November 12, 1957, HFP.

10. George W. Watts to J. B. Duke, August 20, 1903, JBDP.

11. Leyburn, *The Way We Lived*, p. 47.

12. GWH, interview by Reynolds, June 21, 1984.

13. Capital Strategies, "Central Carolina Bank & Trust Company, 1903–1997," HFP; JSH, interview.

14. JSH, Testimony before the subcommittee of the Committee on Banking and Currency, U.S. Senate, *Rural Credits*, March 4, 1914, HFP.

15. Transcribed notes from meeting of Board of Directors, Durham Bank and Trust.

16. Ibid.

17. "Why Durham Is the City to Live in and Do Business in," *Durham Sun*, February 3, 1903.

18. Dr. B. R. Lacy Jr., "A Profitable Partnership," (sermon delivered at Ginter Park Presbyterian Church, February 18, 1962), HFP.

19. "A Night Invasion by the Southern," *Raleigh News and Observer*, March 21, 1905.

20. "The Railroad Taxed with the Costs," *Raleigh News and Observer*, April 9, 1905.

21. JSH to F. P. Venable, January 31, 1903, PP.

22. JSH to Francis P. Venable, January 14, 1905, SHC; Francis P. Venable to JSH, January 16, 1905, SHC.

23. JSH, "Address before the Alumni Association of the University of North Carolina," June 2, 1903, privately published, HFP.

24. George W. Watts to W. W. Moore, March 19, 1909, HFP.

25. Davison, *Davison of Duke*, p. 114.

26. Reynolds, *Watts Hospital*.

27. Ibid.

28. JSH to Mssrs. Kendall-Taylor, December 1, 1910, HFP.

29. Ibid., February 11, 1911, HFP.

30. Flowers and Schumann, *Bull Durham and Beyond*.

31. JSH to Mssrs. Kendall-Taylor, December 28, 1911, HFP.

32. Corina, *Trust in Tobacco*, p. 1.

33. Ibid., p. 117.

34. Ibid.

35. "Efforts Making to Convict Tobacco Trust Official through Criminal Action," *Raleigh News and Observer*, May 31, 1911.

36. "It's the Jail for Trust Magnates, Attorney General Tells Congress as Much," *Raleigh News and Observer*, June 1, 1911.

37. "Settlement of the Tobacco Case," *Durham Sun*, November 9, 1911.

38. "Farmers' Union May Take Action," *Durham Sun*, November 20, 1911.

Chapter Five

1. Hobbs, *North Carolina*, p. 89.

2. George W. Watts to W. W. Moore, March 1, 1908, W. W. Moore Papers.

3. Golf register, Carolina Hotel, Tufts Family Papers.

4. "G. W. Watts is President," *Durham Morning Herald*, April 16, 1913.

5. "Opening Day on Golf Links," *Durham Sun*, April 9, 1912.

6. Leyburn, *The Way We Lived*, p. 164.

7. "Carolina Industries in 1914," *University News Letter* 2, no. 38, NCC.

8. Clarence Poe, Untitled editorial, *Progressive Farmer*, June 7, 1913.

9. Letter to the editor, *Progressive Farmer*, July 19, 1913.

10. Clarence Poe, Untitled editorial, *Progressive Farmer*, July 19, 1913.

11. Ibid., May 2, 1914.

12. JSH, Untitled speech, May 26, 1913, HFP.

13. "Union of Farmers in the Production and Sale of Crops," *Raleigh News and Observer*, August 27, 1913.

14. Report of the Committee Appointed by the Governor of North Carolina on Needs of

North Carolina Farmers with Regard to Credits, Marketing, and Co-operation, Addressed to Honorable Locke Craig for Transmission to American Commission on Finance, Production, Distribution, and Rural Life, 1913, HFP.

15. Ibid.

16. Ibid.

17. JSH, Testimony before the subcommittee of the Committee on Banking and Currency, U.S. Senate, *Rural Credits*, March 4, 1914, p. 39, HFP.

18. Fred Mutchler to JSH, April 13, 1914, ECBP.

19. JSH to Ernestine Noa, July 9, 1914, ECBP.

20. E. C. Branson to JSH, November 14, 1918, ECBP.

21. E. C. Branson to E. K. Graham, February 7, 1914, ECBP.

22. Clarence Poe, "Some New North Carolina Laws," *Progressive Farmer*, April 3, 1915.

23. E. C. Branson, "Farmers Should Organize Cooperative Credit Unions," *Progressive Farmer*, March 8, 1915.

24. JSH to E. C. Branson, November 12, 1915, ECBP.

25. JSH, "Organized Credit: The Paramount Need of the Tar Heel Farmers," (speech delivered to organized farmers of North Carolina, November 16, 1915), HFP.

26. F. W. Risher, "The Dark Corner of Durham and Its Wonderful Development," *Progressive Farmer*, December 25, 1915.

27. JSH to J. Y. Joyner, January 17, 1916, JSHL.

28. Hobbs, *North Carolina*, p. 208.

29. JSH to A. C. Michie, October 3, 1917, JSHL.

Chapter Six

1. GWH, interview by Reynolds, June 21, 1984.

2. Leyburn, *The Way We Lived*, p. 117.

3. Ibid., p. 125.

4. JSH to GWH, July 11, 1917, HFP.

5. JSH to H. G. Buehler, September 14, 1917, HFP.

6. *Alumni Review* 7, no. 8 (May 1919).

7. Ibid., no. 9 (June 1919).

8. JSH to E. C. Branson, May 11, 1917, ECBP.

9. Anderson, *Durham County*, p. 296.

10. JSH to R. D. W. Connor, March 9, 1918, HFP.

11. Governor Thomas W. Bickett to Secretary of War Newton D. Baker, July 10, 1918, in House, *Bickett*, p. 350.

12. JSH to Colonel F. H. Fries, July 2, 1918, HFP.

13. JSH to Edward Kidder Graham, April 26, 1918, JSHL.

14. JSH to Charles L. Raper, May 4, 1918, JSHL.

15. Sullivan, *Over Here*, p. 654.

16. Fox, interview by the author, March 10, 1999.

17. Coates, *University of North Carolina*, p. 38.

18. "Life Insurance Co. Stock Resembled White Elephant," *ESC Quarterly* (Fall 1948).

19. GWH, interview by Leutze, January 30, 1986.

20. JSH to GWH, January 26, 1922, HFP.

21. GWH, interview by Reynolds, June 21, 1984.

22. Fox, interview by Hill, February 8, 1999.

23. Gifford, *Evolution of a Medical Center*, p. 27.

24. Reynolds, "Watts Hospital," p. 93.

25. Minutes of the Board of Trustees, January 27, 1920, University Archives, University of North Carolina.

Chapter Seven

1. JSH, "A Progressive Program for Building and Maintaining a Great Primary System of State Highways in North Carolina," (speech delivered to the North Carolina Good Roads Association, June 1920), NCC.

2. Harriet M. Berry to T. L. Gwyn, July 1, 1920, HMBP.

3. JSH to Charles M. Pritchett, May 31, 1923, JSHL.

4. JSH to O. B. Hester, February 13, 1924, HFP.

5. Fox, interview by the author, March 10, 1999.

6. "Dynamite Attack on Battle Home," *Chapel Hill Weekly*, April 26, 1923.

7. JSH to E. W. James, November 17, 1925, HFP.

8. JSH to H. F. Johnson, April 30, 1926, HFP.

9. JSH to McPharson Beall, December 4, 1926, HFP.

10. JSH to Charles P. Upham, April 7, 1924, HFP.

11. Minutes of the Board of Trustees, January 27, 1920, University Archives, University of North Carolina.

12. Ibid.

13. Ibid., p. 333.

14. Henderson, *First State University*, p. 236.

15. Minutes of the executive committee, Board of Trustees, February 28, 1920, University Archives, University of North Carolina.

16. E. C. Branson to JSH, November 14, 1918, ECBP.

17. Ibid.

18. Ibid., September 9, 1919, ECBP.

19. JSH to E. C. Branson, December 11, 1919, ECBP.

20. "Approve Plan for Joint University and Trinity Medical School Here," *Durham Herald*, December 20, 1922.

21. Harry W. Chase to Dr. R. H. Lewis, January 16, 1923, University Archives, University of North Carolina.

22. GWH, interview by Reynolds, November 17, 1984.

23. Ibid.

24. "John Sprunt Hill Honored at Alumni Assembly," *Alumni Review* 25, no. 4 (February 1936).

25. Wilson, *University of North Carolina*, p. 392.

26. JSH to Dr. Joseph Hyde Pratt, January 8, 1921, HFP.

27. Wilson, *University of North Carolina*, p. 392.

28. Allcott, *Campus at Chapel Hill*, p. 68.

29. Zogry, *University's Living Room*, p. 16.

30. Wilson, *University of North Carolina*, p. 393.

31. JSH to L. M. Gerling, February 13, 1924, HFP.

32. JSH to J. Elwood Cox, May 3, 1924, HFP.

33. Gretchen Case and Maria Karres, "History of the Carolina Inn," CIP.

34. JSH to T. C. Atwood, February 28, 1924, HFP.

35. JSH to Harry W. Chase, September 6, 1924, HFP.

36. "Long Felt Need Has Been Filled," *Raleigh News and Observer*, November 23, 1924.

37. "Opening Dance at the Carolina Inn," *Chapel Hill Weekly*, January 1, 1925.

38. Jonathan Daniels, "Chapel Hill Now Prepared to Entertain Its Visitors," *Raleigh News and Observer*, January 24, 1925.

39. Ibid.

40. "Bal Masque Brilliant Affair," *Durham Morning Herald*, clipping, n.d., HFP.

41. GWH, interview by Leutze, January 30, 1986.

42. GWH, interview by Reynolds, n.d.

43. JSH to J. H. Hamilton, May 5, 1925, HFP.

44. GWH, interview by Reynolds, n.d.

Chapter Eight

1. Fox, interview by the author, March 10, 1999.

2. Brown, *Durham Architectural and Historic Inventory*, p. 265.

3. JSH to William R. Kenan Jr., April 26, 1924, HFP.

4. JSH to Mayor J. P. Allen, December 18, 1923, HFP.

5. JSH, "North Carolina, A Story of Triumphant Democracy," (address delivered at the annual meeting of the Retail Merchants Association, Atlanta, Georgia, January 28, 1924), HFP.

6. JSH to Charles A. Webb, October 4, 1911, JSHL.

7. Swaim, *Cabins and Castles*, p. 89.

8. JSH to L. L. Merchant Construction Company, February 21, 1927, HFP.

9. Ann Hill, note, n.d., HFP.

10. GWH, interview by Reynolds, July 21, 1984.

11. JSH to Miss Mary Wyche, May 8, 1925, HFP.

12. Reynolds, "Watts Hospital," p. 118.

13. Ibid., p. 113.

14. GWH, interview by Reynolds, September 17, 1984.

15. Reynolds, "Watts Hospital," p. 124.

16. "Hospitals Approved for Internships," *Durham Morning Herald*, May 10, 1926.

17. Reynolds, "Watts Hospital," p. 118.

18. GWH, interview by Reynolds, n.d.

19. Reynolds, "Watts Hospital," p. 129.

20. Ibid., p. 132.

21. Gifford, *Evolution of a Medical Center*, p. 59.

22. Historical sketch, The Hospital Care Association Inc., WCDP.

23. Herndon, *Hospital Care Association*.

24. Ibid., p. 59.

25. Jonathan Daniels, "Quail into Cows—A Farm Adventure with a Happy Ending," *Raleigh News and Observer*, February 26, 1933.

26. Ibid.

27. "Quail Roost Farms Garner Large Number of Prizes," *Durham Morning Herald*, October 1930.

28. GWH, interview by Leutze, April 3, 1986.

29. Leonard Tufts to Harriet Morehead Berry, November 10, 1923, HMBP.

30. JSH to E. C. Branson, January 27, 1925, ECBP.

31. Williams Hays Simpson, "Credit Unions in North Carolina," *North Carolina Historical Review* (Autumn 1962): 548.

32. Morrison, *O. Max Gardner*, p. 75.

33. GWH to O. Max Gardner, March 7, 1930, HFP.

34. Ibid.

35. JSH to Louis R. Wilson, December 22, 1917, HFP.

36. Henderson, *First State University*, p. 201.

37. Wilson, *University of North Carolina*, p. 397.

38. JSH to Frank P. Graham, June 3, 1932, JSHL.

39. Morrison, *O. Max Gardner*, p. 73.

40. Bell, *Hard Times*, p. 15.

41. "Oldest Bank in Queen City Closes Doors This Morning," *Durham Sun*, December 4, 1930.

42. Ibid.

43. "Resistance to Gardner's Plan Urged by Hill," *Raleigh News and Observer*, January 11, 1931.

44. JSH, *Facts About State Road Law, Square Deal vs. Pork Barrel*, privately published, January 16, 1931, HFP.

45. Morrison, *O. Max Gardner*, p. 93.

46. "Mirrors and Memories," *Durham Morning Herald*, July 30, 1931.

47. "Durham Joins in Honoring J.S. Hill," *Durham Morning Herald*, July 31, 1931.

48. Ibid.

Chapter Nine

1. GWH, interview by Reynolds, n.d.

2. JSH to Samuel Sloan, November 13, 1931, JSHL.

3. JSH to Alphonsus Cobb, June 26, 1931, JSHL.

4. JSH, Account of personal debts, June 1, 1931, JSHL.

5. JSH to H. L. McKee, November 26, 1931, JSHL.

6. "City Looms as Bright Spot on Nation's Economic Map," *Durham Morning Herald*, November 18, 1931.

7. "Two More Banks Will Close Today," *Durham Morning Herald*, December 29, 1931.

8. Henderson, *North Carolina*, p. 605.

9. JSH to Wade McFarland, December 31, 1931, JSHL.

10. "Don't Rock the Boat," *Durham Morning Herald*, January 1, 1932.

11. Advertisement, *Durham Morning Herald*, January 2, 1932.

12. "Met the Test," *Durham Morning Herald*, January 5, 1932.

13. GWH, interview by Reynolds, n.d.

14. Watts Carr to Judge, January 4, 1932, HFP. In later years, Watts Hill was often quoted as having said that President Hoover had called upon his father to stop the run on southern

banks by making a stand in Durham. There is no evidence that the call was ever made. John Sprunt Hill did relate some years later that he had received a telephone call from the chairman of the U.S. Senate Committee on Banks and Currency. Hill recalled: "[The chairman] referred to the work that we had done here to clean up the wild-cat mortgage companies, and suddenly turned on me with his remark—'this government charges you, in this hour of panic and demoralization with the job of holding Durham; if you hold Durham you can hold North Carolina; if you hold North Carolina you will hold the balance of the South and save it from ruin at the hands of wild-cat mortgage companies.'" The chairman's comment about Hill's "work" on "wild-cat mortgage companies" referred to legislation that Hill had supported when he was a member of the North Carolina Senate. JSH, interview.

15. "John Sprunt Hill Is Advocated as State Treasurer," *Durham Morning Herald*, January 7, 1932.

16. "Recent Heavy Withdrawal Forces First National to Suspend Business Today," *Durham Morning Herald*, January 18, 1932.

17. JSH to Gurney P. Hood, January 22, 1932, JSHL.

18. "Proctor and Copleland Get Two-Year Prison Terms; Judge Scores Bank Heads," *Durham Morning Herald*, June 4, 1933.

19. JSH to A. D. Burrows, March 5, 1932, JSHL.

20. Bell, *Hard Times*, p. 18.

21. JSH to Mrs. Annie W. King, March 17, 1932, JSHL.

22. "Democracy Doomed, Nazi Leader Cries," *Durham Morning Herald*, July 29, 1932.

23. Henderson, *North Carolina*, p. 608.

24. JSH to Francis F. Bradshaw, March 5, 1932, JSHL.

25. JSH to Frank Porter Graham, June 19, 1933, JSHL.

26. "Governor's Road Program is Bitterly Attacked Here," *Durham Morning Herald*, February 5, 1931.

27. "Wants Efficiency Expert to Cure Spending Ills," *Raleigh News and Observer*, January 16, 1933.

28. R. F. Beasley, "Personal Sides of Some Figures in Legislation," *Durham Morning Herald*, clipping, April 1933, HFP.

29. Wade Lucas, "Legislative Personalities," *State*, February 17, 1934.

30. JSH to Mrs. Elizabeth B. Burruss, May 16, 1932, JSHL.

31. "Governor Gives Assurance against Bank Moratorium," *Raleigh News and Observer*, March 4, 1933.

32. "Sounder Banking Will Come out of Crisis, Says Hill," *Durham Morning Herald*, March 7, 1933.

33. "State Bank Plans Outlined by Hood," *Durham Morning Herald*, March 29, 1933.

34. Ibid.

35. Carl Goerch, "The Man of Many Talents," *State*, November 4, 1950.

36. "Tomtitters," *Time*, May 29, 1933.

37. Wade Lucas, "Legislative Personalities," *State*, February 24, 1934.

38. JSH to John A. Park, September 6, 1933, JSHL.

39. JSH to John W. Aiken, October 17, 1933, JSHL.

40. "Save the Y Campaign Will Be Launched on Wednesday," *Durham Morning Herald*, April 28, 1934.

41. "Under the Dome," *Raleigh News and Observer*, February 2, 1935.

42. "Goes to State Capitol with Open Mind," *Durham Morning Herald*, clipping, n.d., HFP.

43. JSH to Acker, Merrall, and Condit Co., February 27, 1913, JSHL.

44. Carr, interview, November 23, 1999.

45. "1934 Is Year of Progress for Durham," *Durham Morning Herald*, January 1, 1935.

46. "Patton Declares Dry Laws Are Futile," *Durham Morning Herald*, November 3, 1934; "Patton Brands Liquor Laws 'Absurd' Class Legislation," *Durham Morning Herald*, February 2, 1935.

47. JSH, Untitled speech (prepared for delivery in North Carolina Senate, April 16, 1937), NCC.

48. "Hill and Morrison Factions Wax Hot over Hill Bill," *Raleigh News and Observer*, February 21, 1935.

49. "Morrison Leads Attack on Hill Liquor Measure," *Raleigh News and Observer*, February 21, 1935.

50. "Durham Senator Prods Morrison," *Raleigh News and Observer*, February 26, 1935.

51. Carl Goerch, "Curses on You!" *State*, May 18, 1935.

52. JSH to the Reverend Gilbreath L. Kerr, March 11, 1935, JSHL.

53. Carl Goerch, "Curses on You!" *State*, May 18, 1935.

54. Carl Goerch, "Funny Experiences," *State*, February 7, 1959.

55. "Charges Secret Enemies Plot Ruin of University," *Raleigh News and Observer*, October 26, 1934.

56. JSH to Mrs. Edwin C. Gregory, June 14, 1935, JSHL.

57. JSH to William T. Hannah, February 3, 1936, JSHL.

58. JSH, *A Study of the New Plan of Operation of the Consolidated University of North Carolina* (n.p., 1936), p. 18, HFP.

59. JSH to Mrs. Annie Martin, June 2, 1933, JSHL.

60. Gretchen Case and Maria Karres, "History of the Carolina Inn," p. 38, CIP.

61. JSH to Howard E. Rondthaler, February 10, 1935, JSHL.

62. "University Alumni Express Appreciation for Hill Gifts," *Durham Morning Herald*, February 13, 1935.

63. JSH to Josephus Daniels, February 10, 1936, JSHL.

64. Carr, interview, November 23, 1999.

Chapter Ten

1. Anderson, *Durham County*, p. 357.

2. Ibid., p. 323.

3. Harris, interview by George Watts Hill Jr.

4. "Watts Hospital Asks City, Council for Special Funds," *Durham Morning Herald*, March 20, 1934.

5. Gifford, *Evolution of a Medical Center*, p. 29.

6. "Blue Cross History," WCDP.

7. "J.S. Hill Secures Club at Pinehurst," *Durham Morning Herald*, November 8, 1934.

8. "Unemployed Talkers Make Threats at Mass Meeting," *Durham Morning Herald*, January 24, 1933.

9. George Watts Hill Jr., "Durham Academy," private collection of Howard E. Covington Jr.

Chapter Eleven

1. Ernest C. Havemann, "Unofficial Body Gives Citizen Way to Aid in Policy Planning," *Washington Daily Star*, March 21, 1939.

2. Egerton, *Speak Now*, p. 188.

3. Francis P. Miller to Frank P. Graham, December 21, 1938, FPGP.

4. GWH, Memo to the Friends of Finland in North Carolina, n.d., HFP.

5. "American Opinion and the War," *New York Times*, June 2, 1940.

6. Miller, *Man from the Valley*, p. 90.

7. "A Summons to Speak Out," June 1940, HFP.

8. GWH to Francis P. Miller, June 7, 1942, FPMP.

9. Jonathan Daniels to Francis P. Miller, June 6, 1940, HFP.

10. R. E. Wood to Francis P. Miller, June 7, 1940, FPMP.

11. GWH to W. Hays Godwin, June 14, 1940, HFP.

12. GWH to Frank P. Graham, June 14, 1940, FPGP.

13. Laurie, *Propaganda Warriors*, p. 37.

14. Joseph J. Spengler to GWH, June 4, 1940, HFP.

15. Miller, *Man from the Valley*, p. 94.

16. GWH, interview by Leutze, January 30, 1986.

17. Miller, *Man from the Valley*, p. 95.

18. Ibid., p. 96.

19. GWH, "Memo of meeting at Century Club," July 25, 1940, FPMP.

20. Robert R. Reynolds to GWH, August 8, 1940, HFP.

21. John H. Kerr to GWH, August 15, 1940, HFP.

22. GWH to John H. Kerr, August 24, 1940, HFP.

23. Goodwin, *No Ordinary Time*, p. 147; Laurie, *Propaganda Warriors*, p. 42.

24. GWH to Josiah Bailey, September 27, 1940, HFP.

25. W. T. Couch to Chester Boothe Blackman, January 17, 1941, HFP.

26. Stuart Cramer to GWH, January 9, 1941, FPGP.

27. "Defend America Now" memo, January 15, 1941, HFP.

28. GWH to W. T. Couch, January 20, 1941, HFP.

29. Stevenson, *Man Called Intrepid*, p. 254.

30. James P. Warburg, "American First?" (transcript of broadcast on behalf of Fight For Freedom Committee, April 24, 1941), HFP.

31. Laurie, *Propaganda Warriors*, p. 41.

32. F. H. Peter Cusick to GWH, March 17, 1941, HFP.

33. GWH to Ulric Bell, December 23, 1941, HFP.

34. "Civilian Defense Council Here May Convene This Afternoon," *Durham Morning Herald*, December 9, 1941.

35. GWH to William B. Terhune, December 22, 1941, HFP.

36. Francis P. Miller to GWH, March 14, 1942, HFP.

37. GWH, interview by Leutze, January 30, 1986.

38. David K. E. Bruce to Commander Francis P. Old, April 18, 1942, HFP.

39. William J. Donovan to Secretary of War Frank Knox, April 21, 1942, HFP.

40. Brinkley, *Washington Goes to War*, p. 119.

41. GWH to B. W. Harris, n.d., HFP.

42. GWH to JSH, June 14, 1942, HFP.

43. Smith, *OSS*, p. 6.

44. David K. E. Bruce to the *New York Times*, February 8, 1959, David K. E. Bruce Papers.

45. Ford, *Donovan of OSS*, p. 134.

46. GWH to JSH, May 1942, HFP.

47. Smith, *OSS*, p. 3.

48. Ann Hill to GWH, June 11, 1941, HFP.

49. GWH to R. A. Ross, June 15, 1942, HFP.

50. Smith, *OSS*, p. 5.

51. Lt. Col. Hugh D. Butler to Major David Bruce, n.d., OSSA.

52. GWH to Major Bruce, September 30, 1942, OSSA.

53. GWH, interview by Leutze, January 30, 1986.

54. Laney Inglehart, "Glencoe was a Fake Combat Zone," *North County News*, clipping, October 1969, HFP.

55. JSH to GWH, March 22, 1943, JSHL.

56. Sargent, interview.

57. GWH, interview by Leutze, January 30, 1986.

58. Ibid.

59. GWH to Mr. Franz Stone, October 30, 1944, OSSA.

60. George Watts Hill Jr., interview by the author, April 4, 2000.

61. Risto Solanko to GWH, November 12, 1941, HFP; GWH to Risto Solanko, November 19, 1941, HFP.

62. GWH to Francis P. Miller, February 4, 1946, FPMP.

Chapter Twelve

1. GWH to JSH, July 11, 1945, HFP.

2. Moorhead, interview.

3. GWH to JSH, July 11, 1945, HFP.

4. Carr, interview, January 8, 2001.

5. Harris, interview by George Watts Hill Jr.

6. Mary Thornton to JSH, April 14, 1944, MTL.

7. Campbell, *Across Fortune's Tracks*, p. 305.

8. GWH to JSH, July 11, 1945, HFP.

9. GWH to D. L. Cannett, April 15, 1949, HFP.

10. JSH to Sample Forbus, April 15, 1942, JSHL.

11. GWH, interview by Reynolds, n.d.

12. Frank Porter Graham to Louis R. Wilson, January 5, 1962, HSL.

13. Reynolds, "Watts Hospital," p. 203.

14. North Carolina Medical Care Commission, "The Good Health Campaign in North Carolina," September 4, 1946, HSL.

15. Graham to Wilson, January 5, 1962, HSL.

16. "Good Health Campaign in North Carolina," HSL.

17. Moorhead, interview.

18. "Good Health Campaign in North Carolina," HSL.

19. Memo, Meeting of Good Health Association, n.d., University Archives, University of North Carolina.

20. Cranford, interview.

21. William Carmichael telegram to Kay Kyser, n.d., University Archives, University of North Carolina.

22. "Good Health Association's Hollywood Program Cut Off," *Durham Morning Herald*, November 10, 1946.

23. Reynolds, *Watts Hospital*, p. 228.

24. Moorhead, interview.

25. "Paul Horvitz, Tar Heel of the Week," *Raleigh News and Observer*, July 22, 1973.

26. David Folkenflik, "Durham Mourns Watts Hill," *Durham Herald-Sun*, January 21, 1993.

27. Tom MacCaughelty, "J. Sprunt Hill, A. H. Graham, Fight Program," *Durham Morning Herald*, February 10, 1949.

28. "City Asked to Reconsider Adding Fluoride to Water," *Durham Morning Herald*, July 30, 1951.

29. H. G. Jones, "Son of Duplin," (remarks prepared for delivery to the Duplin County Historical Society, February 2, 1985), NCC.

30. William B. Whitley, "U.N.C. Negro Admissions Will Be Studied by Group," *Durham Morning Herald*, January 30, 1951.

31. "The Boss of Durham Has Spoken," *Carolina Times*, February 3, 1951.

32. "City Council Turns Down Proposal to Add Fluoride to Water Supply," *Durham Morning Herald*, August 21, 1951.

33. Clark, interview, June 17, 1999.

34. Research paper on the Durham Bank and Trust Company, n.d., HFP.

35. Ibid.

36. Ibid.

37. George Watts Hill Jr., interview by the author, January 8, 2001.

38. David Folkenflik, "Durham Mourns Watts Hill," *Durham Herald-Sun*, January 21, 1993.

39. Simpson, interview.

40. GWH to Bernard S. Dekle, September 24, 1945, HFP.

41. George P. Geoghegan Jr. to Romeo Guest, June 30, 1958, RGP.

42. Simpson, interview.

43. Romeo Guest to Luther Hodges, January 15, 1957, LHP; GWH to Luther Hodges, March 22, 1957, LHP; George Simpson to Robert M. Hanes, February 26, 1957, LHP; Link, *A Generosity of Sprit*, p. 52.

44. Link, *A Generosity of Sprit*, p. 29.

45. Larrabee, *Many Missions*, p. 73.

46. Romeo Guest to George Simpson, December 28, 1957, RGP.

47. GWH to Romeo Guest, November 26, 1957, RGP.

48. GWH to Pearson Stewart, July 7, 1959, LHP.

49. Stewart, interview.

50. GWH, interview by Leutze, January 30, 1986.

51. George Simpson to Luther Hodges, December 10, 1957, LHP.

52. Carr, interview, January 8, 2001.

53. "Pinelands' Lawyer Given Final Draft of Water Pact," *Durham Morning Herald*, April 21, 1958.

54. Pearson Stewart, Memo to file, 1957, RGP.

55. Simpson, interview.

56. George Simpson to Karl Robbins, February 13, 1958, LHP.

57. GWH to William C. Friday, WCFP.

58. GWH, Memo on meeting with Robbins in Durham, February 26, 1958, LHP.

59. J. Edgar Kirk to Luther Hodges, July 3, 1958, LHP.

60. Archie Davis to GWH, September 15, 1958, LHP.

61. GWH to Archie Davis, December 3, 1958, LHP.

62. GWH to A. J. Graham Jr., January 12, 1959, RGP.

63. "Ruffin Approves Change in Erwin Selling Agents," *Durham Morning Herald*, August 22, 1953.

64. Barnes, *From Pads to Palette*, p. 16.

65. Harris, interview by George Watts Hill Jr.

66. George Watts Hill Jr., Untitled speech (remarks prepared for delivery to the Durham Rotary Club, April 3, 1989), HFP.

67. William Hays Simpson, "Credit Unions in North Carolina," *North Carolina Historical Review* (August 1962).

68. Harris, interview by George Watts Hill Jr.

69. "John Sprunt Hill Dies at 92 at Durham Home," *Durham Morning Herald*, July 30, 1961.

70. Phelps, interview.

Chapter Thirteen

1. GWH, interview by Leutze, April 3, 1986.

2. Friday, interview, June 19, 2000.

3. "Charitable Fund Established," *Durham Sun*, August 1, 1961.

4. "John Sprunt Hill," *Carolina Times*, August 5, 1961.

5. Charles Clay, "Is Durham Lagging behind Other Cities?" *Durham Morning Herald*, March 22, 1959.

6. GWH, interview by Leutze, January 30, 1986.

7. Larrabee, *Many Missions*, p. 26.

8. Herbert, interview.

9. Larrabee, *Many Missions*, p. 27.

10. Ibid., p. 77.

11. Ibid., p. 84.

12. "George Watts Hill Building Dedicated," *Hypotenuse* (October 1977).

13. JSH, "Segregation," n.d., NCC.

14. Ruffin, interview.

15. Howard, "Keep Your Eyes on the Prize."

16. Ibid., p. 127.

17. George Watts Hill Jr., interview by Chafe.

18. Carr, interview, January 3, 2001.

19. Spaulding, interview.

20. "More Racial Barriers Fall in Durham," *Durham Morning Herald*, June 5, 1963; Phelps, interview.

21. Howard, "Keep Your Eyes on the Prize," p. 138.

22. Phelps, interview.

23. George Watts Hill Jr., interview by Chafe.

24. George Watts Hill Jr., interview by the author, January 8, 2001.

25. Howard, "Keep Your Eyes on the Prize," p. 139.

26. George Watts Hill Jr., interview by the author, January 8, 2001.

27. Lenox D. Baker to Thomas Pearsall, April 30, 1963, HFP.

28. GWH to Orville Campbell, September 9, 1959, HFP.

29. GWH to Lenox D. Baker, April 24, 1963, HFP.

30. Clark, interview, June 17, 1999.

31. McDevitt, interview.

32. Covington and Ellis, *Terry Sanford*.

33. Friday, interview, August 23, 1999.

34. GWH, interview by Chafe.

35. GWH to Victor Bryant, October 18, 1956, HFP.

36. Friday, interview, August 18, 2000.

37. Berryhill, interview.

38. Friday, interview, August 23, 1999.

39. GWH to Arch T. Allen, August 8, 1957, WCFP.

40. GWH, interview by the Institute of Government.

41. GWH to William C. Friday, May 12, 1961, WCFP.

42. Ibid.

43. GWH, Memo to Preston Reynolds, July 30, 1981, private collection of Dr. P. Preston Reynolds.

44. Friday, interview, August 18, 2000.

45. Friday, interview, June 19, 2000.

46. "Hill to Receive Top Fellowship," *Durham Morning Herald*, August 15, 1963.

47. Reynolds, "Watts Hospital," p. 299.

48. McMahon, interview.

49. Covington and Ellis, *North Carolina Century*, p. 54.

50. DePasquale, interview.

51. GWH, interview by Leutze, January 30, 1986.

52. DePasquale, interview.

53. Jeff Zimmer, "CCB Tradition Makes Paintings Public," *Durham Herald-Sun*, April 28, 1999.

54. Don Frederick, "Boom! Hotel's Gone in Seconds," *Durham Morning Herald*, December 15, 1975.

55. Bullock, interview.

56. Ibid.

57. Ibid.

58. GWH, interview by Leutze, January 30, 1986.

Chapter Fourteen

1. Lawrence Maddry, "Chapel Hill's Image Has Been Harmed," *Chapel Hill Weekly*, clipping, n.d., HFP.

2. Jesse Helms to GWH, June 12, 1957, HFP.

3. GWH to Jesse Helms, June 18, 1957, HFP.

4. Jon Phelps, "Hill Placed among Leaders of Progress in 'New South,'" *Durham Morning Herald*, May 23, 1961.

5. Dwayne Walls, "Watts Hill Jr.: Rich Young Man Who Fits No Pattern," *Charlotte Observer*, March 19, 1961.

6. George Watts Hill Jr., private communication with the author, February 12, 2001.

7. George Watts Hill Jr., Testimony for the Board of Higher Education before the Southern Association of Schools and Colleges, November 28, 1965, HFP.

8. GWH, Memo on conference with Governor Dan Moore, May 7, 1965, HFP.

9. William C. Friday to GWH, April 28, 1965, WCFP.

10. George Watts Hill Jr., interview by the Institute of Government.

11. Link, *William Friday*, p. 124.

12. GWH to Dan K. Moore, December 8, 1965, DKMP.

13. George Watts Hill Jr., Testimony given to the executive committee of the Commission on Colleges of the Southern Association, Richmond, Va., November 28, 1965, HFP.

14. Jesse Helms, "Viewpoint 1238," WRAL-TV, November 30, 1965, HFP.

15. Friday, interview, August 23, 1999.

16. George Watts Hill Jr., interview by Institute of Government.

17. George Watts Hill Jr. and Dr. William Archie, sound recording of meetings, August 12 and 15, 1965, HFP.

18. Ibid.

19. GWH, interview by the Institute of Government.

20. William C. Friday, Memo for the record, n.d., WCFP.

21. Joe Doster, "The Hills Understand and Love Education," *Winston-Salem Journal*, January 23, 1972.

22. GWH, interview by Leutze, January 30, 1986.

23. Ibid.

24. George Watts Hill Jr., interview by the author, April 4, 2000.

25. Paul Horvitz, "End: Influence; Means: Persuasion; Outcome: Success," *Raleigh News and Observer*, July 22, 1973.

26. Bullock, interview.

27. Walker, interview.

BIBLIOGRAPHY

Manuscript Collections
Chapel Hill, North Carolina
University of North Carolina
   North Carolina Collection
      Howard Odum Papers
      Mary Thornton Letterbooks
   Southern Historical Collection
      Harriet M. Berry Papers
      E. C. Branson Papers
      W. T. Couch Papers
      William C. Friday Papers
      Edwin Gill Papers
      Frank Porter Graham Papers
   University of North Carolina Archives
      Carolina Inn Papers
      Early Presidents' Papers
      Trustee Minutes of the University of North Carolina and the Consolidated University of North Carolina
Hill Family Papers
   Papers, letterbooks, and photographs of John Sprunt Hill and George Watts Hill

Charlottesville, Virginia
University of Virginia
   Manuscripts Department
      Francis P. Miller Papers

Durham, North Carolina
Duke University
   Manuscripts Department
      Benjamin N. Duke Papers
      James B. Duke Papers
      Erwin Mills Papers
      Romeo Guest Papers
      Kemp P. Lewis Papers

Eugene Morehead Papers
W. Alexander Smith Papers
Richard Wright Papers
Medical School Archives
Wilburt C. Davison Papers
First Presbyterian Church
Collections

Pinehurst, North Carolina
Pinehurst Archives
Tufts Family Papers

Raleigh, North Carolina
North Carolina Department of Archives and History
Official Papers of Governor O. Max Gardner
Official Papers of Governor Luther H. Hodges
Official Papers of Governor Dan K. Moore

Richmond, Virginia
Union Theological Seminary Library
W. W. Moore Papers
Historical Society of Virginia
David K. E. Bruce Papers

Washington, D.C.
National Archives
OSS Archives

Interviews
Collections of the University of North Carolina
Herbert, George, interview by William Link, May 13, 1991, SOHP
Hill, George Watts, interview by the Institute of Government, February 29, 1972, SHC; interview by James Leutze, January 30, February 4, 16, 18, 20, April 3, 1986, SOHP; interview by Ed Rehkopf, December 1987, University Archives
Hill, George Watts, Jr., interview by the Institute of Government, March 13, 1972
Spaulding, Asa, Jr., interview by Walter Weare, April 14, 1979, SOHP

Hill Family Papers
Angier, Newton Duke, interview by George Watts Hill Jr., March 1999
Clark, Arthur, interview by the author, June 17, 1999, April 27, May 1, 2, 2000
Fox, Frances Hill, interview by George Watts Hill Jr., February 4, 8, June 6, 1999; interview by the author, March 10, August 2, 1999
Harris, B. W., Jr., interview by George Watts Hill Jr., February 9, 1999; interview by the author, August 18, 1999
Hill, John Sprunt, interview by George Watts Hill Jr., April 2, 1953
Walker, Jack, interview by the author, September 18, 2000

Manuscripts Department, Duke University
Hill, George Watts, interview by William Chafe, June 14, 1974
Hill, George Watts, Jr., interview by William Chafe, 1974

Private Collection of Howard E. Covington Jr.
Berryhill, Norma, interview by the author, December 22, 2000
Boyles, Harlan, interview by the author, June 22, 1999
Bullock, Maceo, interview by the author, August 9, 2000
Burns, William, Jr., interview by the author, June 21, 1999
Carr, Watts, Jr., interview by the author, November 23, 1999, January 3, 8, 2001
Cranford, H. C., interview by the author, January 30, 2001
DePasquale, Frank, interview by the author, August 27, 1999
Friday, William C., interview by the author, August 23, 1999, June 19, August 18, 2000
Hill, Anne Hutchins, interview by the author, April 4, 2000
Hill, George Watts, Jr., interview by the author, May 25, April 4, June 2, December 9, 1999, January 5, 8, 2001
McDevitt, John, interview by the author, December 20, 1999
McMahon, J. Alexander, interview by the author, January 13, 2000
Moorhead, John, interview by the author, January 15, 2001
Phelps, Jake, interview by the author, January 3, 2001
Phillips, Joe, interview by the author, August 14, 1999
Ruffin, Ben, interview by the author, February 14, 2001
Sargent, Dudley Hill, interview by the author, December 30, 2000
Simpson, George, interview by the author, January 24, 2001
Stewart, Pearson, interview by the author, n.d.

Private Collection of Dr. P. Preston Reynolds
Hill, George Watts, interview by P. Preston Reynolds, n.d., June 21, July 21, August 16, September 17, November 17, 1984

Published Sources
Ainsley, W. Frank. *Front Porches, Front Parlors: The Historic Architecture of Faison, North Carolina.* Faison: Faison Museum Committee, 1994.
Alger, Russell A. *The Spanish-American War.* Freeport, N.Y.: Books for Libraries Press, 1901.
Allcott, John V. *The Campus at Chapel Hill: Two Hundred Years of Architecture.* Chapel Hill: Chapel Hill Historical Society, 1986.
Anderson, Jean Bradley. *Durham County: A History of Durham County, North Carolina.* Durham: Duke University Press, 1990.
Ashe, Samuel A. *Biographical History of North Carolina from Colonial Times to the Present.* Vol. 1. Greensboro: C. L. Van Noppen, 1905–17.
Barnes, Ernie. *From Pads to Palette.* Waco, Tex.: WRS Publishing, 1995.
Barry, Herbert. *Squadron A: A History of Its First Fifty Years, 1889–1939.* New York: Association of Ex-Members of Squadron A, 1939.
Battle, Kemp P. *History of the University of North Carolina.* Raleigh: Edwards and Broughton, 1907–12.

Bell, John L., Jr. *Hard Times: Beginnings of the Great Depression in North Carolina, 1929–1933.* Raleigh: North Carolina Department of Cultural Resources, Division of Archives and History, 1982.

Boyd, William Kenneth. *The Story of Durham: City of the New South.* Durham: Duke University Press, 1925.

Brands, H. W. *The Reckless Decade: America in the 1890s.* New York: St. Martin's Press, 1995.

Brinkley, David. *Washington Goes to War.* New York: Alfred A. Knopf, 1988.

Brown, Cecil Kenneth. *The State Highway System of North Carolina.* Chapel Hill: University of North Carolina Press, 1931.

Brown, Claudia Roberts. *The Durham Architectural and Historic Inventory.* Durham: City of Durham, 1983.

Brown, Henry Collins. *In the Golden Nineties.* Freeport, N.Y.: Books for Libraries Press, 1970.

Campbell, Walter E. *Across Fortune's Tracks: A Biography of William Rand Kenan Jr.* Chapel Hill: University of North Carolina Press, 1996.

Chernow, Ron. *Titan: The Life of John D. Rockefeller.* New York: Random House, 1998.

Coates, Albert. *The University of North Carolina at Chapel Hill: A Magic Gulf Stream in the Life of North Carolina.* Privately published, 1978.

———. *What the University of North Carolina Meant to Me.* Privately published, 1969.

Columbia University: A History. New York: Columbia University Press, 1904.

Connable, Alfred, and Edward Silberfarb. *Tigers of Tammany: Nine Men Who Ran New York.* Chicago: Holt, Rinehart, and Winston, 1967.

Coon, Horrace. *Columbia: Colossus on the Hudson.* New York: E. P. Dutton, 1947.

Corina, Maurice. *Trust in Tobacco: The Anglo-American Struggle for Power.* New York: St. Martin's Press, 1975.

Corvo, Max. *The OSS in Italy, 1942–1945: A Personal Memoir.* New York: Praeger, 1990.

Covington, Howard E., Jr., and Marion A. Ellis. *Terry Sanford: Politics, Progress, and Outrageous Ambition.* Durham: Duke University Press, 1999.

———, eds. *North Carolina Century: Tar Heels Who Made a Difference, 1900–2000.* Charlotte: Levine Museum of the New South, 2002.

Daniels, Jonathan. *The Time between the Wars: Armistice to Pearl Harbor.* Garden City, N.Y.: Doubleday, 1966.

Daniels, Josephus. *Editor in Politics.* Chapel Hill: University of North Carolina Press, 1941.

Davison, Wilburt Cornell. *Davison of Duke: His Reminiscences.* Edited by Jay M. Arena and John P. McGovern. Durham: Duke University Medical Center, 1980.

Dula, W. C., and A. C. Simpson. *Durham and Her People.* Durham: Citizens Press, 1951.

Durden, Robert F. *The Dukes of Durham, 1865–1929.* Durham: Duke University Press, 1975.

Egerton, John. *Speak Now against the Day.* New York: Alfred A. Knopf, 1994.

Evans, W. McKee. *Ballots and Fence Rails: Reconstruction on the Lower Cape Fear.* New York: W. W. Norton, 1974.

Flowers, John Baxton, III, and Marguerite Schumann. *Bull Durham and Beyond: A Touring Guide to City and County.* Durham: Durham Bicentennial Commission, 1976.

Ford, Corey. *Donovan of OSS*. Boston: Little, Brown, 1970.

Gifford, James F. *The Evolution of a Medical Center: A History of Medicine at Duke University*. Durham: Duke University Press, 1972.

Gilbert, Martin. *A History of the Twentieth Century*. 3 vols. New York: William Morrow and Company, 1997.

Goodwin, Doris Kearns. *No Ordinary Time: Franklin and Eleanor Roosevelt: The Home Front in World War II*. New York: Simon and Schuster, 1994.

Hand-book of Durham, NC. Durham: Educator Company, 1895.

Henderson, Archibald. *The Campus of the First State University*. Chapel Hill: University of North Carolina Press, 1949.

———. *North Carolina: The Old North State and the New*. Chicago: Lewis Publishing Company, 1941.

Herndon, Elisha M. *History of the Hospital Care Association Incorporated, Durham, North Carolina*. Durham: Blue Cross and Blue Shield of North Carolina, 1968.

Hobbs, S. Huntington, Jr. *North Carolina: Economic and Social*. Chapel Hill: University of North Carolina Press, 1930.

House, R. B., ed. *Public Letters and Papers of Thomas Walter Bickett: Governor of North Carolina, 1917–1921*. Raleigh: Edwards and Broughton Printing Company, 1923.

Jacobstein, Meyer. *The Tobacco Industry in the United States*. New York: Columbia University Press, 1907.

Jones, May F., ed. *Memoirs and Speeches of Locke Craig, Governor of North Carolina, 1913–1917: A History, Political and Otherwise, from Scrap Books and Old Manuscripts*. Asheville: Hackney and Moale, 1923.

Kenan, William Rand, Jr. *Incidents by the Way: More Recollections*. [New York?]: Privately published, 1949.

Lankford, Nelson Douglas, ed. *OSS against the Reich: The World War II Diaries of Colonel David K. E. Bruce*. Kent, Ohio: Kent State University Press, 1991.

Larrabee, Charles X. *Many Missions: Research Triangle Institute's First Thirty-One Years, 1959–1990*. Research Triangle Park: Research Triangle Institute, 1991.

Laurie, Clayton D. *The Propaganda Warriors*. Lawrence: University Press of Kansas, 1996.

Lefler, Hugh T., ed. *North Carolina History Told by Contemporaries*. Chapel Hill: University of North Carolina Press, 1934.

Leloudis, James L. *Schooling the New South: Pedagogy, Self, and Society in North Carolina, 1880–1920*. Chapel Hill: University of North Carolina Press, 1996.

Leyburn, James G. *The Way We Lived: Durham, 1900–1920*. Elliston, Va.: Northcross House, 1989.

Link, Albert N. *A Generosity of Sprit: The Early History of the Research Triangle Park*. Research Triangle Park: Research Triangle Foundation, 1995.

Link, William A. *William Friday: Power, Purpose, and American Higher Education*. Chapel Hill: University of North Carolina Press, 1995.

Lord, Walter. *The Good Years: From 1900 to the First World War*. New York: Harper, 1960.

Love, James Lee. *'Tis Sixty Years Since: A Story of the University of North Carolina in the 1880s*. Chapel Hill: University of North Carolina Press, 1945.

Massengill, Stephen E. *Durham, North Carolina: A Postcard History*. Dover, N.H.: Arcadia Publishing, 1997.

Mayer, Grace M. *Once upon a City*. New York: Macmillan, 1958.

Miller, Francis P. *Man from the Valley*. Chapel Hill: University of North Carolina Press, 1971.

Morris, Lloyd. *Incredible New York: High Life and Low Life of the Last Hundred Years*. New York: Random House, 1951.

Morrison, Joseph. *Governor O. Max Gardner*. Chapel Hill: University of North Carolina Press, 1971.

Myers, Gustavus. *History of Tammany Hall*. New York: Burt Franklin, 1917.

Poe, Clarence. *My First Eighty Years*. Chapel Hill: University of North Carolina Press, 1963.

Porter, Earl. *Trinity and Duke, 1892–1924: Foundations of Duke University*. Durham: Duke University Press, 1964.

Reynolds, P. Preston. *Watts Hospital of Durham, North Carolina, 1895–1976: Keeping the Doors Open*. Durham: Fund for the Advancement of Science and Mathematics Education in North Carolina, 1991.

Russell, Phillips. *These Old Stone Walls*. Chapel Hill: Chapel Hill Historical Society, 1972.

Simpson, William Hays. *The Small Loan Problem of the Carolinas*. Clinton, S.C.: Presbyterian College Press, 1941.

Smith, R. Harris. *OSS: The Secret History of America's First Central Intelligence Agency*. Berkeley: University of California Press, 1972.

State Board of Agriculture. *North Carolina and Its Resources*. Winston: M. I. and J. C. Stewart, 1896.

Stevenson, William. *A Man Called Intrepid: The Secret War*. New York: Harcourt Brace Jovanovich, 1976.

Sullivan, Mark. *Over Here, 1914–1918*. Vol. 5 of *Our Times: The United States, 1900–1925*. New York: Charles Scribner's Sons, 1933.

Swaim, Douglas, ed. *Cabins and Castles: The History and Architecture of Buncombe County, North Carolina*. Asheville: Division of Archives and History, North Carolina Department of Cultural Resources, 1981.

Tilley, Nannie May. *The Bright-Tobacco Industry, 1860–1929*. Chapel Hill: University of North Carolina Press, 1948.

———. *The R.J. Reynolds Tobacco Company*. Chapel Hill: University of North Carolina Press, 1985.

Van Noppen, Charles L. *In Memoriam, George Washington Watts*. Greensboro: Privately published, 1922.

Webb, Mena. *Jule Carr: General without an Army*. Chapel Hill: University of North Carolina Press, 1987.

Wilson, Louis R. *Historical Sketches*. Privately published, 1976.

———. *The University of North Carolina, 1900–1930: The Making of a Modern University*. Chapel Hill: University of North Carolina Press, 1957.

Winkler, John K. *Tobacco Tycoon: The Story of James Buchanan Duke*. New York: Random House, 1942.

Winks, Robin W. *Cloak and Gown: Scholars in the Secret War, 1939–1961*. New Haven, Conn.: Yale University Press, 1996.

Winston, Robert Watson. *It's a Far Cry*. New York: Henry Holt, 1937.

Zogry, Kenneth Joel. *The University's Living Room: A History of the Carolina Inn.* Chapel Hill: University of North Carolina, 1999.

Dissertations and Theses

Howard, Chris D. "Keep Your Eyes on the Prize: The Black Struggle for Civic Equality in Durham, N.C., 1954–1963." Honors thesis, Duke University, 1983.

Reynolds, P. Preston. "Watts Hospital, 1895–1976: Paternalism and Race: The Evolution of a Southern Institution in Durham, North Carolina." Ph.D. diss., Duke University, 1986.

Periodicals

Alumni Review
Carolina Times (Durham)
Chapel Hill Weekly
Charlotte Observer
Daily Tobacco Plant (Durham)
Durham Globe
Durham Herald
Durham Herald-Sun
Durham Morning Herald
Durham Sun
ESC Quarterly
Hypotenuse
New York News

New York Times
New York World
North Carolina Historical Review
Progressive Farmer
Raleigh News and Observer
State
Time
University News Letter
Washington Daily Star
Washington Evening Star
Winston-Salem Journal

INDEX

References to illustrations, which appear in this book in three inserts of sixteen pages, are in italic text, and usually consist of two numbers separated by a period. The first number refers to the insert, the second, to the page within that insert.

UNC stands for the University of North Carolina, GWH for George Watts Hill, JSH for John Sprunt Hill, GWW for George Washington Watts, CDAAA for Committee to Defend America by Aiding the Allies.